THE NARNIAN

The Life and Imagination of
C. S. LEWIS

ALAN JACOBS

HarperSanFrancisco
A Division of HarperCollins*Publishers*

HarperCollins books may be purchased for educational, business, or sales promotional use. For information please write: Special Markets Department, Harper-Collins Publishers, 10 East 53rd Street, New York, NY 10022.

HarperCollins Web site: http://www.harpercollins.com
HarperCollins®, 🔖®, and HarperSanFrancisco™ are
trademarks of HarperCollins Publishers.

FIRST EDITION
Designed by Joseph Rutt

Library of Congress Cataloging-in-Publication Data
Jacobs, Alan
The narnian : the life and imagination of C. S. Lewis / by Alan Jacobs.
p. cm.
ISBN–13: 978–0–06–076690–0
ISBN–10: 0–06–076690–5
1. Lewis, C. S. (Clive Staples, 1898–1963. 2. Lewis, C. S. (Clive Staples), 1898–1963—Religion. 3. Lewis, C. S. (Clive Staples), 1898–1963. Chronicles of Narnia. 4. Christianity and literature—England—History—20th century. 5. Christian literature, English—History and criticism. 6. Authors, English—20th century—Biography. 7. Christian biography—England. 8. Narnia (Imaginary place) I. Title.

PR6023.E926Z725 2005
823'.912—dc22
[B] 2005046151

05 06 07 08 09 RRD(H) 10 9 8 7 6 5 4 3 2 1

To my godchildren:
Emma Kienitz Sniegowski
Daniel Martin Woodiwiss
Mary Howard Lin Edgar

"Child," said the Lion, "I am telling you your story, not hers. No-one is told any story but their own."

Contents

Preface and Acknowledgments

The story that follows is almost a biography in the usual sense of the word. It is not quite so strictly chronological as biographies usually are, and it omits certain details that a responsible biographer would be obliged to include. For instance, C. S. Lewis spent many summers earning extra money by serving as an "outside examiner" for British schools and universities. Though this activity took up many months of his life, it is mentioned only once, briefly, in these pages. Likewise, though Lewis took many driving or walking tours in England, Wales, and Ireland during his vacations, these too I leave unchronicled. From other biographers one can learn when he visited Cambridge to meet with other examiners and discover what sites he and his brother visited when they took a holiday in Wales.

I have neglected these matters because my chief task here is to write the life of a mind, the story of an imagination. The seed of this book is a question: what sort of person wrote the Chronicles of Narnia? Who was this man who made—and, in a sense, himself dwelled in—Narnia? What knowledge, what experience, what history made a boy from Ulster who grew up to profess English literature at Oxford turn, when he was nearly fifty, to the writing of stories for children—and stories for children that would become among the most popular and beloved ever written? The tale turns out to be a curious and (I think) fascinating one: in some ways revelatory of the main currents of intellectual life in twentieth century Europe, in other ways unique to one man's strange experience. But in any case this story traces the routes of Lewis's imagination far more closely than it traces the routes of his holiday itineraries.

Those byways of imagination are worth tracing because in his lifetime Lewis was a famous and influential man, as a scholar, as a writer of fiction, and above all as a controversialist on behalf of the Christian faith. Since his death his fame as a writer of children's books has probably put his other achievements in the shade—at least if one goes by sales figures—but he remains for many Christians a figure of unique authority. Long ago the writers of books and articles concerning "What C. S. Lewis Thought About *X*" ran out of subjects and began to write books and articles concerning "What C. S. Lewis *Would* Have Thought About *X* if He Had Lived Long Enough to See It." For someone who cares about the quality of Christian reflection on contemporary culture, this tendency is rather discouraging, but it indicates that Lewis has—because (as we shall see) he *earned*—a reputation for thinking clearly and writing forcefully about a wide range of subjects of concern to Christians, and indeed to many other people as well. And as discouraged as I can become by overreliance on Lewis, that doesn't prevent me from returning to his books again and again for pleasure and instruction alike; I rarely come away from such a reencounter disappointed.

Of course, many people despise Lewis, a fact not unrelated to his great stature among Christians. I even know a man who says that he lost his faith largely because of Lewis's *Mere Christianity*: he figured that, since all his devout friends told him that it was the last word on what Christian belief is all about, then if he loathed the book he was honor-bound to loathe Christianity as well. And public attacks on Lewis continue to this day; indeed, they have intensified in recent years, as first a play and now a film based on the first Narnia book, *The Lion, the Witch, and the Wardrobe,* have appeared, thus bringing Lewis back to the attention of anyone who might happen to have forgotten him. But of course no one bothers to attack a trivial figure; the violence of the protests (some of which we consider later in this book) testifies to the power—and therefore, from a certain perspective, the danger—of Lewis's writings. The English satirical novelist Kingsley Amis had something like this in mind when he said that Lewis was "big enough to be worth laughing at." That phrase is often quoted, but rarely does one hear that Amis also said that Lewis was someone "whom I respect highly"—indeed, when Amis began his career as a teacher at University College of Swansea in Wales, his lectures on Renaissance literature were given straight from the notes he had taken while listening to Lewis's Oxford lectures.

But if Christians, and some opponents of Christianity, think first of Lewis's religious writings, millions of readers know him only as the maker of Narnia—and many of those have no idea that he was a Christian or that the stories enact Christian themes. One such reader is J. K. Rowling, author of the Harry Potter books, who once said in an interview, "I adored [the Narnia books] when I was a child. I got so caught up I didn't think C. S. Lewis was especially preachy." She then added, "Reading them now I find that his subliminal message isn't very subliminal at all"—but nevertheless many people, children and adults, don't get that message, or don't even imagine that the books *have* a message: they are simply, as the young Joanne Rowling was, "caught up" in the narratives. Likewise, Neil Gaiman, a gifted writer of highly acclaimed (but also rather disturbing) fantasies for adolescents and young adults, remembers reading the Narnia books as a child and feeling "personally offended" when he discovered, while in the middle of *The Voyage of the "Dawn Treader,"* that its author had a "hidden agenda." Yet, he added, "I would read other books, of course, but in my heart I knew that I read them only because there wasn't an infinite number of Narnia books to read." Moreover, "C. S. Lewis was the first person to make me want to be a writer. . . . I think, perhaps, the genius of Lewis was that he made a world that was more real to me than the one I lived in; and if authors got to write the tales of Narnia, then I wanted to be an author."

By contrast, for many Christians the books are almost manuals of faithful religious practice: I once told a Christian friend that I thought the Harry Potter books better than the Narnia books, only to have him reply, "Maybe—but does Harry Potter form children in the character of Christ?" Books that can appeal so strongly to such different kinds of readers are extraordinary books indeed, and fascination with them shows no signs of slowing. Anyone who can write books like that is a person whose life is worth knowing about.

My first thanks must go to Mickey Maudlin, my editor at Harper San Francisco, who explained to me why it made sense for me to write this book. The task has been a joyful one, but I am not sure I would have had sense enough to take it on had it not been for Mickey's clarity of mind and firmness of purpose. Thanks also other folks at Harper who have worked hard on this book: Cindy DiTiberio, Claudia Boutote, Laina Adler, Terri Leonard, and especially Cindy Buck, who did a remarkable job copyediting the manuscript.

I am very grateful for friends who have assisted me in various ways during the writing of this book. John Wilson offered support and encouragement early in the project, when I most needed them. Jay Wood has been remarkably patient with my tendency to wander into his office and start talking about Lewis; conversations with him have helped me through some sticky places in the narrative. Matt Vinson read drafts of the first few chapters and offered valuable critical commentary. Jessica Dwelle read a late version of the manuscript and, at a time that was perfect for me but inconvenient to her, gave me an intelligent and useful response. My agent, Christy Fletcher, made it possible for me to focus on writing this book, and at one or two crucial junctures helped me maintain my sanity.

My wife, Teri, and my son, Wesley, have, as always, brightened my life, given me joy, held me up in hard times, and sometimes managed to convince me that I am a competent writer who knows what he's doing. Certainly they have doubted this less often than I have. But Teri did still more: she painstakingly read the manuscript; she offered insight, commentary, challenge, correction, encouragement, plenty of hot coffee, and (above all) constant love. Clichés become clichés for a reason, so I do not hesitate to say: I don't know what I would do without her.

In writing this book, I have been blessed in having an office a short stroll away from the finest collection of Lewis research materials in the world, the Marion Wade Center at Wheaton College. Chris Mitchell, Marjorie Mead, and Heidi Truty have been unfailingly helpful and supportive and have graciously refrained from noting—in my presence anyway, which is what counts—that they know more about Lewis than I ever will. I also must note that every writer on Lewis—every *reader* of Lewis—owes a great debt to Walter Hooper, who as literary executor has spent the last forty years getting Lewis's multitudinous writings before the public.

Finally, a word to any lovers or scholars of Lewis who happen to read this book and take umbrage at some claim, description, or argument I have made in these pages. As Beatrice says of Benedick, "I know you of old"—so well, indeed, that some years ago I made a great vow never to write another word about Lewis, that I might never again feel your wrath. That vow I have, obviously and quite spectacularly, broken, and I suppose I must live with the consequences. But before you write, or call, or fax, or e-mail me with your words of chastisement, please hear me: I am sorry. Indeed, I repent in sackcloth and ashes. I bow to your wisdom and knowledge, and I promise that I will not make such mistakes again. And do you know why? Because I will never, ever write another word about C. S. Lewis.

Introduction

I n March 1949 C. S. Lewis invited a friend named Roger Lancelyn
Green to dinner at Magdalen College of Oxford University, where
Lewis was a tutor; Green, though he had not been Lewis's pupil,
had attended many of his lectures a decade earlier, and their friendship
had grown over the years. It was scarcely unusual for Lewis to make
such an invitation—he had many friends and enjoyed their company
greatly and often—but it must have been especially refreshing for him
at that moment to contemplate an evening of food, wine, and conversation, for his life was very miserable.

He lived with his brother and an elderly woman named Mrs.
Moore whom he often referred to as his mother—though, as we shall
see, she was not his mother—and both of them were unwell and de-
pendent upon him for their care. Just a few days before his dinner
with Green he had written to an American friend that he was "tied to
an invalid," which is what Mrs. Moore had become, confined to bed
by arthritis and varicose veins. For her part, Mrs. Moore proclaimed
that Lewis was "as good as an extra maid in the house," and she certainly *used* him as a maid, to his brother's constant disgust; she seems
also to have become obsessive and quarrelsome in her later years,
worried always about her dog and constantly at odds with the domestic help. Lewis had been able to hire two maids to help with
cleaning and nursing when he had to be at Magdalen, where he kept
up a grueling round of lectures, tutorials, and correspondence-keep-
ing, but for a time one of the maids became unstable (she was undergoing some sort of psychiatric treatment), and he occasionally had to

return home to sort out conflicts the maids had with each other and with Mrs. Moore.

In 1947 he had been asked, by the Marquess of Salisbury, to participate in meetings, along with the Archbishops of Canterbury and York, to discuss the future of the Church of England (of which Lewis was a member), but had had to decline: "My mother is old and infirm . . . and I never know when I can, even for a day, get away from my duties as a nurse and a domestic servant. (There are psychological as well as material difficulties in my house.)" In the intervening two years the miseries had if anything intensified, and there are dark hints in some of Lewis's writings that the suffering shook his Christian faith to the core. Though he had written, and written recently, of the joys of heaven, in the year of the Marquess's letter he found himself consumed by a "horror of nonentity, of annihilation"—that is, of finding that the God in whom he had trusted had no eternal life to offer.*

As one might guess from Lord Salisbury's invitation, Lewis was a famous man, in America as well as in Britain (within a few months of receiving that letter he would find himself on the cover of *Time* magazine), and he was besieged daily by a blizzard of letters. Lewis, who was determined to answer every correspondent, was normally assisted by his brother, Warnie, who typed dictated or drafted letters and kept the files organized, but at the beginning of March 1949 Warnie was in Oxford's Acland Hospital, having drunk himself into insensibility. (He would go on such destructive binges occasionally for the rest of his life.) When Warnie was released, on March 3, he was not strong enough to fend fully for himself, so his brother had to take care of him as well as Mrs. Moore and Bruce, the elderly dog with whose welfare Mrs. Moore was so preoccupied. For a time Lewis worked away at the correspondence by himself, while continuing his labors at Magdalen. Warnie wrote in his diary, "His kindness remains unabated," but his brother's resources were failing. In early April Lewis wrote to a friend who had reproached him for not replying promptly to a letter, "Dog's stools and human vomit have made my day today: one of those days when you feel at 11 A.M. that it really must be 3 P.M." Two months

---

* Here is the comment in its context: "I have, almost all my life, been quite unable to feel that horror of nonentity, of annihilation, which, say, Dr. Johnson felt so strongly. I felt it for the first time only in 1947. But that was after I had long been reconverted and thus began to know what life really is and what would have been lost by missing it."

later he collapsed at his home and had to be taken to the hospital. He was diagnosed with strep throat, but his deeper complaint was simply exhaustion, and his doctor was concerned about stress to his heart.

Though the breakdown was still to come, such, in outline, was C. S. Lewis's world the evening he had his friend Roger Lancelyn Green to dinner at Magdalen's high table, and to his rooms for talk afterward. It is unlikely that Green had any idea how miserable his friend had been, and he surely could not have suspected that Lewis would soon be in the hospital. That evening Lewis was a charming host, and (Green wrote in his diary) they had "wonderful talk until midnight: he read me two chapters of a book for children he is writing—very good indeed, though a trifle self-conscious." This book would eventually become *The Lion, the Witch, and the Wardrobe,* the first story about a world called Narnia.

Many years later, in the biography of Lewis that Green wrote with Walter Hooper, he added a brief commentary on that diary entry (referring to himself in the third person): "Nevertheless it was a memorable occasion which the listener remembered vividly, and remembered his awed conviction that he was listening to a book that could rank among the great ones of its kind." It is hard not to see this as a case of revisionist memory—like the tale of some old baseball scout who claims that he knew from the first time he laid eyes on a seventeen-year-old shortstop that one day the boy would be in the Hall of Fame. If Green had had an "awed conviction" of the book's potential greatness, surely that would have been recorded in the diary entry written so soon after the "memorable occasion." Perhaps, after all, the draft chapters that Lewis read really *were* no more than "very good"—isn't that sufficient praise?—and perhaps they really *were* marred to some degree by self-consciousness. After all, Green and Hooper note on the same page of their biography that Lewis got "stuck" for quite some time and couldn't get the story past its opening chapters. Lewis himself had written in a letter some time earlier, "I have tried [to write a children's story] myself but it was, by the unanimous verdict of my friends, so bad that I destroyed it." And according to Green's later recollections, Lewis had already tried out the story on his friend J. R. R. Tolkien and had received a pronounced negative response. It might even be that Green was too generous to his beloved guide and friend: perhaps the story he read that night wasn't good at all—yet.

But whether what Lewis read to Green was any good seems beside the point: what is remarkable about the scene is that in the midst of all his miseries the writing of a *story for children* is what Lewis had turned to. I have said that he was already famous, but his fame was chiefly that of a controversialist—a polemical contender for Christianity. Certainly that was the thrust of *Time*'s cover story, which emphasized Lewis's then-forthcoming book arguing for the validity of belief in miracles. He was also a highly accomplished scholar, perhaps already (in his midforties) the most accomplished on the Oxford English faculty. He had written fiction too, but of a highly intellectual character; a bachelor with no children of his own, he had relatively few friends whose children he knew. He would not seem to be a likely candidate to be writing a children's book.

Moreover, he was never an aficionado of children's books—even in the year before his death, he could tell a correspondent, "My knowledge of children's literature is really very limited. . . . My own range is about exhausted by Macdonald, Tolkien, E. Nesbit, and Kenneth Grahame"—and he never read *The Wind in the Willows* or Nesbit's stories of the Bastable family until he was in his twenties. Yet he never outgrew the love of the children's stories he *did* know. Once he discovered *The Wind in the Willows*, it was forever precious to him, both for the sheer charm of its story and for the main characters, whom he considered beautifully drawn examples of certain distinctively English "types." (He told a friend that he always read Grahame's masterpiece when he was in bed with the flu.) Perhaps most telling of all, in 1942, when presented with an opportunity to visit England's Lake District, he was primarily eager to do so in order to make a "pilgrimage" to visit Beatrix Potter, of Peter Rabbit fame, who, though elderly, still lived there. (Alas, she died the next year without receiving a visit from Lewis.) "She has a secure place among the masters of English prose," he wrote—a verdict that he would have issued, perhaps in slightly different language, when he was five years old, and from which he surely never wavered.

You can see Lewis's love of children's stories in the oddest places and in the most charming ways. In one of his most learned and scholarly books, *A Preface to "Paradise Lost"*—and *Paradise Lost* is as sober and serious and adult a poem as one could imagine—Lewis quotes his eighteenth-century predecessor at Magdalen College, Joseph Addison: "The great moral which reigns in Milton is the most universal and most useful that can be imagined, that Obedience to the will of God makes men happy and that Disobedience makes them miserable." Lewis then notes that a fellow literary critic, E. M. W. Tillyard, called

Addison's comment "vague," and having stated that Tillyard's claim "amazes" him, off he goes:

> Dull, if you will, or platitudinous, or harsh, or jejune; but how *vague?* Has it not rather the desolating clarity and concreteness of certain classic utterances we remember from the morning of our own lives; "Bend over"—"Go to bed"—"Write out *I must do as I am told* a hundred times"—"Do not speak with your mouth full." How are we to account for the fact that great modern scholars have missed what is so dazzlingly simple? . . . It is, after all, the commonest of themes; even Peter Rabbit came to grief because he *would* go into Mr. McGregor's garden.

This is as delightful as it is wise: any literary critic who can, in the course of a few sentences, take us from the great Milton's account of the Fall of Humanity, in twelve books of stately and heroic blank verse, to Beatrix Potter's rather humbler account of Peter Rabbit's rather humbler troubles, is a critic of (to put it mildly) considerable range. And the *naturalness* with which he achieves this!—clearly it never occurs to Lewis to imagine that there is some great disjunct between Milton's world and Beatrix Potter's, and once he puts the likeness before us it's easy for us to see too. After all, leaving aside the one fact that Adam and Eve's decision was disastrous for all of us, while Peter's was (nearly) disastrous just for himself, the two stories have a great deal in common. But it takes someone of Lewis's peculiar stamp to recognize (and more, to declare, in a public, academic setting) the ethical shape of a narrative world in which obedience to Just Authority brings happiness and security, while neglect of that same Authority brings danger and misery. Few writers other than Lewis could open to us that sphere of experience in which John Milton and Beatrix Potter can be seen as laborers in the same vineyard—that sphere in which a *moral* unity suddenly seems far more important than those otherwise dramatic differences in time, genre, and purpose.

And it was not just a few children's classics of the past about which Lewis was enthusiastic. Lewis served as almost a midwife to many children's stories, including those of Green (drafts of whose books he often read and responded to) and, most famously, those of his friend and Oxford colleague Tolkien. In 1932 Tolkien took the chance of reading aloud to Lewis a story he had written. Lewis adored it and insisted that others would too—he badgered Tolkien into seeking to have it published, which eventually he did, in 1938: the story was called *The Hobbit*. So those who knew Lewis best were not surprised at all when he brought forth drafts of *The Lion, the Witch, and the Wardrobe,* or when he published it, in late 1950. But perhaps they would have been surprised had they known that that story, and the six that followed it into Narnia, would bring him greater fame and influence than all his other books combined, making his name known all over the world. The Chronicles of Narnia have been translated into more than thirty languages and, worldwide, have sold more than eighty-five million copies. No one could have guessed that *that* was the future of the little story for children that Lewis was struggling with—along with all the other things he was struggling with—that evening in 1949 when he invited Green to dinner.

In 1944, when Lewis was beginning to be quite famous—though not nearly as famous as Narnia would later make him—the American publishing house Macmillan asked him for a brief biographical sketch that they could include in his books. Macmillan had started to publish his more popular ones the year before and clearly expected their audience to want to know something about the life of this remarkable writer. Lewis was not especially interested in writing or talking about himself; indeed, his close friend Owen Barfield thought this one of Lewis's more noteworthy traits ("there was so much else, in letters and in life, that he found much *more* interesting!"). But when asked for a statement he would sometimes comply; some years later he wrote a whole book (*Surprised by Joy*) to satisfy the curious. Here's what he sent to the people at Macmillan:

> I was a younger son, and we lost my mother when I was a child. That meant very long days alone when my father was at work and my brother at boarding school. Alone in a big house full of books. I suppose that fixed a literary bent. I drew a lot, but soon began to write more. My first stories were mostly about mice (influence of Beatrix Potter), but mice usually in armor killing gigantic cats (influence of fairy stories). That is, I wrote the books I should have liked to read if only I could have got them. That's always been my reason for writing. People won't write the books I want, so I have to do it for myself: no rot about "self-expression." I loathed school. Being an infantry soldier in the last war would have been nicer if one had known one was going to survive. I was

wounded—by an English shell. (Hence the greetings of an aunt who said, with obvious relief, "Oh, so *that's* why you were wounded in the back!") I gave up Christianity at about fourteen. Came back to it when getting on for thirty. An almost purely philosophical conversion. I didn't *want* to. I'm not the religious type. I want to be let alone, to feel I'm my own master: but since the facts seemed to be the opposite I had to give in. My happiest hours are spent with three or four old friends in old clothes tramping together and putting up in small pubs—or else sitting up till the small hours in someone's college rooms talking nonsense, poetry, theology, metaphysics over beer, tea, and pipes. There's no sound I like better than adult male laughter.

The sentence fragments, colloquialisms, and general bluntness of tone—all uncharacteristic of Lewis's public writings—suggest that he dashed this off without editing it, perhaps without even thinking about it too seriously. Lewis undoubtedly expected the people at Macmillan to recognize this as a rough pile of facts from which they were at liberty to construct a more formal narrative. (As it happened they did not, and published this scribbled note just as they received it.) But the very casualness of the paragraph is what makes it interesting: what we have here is something like the self-understanding that came readily to Lewis's mind, the basic narrative *shape* of his experience. (When he got around to writing *Surprised by Joy*—which is something like a three-hundred-fold expansion of the paragraph for Macmillan—he subtitled it "The Shape of My Early Life.") Much is revealed in these few sentences that will govern the story I wish to tell.

It's clear that the foundational elements are the early death of his mother and his subsequent aloneness—not necessarily loneliness, but a kind of personal and intellectual independence forged in solitude. The last thing he wants is to achieve "self-expression"; he's not interested in sharing his "self" with others. Thus his hatred of school, more particularly the English public school with its determination to socialize boys into a certain kind of citizenship, its manifold schemes of regimentation; thus his sense that if people won't write the books he likes, he'll just have to write them himself. Note also the stubbornness: he's not going to start liking a certain kind of story just because it's the kind that people nowadays write—he will continue to stick with his own preferences, even if they cause him the enormous trouble of becoming an author. A few years earlier he had written—in a scholarly

study of medieval allegory, of all things—that his "ideal happiness . . .
would be to read the [Renaissance] Italian epic—to be always convalescent from some small illness and always seated in a window that
overlooked the sea, there to read these poems eight hours of each
happy day." In this vision of bliss, there's no writing, because writing
is work—and a convalescent can't be expected to work, now can he?
(I might add that this paradise has no *people* in it either, at least not
during the reading day.)

And clearly Lewis is a man who values friendship above almost all
else—look at how he concludes his little self-portrait—but equally
clearly, his core convictions have not been formed while walking country lanes or warming his feet around a shared fire; rather, he has
worked out his beliefs alone, in houses full of books. "I am a product," he would later write, "of long corridors, empty sunlit rooms, up-
stairs indoor silences, attics explored in solitude, distant noises of
gurgling cisterns and pipes, and the noise of wind under the tiles. Also,
of endless books." Describing a period of his childhood when a "small
illness" kept him at home when he otherwise would have been at
school, he writes with evident nostalgia, "I entered with complete satisfaction into a deeper solitude than I had ever known."

In the "endless books" that peopled his solitude, Lewis discovered a
range of interests ("nonsense, poetry, theology, metaphysics") that, nur-
tured and matured, would almost all find their way into his career as a
writer. The books by Lewis that Macmillan published in the years 1943
and 1944 alone (though some of them had been written several years
earlier) included two science fiction novels, a theological treatise about
suffering, a satire in the form of letters from a devil, and two brief works
in explanation and defense of the Christian faith. It is so hard to imagine
one person managing all these kinds of writing—plus works of serious
scholarship and still another kind of writing that we will soon turn our
attention to—that one can understand why Owen Barfield once wrote
an essay about his famous friend called "The Five C. S. Lewises."

And yet the chief point of Barfield's essay is that what's really remarkable about Lewis is not the *diversity* of his writings, but the
unity—the sense that something ties them all together. But what precisely *is* this alleged unity? What does it consist in? Barfield's attempt
to answer this question is tentative but highly intriguing:

> I am not sure that anyone has succeeded in locating it. Some have
> pointed to his "style," but it goes deeper than that. "Consistency"?

Noticeable enough in spite of an occasional inconsistency here or there. His unswerving "sincerity" then? That comes much nearer, but still does not satisfy me. Many other writers are sincere—but they are not Lewis. No. There was something in the whole quality and structure of his thinking, something for which the best label I can find is "presence of mind." If I were asked to expand on that, I could say only that somehow what he thought about everything was secretly present in what he said about anything.

Whether or not Barfield has rightly identified this "presence of mind" as *the* unifying feature of Lewis's writings, and indeed of his character, it is surely a notable trait, one that we see repeatedly in the course of this book. Certain Lewisian themes, ideas, concerns, and convictions can find their way into almost anything he writes, for almost any audience. But even if we agree that Lewis is particularly, even uniquely, characterized by such omnivorous attentiveness, one might go further and ask what *kind* of attentiveness it was—what, specifically, was present to his mind.

And here I would like to suggest something that is the keynote of this book: my belief that Lewis's mind was above all characterized by a *willingness to be enchanted* and that it was this openness to enchantment that held together the various strands of his life—his delight in laughter, his willingness to accept a world made by a good and loving God, and (in some ways above all) his willingness to submit to the charms of a wonderful *story,* whether written by an Italian poet of the sixteenth century, by Beatrix Potter, or by himself. What is "secretly present in what he said about anything" is an openness to delight, to the sense that there's more to the world than meets the jaundiced eye, to the possibility that *anything* could happen to someone who is ready to meet that anything. For someone with eyes to see and the courage to explore, even an old wardrobe full of musty coats could be the doorway into another world. It is the sort of lesson a child might learn—even a stubborn, independent child—if his mother has died and his father and brother are often away and he spends his days alone in an old house full of books, thinking and drawing and writing and thinking some more.

After all the Narnia books were done, he wrote a little essay in which he explained that the stories began when he started "seeing pictures in [his] head"—or rather, when he started paying attention to pictures he had been seeing all along, since the "picture of a Faun carrying

an umbrella and parcels in a snowy wood," which we find near the beginning of *The Lion, the Witch, and the Wardrobe,* first entered Lewis's
head when he was sixteen years old. It was only when he was "about
forty" that he said to himself, "Let's try to make a story about it." As
we have seen, it was a particularly trying time in his life when he wrote
the first tale of Narnia. Yet something—some instinctively strong response to the offer of enchantment, I would say, perhaps all the
stronger because of the difficult circumstances in which the offer presented itself—made him start writing, even though he "had very little
idea how the story would go." (It was only when the great lion Aslan
"came bounding into it" that "He pulled the whole story together, and
soon He pulled the six other Narnian stories in after Him.")

What made Lewis write this way, and why it is such a good thing
that he was able to write this way—these are hard things to talk about
without being (or at least seeming) sentimental, yet they are necessary
to talk about. In most children but in relatively few adults, at least in
our time, we may see this willingness to be delighted to the point of
self-abandonment. This free and full gift of oneself to a story is what
produces the state of enchantment. But why do we lose the desire—or
if not the desire, the ability—to give ourselves in this way? Adolescence introduces the fear of being deceived, the fear of being caught
believing what others have ceased believing in. To be naïve, to be
gullible—these are the great humiliations of adolescence. Lewis seems
never to have been *fully* possessed by this fear, though at times in his
life he felt it: "When I was ten, I read fairy stories in secret and would
have been ashamed if I had been found doing so. Now that I am fifty I
read them openly. When I became a man I put away childish things,
including the fear of childishness and the desire to be very grown up."
But even in his adolescent unbelief he was always capable of a kind of
innocent delight; his greatest and deepest affection was always reserved for the bards, the tellers of tales—and the taller the tales the
better. It was Wagner's vast landscapes of heroic myth that captured
him, and the gentler "Faerie" world of the English imagination, from
Spenser to Tennyson and William Morris and (above all) George Mac-
Donald. He once wrote that stories that sounded "the horns of
Elfland" constituted "that kind of literature to which my allegiance
was given the moment I could chose books for myself." It was therefore perhaps inevitable that he would become a scholar of medieval
and Renaissance literature, and unsurprising that his first work of fiction would be an elaborate allegory based on Bunyan's *Pilgrim's*

Progress (that alluring sugared spiritual medicine for so many generations of English children) and that he would consume works of fantasy and then science fiction—in which genre he would write his first novels. It was probably not likely that such an *open* mind would remain atheist long, though Lewis did manage to hold out as an unbeliever until he was nearly thirty.

One could say, then, that Lewis remained in this particular sense childlike—that is, able always to receive pleasure from the kinds of stories that tend to give pleasure to children. This trait in him was evident to his close friends, though they described it in different ways. I think his friend Owen Barfield has this childlikeness, or some component of it, in mind when he refers to "a certain psychic or spiritual immaturity . . . which is detectable in some of his religious and philosophical writings." Ruth Pitter—a poet who was a close friend of Lewis's for some years—makes a similar but more comprehensive statement: "In fact his whole life was oriented & motivated by an almost uniquely-persisting child's sense of glory and of nightmare. The adult events were received into a medium still as pliable as wax, wide open to the glory, and equally vulnerable, with a man's strength to feel it all, and a great scholar's & writer's skills to express and to interpret." Surely Lewis himself would have said that when we can no longer be "wide open to the glory"—risking whatever immaturity thereby—we have not lost just our childlikeness but something near the core of our humanity. Those who will never be fooled can never be delighted, because without self-forgetfulness there can be no delight, and this is a great and a grievous loss.

When we talk today about receptiveness to stories, we tend to contrast that attitude to one governed by reason—we talk about freeing ourselves from the shackles of the rational mind and that sort of thing—but no belief was more central to Lewis's mind than the belief that it is eminently, fully rational to be responsive to the enchanting power of stories. As we see in detail later on, Lewis passionately believed that education is not about providing information so much as cultivating "habits of the heart"—producing "men with chests," as he puts it in his book *The Abolition of Man*, that is, people who not only *think* as they should but *respond* as they should, instinctively and emotionally, to the challenges and blessings the world offers to them. It was with this idea in mind that Lewis dedicated *A Preface to "Paradise Lost"* to his friend and fellow writer Charles Williams. In his dedicatory letter he fondly remembers a series of lectures that Williams gave at Oxford about the poetry of Milton: "It is a reasonable hope," Lewis writes, "that of those who heard you in Oxford many will understand that when the old poets made some virtue their theme they were not teaching but adoring, and that what we take for the didactic is often the enchanted." Lewis is known as a moralist, but I think we can infer from this comment that his teaching is often a function of his adoration—so that the moral elements of his writing are not so easily distinguished from the enchantment of storytelling and story-loving. It is the merger of the moral and the imaginative—this vision of virtue itself as adorable, even ravishing—that makes Lewis so distinctive.

Oddly enough he achieves this merger most perfectly in his children's books. I say "oddly" because Lewis was quite aware of the restraints and limitations imposed on a person writing for children: "Writing 'juveniles' certainly modified my habits of composition. Thus (a) It imposed a strict limit on vocabulary. (b) Excluded erotic love. (c) Cut down reflective and analytical passages. (d) Led me to produce chapters of nearly equal length for convenience in reading aloud." But, he added, "all these restrictions did me great good—like writing in a strict metre." I think we can infer from the context that writing for children forced him to concentrate on what was most essential—in the story, yes, but also in his own experience. In writing these tales for children, he found something like the bedrock of his own imagination and belief.

In 1954, when Lewis had finished writing the Narnia books (though *The Last Battle* remained to be published), he got a letter from the leadership of the Milton Society of America informing him that they wanted to honor him for his contribution to the study of John Milton's poetry—by which the Society meant, primarily, *A Preface to "Paradise Lost."* They also asked him to "make a statement" about his published works. Looking them over—noting the presence of novels, literary history and criticism, poetry, Christian apologetics—he admitted that his works amounted to a "mixed bag." Nevertheless, he wished to insist that through them all "there is a guiding thread."

> The imaginative man in me is older, more continuously operative, and in that sense more basic than either the religious writer or the critic. It was he who made my first attempt (with little success) to be a poet. It was he who, in response to the poetry of others, made me a critic, and in defense of that response, sometimes a critical controversialist. It was he who, after my conversion led

me to embody my religious belief in symbolic or mythopoeic forms, ranging from *Screwtape* to a kind of theologised science-fiction. And it was, of course, he who has brought me, in the last few years to write the series of Narnian stories for children; not asking what children want and then endeavouring to adapt myself (this was not needed) but because the fairy-tale was the *genre* best fitted for what I wanted to say.

I think Lewis's message here, though couched in the politest of terms, is quite clear. He is honored by the approval of the Miltonists, but he also must admit that he is not really one of them—he is not one for whom scholarship is an end in itself or a life's calling. He wrote as a "controversialist" about Milton, he sought to rescue Milton from misinterpretation, not because it was his vocation to do so, but rather because he loved Milton's poetry and wished to defend it against those who would slight it or attack it. At the heart of his impulse to write, then—to write even scholarly works of literary criticism—was the warm and passionate response to literature of an "imaginative man." A deeply learned book about John Milton is important to its author largely because it witnesses to something else: a child's love of the rhythms of verse and the excitements of story. And it would seem that Narnia taught him this about himself: that, in the forty years since his childhood in Belfast, Northern Ireland, he hadn't really changed very much. The same impulse that had produced *The Allegory of Love* and *Miracles* and *Mere Christianity* also produced the Chronicles of Narnia, but it was only Narnia that *revealed* that truth to him. Aslan has gifts for everyone, and perhaps that was what he gave Lewis: a certain, and very important, piece of self-knowledge.

Clearly Lewis's imagination was a transforming one: he took the people he knew and loved, the great events he experienced, the books he read, and swept them all together into the great complicated manifold world of Narnia. (As A. N. Wilson shrewdly writes, the "whole theme" of the Narnian books is "the interpenetration of worlds, and [Lewis] poured into them a whole jumble of elements.") Or perhaps this is a better way to say it: Lewis could make Narnia because the essential traits of Narnia were already in his mind long before he wrote the first words of the Chronicles. His reading and his other experiences had formed him that way. He was a Narnian long before he knew what name to give that country; it was his true homeland, the native ground to which he hoped, one day, to return.

At the darkest moment in the first tale of Narnia, when Aslan's tortured and humiliated body lies stone dead on the Stone Table, Lewis tells us what Susan and Lucy are feeling:

> I hope no one who reads this book has been quite as miserable as Susan and Lucy were that night; but if you have been—if you've been up all night and cried till you have no more tears left in you—you will know that there comes in the end a sort of quietness. You feel as if nothing was ever going to happen again.

Obviously, only one whose misery had taken him to this devastated "quietness" could write these sentences. Lewis had known such misery as a child; he knew it again as a middle-aged man. Yet it was quite directly out of this misery that a story for children came—at first a bumbling story, flat and uninspired, but one that Lewis could not ignore. As he wrote when all the Narnia stories were done, it was only when the great lion Aslan "came bounding into it" that he stopped bumbling and the story began to move in its proper course: "He pulled the whole story together, and soon He pulled the six other Narnian stories in after Him." And into Narnia he also pulled Lewis; and then, us.

ONE

"Happy, but for so happy ill secured . . ."

When Clive Staples Lewis was four years old, in 1902 or 1903, he quite suddenly announced to his mother, father, and older brother that from that day forth he would no longer be known as Clive, but rather as "Jacksie." To no other name would he answer. Eventually he allowed slight modifications—Jacksie yielded to Jacks, and then, finally, to Jack—but never again would he be Clive. Except to teachers and others whom he knew only formally, he remained Jack to the end of his days, sixty years later.

Such boldness indicates a precocious self-assurance, and surely the indication is correct: it was only a few years later that Jack interrupted his father in his study in order to announce, "I have a prejudice against the French." When his father asked him why, he replied, "If I knew *why* it would not be a prejudice." So, self-assurance, yes, but also an assurance of being loved—the expectation of tolerance, affection, and even indulgence that is so often found in the youngest child of a family.

And the Lewis family was a happy one, according to that model of domesticity adored and nearly perfected by the Victorians: the paterfamilas, his Angel in the House, and children (in this case sons) respectful of Papy and adoring of Mamy. When Jack was six they had moved from a semidetached house in Dundela, an inner suburb of Belfast, Ireland—*Northern* Ireland would not exist, as such, for another few decades—into a rambling, expansive, new brick house in more prestigious Strandtown and had filled it with books. They called it Leeborough, or, more familiarly, Little Lea. It possessed a garden, and the servants were kind. Once the family took a holiday in France. It was ideal—but when, half a century later, Jack wrote about his childhood in his book *Surprised by Joy,* he prefaced the first chapter with a quote from Milton's *Paradise Lost,* a dark statement from Satan, musing on the occupants of the Eden into which he peers: "Happy, but for so happy ill secured."*

Lewis's mother was named Florence Hamilton; she was called Flora. She had been born in County Cork in 1862, the daughter of an Anglican priest who throughout much of her childhood led a church in Rome. In 1874 he returned to Ireland to become the rector of St. Mark's Church in Dundela. The Reverend Thomas Hamilton could be so deeply moved by Christian faith and doctrine that he actually wept during his own sermons. Like many Ulster Anglicans, he despised Catholics and thought them not only un-Christian but positively Satanic, but he was not simply and uniformly reactionary. He was for his time and place unusually supportive of women's education: when the brand-new Royal University of Ireland (founded in 1878, and now called Queen's University) announced that from the outset it would accept women as students and give them the same rights and privileges as men—something then unthinkable at Oxford or Cambridge—he sent his daughter Flora. She performed very well indeed, in 1885 taking a first (that is, a first-class degree) in logic and a second in mathematics.

A year later a young man named Albert Lewis asked her to marry him; she refused. This appears not to have deterred him, since in 1893 she agreed to his renewed proposal, though she made no pretense of ecstatic transport or (it would seem) anything like a sense of romance. "I wonder do I love you?" she wrote to Albert, as though considering a problem in logic. "I am not quite sure. I know that at least I am very fond of you, and that I should never think of loving anyone else." She would never, in her letters at least, confess to having fallen in love with Albert, but those letters do grow much more affectionate over time,

---

* Ah! gentle pair, ye little think how nigh
  Your change approaches, when all these delights
  Will vanish, and deliver ye to woe;
  More woe, the more your taste is now of joy;
  Happy, but for so happy ill secured
  Long to continue, and this high seat your Heaven
  Ill fenced for Heaven to keep out such a foe
  As now is entered. (*Paradise Lost,* IV.365ff)

and she reveals to him more and more of her personality. Especially notable is a witty parody of some of the preaching she had heard, a careful exegesis of that famously difficult text "Old Mother Hubbard, she went to the cupboard." Given the extraordinary skills as a satirist and parodist her younger son would later exhibit, one wonders whether this sort of gift could be hereditary.

This Albert Lewis had been born in the same county as Flora, in the city of Cork itself; he was a year younger. When Albert was still an infant his father—who was in the shipbuilding business—moved to Dublin, and then later to Belfast. Albert was sent for his chief education to Lurgan College in County Armagh (an Irish imitation of the English prep school), whose headmaster, an Ulster Scot named W. T. Kirkpatrick, would prove to be a central figure in the later history of the Lewis family. We will hear much more of him later.

After graduating from Lurgan in 1879, Albert was "articled" to a firm of solicitors in Dublin—that is, taken on as a kind of apprentice. Five years later he qualified as a solicitor and soon moved to Belfast to start his own practice. As an attorney he excelled. He was, his younger son would later write, "sentimental, passionate, and rhetorical," and while these qualities may have made him sometimes difficult to live with, they were of great value in the courtroom. "Woe to the poor jury man who wants to have any mind of his own," wrote Albert's former teacher Kirkpatrick; "he will find himself borne down by a resistless Niagara." Perhaps Flora Hamilton had a similar experience; at any rate, the man she married in 1894 was a man on the rise, and he would eventually become a significant figure in the public life of Belfast. At his death in 1929 the newspaper obituaries would be prominent, long, and effusive.

In a sense Albert Lewis, and the Lewis family, grew along with Belfast. A hundred years earlier it had been a town of little more than 20,000 people; by the time Jack Lewis was born it had grown into an energetic (if politically riven) city of more than 350,000. Shipbuilding had been the key to its growth—during Jack's childhood about one-fourth of all the men in Belfast worked in the shipyards in one capacity or another—and if Dublin was the political and cultural capital of Ireland, Belfast was equally clearly its industrial and economic powerhouse. It had become a place for the nouveau riche and nouveau bourgeois alike to thrive, and the Lewis family found their place somewhere between the two groups. They became part of a circle of people who loved books and the arts, who brought a cultural richness and sensitivity to this city of steel and shipyards and barely suppressed sectarian hatreds. It was a circle that Jack Lewis would always remember with great fondness and respect; even after many years in Oxford he would insist that "we Strandtown and Belmont people had among us as much kindness, wit, beauty, and taste as any circle of the same size that I have ever known." He did not have to come to Oxford, or anywhere else in England, to discover such virtues.

Flora Lewis gave birth to Warren in 1895, and to Clive (Jacksie-to-be) in 1898. Though the family was not quite as characteristically late-Victorian as it seemed to be—Flora being rather too much of an intellectual, and a highly rational intellectual at that, to fit perfectly the role of Angel in the House—the children certainly knew little but peace, harmony, and profound security. But sometime in 1907 Flora began experiencing frequent and increasingly severe abdominal pain; in February 1908, she underwent an exploratory operation. As was common in that time, it was conducted in her home. The doctors discovered abdominal cancer, and there was, of course, nothing that they could do. Shut up in her sickroom, she saw less and less of her family. The adult Jack would remember a night in his childhood when he was "ill and crying both with headache and toothache and distressed because my mother would not come to me. That was because she was ill too." On the twenty-third of August she died.

Jack had prayed for her to live. The Lewises were a Christian family, though it appears in a rather bland, Anglican sort of way: "I was taught the usual things and made to say my prayers and in due time taken to church. I naturally accepted what I was told but I cannot remember feeling much interest in it." He is at some pains to insist that in his childhood "religious experiences did not occur at all," and he makes no exception for his failed prayers for his mother's healing: "My mother's death was the occasion of what some (but not I) might regard as my first religious experience." One might think that a child's desperate but unanswered prayers for his mother's life to be spared would count as a "religious experience," though a bitter one, but the adult, Christian Lewis contends that the belief that motivated his prayers "was itself too irreligious for its failure to cause any religious revolution. . . . A 'faith' of this kind is often generated in children and . . . its disappointment is of no religious importance." What on earth does he mean by this?

Chiefly he means that when he was a child he conceived of God merely as a kind of "magician"—a being who had power to do miraculous things and to whom one might turn when in need of a miracle. He also had come to believe that *his* task, in coming before this magician, was to "produce by will a firm belief that [his] prayers for her recovery would be successful"—that is, he had gotten the idea that praying "in faith" was a matter of convincing yourself that what you were asking for would be granted. (After Flora had died he strove to convince himself that God would bring her back to life.) In short, young Jack was thinking of prayer as a kind of *technique*—a task that had to be managed in just the right way, according to approved procedures, or it wouldn't work. We see here for the first time a theme that will resonate powerfully in Lewis's adult work, the link between magic and technique or technology—and the opposition of magic and technology to truly religious experience. But at the time he had no sense of God as a "Savior" or as a "Judge" or even as a Person with whom one might have a personal exchange, and consequently (he argues), what happened when his prayers were not granted had nothing to do with religion as such. Nor, he contends, would anything religious have happened had his mother been healed, or even brought back from the dead.

Well, one sees his point. It is true that any truly Christian understanding of God will see him as something much more, and wholly other, than a magician—that is, as someone whose value lies in his ability and willingness to satisfy our desires. But it is hard to imagine that many young children (especially those whose mothers are dying) would be likely to separate their desires from their recognition of God as Savior and Judge. Perhaps children cannot yet think of God that more mature way at all; if so, what Lewis is really saying is that children do not have religious experiences. But even if one were to grant that point, surely it is still true that the kind of prayers that young Jack prayed were as close to genuine religion as he could manage, and that the failure of those prayers had some significance for his later thinking about religion. The adult Lewis resists this: "My disappointment produced no results beyond itself. The thing hadn't worked, but I was used to things not working, and I thought no more about it."

I take his word that he "thought no more about it." But it seems oddly perverse for Lewis to say that his experiment in prayer—or, if he would prefer, in practical magic—"produced no results beyond itself." If a child is deeply *confirmed* in a preexisting belief that "things" aren't going to "work"—that the universe will always find a way to resist his will and thwart his desires—I call that a result, just as it would have been a result had that preexisting belief been overturned by the healing or resurrection of his mother. And if Flora *had* been cured—and still more if she had been brought back to life—surely there would have been significant results for her son and his understanding of what "religious experience" is.

Why is Lewis so insistent that there was nothing truly religious about his childhood prayers for his mother's life? In part, his insistence must be his attempt to uphold a set of beliefs about what Christianity really is, or really should be—and to that point we cannot return until much later in this book. But I also think he has a great resistance to anything like a "Freudian" explanation of his spiritual history—and in the Freudian account, childhood experiences are usually definitive for later life. Lewis hated Freudianism, and he also wanted to preserve his own way of telling the story—which it is his task in *Surprised by Joy* to tell—of his eventual conversion to Christianity. His mother's death had nothing to do with that conversion as he understands it. But his insistence on the religious insignificance of Flora Lewis's death, and of his denied prayers for her recovery, has a curious effect on his narrative: it makes the loss of his mother seem less devastating to him than it actually was.

In light of this passage in his autobiography, it is illuminating to turn to *The Magician's Nephew*—a story that, like all the Narnia books, Lewis was writing at precisely the same time he was writing *Surprised by Joy*. When we first meet its protagonist, a boy named Digory Kirke, he's crying, and so miserable that he doesn't care who knows it. He tells Polly—the girl who catches him crying in the back garden of a London brownstone—that she would cry too in his situation.

> "And so would you ... if you'd lived all your life in the country and had a pony, and a river at the bottom of the garden, and then had been brought to live in a beastly Hole like this. ... And if your father was away in India—and you had to come and live with an Aunt and an Uncle who's mad (how would you like that?)—and if the reason was that they were looking after your Mother—and if your Mother was ill and was going to—going to—die." Then his face went the wrong sort of shape as it does if you're trying to keep back your tears.

Perhaps one should not read too much into typography, but I can't help noticing that in Digory's speech "father" appears in lower case and "Mother" in upper case—as though "father" is just a description but "Mother" a proper name.

In any case, Digory does not pray for his mother's healing. The people in the Narnia stories who come from our world give little evidence of being Christians: the cabby in *The Magician's Nephew* (the one who becomes King Frank, the first King of Narnia) sings hymns, but this seems to be a function of his rural Anglican upbringing rather than of any particular devotion; only at a few points in *The Last Battle* do we get meaningful direct references to Christianity as such. (Meaningful *indirect* references are, of course, another matter.) So Digory does not pray, and until a certain point in the story he does not even seem to *hope:* that his mother is "going to die" he takes as a given.

But then, after having traveled to the Wood Between the Worlds and to desolate Charn, and having returned, he overhears his aunt saying that "it would need fruit from the land of youth to help [Digory's mother] now. Nothing in *this* world will do much." And hearing this, what Digory suddenly realizes is that "he now knew (even if Aunt Letty didn't) that there really were other worlds," and that perhaps in one of them there really *could* be fruit that had the power to cure his mother. What he then thinks is noteworthy:

> Well, you know how it feels when you begin hoping for something that you want desperately badly; you almost fight against the hope because it is too good to be true; you've been disappointed so often before. That was how Digory felt. But it was no good trying to throttle this hope. It might—really, really, it just might be true. So many odd things had happened already. And he had the magic Rings. There must be worlds you could get to through every pool in the wood. He could hunt through them all. And then—*Mother well again*. Everything right again.

At this point, what Digory has that young Jack Lewis did not have is, simply, this: "So many odd things had happened already." He has been given no certainty of power, but rather a glimpse of infinite possibility: "It might—really, really, it just might be true." And later in the book he is given more than possibility: he stands in a perfect Garden, holding in his hand the very fruit that can heal his mother, and in his pocket lies the ring that will take him to her.

But he does not touch the ring, for two reasons. The first is that he remembers that he has made a promise to Aslan to bring the fruit back to him (and his mother, he knows, would want him to keep a promise). The second is that the Witch who tries to convince him to bring the fruit to his mother rather than to Aslan also suggests that he leave his friend Polly behind—and when she says that, "all the other words the Witch had been saying to him [sound] false and hollow." So Digory returns to Aslan with the fruit. But he knows that he has been faced with "the most terrible choice," and after making that choice, "he wasn't even sure all the time that he had done the right thing."

What reassures him, though, is a memory—a memory of his first real conversation with the great lion Aslan, in which he pleaded for his mother's life:

> "But please, please—won't you—can't you give me something that will cure Mother?" Up till then he had been looking at the Lion's great front feet and the huge claws on them; now, in his despair, he looked up at its face. What he saw surprised him as much as anything in his whole life. For the tawny face was bent down near his own and (wonder of wonders) great shining tears stood in the Lion's eyes. They were such big, bright tears compared with Digory's own that for a moment he felt as though the Lion must really be sorrier about his Mother than he was himself.

It is the memory of Aslan's tears that convinces Digory that he has done the right thing in rejecting the Witch's advice. It is because of the Lion's great compassion that Digory accepts Aslan's statement that, had Digory given his mother that fruit, someday both of them "would have looked back and said it would have been better to die in that illness." Though at this statement Digory must give up "all hopes of saving his Mother's life," he tells himself—and he really believes—that "the Lion knew . . . that there might be things even more terrible than losing someone you love by death."

The choice that Digory faces is, fundamentally, between magic and faith. Magic is power; magic *compels*. Through the magic of the fruit and the ring, Digory could give his mother life. (And in the world of Narnia the power of magic is real: when Polly suspects that magic used "in the wrong way" won't work, Aslan tells her that indeed it will work—but perhaps not in the way its user suspects. "All get what they want: they do not always like it.") What Aslan suggests to Digory is that, though sometimes we lose sight of this, mere biological life is not what we want, but rather the grace of love that, in *our* experience, is possible only when we also have biological life. And Digory trusts Aslan—has faith in him—not because he can really understand what

Aslan is telling him, but because of those tears. Because of those tears, Digory lays aside the compelling power of magic and decides to live by faith—even if it means that he must abandon the hope of curing his mother. (One could say that this decision marks Digory's first "religious experience.") But at the moment that Digory gives up that hope, Aslan restores it to him: he gives Digory another apple, and that apple heals his mother. It is tempting to say that Lewis gives to his character Digory what God would not give to young Jack. But then, in this world we always see what is taken away; what restoration awaits us, and the ones we love, we cannot yet see.

Flora Lewis had a calendar that featured a daily quotation from Shakespeare; the lines on the day of her death offered this speech from *King Lear:*

> Men must endure
> Their going hence, even as their coming hither:
> Ripeness is all.

The family preserved that page from the calendar as a memorial to the woman whom Albert called "as good a woman, wife and mother, as God has ever given to man." Fifty-five years later Warnie would have those first six words—*Men must endure their going hence*—inscribed on his brother's grave.

It is a curious feature of the Narnia books that almost all of the children in them are, in one way or another and for one reason or another, homeless. The Pevensie children, who inaugurate the series in *The Lion, the Witch, and the Wardrobe* and return for several later volumes, have parents but seem never to be with them: either the children have been sent to the countryside to avoid the dangers of the London Blitz—the book takes place during the Second World War—or they are on their way to their various boarding schools, or their parents have gone to America. Eustace Scrubb, whom we first meet in *The Voyage of the "Dawn Treader,"* also has parents, but they are—in Lewis's view of things—so eccentric and disconnected from reality ("They were vegetarians, non-smokers and teetotalers and wore a special kind of underclothes," and they insisted that Eustace call them by their first names) that they scarcely deserve the name of parents, and their home is, correspondingly, anything but homey. We never hear a word about the parents of Jill Pole (from *The Silver Chair*), but since they send her to the same "progressive" school that Eustace attended, we may draw inferences; in any case, as far as Lewis was concerned, simply being an English public school student is itself a kind of homelessness (as we shall see). Even the most notable children among the Narnian characters, Caspian and Shasta, are orphans. And then there is Digory Kirke himself, on the verge of becoming a true orphan, but even in the state in which we meet him he is cut off from his father by distance and from his mother by her illness.

None of these children, then, is homeless in the strictest sense of that word, but all of them are somehow disjointed, partly or wholly uprooted; where they live is never quite home—not as Jack knew home before his mother died. "With my mother's death," he later wrote, "all settled happiness, all that was tranquil and reliable, disappeared from my life." He is quick to say that his life was not without happiness—"but no more of the old security." At Little Lea, after his mother's death, familiar and sweet though the surroundings were, he could never be what he had been, insofar as nothing could ever be quite "settled" and "reliable" again. A month after the operation that discovered his mother's cancer, nine-year-old Jack recorded in his diary that he had been reading *Paradise Lost* and making "reflections thereon." One can only guess what those reflections might have been, but certainly he would have much more to reflect on in the coming months and years. For the rest of his life he would have a powerful sense of blessings fled and irrecoverable—though it would be a long time before he could learn to hope for other blessings, some possibly greater than the ones forfeited. At the end of Milton's poem the archangel Michael tells Adam that, though what he has lost is glorious, he will ultimately achieve something more glorious still: "a Paradise within thee, happier far."* But as he and Eve are leaving their perfect garden, passing the fearsome guardians whose flaming swords will forever bar any return, Adam (despite his pious protestations to the contrary) must have a great deal of difficulty taking the angel's word for it.

---

*From the end of the final book of the poem:
  Only add
  Deeds to thy knowledge answerable; add faith;
  Add virtue, patience, temperance; add love,
  By name to come called Charity, the soul
  Of all the rest: then wilt thou not be loth
  To leave this Paradise, but shalt possess
  A Paradise within thee, happier far.

It is noteworthy that Lewis laments the absence, not of love and affection, but of stability and reliability. His father loved Jack and Warnie but, as a "sentimental, passionate, and rhetorical" man, was not well equipped to calm his sons' fears and ease their anxieties. Rather, in his grief he seems to have continually disrupted whatever emotional equilibrium his sons—especially his younger son—managed to retain. (As if the death of his wife were not enough, Albert's father had died in April, and his brother Joseph would die two weeks after Flora.) As Jack would write decades later, his father's "nerves had never been of the steadiest and his emotions had always been uncontrolled. Under the pressure of anxiety his temper became incalculable; he spoke wildly and acted unjustly." In his biography of Lewis, A. N. Wilson refers to this comment as "merciless," but it is hard to see how one can make that judgment without knowing just what sorts of wild things Albert said or what unjust deeds he performed. (Warnie fully shared Jack's view of the general defects of their father's character—especially his "smothering tendency to dominate the life and especially the conversation of the household"—and such shortcomings were unlikely to have been remedied by grief.) In any case, immediately after the passage that Wilson deplores Lewis goes on to say that what his father suffered in those days after his beloved wife's death constituted a "peculiar cruelty of fate." Whatever happened and whoever was to blame for it, what remains abundantly clear is that the boys fled from their father whenever possible into their own company, and despite the fact that they continued to live in their comfortable house, surrounded by friends and family, they increasingly came to feel like "two frightened urchins huddled for warmth in a bleak world." The loss of their mother led to the loss (in a different way) of their father, and the damage Albert inadvertently did in those miserable days to his relationship with his children did not heal for years and years—if indeed it was ever fully remedied.

What happened to Jack after that is something he describes in different ways, and there are three components to it. The first I have already mentioned in the introduction: he discovered solitude. And now, perhaps, we can better see why Jack treasured it so: when his father walked out the door, on his way to his law office, wild words and unjust acts departed with him. But Jack also discovered his brother, Warnie—or it might be better to say that he and Warnie together began to discover new worlds within what they called the Little End Room.

In 1905, shortly after the family had moved to Little Lea, Warnie started school at the Wynyard School in Hertfordshire, England.

(Albert Lewis had devoted thorough research and great energy to the task of finding the best possible education for his elder son; nevertheless, as Roger Lancelyn Green and Walter Hooper write, "of all the schools in the British Isles he seems to have chosen the very worst." We shall see why they say so in the next chapter.) English preparatory schools, public schools, and universities then all ran—and for the most part still run—on a three-term academic calendar: from October to mid-December, from late January to early April, and from early May to early July. As a result, after starting school Warnie was together with his brother—who remained at Little Lea, receiving visits from tutors—for about five months of the year. During those five months the brothers would spend an extraordinary amount of time in the attic room they had claimed for themselves and turned into a playroom. It was there in the Little End Room that each boy created an imaginary world, and there that they learned to fuse their worlds into a single one.

Their endeavors had begun when they still lived in Dundela, before Little Lea had been built. (If their father's emotional instability drove them closer to each other, it was certainly not the first cause of their time spent together. Warnie himself, prosaically but probably accurately, attributed their play habits chiefly to the raininess of Ireland, which so regularly drove the boys indoors.) Jack was exceptionally bright, and it would seem that from early on Warnie treated him as the equal that, in effect, he was. Warnie, dreaming of Empire and probably having already read Kipling's stories, constructed an imaginary India; his first tale, Jack later recalled, was entitled *The Young Rajah*. Jack had developed an early fascination with Beatrix Potter's tales, and especially her illustrations, which in one of his last books he says were "the delight of my childhood. . . . The idea of humanised animals fascinated me perhaps even more than it fascinates most children." So Jack created Animal-Land, where what he and Warnie called "dressed animals" could have plenty of room for adventure.

What is curious—and especially significant for those who wish to understand Narnia—is that India and Animal-Land were eventually fused into a single world, called Boxen. The chronology of this important event is not very clear. In his autobiography *Surprised by Joy*, Lewis writes about it in a chapter that deals with his early adolescence, yet Boxen is already mentioned in letters that Jack wrote to Warnie when Jack was at Little Lea and Warnie at Wynyard—that is, in 1906 or 1907, possibly less than a year after the family had moved, when Jack was about eight. ("At present Boxen is *slightly* convulsed. The news has just reached her that King Bunny is a prisoner.") So it would appear that the decision to link their imaginary worlds came quite early. But whenever it happened, the brothers' alliance indicates an early willingness on Jack's part to think of imaginary worlds as having permeable boundaries and negotiable contours and characters. The sort of boy who thinks that worlds as different as Animal-Land and India could be joined might well grow up to be the sort of man who thinks that one can put talking animals, fauns, witches, and Father Christmas in the same book, with Bacchus and Silenus in its sequel. It's not the sort of practice that every storyteller finds attractive—J. R. R. Tolkien, for one, despised it, as we shall later see—but clearly Jack acquired a taste for this kind of syncretism from a very early age and never lost it. In fact, a taste for syncretism is one of his cardinal traits, and it ultimately became for him a matter of theological principle.

One might also imagine another important link between Boxen and Narnia: the talking animals themselves. But Lewis himself did not think the connection significant, because the two narrative worlds were so radically at odds: "Animal-Land had nothing whatever in common with Narnia except the anthropomorphic beasts. Animal-Land, by its whole quality, excluded the least hint of wonder. . . . There was no poetry, even no romance, in it. It was almost astonishingly prosaic." The Animal-Land stories, and later the Boxen stories, are more Anthony Trollope than Beatrix Potter: they are full less of heroic battles (which one might reasonably expect from a child's story, and receive with some gratitude) than they are of, strangely enough, *politics*—the one topic one would imagine that a young boy in early-twentieth-century Ulster would want to avoid. Yet not only was Animal-Land and then Boxen full of it—in the letter I quoted in the previous paragraph the kidnapping of King Bunny leads to riots that "the able general Quicksteppe" seeks to quell by formulating plans to rescue the king—but by the time he was fourteen Jack had written an entire political novel. Warnie has a reasonable explanation for this: remembering that his father always insisted that the boys sit quietly and listen to the adults' talk when visitors came to Little Lea, he notes that this experience convinced Jack that "grown-up conversation and politics were one and the same thing, and that everything he wrote must be given a political framework." (The inference is that young Jack wanted his writings to be somehow "adult.") However, Warnie continued, "the long-term result was to fill him with a disgust [for] and revulsion from the very idea of politics before he was out of his teens." That the adult Jack Lewis was as apolitical, or antipolitical, as Warnie claims is true only in a certain sense, but certainly Warnie helps us understand why the fundamental narrative character of Boxen is so alien to that of Narnia.

(While the animals of Boxen, in Jack's many drawings, wear the clothing of Victorian gentry and aristocracy, the animals in Narnia are almost never dressed, though I suppose Reeipcheep the valiant Mouse needs a swordbelt. In *Prince Caspian*, Trufflehunter the Badger is offered armor in preparation for battle, "but it said it was a beast, it was, and if its claws and teeth could not keep its skin whole, it wasn't worth keeping." This is the proper attitude for a Talking Beast of Narnia, and is forgotten only by the abysmal Ape Shift, who, to maintain the fiction that he is the representative of Aslan Himself, decides that he needs not only a scarlet jacket but also "jeweled slippers on his hind paws which would not stay on properly because, as you know, the hind paws of an Ape are really like hands." And it is not long after he assumes his clothing that Shift declares himself to be a Man.)

But there is probably another explanation for young Jack's "political novel"—one that complements rather than supplants Warnie's. Jack once wrote of those "endless books" that filled Little Lea: "Nothing was forbidden me. In the seemingly endless rainy afternoons I took volume after volume from the shelves," some of them "books suitable for a child" and others "books most emphatically not." Like many bright children, he seems to have graduated almost instantly from books of the nursery, like Beatrix Potter's tales, to adult books. (Less commonly, he later found his way back to the works of childhood that he had missed in his juvenile years.) Among the house's adult books were many, if not all, of the fifty-eight novels of Anthony Trollope, who was a favorite of Albert's; Jack later speculated that through characters such as Phineas Finn, Trollope's ambitious young Irishman in the British Parliament, Albert vicariously gratified his own secret political aspirations. Indeed, it would seem that Little Lea contained an extensive library of eighteenth- and nineteenth-century fiction and journalism: Jack read (to name just a few items) not only quite recent work by Sir Arthur Conan Doyle but also the romances of Sir Walter Scott, a "lavishly illustrated" edition of *Gulliver's Travels*, and volume after volume of the satirical magazine *Punch* (to which, years later, Jack would contribute poems, though always under a pseudonym).

There were surely books of adventure and even fantasy in the house, either already owned by the family or bought for Warnie and Jack: the Conan Doyle he mentions was *Sir Nigel,* a characteristic piece of late-Victorian medievalism, and though he did not discover E. Nesbit's Bastable books until adulthood, he did as a child read her *Five Children and It*—"It" being a Psammead, or sand fairy, and a rather ill-tempered one at that—and its two sequels. His parents might have bought the Nesbit stories for themselves, since, as Gore Vidal pointed out many years ago, she wrote *about* children more than she wrote *for* them, but it would appear that the tastes of both Albert and Flora ran to the more prosaic:

> What neither of [my parents] had the least taste for was that kind of literature to which my allegiance was given the moment I could choose books for myself. Neither had ever listened for the horns of elfland. There was no copy of either Keats or Shelley in the house, and the copy of Coleridge was never (to my knowledge) opened. If I am a romantic my parents bear no responsibility for it. . . . My mother, I have been told, cared for no poetry at all.

The phrase "horns of elfland" comes from a poem by Tennyson—

> O hark, O hear! how thin and clear,
>   And thinner, clearer, farther going!
> O sweet and far from cliff and scar
>   The horns of Elfland faintly blowing.

—and it encapsulates something that would later be dear to Lewis, something that saturates his Narnian tales, and indeed saturated much of his life. It is the distinctively English world called Faery.

I do not know of anything harder to explain than the land of Faery. It is, first of all, an alternate Britain—Britain seen in a distorting mirror, a mirror one can pass through. (And passing through a mirror is exciting and, at the same time, terrifying.) I say "Britain" rather than "England" because much of Faery mythology has its roots in a Celtic culture that preceded the coming of the Anglo-Saxons and has continued in various permutations in Ireland and England's "Celtic fringe" (Scotland, Wales, Cornwall). It is no accident that two of the people most influential in shaping the Victorian obsession with the world of

Faery were Scots: Andrew Lang (in his series of story collections called
Fairy Books) and George MacDonald.

But before we can begin to say what Faery is, we had best say what
it is not. It has nothing to do with "fairies" in the usual sense of that
term—that is, tiny creatures with butterfly wings, like Disney's
Tinkerbell. Those are a corruption of the original idea of Faery: J. R. R.
Tolkien, in his seminal essay "On Fairy-Stories," refers to them as
"that long line of flower-fairies and fluttering sprites that I so disliked
as a child." Tolkien gives credit to Andrew Lang for protesting against
this infantilization and miniaturization, but he chastises Lang for
classifying almost any story that is not completely realistic as a fairy
story—including even Gulliver's voyage to Lilliput! He further blames
Lang for helping to redescribe the fairy-tale world as a world for children; to Tolkien this it most emphatically is not, except insofar as children are simply people.

Tolkien himself is not interested in fairies, and not much in the
kinds of stories that are usually called fairy tales; but he is passionately
fascinated by Faery itself: a place, a world, that sometimes overlaps
with Britain but is fundamentally Other than it. Knowledge of this
place goes far back in British history; something like it is known in
other cultures, but Faery proper depends for much of its character on
the gentleness of British landscapes—their greenness, whether the
green of Irish fields or of ancient English forests, their lack of out-
size mountains or dramatic weather, their essential homeliness. That
homeliness is painted nowhere better than in Tolkien's writings about
the Shire. It is this simple, gentle world with which Faery overlaps—
Faery introduces into this unthreatening scene an element of *danger*, of
the wild and unpredictable. Faery is first of all a reminder that Nature
is not as gentle as, in Britain, it often seems. Though the dictionaries
often refer to fairies as "supernatural" beings, for Tolkien this is a
gross error:

> *Supernatural* is a dangerous and difficult word in any of its
> senses, looser or stricter. But to fairies it can hardly be applied,
> unless *super* is taken merely as a superlative prefix. For it is man
> who is, in contrast to fairies, supernatural (and often of diminu-
> tive stature); whereas they are natural, far more natural than he.
> Such is their doom.

For Tolkien, fairies are simply the residents of Faery, and as such
are Nature embodied in human or humanlike forms, and if one

thinks for five minutes about how Nature works—its beauties side by side with what in the human world would be shocking cruelties—one can see that true faeries are not likely to be diminutive and harmlessly cute. Faery is a world in which the forces of Nature take on sentience, will, active power. It is therefore a world equally capable of enchanting us and destroying us. "The trouble with the real folk of Faerie," writes Tolkien, "is that they do not always look like what they are; and they put on the pride and beauty that we would fain wear ourselves. At least part of the magic that they wield for the good or evil of man is power to play on the desires of his body and his heart." A man who finds himself in Faery will be overcome by desire, but what happens when he gains what he desires? In his wonderful story "Smith of Wooton Major," Tolkien calls it "that perilous country"; the protagonist, Smith, travels in Faery under the protection of a magical star on his forehead, but even so, "he soon became wise and understood that the marvels of Faery cannot be approached without danger."

Something of the same idea appears early in Lewis's science-fiction novel *That Hideous Strength,* the final volume of his Space Trilogy, when Dr. Dingle is meditating on Thomas Malory's great gathering of the Arthurian legends, the *Morte d'Arthur:*

> You've noticed how there are two sets of characters? There's Guinevere and Lancelot and all those people in the centre: all very courtly and nothing particularly British about them. But then in the background—on the other side of Arthur, so to speak—there are all those dark people like Morgan and Morgawse, who are very British indeed and usually more or less hostile though they are his own relatives. Mixed up with magic.... Merlin too, of course, is British though not hostile.

The "dark people" are connected with Faery—the "Morgan" he refers to is Arthur's archenemy Morgan le Fay, that is, Morgan the Fairy—and are always at least potentially "hostile." But not intrinsically and necessarily so: as Dingle says later in that book, "there might be things neutral in relation to us.... There used to be things on the earth pursuing their own business, so to speak. They weren't ministering spirits sent to help fallen humanity; but neither were they enemies preying upon us." Such neutrality carries its own dangers: such powers' lack of overt hostility can mask their serene indifference to human suffering. One hears echoes of this in Tolkien's portrayal of many of the Elves in *The Lord of the Rings,* those for whom the agonies of Middle Earth are simply no longer their problem. This is the true relation of Faery to our world.

I call "Smith of Wooton Major" the best brief introduction to Faery because, as I have said, Faery cannot really be described or explained: it must, if only in the form of fiction, be experienced. The marvels and dangers of Faery are cast in epic scope in *The Lord of the Rings,* but in a somewhat displaced way, because Faery there is made to serve Tolkien's own distinctive mythology. In Lothlorien, perhaps, we see most perfectly the sweet and lovely side of Faery—Aragorn tells Boromir that it is "fair and perilous; but only evil need fear it, or those who bring some evil with them"—but the dangers in *The Lord of the Rings* are perhaps too overt to be truly Faery-like. The *surreptitiousness* of Faery's true dangers is harder to capture; I have seen it done nowhere better than in Susanna Clarke's extraordinary novel *Jonathan Strange and Mr. Norrell* (2004). That surreptitiousness lies primarily in the old idea that Faery overlaps our world—that one can, unwillingly and unwittingly, pass from one into the other. The boundaries are unclear and sometimes nonexistent. This is part of the beauty of Faery—and also, of course, part of the danger, but the danger is part of the attraction, and it was in part this danger that young Jack Lewis heard when he first attended to "the horns of elfland."

In Faery are the seeds and roots of Narnia. But Narnia, as we shall see, is something other than Faery.

In the aftermath of Flora's death, the horns of elfland were scarcely audible to Jack. There he was in the Little End Room with Warnie, day after rainy day—Christmas, Eastertide, summer—writing and drawing for hours at a time, making maps that linked India and Animal-Land, narrating the history that led to the two lands joining to form Boxen. When we consider the misery the boys must often have felt, it is perhaps not so surprising that the romantic and fantastic were so absent from their shared imaginative world. Perhaps the very prosaicness of Boxen—the dry, historiographical character of much of the story—was a relief from the intensity of feeling. And when Warnie was away Jack wandered the house—servants were there, to be sure, but they obviously left him to his own devices—and learned the virtues and pleasures of solitude. After the death of his mother, solitude was more reliable, more secure, than anything else Jack knew.

"Coarse, brainless English schoolboys"

I n *The Silver Chair* we meet Jill Pole and become reacquainted with Eustace Scrubb at the school they attend: Experiment House, it is called.

It was "Co-educational," a school for both boys and girls, what used to be called a "mixed" school; some said it was not nearly so mixed as the minds of the people who ran it. These people had the idea that boys and girls should be allowed to do what they liked. And unfortunately what ten or fifteen of the biggest boys and girls liked best was bullying the others. All sorts of things, horrid things, went on which at an ordinary school would have been found out and stopped in half a term; but at this school they weren't. Or even if they were, the people who did them were not expelled or punished. The Head said they were interesting psychological cases and sent for them and talked to them for hours. And if you knew the right sort of things to say to the Head, the main result was that you became rather a favourite than otherwise.

Clearly this is a "progressive" school, with its identification of psychology as the master science, its emphasis on understanding rather than correcting or punishing errant students, and its belief that children require personal freedom rather than rules if they are to flourish. Here are, fully embodied, the basic educational principles that in America we associate with the philosopher of education John Dewey, though many of those principles find their origin ultimately in the eighteenth-century French thinker Rousseau. The core beliefs of this model of education are that children are innocent, imaginative, and generous of spirit and that being socialized into a rigorous system of school discipline—a system reflecting the priorities and the defects of adult society—corrupts their innocence, silences their imagination, and transforms their generosity into competitive hostility. The obvious sarcasm with which Lewis treats Experiment House tells us that our author is very much an educational traditionalist: a defender of same-sex schooling, a believer in discipline, a skeptic regarding modern psychology. And so he was. Moreover, one might very well assume, upon reading this passage, that our author would hold up as a shining counterexample to Experiment House the great tradition of the English public school. *There,* surely, is true order, true discipline—true education.

Yes, one might infer that such is our author's view, but one would be so, so wrong. It is more telling than most readers know that, in the last tale of Narnia, Aslan describes the passage from a dying world to eternal life thus: "The term is over: the holidays have begun." Holidays are Heaven; school is, well, . . . death. Lewis had an almost frankly theological—more specifically, eschatological (that is, pertaining to the Last Things)—view of this matter. "Life at a vile boarding school is in this way a good preparation for the Christian life, that it teaches one to live by hope. Even, in a sense, by faith; for at the beginning of each term, home and the holidays are so far off that it is as hard to realize them as to realize heaven." And near the end of his life he wrote to a child who had read his Narnia tales, "I was at three schools (all boarding schools) of which two were very horrid. I never hated anything so much, not even the front line trenches in World War I. Indeed the story is far *too* horrid to tell anyone of your age."

Less than a month after his mother's death, Jack was sent to England to attend Wynyard School, where Warnie had begun school three years before. In America a preparatory or "prep" school gets people ready for university; in England, traditionally, it is the school that "prepares" a student for secondary education, usually a public school—which is what in America would be called a *private* school. Since the English often refer to public schools as "colleges"—because a collegiate institution, technically, is one in which the pupils live together in dormitories—it's all very confusing. (Most of the terminology is derived from medieval monasticism.) According to a practice that became common among the gentry in the nineteenth century and eventually worked its way a rung or two down the social ladder, English children would attend—as boarders—a preparatory school starting at age eight or nine or ten and then typically moved on to a public school three or four years later. For some, graduation from public school—some of the most famous of which are Eton, Harrow, Winchester, and Rugby—would mark the end of their education. Others would continue on to Oxford or Cambridge; still others might attend Sandhurst, the military academy that is the English equivalent of West Point. But almost all of them would start, as very young boys, by being sent away from home and family to live seven months each year at a preparatory school.

To Americans such a practice seems strange at best and at worst barbaric, and indeed, it has come under increasingly critical scrutiny in recent years in Britain, for all the obvious reasons. Among the English intelligentsia, it has been fairly widely condemned for much longer: George Orwell, for instance, at almost the same time that Lewis was writing of his school experiences in *Surprised by Joy,* wrote an incandescently bitter essay about his own school days, during which he was afflicted by teachers whom he thought to be "terrible, all-powerful monsters" and regularly subjected to "irrational terrors and lunatic misunderstandings," all in a context of filth, inedible and inadequate food, institutionalized social snobbery, and the constant threat of flogging. He further asserted that "the characteristic faults of the English upper and middle classes may partly be due to the practice, general until recently, of sending children away from home as young as nine, eight, or even seven." (Each of the Lewis boys was nine when he first crossed the Irish Sea to go to school at Wynyard.) For about 150 years, however, such a system of education was considered utterly necessary to the making of English gentlemen. And English gentlemen were what Albert Lewis wanted his sons to become. He may also have wanted to get Jack away from a home that was a constant reminder of death.

Lewis's biographer A. N. Wilson writes shrewdly about the choice that Albert faced: to allow the boys to develop a stronger Irish identity by going to school in their native land, or to pour them into the mold of the English public-school boy in hopes that they would develop the social skills, and perhaps also the social contacts, that would serve them well in any vocation anywhere in Britain or its colonies. One could say that the appeal of this second choice was mere snobbery, or, in a slightly less pejorative formulation, a function of upward mobility. The Lewises, as we have seen, were very much an upwardly mobile family; such families like to give their children the very best of everything, and as Wilson writes, "The 'best' in this context meant an English public school."

As Wilson also points out, Albert may have been led by an unquestionably legitimate political concern as well: it was not clear at the turn of the twentieth century whether there was much of a future for Protestants in Ireland. (It would be more than twenty years before the plan for separating the northern counties of Ulster from the Catholic-dominated rest of the island would be accepted as the least of the many evil choices.) If it became necessary for beleaguered Protestants—even relatively gentle and nonsectarian Protestants like most of the Lewis family—to leave Ireland, it would be better for the boys if they had an English education.

Moreover, it was widely believed at the time that going away to school was good for young boys—it led them to "cut the apron strings," to escape from the excessively feminine world of Victorian domesticity, to learn independence. When Albert was considering the option of sending Warnie to Campbell College, the best school in Belfast itself, his former teacher, Mr. Kirkpatrick, wrote in opposition: "It will be good for the boy himself to be away, and look to his home as a holiday-heaven." Concerns like Orwell's were dismissed as mere timidity or overscrupulousness; boys who suffered as Orwell did were likewise dismissed as mama's boys or sissies. So off to school Warnie went, and three years later, so did Jack.

Some of the English public schools had been around for a very long time—the oldest of them, Winchester College, accepted its first students in 1394—but they began to assume the character that Warnie and Jack experienced only after 1828, when Thomas Arnold became headmaster at Rugby. Arnold stressed the importance of educating not just English gentlemen but Christian gentlemen, and educating them not just intellectually but also socially. It was Arnold who developed what would come to be known as "muscular Christianity"—that is, an emphasis on sports (or "games") as a builder of character. He also specialized, in his frequent preaching at the school chapel, in a kind of sermon that today would be called "motivational speaking." And— what would be most telling for Jack Lewis and many like him—he instituted a form of social organization for the students in which the teachers appointed leaders, called "prefects," who were responsible for guiding and, if necessary, disciplining their fellow students. It was, depending on your view of things, either a system for democratizing school leadership and empowering students or else a sly means of co-opting the best and the brightest boys to do the headmaster's dirty work. To some children the prefects were heroes, to others they were bullies and tyrants—and in the usual order of things, some prefects must have been the one, some the other, and many a mixture of the two. So it was in Thomas Arnold's Rugby School, so it is in Albus Dumbledore's Hogwarts School of Witchcraft and Wizardry, and so, surely, it was at the schools that the Lewis boys attended. But what they *felt* about their school and their prefects we shall see.

In any case, prefects came into the mix in the public school (that is, the secondary school) years: preparatory schools, especially small ones such as Wynyard, tended to be run more simply and straightforwardly by the masters. The school that Albert Lewis, after careful study and deep reflection, chose for his sons was run quite autocratically by a man who had already been prosecuted for cruelty to his students and who, within a very few years, would be certified as insane.

His name was Robert Capron, and, as a young Anglican priest, he had founded Wynyard School (in Watford, Hertfordshire) in 1881, so he had been running it for about a quarter-century when Warnie arrived. By this time he had a son and three daughters, all adult, and they and his wife lived in obvious terror of him. Warnie and Jack could see this because the whole family helped Capron—"Oldie," as he was called by his students, though, of course, behind his back—run the school, such as it was. In *Surprised by Joy,* Lewis describes his experiences at Wynyard in a tone of near-incredulity, as though he's not sure he can trust his own memories. "When really angry [Oldie] proceeded to antics; worming for wax in his ear with his little finger and babbling, 'Aye, aye, aye, aye. . . .' I have seen him leap up and dance round and round like a performing bear." Oldie once flogged a boy he despised by making the child bend over at the far end of the schoolroom, so that he could take a long run at his target to ensure maximum impact with his cane—like a cricketer running up to the wicket to bowl. The boy, Lewis adds, was being flogged simply for having made a mistake in geometry; Oldie hated him not for that but for being the son of a dentist. Like the headmaster at Orwell's school, Oldie held in his mind a strict social hierarchy and seems to have thought it part of his job to reinforce the existing social strata. Warnie and Jack occupied a sufficiently high stratum to avoid being afflicted by the wildest of Oldie's rages.

In his first letter from Wynyard, announcing his safe arrival, Jack wrote to his father, "Missis Capron and the Miss Caprons are very nice and I think I will be able to get on with Mr. Capron though to tell the truth he is rather eccentric." At the end of November he wrote, "In spight of all that has happened I like Mr. Capron very much indeed." And Jack had some reason to like him, for, by his own admission, he had quickly and permanently fallen into Oldie's good graces, such as they were. Jack "escaped [the] worst brutalities" of Wynyard, Warnie later wrote, because "he amused the headmaster who even made something of a pet of him, so far as was possible for such a man."

The implication of Warnie's comment is that he himself was not so fortunate. While I have just said that Warnie and Jack were socially "safe"—at least in comparison to the poor dentist's son—Capron seems to have decided at some point in the autumn of 1908 that Warnie wasn't working as hard as he should, and the headmaster made a point of telling Albert Lewis. (Could it be that Warnie was put in the shade by his younger but more gifted brother?) "I am very sorry you are so much annoyed at Mr. Capron's letter," wrote the loyal younger brother in late October, "but it is quite untrue, Warnie is not lazy." Yet even before that (in fact, just a few days after the boys' arrival) Jack was begging his father to take both of them out of school and bring them home. Even if one is not the chief target of a lunatic's wrath, it must be unnerving for a nine-year-old boy—especially one used to being cared for, even pampered, in a loving home—to be in regular contact with said lunatic.

Albert Lewis refused to yield to his sons' pleas. Presumably he thought that things could not be as bad as they were making out; apparently he also did not wish to admit that scrupulous research could have led him so far astray. Plus, Capron was sending him letters full of praise for Jack, and in any case, Warnie would be finished with Wynyard and moving on to public school at the end of the year. So the boys stayed on at the school that in his autobiography Jack called "Belsen." (Lest anyone miss the point, the chapter describing it is entitled "Concentration Camp.")

We should not be deceived about his reasons for using such metaphors. Yes, Oldie was crazy; moreover, the students learned next to nothing. "Intellectually, the time I spent at Oldie's was almost entirely wasted," Jack wrote; "if the school had not died, and if I had been left there two years more, it would probably have sealed my fate as a scholar for good." Warnie's view was the same: "In spite of Capron's policy of terror, the school was slack and inefficient, and the time-table [the schedule of classes], if such it could be called, ridiculous." But even if Oldie had been a paragon of virtue and the school a model of efficiency, Jack likely would have thought of it as a prison camp anyway—a well-run prison perhaps, but a place of incarceration nonetheless. And as we shall see, Jack never could acclimate himself to the chief features of boarding school life: strictly imposed regimentation, enforced social hierarchy, and a complete absence of solitude. It was his hatred of these aspects of school life that led him to think of holidays from school—*any* school—as something akin to an Ascent into Heaven.

In the summer of 1909, Warnie left Wynyard and later that year began attending Malvern College in the Malvern Hills of Worcestershire. Jack had to struggle on in Belsen until the summer of 1910, when the school collapsed because Capron could no longer attract enough students (though he told Albert Lewis that it was his own decision to give up teaching). Once the school closed, Capron found his way back into pastoral ministry, taking up the care of a nearby parish church, where he almost immediately began flogging the choirboys. When the churchwardens tried to intervene, he simply caned them as well for their presumption. Unsurprisingly, he was soon found to be insane, and less than eighteen months after closing his school he died in an asylum in Kent.

Faced with the need to make a decision about where his younger son should go to school, Albert Lewis did an interesting thing: rather than finding another English school, he decided to send Jack to Campbell College, in their own neighborhood of Belmont, not much more than a mile from Little Lea. As it turned out, Jack liked Campbell well enough, in part because its social structure was rather more entertaining than what he had known at Wynyard—"There were real fights at Campbell, with seconds, and (I think) betting, and a hundred or more roaring spectators"*—and also because, thanks to an excellent English master whom he called Octie (his real name was Lewis Alden), he learned quite a lot. But incomparably the best thing that happened

---

* In this, as in many other things, the Irish schools lagged behind the English ones: in 1825 at Eton, the fifteen-year-old son of the Earl of Shaftesbury was killed by a classmate in a fight of this kind, after which the English schools became stricter in such matters.

to him while he was at Campbell was this: in November 1910, having been at Campbell little more than a month, he developed a bad cough and was sent home, never to return.

Apparently Albert Lewis had already grown uncomfortable with the idea of Jack's attending an Irish school, because in the very letter in which he tells Warnie that Jack has just fallen ill, he asks Warnie to investigate Cherbourg, a preparatory school in Malvern. "I am strongly inclined to send Jacko there until he's old enough to go to the College"—that is, Malvern College. Strangely, Albert had written to Capron asking his views about where to send Jack. More strangely, Capron wrote back with sound advice: "Jacko has his peculiarities and I think it very essential that he should go to a SMALL school where the Hd.Master himself might take an interest in him." He feared that a school such as Cherbourg would be too large and impersonal, which was true. Albert, of course, ignored him.

It is not clear why Albert was so determined not to send Jack back to Campbell. Perhaps he felt that Jack would be damaged by a long-term stay at Campbell—socially damaged, that is; intellectually he was infinitely better off than he had been at Wynyard. Lewis does say in his autobiography that at Campbell "the population was socially much more 'mixed' than at most English schools; I rubbed shoulders there with farmers' sons." Probably Jack could have returned to school within a week or two, but Albert kept him at home for the rest of the autumn. Perhaps he saw the chance slipping away of making his younger son into an English gentleman. Warnie would write years later that "the experiment [of sending Jack to Campbell] was for some reason or another not a success," which indicates that he remained ignorant of Albert's thinking—as do we all.

In any event, to Jack his confinement during illness was the best possible situation. As I have already noted, Jack's "ideal happiness" was "to be always convalescent from some small illness and always seated in a window that overlooked the sea, there to read [the Italian epic] eight hours of each happy day." Well, Little Lea could boast no ocean views, and Jack had not yet discovered Ariosto and Tasso, but in other respects this time was as close to perfection as he would ever get. For two blessed months, he had the experience each weekday morning of saying good-bye to his father—off to his firm after breakfast—and then looking forward to something like nine or ten hours of peaceful reading, interrupted only by lunch and tea. There were people in the house (a cook and a housemaid) to care for him, but none to bother him. He had the solitude that he always craved and that had been so utterly absent from life at Wynyard and, for that matter, at Campbell, which he had felt was "very like living permanently in a large railway station."

(Periods of aloneness were so dear to him that he seems to have thought them more common than they actually could have been. For instance, in his preface to *The Allegory of Love,* his first scholarly book, he speaks of "the inestimable benefit of a childhood passed mostly alone," but this cannot be an accurate description. Though Warnie went to school three years before he did, their mother was still alive and in fact taught Jack French and Latin; after her death the boys were always home on holiday together. It's hard to imagine that Jack *could* have been alone very often—except during his post-Campbell convalescence. Perhaps his exaggeration of those times of solitude into the normal state of his childhood reflects their importance to him.)

One benefit of his time under the tutelage of Octie, however brief, may have been that he was now better prepared to take advantage of the opportunity to read. While he was at Wynyard, he later felt, there had been "a great decline in [his] imaginative life." He read "twaddling school stories" and a great deal of historical fiction, most of it bad. "My reading now was mostly rubbish." But in Jack's brief time at Campbell, Octie had shown him a better way: for instance, he had his boys read Matthew Arnold's adaptation of an episode from an old Persian epic, *Sohrab and Rustum* (1853). It was a vigorous, heroic tale, but above all it was in *verse:* through Octie's teaching of it, Jack became acquainted, perhaps for the first time, with the power of poetic language, especially the rhythm and propulsion it can give to a story. In this sense the brief time at Campbell may have been more decisive than even Lewis himself thought, for narrative verse would become one of the great loves of his life. He wrote books about Spenser's *Faerie Queene* and Milton's *Paradise Lost,* and almost everything he discusses in *The Allegory of Love* is narrative poetry. As a young man, he produced long stories in verse himself—the second book he ever published, *Dymer,* is such a work—and had he proven to be very good at it he might never have turned to prose at all. The telling of a tale in noble metrical language—probably, though not necessarily, also in rhyme—struck him as the highest kind of literature, and the kind that gave the greatest pleasure. The same could be said about his friend-to-be, J. R. R. Tolkien. Although it may seem odd that neither of them is at all known for the kind of literature they most loved, the fact is that neither of them was greatly skilled at producing it. And perhaps more important, sometime in the twentieth century the audience for narrative poetry (weakened in the previous century) almost completely disappeared.

In their adolescence and young adulthood, Lewis and Tolkien were unusual but not unique in their love of poetic storytelling, their sense of its centrality. It was a transitional period in Western education, and in Western ideas about literary greatness. We are now accustomed to thinking of the novel as the major literary form, but the novel as a genre is only three hundred years old; for the first hundred or more years of its existence writers thought of it as a light and popular form, not worthy to be compared with the epic, or poetic tragedy. Goethe wrote novels, but he knew that *Faust* was his masterpiece. Because Wordsworth had the highest of poetic aspirations, he sought to write an epic, though of a curious kind: he called it *The Prelude* because he hoped it to be the doorway to something even more ambitious. Keats explored epic narrative verse before his early death. For such writers, the achievements of novelists, however entertaining and even morally instructive, were something lighter and less: Dickens, on this account, would be an entertainer more than an artist. In thinking thus they were looking back toward the universally recognized great works of the Western canon, all of them without exception in verse: Homer, Sophocles, Virgil, Dante, Milton. (Only Shakespeare, among the giants, freely mixed verse and prose.)

The English and Irish public schools of the nineteenth century were also inheritors of this tradition. Boys could read novels if they chose, but in their spare time—no one would ever think of *teaching* prose fiction. The idea of teaching literature in one's own language at all was a recent development; therefore, the literature taught would have to be of the highest and most challenging quality.

Yet the expectation was also that boys would find some pleasure in the verse: Lewis was educated in a time when it was still possible for people to be delighted by rhyme and rhythm, even when extended over hundreds of pages. Albert Lewis was not at all unusual in adoring Thomas Babington Macaulay's *Lays of Ancient Rome* (1855)—for untold thousands of Victorian public school boys, Macaulay's stirring verse made the history of Rome come to life:

Just then a scout came flying,
All wild with haste and fear:

"To arms! to arms! Sir Consul:
Lars Porsena is here."
On the low hills to westward
The Consul fixed his eye,
And saw the swarthy storm of dust
Rise fast along the sky.

So, strange though it may seem to us—a people who tolerate rhyme and meter only in songs and in brief lyric poems—Octie taught Arnold's *Sohrab and Rustum* not just because he thought it was good, but also because he thought it was *fun*. And that is how young Jack Lewis received it. But because there was no longer an audience for narrative verse by the time he and Tolkien wrote their own stories, they wrote in prose. The virtues they loved in the story-poems of their youth found new life in their fiction, especially in Tolkien, but to a lesser degree even in the Narnia books. Some of the nobility and solemnity of poetic rhythm emerges in their work, and readers today find a pleasure in that very like the pleasure that young Jack Lewis found in Arnold's poem.

In any case, Octie did Jack a great service by raising his standards and reminding him that there was a world of literature that far transcended the "twaddling school stories" he had grown addicted to while at Wynyard. And in his solitude, while it lasted, Jack could explore that world to his heart's content. Interestingly, during this period he read many fairy tales and became particularly enamored of Dwarfs (or, as Tolkien would later insist, Dwarves). When he was alone, his inner life grew and developed, and we will soon explore the contours of that inner life. But first, the external world remains to be dealt with.

Jack began school at Cherbourg in January 1911; he had recently turned twelve years old. He would leave Cherbourg in the summer of 1913, writing a valedictory poem ("Alas! What happy days were those"), but in most respects the place seems to have made little impression on him. He speaks well of the headmaster, who had the benefit of sanity, and under whom Jack did well in Latin and English, but such comments are brief; he says that at Cherbourg he made his first real friends, but further comments on that point are nonexistent. He relates a funny anecdote about his and his classmates' worship of a new young master whom they called "Pogo"—"Pogo was a wit, Pogo was a dressy man, Pogo was a man about town, Pogo was even a lad"—and how Pogo led him, for the first and last time in his life, to take an interest in being a "dressy man" himself. ("Up till now I had committed nearly every other sin and folly within my power, but I had not yet been flashy.") But though funny, the story doesn't tell us much—except, perhaps, that Jack was entering that stage of early adolescence (he was thirteen and a half when Pogo came to Cherbourg) when conforming to the tastes and interests of the crowd assumes paramount value. "I began to labor very hard to make myself into a fop, a cad, and a snob."

But these social aspirations were not to last long, for this was not a field in which Jack could excel. He was physically awkward and thus, though large for his age, no good at games (much less at being "dressy"), and of course, he was not only exceptionally intelligent but exceptionally bookish. Indeed, he did manage to turn himself into a snob, but an *intellectual* one—a prig and a highbrow, as he would later term himself—not a social one like Pogo and his young worshipers. His letters home to his father became increasingly marked by his frustration with the ignorance and shallowness of his classmates. As the years of adolescence went on, Jack paid a stiffer and stiffer price for his idiosyncratic abilities and preferences—and this price would become greater still as he became more fully aware of just how idiosyncratic he was. He writes that Pogo "made sad work of certain humble and childlike and self-forgetful qualities which (I think) had remained with me to that moment," but surely Pogo was simply the instrument by which a self-consciousness was achieved that would have been achieved soon anyway. That is what adolescence *is*.

Though real afflictions beset him at Cherbourg, they were largely internal ones, and we shall deal with them in due course. The external afflictions—the social ones—hit him hardest when he had left Cherbourg and moved on to Malvern College, which he did in September 1913. This was a movement for which he and his whole family had had high hopes. Perhaps this would have been so even if Warnie had not preceded him to Malvern—for all the students at Cherbourg "lived under the shadow of the Coll" (as they called it) and desired nothing more than to rise to its eminence—but the hopes were intensified by the success Warnie had found there. Warnie was, and would always be, good-natured and rather "cheery," and he was popular with students and masters alike. He thought Malvern wonderful and expected that Jack would too.

The story of how Jack blundered his naïve way into social trouble at Malvern, especially with the prefects, is told at length in *Surprised by Joy,* and I will not rehearse fully here. He had trouble catching on to the complicated system of rules and obligations, and he hated all the games; as a result, he quickly found himself the regular victim of a prefectual system that allowed the prefects, not to "take points away"—as they do at Harry Potter's Hogwarts—but instead to administer physical punishments. So when, in his first term at Malvern, Jack got confused about which games he was obliged to play, he eventually discovered that he had "committed the serious crime of 'Skipping Clubs'" and would be punished by being publicly flogged, not by one of the schoolmasters but by the highest of the prefects, the "Head of the Coll."

Lewis actually doesn't talk much of prefects but rather of "Bloods," that is, the social aristocracy of the Coll. At many public schools there was little overlap between the aristocracy and the prefecturate—that is, the students whom the other students worshiped had little in common with those praised and promoted by the masters. But at Malvern, Lewis asserts, the Bloods were almost always prefects as well, which made them doubly powerful—indeed, something like omnipotent. That Jack had made his mistake about Clubs because a Blood lied to him soured him still further on the system; that his early public humiliation served to make him a permanent target for "fagging" made any sort of reconciliation between Jack and the Coll impossible.

The fagging system was one wing of the great edifice of Bloodery. Its rules were simple: non-Bloods had to perform whatever services Bloods required of them: shoe shining, clothes brushing, housekeeping, tea making. It was never, ever possible for an underling to plead any excuse, and refusal would have been repaid by something far worse than public caning. Curiously, the one place of refuge was the library—one could not be fagged there—so Jack's great ambition on almost every day of school was to make it to the library before being called upon by a Blood in need. And of course, there was no place he would rather have been than the library, even if there had been no fagging and no Bloods. But he rarely got there.

Jack's life at the Coll would steadily deteriorate throughout the school year—a situation made still worse probably by the absence of Warnie, who had moved on to work with a tutor (his father's old teacher, Mr. Kirkpatrick) just before Jack's arrival. This was not a voluntary move on Warnie's part. He had become a Blood, and such a Blood that he was considered a candidate for Head of the Coll. But one dark day he was caught smoking—a great crime in those days, though he and Jack both were already regular smokers—and was threatened with immediate expulsion. However, a saving compromise was worked out: Warnie lost his status as a prefect and agreed to leave the Coll at the end of the term. His academic record already being spotty, he was sent to Mr. Kirkpatrick (then living in Surrey, having left Ireland some years before) to get him ready for the entrance examination to Sandhurst, the military academy. With Warnie's departure, Jack had none of the protection that could be offered by a brother who was also a Blood.

The daily games at Malvern tired Jack, fagging wore him out completely; and all this was added to an enormous load of schoolwork, because—thanks to a scholarship he had won at the end of his Cherbourg time—he had been placed in an unusually high form for a boy his age. Early in his first term at the Coll he was already writing to his father, "The work here is very heavy going, and it is rather hard to find time for it in the breathless life we live here."

"No true defender of the Public Schools will believe me if I say that I was tired." (And indeed, some of his classmates responded to the publication of *Surprised by Joy* by strenuously denying that there was anything especially unpleasant about the fagging system—just as Orwell's classmates would equally strenuously protest the critique of *his* school in "Such, Such Were the Joys." The world appears to be full of people who believe that if they did not have a particular experience in a particular context, no one else could have either.) "But I was— dog tired, cab-horse tired, tired (almost) like a child in a factory."

And—it's hard to blame him for this—he let his frustration show. "Worst of all, there was my face. I am the kind of person who gets told, 'And take that look off your face, too.'" Lewis denied that he ever had a look of insolence on his face when told that, but Warnie recalled returning to the Coll for a visit near the end of Jack's first term and having a different impression. The occasion was a house supper (a gathering for past and present members of a particular house, or dormitory, within the Coll), and Warnie recalled it's being "a noisy, cheerful function"—except for "Jack's gloom and boredom," which were "glaringly obvious to all," and which were "not tending to increase his popularity with the House." Apparently even Warnie thought that Jack should take that look off his face. In the spring of 1914 Warnie wrote to his father that if Jack "has made himself unpopular, he has only himself to thank for it.... I feel it intensely that my brother should be a social outcast in the House where I was so happy." What Warnie felt so "intensely" was both shame and compassion—but perhaps mostly shame—plus sheer annoyance that Jack would so desper-

ately loathe a place that Warnie had loved and had been forcibly expelled from. Jack's hatred of Malvern would mark a cooling in the
brothers' relationship that would not be fully corrected for several
years. They seem to have corresponded hardly at all in this difficult period, preferring instead to talk *about* each other in letters to their father.

(The making of Boxen would continue, to some extent, during the
holidays, but by this time "the classical period" of their boyhood had
come to an end. However, their shared frustration with their father's
eccentricities, which was the one immovable foundation of their
bond—which they called Pigiebotianism, a joke that derived from a
nurse who once said that if they didn't behave she would spank their
"pigiebottoms"—continued to link them when nothing else did. They
made almost a system of it, talking even of "Pigiebotian ethics." The
need to have a common Pigiebotian front against the P'daitabird—as
they invariably called Albert, mocking his excessively "Oirish" pronunciation of "potato"—was the one need they would share as long
as Albert lived. But the Malvern crisis set them at odds in almost every
other way.)

Jack's letters of the time have one great theme: his pleas for his father to somehow get him out of Malvern. "Not only does this persecution [from the Bloods] get harder to bear as time goes on, but it is
actually getting more severe.... All the prefects detest me and lose no
opportunity of venting their spite.... Please take me out of this as
soon as possible." Such is the refrain. Added to it are plentiful expres-
sions of sheer contempt for his classmates, with special emphasis on
their Englishness: "These brutes of illiterate, ill-managed English prefects are always watching for an opportunity to drop upon you," he
tells his father; to a friend he refers to them as "coarse, brainless English schoolboys." His entire experience at Malvern he sums up as "all
this unpleasantness in a foreign land," and he is thankful that at least
"it teaches one to love home and things connected with home all the
more, by contrast." At Malvern Jack seems to have become Irish.

And a social critic as well: he denounces the entire institution of the
Public School with an intensity that reminds one of Orwell and that is
quite surprising in light of the older C. S. Lewis's reputation as a
conservative: "This place [Malvern] is a failure.... These places are
doomed.... If you came back in a couple of hundred years, there
would be no Public Schools left.... I for one will be glad to be rid
of them all, and would like to see the day when they are abolished."
The gleeful malice with which he contemplates the destruction of this

institution of the English ruling classes is pretty palpable, and one may well wonder why Lewis didn't end up becoming just the kind of socialist that public school made of Orwell. In *Surprised by Joy*, Lewis asks himself this very question and concludes that it was simply his "Romanticism"—his deeply ingrained preference for living in a world of imagination—that prevented him from following that path. Orwell's experience energized him politically, as happened with many others; Lewis quite forthrightly says that the "bitter, truculent, skeptical, debunking, and cynical *intelligentsia*" of twentieth-century England was largely made up of "products of the system." Lewis's own misery, by contrast, seems to have made him withdraw from the political realm and become more inward-looking—though perhaps it is telling that Dymer, the hero of Jack's first book-length poem (published in 1927), begins his exile from the Perfect City by whacking a schoolmaster in the head and killing him stone dead.

"It was, of course, to turn us into public-school boys that my father had originally sent us to [Malvern]; the finished product appalled him." Given his hatred of the place, it might seem odd that the adult Lewis would look back and see himself as a characteristic artifact of it. Yet he is right. If the "coarse, brainless English schoolboys" were social snobs, he would become an intellectual one. If they looked down on him for his physical ineptitude, he would sneer at their illiteracy. He joined a long-standing war in the world of English education: that of the Hearties and the Aesthetes. And just as it is in the nature of the Hearties to look with pity or contempt on those who are "useless at games," it is in the nature of the Aesthetes to turn the same gaze on the intellectually inferior and culturally backward. To judge from Jack's letters, it would be many years before his priggishness abated, and in fact, only his conversion to Christianity put it finally to death.

A knowledge of Lewis's miseries in school reveals that some scenes in the Narnia books are more important than they might appear. In *The Lion, the Witch, and the Wardrobe,* when Edmund is being nasty to his younger sister, Lucy, their older brother, Peter, tells him, "You've always liked being beastly to anyone smaller than yourself; we've seen that at school before now." But after Edmund has met Aslan and fought on Aslan's behalf, we have this scene:

> When at last [Lucy] was free to come back to Edmund she found him standing on his feet and not only healed of his wounds but looking better than she had seen him look—oh, for ages; in fact

ever since his first term at that horrid school which was where he began to go wrong. He had become his real old self again and could look you in the face.

Edmund, then—the "bitter, truculent, skeptical" Edmund (as we might call him) who lies about his experience in Narnia and joins with the White Witch to overturn a power structure that leaves him always subservient to his older brother, Peter—is a "product of the system" as much as George Orwell was. (And if Peter attends the same "horrid school," which is likely, then perhaps Peter—who apologizes to Aslan for his treatment of Edmund—has been a little too much of a Blood.) Though Edmund's public school was no doubt far more traditional than Eustace Scrubb's, the *Lord of the Flies*–like social dynamic of the strong oppressing the weak is just as pervasive at Experiment House as it was at Jack's own Malvern. Before he went to Narnia, Eustace was the kind of person who spent his time "sucking up to Them, and currying favour, and dancing attendance on Them," as Jill Pole says in the opening chapter of *The Silver Chair*. After Narnia, he stops doing that, even if it means suffering "torture." When Lewis describes his young self as a prig and a highbrow, he is describing someone more like the pre-Aslan Edmund and Eustace than like their post-Aslan selves. And when he suggests that it was only a kind of *conversion* that put an end to their nastiness, we may reflect that his own conversion did not take place until he had been out of school for fifteen years. Lewis clearly believed that the social pressures of school had long-term effects. We can see them with perfect clarity in *That Hideous Strength* in the character of Mark Studdock, whose childhood quests to belong to the "Inner Ring" lead him as an adult—and a highly educated and intelligent adult at that—inexorably into the web of the evil regime of the National Institute of Co-ordinated Experiments, or NICE. ("Stone had the look which Mark had often seen before in unpopular boys or new boys at school . . .—the look which was for Mark the symbol of all his worst fears, for to be one who must wear that look was, in his scale of values, the greatest evil.")

But such reflections belong to the far future; for now, we still have a miserable young boy grieving his imprisonment at Malvern. Albert Lewis may have been a stubborn man, but he was a loving father, and he was genuinely grieved by Jack's pleas for release. Whether it was Jack's own fault or not, the boy was truly and deeply miserable, and Albert's response was truly and deeply empathetic. To Warnie's letter saying that Jack "has only himself to thank" for his misery, Albert replied, reasonably and compassionately, "He is not altogether to blame for it. Boys, like men, are of course cast in different molds, and I honestly confess than knowing Jack's mind and character, I am not greatly surprised to find him and a Public School unsuited to one another. In saying that I blame neither the one nor the other. He is simply out of his proper environment." Warnie agreed that Jack could never thrive at Malvern and needed to be taken out of there if at all possible. But even so, Albert might well have sent Jack back there for another year or more had not an attractive alternative presented itself. That alternative was Mr. Kirkpatrick.

He was a man for whom Albert Lewis had great affection and respect in any case, but he had also done wonders for Warnie. Originally he had not had high hopes: though admiring Warnie's "good nature," Kirkpatrick had said flatly that "it is too late now to make him interested in knowledge." Nevertheless, in just a few months he provided Warnie with enough knowledge that he not only got into Sandhurst but won a "prize Cadetship." (Out of 201 successful applicants, Warnie ranked twenty-first.) And if he could do all this for Warnie, perhaps he could also solve some of the problems of Albert's younger son. In the hope of warming Kirk up to the idea of taking on another resident pupil—a prospect that did not, in principle, delight the old man—Albert took the liberty of sending him a sample of Jack's translations from Latin poetry. Kirk replied, "The verse translation which you enclose takes away by breath. It is an amazing performance for a boy of his age—indeed a boy of any age. The literary skill is one which practiced masters of the craft might envy." In the spring of 1914, Kirk agreed to Albert's proposal that in September Jack would move to Surrey to live with and be taught by the man whom they called "the Great Knock."

But this narrative has continued long enough without considering the other half of Jack's story: his inner life. However, this is not a straightforward proposition, because this extraordinarily gifted boy was developing in several ways, and on several levels, at once. What I have called his inner life was not a unitary thing, but rather a stratified, complex set of experiences with complex interrelations. The intricacy of the adult Lewis—all that made his friend Barfield say that there were "five C. S. Lewises"—was already evident in Jack's early teens. Three kinds of experiences, which may or may not be related, factor

into this story. Lewis seemed to think that they were not related; I
have a sense that they may be.

The first is Christianity. I have already noted Lewis's denial that he
had had any truly "religious experience" when he prayed for his
mother's healing and then, after her death, for her resurrection. It was
when he was attending Wynyard, of all places, that real Christian
faith became part of his life for the first time. Though Oldie may have
been a vile old sadist, the local church—which the boys were expected to attend weekly—proved to be something far different and
better. Jack's first response to it was thoroughly negative: soon after
his arrival in the fall of 1908 he wrote to his father, "I do not like
church here at all because it is so frightfully high church that it might
as well be Roman Catholic." The Ulster Anglicanism Jack had known
up to then was thoroughly Protestant, with a simplified liturgy, and
certainly none of the "smells and bells" he encountered in the church
at Watford; in fact, it is not clear that he ever fully reconciled himself
to those Anglo-Catholic trappings. But "what really mattered was
that here I heard the doctrines of Christianity (as distinct from general 'uplift') taught by men who obviously believed them." Though
Lewis does not draw the comparison, one must infer that "uplift"
was the usual fare back home at St. Mark's in Dundela and that
young Jack was responding in a quite intellectual way to the offering
of something more substantive.

But emotionally his primary response to the doctrines he encountered was fear: "I feared for my soul. . . . I began seriously to pray and
to read my Bible and to attempt to obey my conscience." Oddly, he
says that "the effect" of this fear was "entirely good," because it
prompted him to these virtuous deeds. Though indeed "the fear of the
Lord is the beginning of wisdom" (Psalm 111:10), I am not sure the
rest of his story bears out the adult Lewis's judgment. But in any case,
from about the ages of ten to twelve or thirteen Jack was a Christian
believer, and a dutiful one—perhaps too dutiful. He seems to have
worked very hard at being a Christian: not content to pray, he was determined that his prayer should achieve what he called "realization,"
that is, "a certain vividness of the imagination and the affections." It is
hard not to believe that this determination was related to the fear: on
some level did Jack believe that an un-"realized" prayer would not
save him from the judgment he feared? Of the idea that God is gracious and merciful we get no hint in Lewis's description of his childhood religion. Prayer was but a duty and a burden, and (because he

could never be confident that his prayers had indeed been "realized") a burden that was almost literally maddening.

He was released from this burden by an odd combination of factors. First among them was something that emerged from his studies: as he wrote many years later, "My [Christian] faith was first undermined by the attitude towards *Pagan* religion in the notes of modern editors of Latin & Greek poets at school. They always assumed that the ancient religion was pure error"—that is, that the beliefs of pre-Christian cultures were just superstitious nonsense. Possibly these editors were Christians themselves and merely sought to denigrate other religions, or perhaps they were unbelievers who thought *all* religious belief superstitious. In any event, the effect on young Jack was to extend their critique to his own religion: "Hence, in my mind, the obvious question 'why shouldn't ours be equally false?'"

After this intellectual challenge came the bumbling and thoughtless intervention of a matron (a kind of all-purpose nurse and dorm mother) at Cherbourg School named Miss Cowie. Miss Cowie was a highly recognizable English type: a warmhearted, kindly enthusiast for the world of Spirit—the sort of person who today would be called a proponent of New Age spirituality. "She was ... floundering in the mazes of Theosophy, Rosicrucianism, Spiritualism; the whole Anglo-American Occultist tradition"—a tradition that flourished in the years of Lewis's childhood. The influence of this weird world on Lewis's life and character is great, though usually neglected by his biographers: Lewis wrote in *Surprised by Joy* that Miss Cowie's suggestions of a hidden spiritual reality "started in me something with which, off and on, I have had plenty of trouble since—the desire for the preternatural, simply as such, the passion for the Occult." It is noteworthy that Lewis does not speak of this "trouble" in the simple past tense; the grammar suggests that at the time of writing—which was the time of the writing of the Narnia books—he was still not untroubled by it. (In fact, he would be tempted by "the desire for the preternatural" even at the end of his life, after the death of his wife.) This does not mean, of course, that he *embraced* any form of spiritualism, but it does suggest that the thirst spiritualism promises to quench was one he still felt.

This "tradition"—this movement, or set of movements—had grown strong in England near the end of the nineteenth century; it was usually associated with some sense of "wisdom from the East," though a lot of cultures lay east of England. Sometimes the East meant Russia—as in the case of Madame Blavatsky, whose book *The Secret*

Doctrine (1888) was essentially the founding document of Theosophy, or somewhat later mystics such as Gurdjieff and Ouspensky—but perhaps more often India was the source. At about the same time Madame Blavatsky was flourishing, Swami Vivekananda was bringing to the West the all-religions-are-one message of his master Sri Ramakrishna. (He was the most dynamic figure at the Parliament of Religions held in Chicago in 1893.) The Ouija board was also a product of this ferment, and all over England and America people were holding séances to speak with their beloved dead.

Messages of spiritual oneness and the possibility of occult experience were especially appealing to people whose belief in orthodox Christianity had been shaken, or destroyed, by the aggressive "scientific" agnosticism or atheism espoused by many followers of Darwin or by the philosophical atheism of (for example) many Marxists. A characteristic *fin de siècle* figure in England was the great political agitator, and early advocate of birth control, Annie Besant (1847–1933), who moved from a youthful orthodox Christianity to doubt to atheism—and then to passionate advocacy of Madame Blavatsky's Theosophy. Besant lived the last decades of her life in India, which she had chosen as her spiritual home.

Another characteristic figure, one (as we shall see) closer to Lewis, was the poet William Butler Yeats. "I am very religious," he once wrote, "and deprived by Huxley and Tyndall, whom I detested, of the simple-minded religion of my childhood, I had made a new religion." (Thomas Henry Huxley and John Tyndall, a scientist and a doctor, respectively, were among the most prominent Victorian opponents of Christianity.) As early as 1887, when he was just twenty-two, Yeats was initiated into a society called the Hermetic Students—"Hermetic" referring to an ancient legendary magician, Hermes Trismegistus, and more generally to secret spiritual knowledge. Later he would be admitted into the Order of the Golden Dawn, an organization that also attracted Aleister Crowley, a black magician and Satanist who liked to refer to himself as "the Beast of the Apocalypse." Yeats was no Satanist, but the "new religion" he made developed into something that, at precisely the time when Jack Lewis was falling under the sway of Miss Cowie, he was happy to call simply "Magic"—"what I must call the evocation of spirits, though I do not know what they are."

The appeal of all this to young Jack is evident. His experience with Christianity was, as we have seen, almost completely a matter of painful and fearful duty. He struggled incessantly to form prayers that he could believe were completely valid, but he never knew whether he had achieved that goal. He was on a spiritual treadmill with no hopes of getting off. What Miss Cowie's mushy spiritualism held out to him was the possibility of there being Something out there, some Higher Power, or Deeper Meaning, or Spirit World—in short, a version of the transcendent that gave richness of possibility but made no *demands* on anyone. "From the tyrannous noon of revelation I passed into the cool evening of Higher Thought, where there was nothing to be obeyed, and nothing to be believed except what was either comforting or exciting." Freed from the burdens of prayer, by the time he left Malvern Jack had ceased to be a Christian. "And oh, the relief of it!" As he grew older the hermetic—that is, the secretive—aspects of the occult recommended themselves to him: "The idea that if there were Occult knowledge it was known to very few and scorned by the many became an added attraction: 'we few' . . . was an evocative expression for me." As he became increasingly aware of his power to learn the knowledge of scholars, perhaps the possible acquisition of this more esoteric but also practical wisdom became even more desirable. Certainly the older Lewis felt that he had been in real danger at that time of his life: "If there had been in the neighbourhood some elder person who dabbled in dirt of the Magical kind (such have a good nose for potential disciples) I might now be a Satanist or a maniac."

So the first kind of experience that shaped the adolescent Jack Lewis was the Christian religion; the second was Miss Cowie's spiritualism, which replaced that religion when it had been undermined by classical scholarship. Yet more important than either of them, and somehow related to both, was his imaginative life—his instinctive aesthetic responses to art but also to the natural world. And these responses came to center on something that, by the time he was a young adult, he had come to call "Joy." He would always stick with that terminology, even though to most readers it is misleading—it is what the title of his autobiography refers to, which should give us an idea of how important Joy was to him. In his first reference to it in his autobiography, he calls it by a more common name: remembering his youthful response to the sight of the Castlereagh Hills from his nursery window, he writes, "They taught me longing—*Sehnsucht*; made me for good or ill, and before I was six years old, a votary of the Blue Flower."

Of all Lewis's books, *Surprised by Joy* may be the fullest of unexplained and arcane literary references—it is as though in telling his own story he momentarily forgets that almost none of his readers is as learned as he—and for today's reader this invocation of the "Blue Flower" will be one of the most arcane ones. He is thinking of Novalis—the pen name of the German Romantic writer Friedrich von Hardenberg, who died in 1801 at the age of twenty-nine. The protagonist of Novalis's unfinished allegorical novel *Heinrich Von Ofterdingen* becomes obsessed by a vision of a blue flower, which he first encounters in a stranger's tales and then in dreams:

> There is no greed in my heart; but I yearn to get a glimpse of the blue flower [*aber die blaue Blume sehn' ich mich zu erblicken*]. It is perpetually in my mind, and I can write or think of nothing else. . . .
>
> Often I feel so rapturously happy; and only when I do not have the flower clearly before my mind's eye does a deep inner turmoil seize me. This cannot and will not be understood by anyone. I would think I were mad if I did not see and think so clearly. Indeed since then everything is much clearer to me.

He "yearns" or "longs" (*sehn*) for the flower—and yet nothing that he can grasp seems so desirable as that longing itself. This is the paradox of *Sehnsucht*: that though it could in one sense be described as a negative experience, in that it focuses on something one cannot possess and cannot reach, it is nevertheless intensely seductive. One cannot say it is exactly *pleasurable*—there is a kind of ache in the sense of unattainability that always accompanies the longing—and yet, as Lewis puts it, the quality of the experience "is that of an unsatisfied desire which is itself more desirable than any other satisfaction." This is why he called it Joy: because the word *longing* fails to convey the desirability of the feeling itself. No one, presumably, *wants* to be in a state of longing, but anyone would want to experience Joy.

Young Jack found a version of the search for Joy when he looked on the Castlereagh Hills; another when he read Beatrix Potter's *Squirrel Nutkin,* with its evocation of the longings peculiar to Autumn; and still another when he read one of Henry Wadsworth Longfellow's "Norse Ballads":

> I heard a voice, that cried,
> "Balder the Beautiful
> Is dead, is dead!"

And through the misty air
Passed like the mournful cry
Of sunward sailing cranes.

In his adolescence he would become obsessed with seeking Joy, and the obsession would continue through his early adulthood. In the diary he kept between 1922 and 1927 he records every manifestation of it, however fleeting or weak. The desire for desire, the quest for Joy, would lead him from Longfellow to everything else Norse and more generally northern—and fortunately for him, this was a taste easily satisfied in his day, thanks to the enormous popularity of Richard Wagner's music. Just seeing a description of Margaret Armour's translation of *Siegfried and the Twilight of the Gods*—which Jack did around Christmas of 1911—renewed and inflamed his craving for Joy. (It also complemented Octie's teaching and helped to draw him out of the world of fictional "rubbish" in which he had been floundering.) Jack moved from Armour's book, with its illustrations by Arthur Rackham, to recordings of Wagner's operas themselves, and from there to all manner of Norse and Germanic legends and tales. He even wrote a verse tragedy called *Loki Bound,* in which (as he saw later) Loki's rebellion against the other gods of the Norsemen is a disguised version of Jack's own rebellion against the power structure of the Coll. Thor, it turns out, is a prototypical Blood: Loki sees right through him—and presumably as a result is told to take that look off his face. (But there is something odd about Jack's identification with Loki, for Loki, after all, is the one who, in pure malice, causes the death of Balder the Beautiful.)

Having reawakened Joy—in or around his thirteenth year—Jack was on the way to becoming himself. Nothing was closer to the core of his being than this experience: "In a sense the central story of my life is about nothing else." But only in a sense: later he would discover that his quest for Joy had always been based on misunderstanding. But that would not be for many years; and what Joy *really* stood for he would only then understand and embrace. In the meantime his quest for Joy, along with his interest in occult spiritual experience, would do for him what his youthful Christianity had manifestly failed to do. If his experiments in prayer had been nothing but onerous duty, had given him nothing but a sense of ever-encroaching obligations that he could never quite meet, these other experiences suggested a more open inner world, a world where delight was still possible, and something more than delight—a world always on the verge of disclosing something beautiful and infinite, but undemanding, and not so threatening that a bold boy couldn't risk the dangers.

Indeed, it was in Christian faith that the real dangers lay: those invoked by the specter of dreary and unachievable obedience. Twenty years later Lewis would write an allegorical story called *The Pilgrim's Regress*, which features a young man named John who lives in fear of a great and all-powerful figure called The Landlord. Once John begins to suspect that the Landlord is not the ogre he once believed him to be, he tells a character named Father History, "I am terribly afraid. I am afraid that the things the Landlord really intends for me may be utterly unlike the things he has taught me to desire." In other words: what if God leaves no room for Joy? Better, then, to keep that God at arm's length—farther, if possible.

THREE

"Red beef and strong beer"

I n all the misery of life at Malvern, Jack had found one great blessing: Harry Wakelyn Smith, the Latin master, whom the boys
called Smugy—or Smewgy, in the phonetic spelling Lewis used in
Surprised by Joy.* In many ways Smith continued the work that Lewis
Alden had begun at Campbell: when he told the boys that one line by
Milton ("Thrones, Dominations, Princedoms, Virtues, Powers"—the
salutation of an address by Satan to his fellow demons) had made him
happy for a week, he was reinforcing the idea of verse as pleasure and
delight. An exceptionally demanding teacher, he was also the chief reason Jack felt overwhelmed by academic work, but, though the boy
was not above complaining to his father about Smith's requirements,
he also made it clear that he admired Smith unreservedly and rejoiced
in what he was learning. "How can people advocate a 'modern' education? What could be better or more enjoyable than reading the
greatest masterpieces of all time, under a man [Smith] who has made

---

* The fondness for campy or childish nicknames—characteristic of the period rather
than of Jack personally—grows tiresome after a while. In "Such, Such Were the Joys,"
Orwell says that they called their headmaster Sim and his wife Bingo, though this is a
disguise: they actually called the headmaster Sambo and his wife Flip. Orwell and
Lewis also both gave fictional names to their schools: for Orwell, St. Cyprian's becomes
Crossgates, while for Lewis Cherbourg becomes Chartres, Malvern Wyvern, and of
course Wynyard Belsen. Their stories echo each other in striking and curious ways, but
wholly accidental ones. Lewis was still working on his book when Orwell died, and
Orwell's essay was published only after *Surprised by Joy* was completed—and not in
England until long after Lewis's death. In any case, rather than add a Smugy to our collection of Oldie, Octie, Pogo, and the Great Knock, I'm going to call this man Smith.

them part of himself?" But in his letters home Jack also worries that Smith might learn about his unhappiness or his struggles to keep up academically: "My chief dread is that he may get a bad impression, and I prize his opinion as much as anyone." And he certainly did not want Smith to know that he was getting ready to leave Malvern—indeed, though he learned in the spring of 1914 that he would go to study with Mr. Kirkpatrick in the fall, he kept it a close secret.

The first thing Jack had noticed about Smith was his *manner,* which was utterly at odds with what the Coll otherwise presented: "Amidst all the banal ambition and flashy splendors of school life he stood as a permanent reminder of things more gracious, more humane, larger and cooler." (When Lewis became a teacher himself, he modeled his deportment largely on that of Smith.) But Smith also began to make Jack a scholar: he demonstrated that a concern for the grammatical and syntactical details of a classical text was intimately, even necessarily, linked with a concern for its literary quality. Forced to study both Latin and Greek more attentively than he had ever done before, Jack for the first time "tasted the classics as poetry." He had acquired a taste that would serve him well for the rest of his life—and would begin to serve him well very soon, once he began studying with the Great Knock.

When Jack first arrived in Surrey, he tells us in *Surprised by Joy,* he had steeled himself for an unpleasant meeting with Mr. Kirkpatrick. "We [he and Warnie] had heard about him all our lives and I therefore had a very clear impression of what I was in for. I came prepared to endure a perpetual lukewarm shower bath of sentimentality." Particularly vivid in Jack's mind was a favorite story of his father's in which Kirkpatrick, as headmaster of Lurgan College, had comforted a miserable young Albert by "rubbing his dear old whiskers against my father's youthful cheek." Confronted by the tall, gnarled old man at the Great Bookham railway station, Jack's "cheek already tingled in anticipation. Would he begin at once?"

So begins one of the funniest and most delightful passages in all of Lewis's writing: the story of his encounter with Mr. William T. Kirkpatrick—or Kirk, or the Knock, or the Old Knock, or the Dear Old Knock, or the Great Knock. It is rather difficult to believe that Lewis's description of their first meeting is wholly *accurate*—after all, Warnie had just finished a period of studying with Kirk and was in an excellent position to confirm or contradict his father's account of "the arch-sentimentalist." But perhaps, given the tension in the brothers' relationship at the time, Warnie let Jack twist in the wind, ever fearful of an onslaught of saccharine emotion that Warnie knew would never come.

It would never come because, as Jack would soon discover, "if ever a man came near to being a purely logical entity, that man was Kirk." Even on the walk from the railway station to Kirk's house he subjected Jack, not to a "lukewarm shower bath of sentimentality," but to a relentless exposure of the boy's ignorance and unreason—all because Jack had carelessly ventured the comment that the scenery of Surrey was "wilder" than he had expected. It did not take long for Kirk to demonstrate, with a terrifying absoluteness, that Jack "had no clear and distinct idea corresponding to the word 'wildness,'" and, moreover, had no justification for having "any opinion whatever" about Surrey's flora, fauna, or geology.

"By this time," writes Lewis—who, nearly forty years later, seems still rather shaken by the memory—"our acquaintance had lasted about three and a half minutes; but the tone set by this first conversation was preserved without a single break during all the years I spent at Bookham." And he loved every minute of it: "Some boys would not have liked it; to me it was red beef and strong beer." Under Kirk's guidance he developed the skills in logic and argumentation that so far in his life had gone undeveloped, and perhaps unrecognized—though his mother had been a logician and mathematician, his "sentimental, rhetorical, and passionate" father had dominated his childhood, and it was only now that this other side of his inheritance came into its own. Later in life he would become famous—to his opponents, notorious— for his zeal in debate, but without the tutelage of Kirk it is unlikely that he ever would have become nearly so skillful. His final words on Kirk in *Surprised by Joy* are heartfelt and moving: "My debt to him is very great, my reverence to this day undiminished."

Kirk was a character of the first order, and so it is not surprising perhaps that versions of him find their way into Lewis's fiction. The most direct portrayal is McPhee in *That Hideous Strength*. McPhee's attraction to goodness keeps him in the company of Ransom, the "Director" of a small company of people who are engaged in profound spiritual warfare with the forces of evil, but McPhee's inability to accept the supernaturalism of the company's beliefs makes him always marginal to them. There is a sad honesty in this portrayal: one does not know quite whether to commend McPhee for his integrity or lament his stubbornness, but in either case, he is missing out on something beautiful. He is loved by all, especially Ransom, but pitied a bit too. At the end of the story, having been confronted with miracle after miracle, McPhee tells Ransom, "If I ever take to religion, it won't be your kind." (But his last words to Ransom are perhaps tellingly, "God bless you.")

This is all consistent with the real Kirk, who, as a young man in Ulster, had trained for the Presbyterian ministry but had given it up when he lost his faith. By the time Jack studied with him he had long been a convinced atheist, "a 'Rationalist' of the old, high and dry nineteenth-century type.... At the time when I knew him, Kirk's Atheism was chiefly of the anthropological and pessimistic kind. He was great on *The Golden Bough* and Schopenhauer"—as indeed were many late-Victorian atheists. The work of Arthur Schopenhauer provided a specifically philosophical basis for pessimism, that is, the belief that misery and disorder provide a kind of negative but overwhelming case against the existence of a good and loving God. For Schopenhauer, human reason is enslaved to human will, and human will to human desire; the result is a pointless and probably inescapable cycle of suffering that we inflict on ourselves and others. As England's great *poetic* pessimist, A. E. Housman (a near-contemporary of Kirk's), put it:

> Therefore, since the world has still
> Much good, but much less good than ill,
> And while the sun and moon endure
> Luck's a chance, but trouble's sure,
> I'd face it as a wise man would,
> And train for ill and not for good.

This advice Jack took, especially since he was temperamentally inclined that way anyhow: from his earliest childhood, he says, he had developed "a settled expectation that everything would do what you did not want it to do." From a series of experiences as varied as his intractable physical clumsiness and the death of his mother, he had learned that he could not expect anything to work out as he hoped. He was a Schopenhauerian long before hearing of Schopenhauer from Kirk.

(In a letter to his father in November 1915, he mentions that he has been reading a library copy of Schopenhauer's *The World as Will and Idea* and finding it "abstruse and depressing," but he goes on to note that "Kirk, I need hardly say, is strong on him, and will talk on the subject for hours." He does not tell his father how deeply he shares Kirk's estimation of Schopenhauer, and indeed, at this point in his life he was at some pains to hide his atheism from his father. In December 1914 he had allowed himself to be confirmed at St. Mark's in Dundela in full awareness that he believed nothing of what he was publicly claiming to believe—something that he later thought of as "one of the worst acts" of his life.)

A different case against God, or at least against Christianity, is provided by *The Golden Bough*, Sir James Frazer's massive, multivolume study of ancient religious practices in Europe and the Middle East. (The first version of it appeared in two volumes in 1890, and additional volumes would continue to be published until 1920.) Frazer's exploration of "dying-god myths"—along with other common religious practices that, Frazer argued, emerged from the cycle of the seasons—convinced many intellectuals that Christianity was a late, unoriginal, and not especially appealing version of an archaic religious habit. Though Frazer's book is little read now, it was one of the most influential books of the first half of the twentieth century, and its impact on literature was especially great: it is hard to imagine many of the great modernist writers without it, especially Joyce, Yeats, and T. S. Eliot. (Eliot's poem *The Waste Land* in particular is almost a summary of *The Golden Bough*.)

From the time he studied under Kirk, young Jack Lewis took Frazer's argument for granted; a fundamental and essential piece of his intellectual equipment, it incidentally confirmed him in his earlier loss of Christian faith. For those who had learned from Frazer, spiritual experience was only religion, religion was only myth, and myth was only an intellectual formulation of agricultural cultures' need to adapt themselves to, and give meaning to, the changes of the seasons and the unpredictability of weather. Jesus Christ, Osiris, even Balder the Beautiful—they were all articulations of one of the basic features of material existence: that at one time of the year things come to life, and at another they sink into the earth. (Frazer explores at great length his belief that the myth of Balder is closely associated with the many different "fire-festivals" practiced throughout Europe; he comes to the conclusion that Balder is a personification of the oak tree.) This radically materialist view of myth was one that, later in life, C. S. Lewis would devote a great deal of energy to refuting—but largely because in his teenage years it had been his settled conviction.

Yet even when he was at his most pessimistic, "Balder the Beautiful / Is dead, is dead" still cut through him like a knife. Why was that, given the false promise of the myth? Better not to ask—and indeed, it seems, he did *not* ask. "The two hemispheres of my mind were in the sharpest contrast. On the one side a many-islanded sea of poetry and myth; on the other a glib and shallow 'rationalism.' Nearly all that I loved I believed to be imaginary; nearly all that I believed to be real I thought grim and meaningless." A life riven by such deep inner chasms could not have been easy to live; the wonder is that Jack held these opposite tendencies in tension as long as he did. He had already become an exceptionally self-disciplined person in many respects—Kirk would write to Albert about the boy's "fixity of purpose, determination of character, persevering energy"—and nowhere were those traits more evident than in the terrible task of sustaining a dramatically divided self throughout the years of adolescence and, as we shall see, young manhood.

If the "anthropological and pessimistic" Kirk appears straightforwardly in the character of McPhee, it is in a somewhat disguised or altered form that he appears in the Narnia books as Professor Kirke—Digory Kirke of *The Magician's Nephew* all grown up. It is true that the Professor has some of Kirk's most pronounced mannerisms: for instance, in *The Lion, the Witch, and the Wardrobe,* when Peter and Susan Pevensie disbelieve Lucy's story of the magical wardrobe and believe Edmund's claim that they were just pretending, he subjects them to the kind of dialectical workout that Jack had regularly received from his tutor:

"For instance—if you will excuse me for asking the question— does your experience lead you to regard your brother or your sister as the more reliable? I mean, which is the more truthful?"

"That's just the funny thing about it, Sir," said Peter. "Up till now, I'd have said Lucy every time."

"And what do you think, my dear?" said the Professor, turning to Susan.

"Well," said Susan, "in general, I'd say the same as Peter, but this couldn't be true—all this about the wood and the Faun."

"That's more than I know," said the Professor, "and a charge of lying against someone whom you have always found truthful is a very serious thing; a very serious thing indeed."

"We were afraid it mightn't even be lying," said Susan. "We thought there might be something wrong with Lucy."

"Madness, you mean?" said the Professor quite cooly. "Oh, you can make your minds easy about that. One has only to look at her and talk to her to see that she is not mad."

"But then," said Susan and stopped. She had never dreamed that a grown-up would talk like the Professor and didn't know what to think.

"Logic!" said the Professor half to himself. "Why don't they teach logic at these schools? There are only three possibilities. Either your sister is telling lies, or she is mad, or she is telling the truth. You know she doesn't tell lies and it is obvious that she is not mad. For the moment then and unless any further evidence turns up, we must assume that she is telling the truth."

What could be more Kirkian than this Socratic inquisition? Yet there is a difference. What that difference is becomes clearer when we hear from the Professor again, in the last pages of the final Narnian story, *The Last Battle*. There Peter and Susan Pevensie are puzzled to find themselves in what seems to be Narnia—puzzled because Aslan had told them they would not return there. But the Professor—or, as he is now called, the Lord Digory—explains that the Narnia where they had become High King and Queen

"... was only a shadow or copy of the real Narnia, which has always been here and always will be here.... And of course it is different; as different as a real thing is from a shadow or as waking life is from a dream." His voice stirred everyone like a trumpet as he spoke these words: but when he added under his breath "It's all in Plato, all in Plato: bless me, what *do* they teach them at these schools!" the older ones laughed. It was so exactly like the sort of thing they had heard him say long ago in that other world where his beard was grey instead of golden.

And *almost* exactly like the sort of thing the Kirk who taught the Lewis family would say. That Kirk might well have deplored the schools' failure to teach logic, but he scarcely would have lamented ignorance of Plato in the same terms. For Mr. Kirkpatrick, what Plato taught—or at least the part of his teaching that involved a spiritual realm higher than ours, and perfected—is mere illusion, a sentimental distraction from the real, hard, cold facts of the case, the facts that pessimism squarely faces.

Why does Lewis do this? Why does he transform Kirk into Kirke, the Schopenhauerian pessimist into the Platonic idealist? It is best to think of it as a *gift*. Lewis grants to this fictional version of his old teacher something that Kirk was not granted in his earthly life: a vision of Narnia, an entry into another world. Professor Kirke, in fact, does not tell Peter and Susan the whole story: he believes Lucy, not just because it is the most logical thing to do (indeed his argument is not very logical), but because when he had been a little boy in London with his dying mother, he himself found a way into Narnia and watched that world come into being at the command of Aslan, and from it he brought back an apple that restored his mother to life and health. Digory Kirke is Lewis's picture of what William T. Kirkpatrick *might* have been—had he ever found a way into Narnia.

Strangely, Digory Kirke is also what young Jack Lewis might have been had *he* found his way into Narnia when it was not too late to save his dying mother, Flora. Moreover, the argument about Lucy's reliability that Lewis puts in the mouth of the old Professor—"There are only three possibilities"—will remind many readers of one of the most famous passages in the writings of C. S. Lewis the Christian apologist:

> I am trying here to prevent anyone saying the really foolish thing that people often say about Him: "I'm ready to accept Jesus as a great moral teacher, but I don't accept His claim to be God." That is one thing we must not say. A man who was merely a man and said the sort of thing Jesus said would not be a great moral teacher. He would either be a lunatic—on a level with the man who says he is a poached egg—or else he would be the Devil of Hell. You must make your choice. Either this man was, and is, the Son of God: or else a madman or something worse. You can shut Him up for a fool, you can spit at Him and kill him as a demon or you can fall at his feet and call Him Lord and God. But let us not come with any patronizing nonsense about His being a great human teacher. He has not left that open to us. He did not intend to.

At moments like these, Lewis's "reverence" for Kirk comes close to identification. One can almost hear him muttering under his breath, "Logic! What *do* they teach them at these schools?"

Kirk worked Jack hard, no doubt, but everything about Jack's life at Bookham savored of liberation. He was freed from games, freed from fagging—freed from almost every sort of social accountability. He was never flogged, and no one told him to take that look off of his face. What he studied—primarily the greatest writers of Greece and Rome, though he also studied German and Italian and (under Kirk's wife) French—he mostly loved, and what he did not love he could easily tolerate. Above all, perhaps, his daily life had a shape that he found—and for the rest of his life would find—ideal. "If I could please myself I would always live as I lived there." The form of his life is well and thoroughly described in a letter he wrote to his friend Arthur Greeves—about whom more soon—in October 1915, about a year after he first came to Bookham. He was sixteen years old, soon to be seventeen.

> You ask me how I spend my time, and though I am more interested in thoughts and feelings, we'll come down to facts. I am awakened up in the morning by Kirk splashing in his bath, about 20 minutes after which I get up myself and come down. After breakfast & a short walk we start work on Thucydides—a desperately dull and tedious Greek historian (I daresay tho', you'd find him interesting) and on Homer whom I worship. After quarter of an hour's rest we go on with Tacitus till lunch at 1. I am then free till tea at 4:30; of course I am always anxious at this meal to see if Mrs K. is out, for Kirk never takes it. If she is I lounge in an arm chair with my book by the fire, reading over a leisurely and bountiful meal. If she's in, or worse still has "some people" to tea, it means sitting on a right angled chair and sipping a meagrue allowance of tea and making intelligent comments about the war, the parish and the shortcomings of everyones servants. At 5, we do Plato and Horace, who are both charming, till supper at 7.30, after which comes German and French till about 9. Then I am free to go to bed whenever I like which is usually about 10.20.

(Note the condescension toward Plato, who is merely "charming": it is Homer whom he "worships.") It is a scholar's life, and though he makes petty complaints to Arthur, Jack adored it and throve within it. It was everything school had not been: peaceful, solitary, socially undemanding—tea with the ladies was nothing compared to being fagged by Bloods—and filled with long uninterrupted periods of study and reflection.

If one wonders what he did with that free time between lunch and teatime, the answer is simple: he walked. He seems to have developed his love of walking when he was at Malvern—at least, that is when his letters first refer to it. ("The other day we went off for a ripping walk over the hills, right across into Wales, a good step on the other side, and home through a sort of cutting.") Going for long walks was one of the great pleasures of Lewis's life until illness, at the end of his life, made him virtually immobile. In his love of such peregrination Lewis joined a great English tradition, though not an especially ancient one. Of course, before the advent of the many forms of motorized transport almost everyone had to walk almost everywhere, but sometime around the beginning of the nineteenth century people—especially artists and intellectuals—had begun to think of walking as an activity worthy of note and even celebration. The Wordsworths and their friends seem to have walked all over England and Scotland, often wearing their shoes down to nothing along the way. Thomas de Quincey, after his first meeting with Coleridge in 1807, was so exalted by the experience that, leaving Coleridge's house around 10:00 p.m., he decided to walk home—home in his case being Bristol, some forty miles away.

That de Quincey did it is extraordinary, but what is more important is that he chose to tell the tale. (He makes a point of mentioning the forty miles.) Even before the first railway engines, and long before automobiles or even bicycles, walking was beginning to take on a bit of romance. By the time Lewis was a child, the romance had flowered, and people who chose to walk when they could ride something were aware that they were making a distinctive choice. After the Great War, organizations sprang up to support the habit: the Ramblers' Association to get walkers together and help them plan their trips, and the Youth Hostel Association to give them places to sleep and eat during their rambles. But by this time Lewis's habits had long been formed.

He would usually take his daily walks—often a short one in the morning and a much longer one after lunch—alone. These were times of meditation and reflection and, after he became a Christian, prayer; they were also part of his quest for Joy, because particular landscapes, or certain views of those landscapes, would sometimes set off the much-desired longing. But he liked equally well long walks with friends—especially if they didn't talk much along the way—and in adulthood he and his companions would often go off for jaunts of several days, staying overnight in little inns and pubs. When one stops to think about it, there is a great deal of walking in Narnia: in almost every book some of the characters set off on long journeys by foot, and even in *The Voyage of the "Dawn Treader"* a few of them feel the need to hop off the ship to take a stroll across the island of Felimath. Likewise, when considered from a certain point of view, *The Lord of the Rings* is hardly anything *but* friends going on long—really long—walks together. It is true that few of these fictional journeys are voluntary and still fewer are pleasant, but they are always interesting, and for Lewis and Tolkien alike there is something intrinsically adventurous about a "ripping walk." (However, though Lewis and Tolkien were close friends indeed, Tolkien rarely accompanied Lewis and company on their rambles.)

If Jack had developed the habit of walking while at Malvern, and continued it in Surrey, he extended it to his holidays back home in Ireland. He early on became very aware of the ways in which the Irish landscape—especially as it stretched out northwards from Little Lea, which was then at the very edge of Belfast suburbia—differed from any of the English ones he had come to know. When writing about the contours of County Down in *Surprised by Joy*, he becomes more overtly Irish than at any other point in that story. His use of pronouns is particularly noteworthy: "The woods, for we have a few, are of small trees, rowan and birch and small fir," and, "You must not spread over this landscape your hard English sunlight." It is as though he is claiming some ownership of the landscape and keeping the alien English at a distance. Even though he loved his walks around Malvern and in Surrey, he was prone to nostalgia for Ireland. When still at Malvern he wrote to a Strandtown friend:

> Where is your favourite walk? . . . County Down must be looking glorious just now: I can just picture the view of the Lough and Cave Hill from beside the Shepard's Hut. Sometime next holy-days, you and I must make a journey up their before breakfast. Have you ever done that? The sunrise over the Holywood Hills, and the fresh stillness of the early morning are well worth the trouble of early rising, I can assure you.

This "Strandtown friend" was Arthur Greeves, whom Jack had come to know fairly recently. He had lived across the road from the Lewises for years, but Warnie and Jack had been unresponsive to his overtures of friendship. Arthur was a sickly and coddled child, thought by his mother too delicate for school—though for a time he attended Campbell College—and was perhaps insufficiently robust for the Lewis boys. (He was just Warnie's age.) But in April 1914, when Jack was on holiday before his final term at Malvern, he was told that the then-bedridden Arthur would appreciate some company, and as an act of charity he paid a visit—only to be very surprised by what he discovered:

> I found Arthur sitting up in bed. On the table beside him lay a copy of *Myths of the Norsemen.*
> "Do *you* like that?" said I.
> "Do *you* like that?" said he.
> Next moment the book was in our hands, our heads were bent close together, we were pointing, quoting, talking—soon almost shouting—discovering in a torrent of questions that we liked not only the same thing, but the same parts of it and in the same way; that both knew the stab of Joy and that, for both, the arrow was shot from the North. Many thousands of people have had the experience of finding the first friend, and it is none the less a wonder; as great a wonder (*pace* the novelists) as first love, or even a greater. I had been so far from thinking such a friend possible that I had never even longed for one; no more than I longed to be King of England. . . . Nothing, I suspect, is more as-tonishing in any man's life than the discovery that there exist people very, very like himself.

With Arthur, Jack explored not only the wonders of story and myth, but (insofar as Arthur's health allowed) the treasures of County Down. And though they were very alike in some respects, they were sufficiently different that Jack could learn from Arthur. For instance, it was from Arthur that Jack first learned to appreciate the "homely" as much as the dramatic landscapes of Norse myth, with their mighty mountains, deep fjords, and "sunward-sailing cranes." Arthur taught Jack to love the sight of a row of cabbages in a farmhouse garden and helped him appreciate the very ordinariness of the Victorian novelists.

They were different in other ways too. Arthur, always a religious person, seems to have been distressed by Jack's blunt unbelief. And later in life Jack would say quite frankly, "He was not a clever boy, he was even a dull boy; I was a scholar. He had no 'ideas.' I bubbled over with them." But what young Jack did not know was that, over the long haul, Arthur was to have a greater influence over him than he had over Arthur. By middle age, having learned that, he would write, "I learned charity from him and failed, for all my efforts, to teach him arrogance in return."

Over the years the friendship waxed and waned and waxed again. The two could be at odds for years together but then draw back together in mutual, deep affection. They were not always good for each other; even before he became a Christian, Jack would come to think that he and Arthur were too frank with each other about their sexual preferences and fantasies. (Arthur confessed his homosexuality to Jack—which seems to have had no effect whatever on their friendship—and Jack, in correspondence and conversations with Arthur, would indulge in mildly sadomasochistic fantasies: there are often references in letters to women he'd like to spank, and for a while he signs his letters "Philomastix"—"whip-lover.") But only his brother, Warnie, meant more to Lewis, and was a part of Lewis's life for longer, than Arthur. In 1963—as it turned out, the last year of Lewis's life—he planned a vacation in Ireland with Arthur, but he suffered a major heart attack and was forced to cancel his plans. Lewis was always reserved in his correspondence, even with the people closest to him, so one can but imagine the pain that underlay one of his last letters to his friend: "But oh Arthur, never to see you again!"

The long walks with Arthur through the Holywood Hills had another benefit for Jack: they kept him away from his father. One of the consequences of Albert's bereavement was an ever-increasing desire on his part to be intimate with his children—to be "one of the boys." When at home, Jack was "closely tethered" to his father on evenings and weekends, "and felt this something of a hardship, since these were the times when Arthur was most often accessible." It was out of the question for Arthur to visit Jack at Little Lea, for reasons Warnie would explain much later:

> Jack would have liked to return Arthur's hospitality: had this been arranged, my father would certainly have welcomed his son's friend very cordially, but not for a moment would it have occurred to him that the two boys might want to talk together, alone. No: he would have joined them, inescapably, for a good talk about books, doing nine-tenths of the talking himself, eulogizing his own favourites without regard to their interests. Two

bored and frustrated youths would have been subjected to long readings from Macaulay's essays, Burke's speeches, and the like, and my father would have gone to bed satisfied that he had given them a literary evening far more interesting than they could have contrived for themselves.

Though there is much excellent intentional comedy in *Surprised by Joy*, there is unintended comedy as well—though with a melancholy tinge—in Lewis's attempts to describe his father and their relationship. He knows that Albert was a good and loving and generous father, and he feels strongly that among the greatest sins in his life were sins against Albert—and yet he cannot resist telling yet another story that reveals just how maddening it must have been to live with the man. A. N. Wilson says that Lewis's portrait of his father is "devastatingly cruel," which is at best an exaggeration; affection and frustration are always warring in the depiction of Albert, who, if the Lewis brothers are to be trusted at all, legitimately prompted both. "He had," writes a still-exasperated, middle-aged Lewis,

> more power of confusing an issue or taking up a fact wrongly than any man I have ever met.... Some facts must have been asked for and told him, on a moderate computation, once a week, and were received by him each time as perfect novelties. But this was the simplest barrier. Far more often he retained something, but something very unlike what you had said. His mind so bubbled over with humour, sentiment, and indignation that, long before he had understood or even listened to your words, some accidental hint had set his imagination to work, he had produced his own version of the facts, and believed that he was getting it from you.... [And] his own version, once adopted, was indelible, and attempts to correct only produced an incredulous "Hm! Well, that's not the story you *used* to tell."

No wonder Jack took such long walks. He and Warnie knew the P'daitabird was funny—they kept a record of his more peculiar sayings in a book they called "P'daita Pie." Their gibes were superficially good-humored and even affectionate, but there was an undercurrent of something like contempt in them. Jack's letters to his father from this period remain openly pleasant and friendly, only occasionally revealing a bit of an edge. Perhaps because he was gaining intellectual confidence under Kirk's tutelage, or perhaps just because he was a teenager, Jack could not resist the occasional priggish dig: at age fifteen, he writes from Kirk's house, in response to a mention by Albert of the essays of Francis Bacon, "By the way, who is your friend Lord Bacon? I don't remember any such name in English literature: in fact the name Bacon itself never occurs, to my knowledge, except as the family name of Lord Verulam. (Ahh! A body blow, eh?)" Jack's point is simply that after Bacon was created Baron Verulam in 1618, the proper way to address him would have been as Francis Bacon, Lord Verulam, never Lord Bacon. He is correct, of course, but such cheap pedantry in so young a boy!—and how sad to see him rejoicing in this trivial "victory" over his father.

His letters from the period reveal him to have been consistently and grossly patronizing to Arthur as well. He lists the words that Arthur misspells, calling them "gems of Arthurian style"—this though he is himself an erratic speller at best. When Arthur expresses hurt feelings over a misunderstanding regarding holiday plans, Jack becomes positively Olympian:

> Now what is your grievance—for grievance you must have or you would not write such good grammar. Is it because I won't throw up my previous invitation in favour of yours? That would be rude. Is it because I will not accompany you on another holyday? That is selfish of you.... Is it because I mildly suggested that you need not go for a holyday? There was never any obligation on your part to accept such a scheme.... How funny that I always prove everything I want in argument with you but never convince you!

In short, Jack Lewis in his middle teens was a thoroughly obnoxious, arrogant, condescending intellectual prig. (But then, so was I at the same age, and with much less justification for my self-confidence.)

I mentioned earlier Kirk's praise for Jack's perseverance and intellectual industry. He had quickly realized that Jack was a very different character than his older brother. If he had judged that it was too late to make Warnie interested in knowledge, in Jack he saw a boy who was not likely to be interested in anything else. Strict though Kirk was, when writing to Albert he did not stint his praise for Jack: "He has read more classics than any boy I ever had—or indeed I might add than any I ever heard of, unless it be an Addison or Landor or Macaulay. These are people we read of, but I have never met any." Jack was seventeen at the time, and Kirk was already comparing him to great English men of letters, but even earlier Kirk, freely confessing Jack's superiority to himself, had flatly told Albert, "He is the most brilliant translator of Greek plays I have ever met." And it was not just the breadth of his reading that set him apart, but also, and equally, the quality of his mind: "As a dialectician, an intellectual disputant, I shall miss him, and he will have no successor. Clive can hold his own in any discussion, and the higher the range of the conversation, the more he feels himself at home."

However, when Kirk told Albert that Jack "was born with the literary temperament and we have to face that fact with all it implies," he was not simply praising the boy: he was also commenting on Jack's lack of fitness for any sort of life other than the literary or the scholarly. At any time a boy with such a temperament would be in a difficult position, because there are few ways to make a living as a writer or scholar. But in the years following 1914 something else was clouding Jack's future: the Great War.

Tensions had been building in Europe for some time as the various powers—France, Germany, Russia, England, the Austro-Hungarian Empire—jockeyed for power and influence on the Continent. The Balkans were the focus of greatest attention and unease. For the previous fifteen years there had been peace conferences, summits on international law and conflict mediation, the establishment of tribunals, but alliances had also been forged such that a single country deciding to risk war could cause all the dominoes of Europe to fall. In the newspapers some writers said that war was inevitable; others thought that all the efforts toward reconciliation could still pay off or that no country would be foolish enough to risk war in such a volatile environment.

It was in the midst of all this debate and speculation that Warnie went to study with Kirk, took his entrance examination for Sandhurst, and began his cadet program there in January 1914. How Her Majesty's Government felt about the likelihood of war may be judged from this: soon after Warnie's arrival the usual two-year cadet program was compressed into nine months.

On the twenty-eighth of June, the Crown Prince of the Austro-Hungarian Empire, Franz Ferdinand, was assassinated, along with his wife, Sophie, in the streets of Sarajevo, Bosnia (which had recently been annexed by the Austrians, prompting enormous nationalist resentment). The dominoes soon began to fall. Austria-Hungary blamed Serbia for the assassination and precisely one month after Franz Ferdinand's death declared war on Serbia. Austria-Hungary's ally Germany demanded that the other Great Powers stay out of the conflict, but Russia began to mobilize its army to defend *its* ally, Serbia; so on August 1 Germany declared war on Russia and, having received no response from France to its ultimatum, two days later declared war on that country as well. When Germany violated Belgian neutral ground on its way to France, Britain protested and, when the protest was ignored, entered the war. What we usually call World War I, but what was then (and more properly) called the Great War, had begun.

Warnie was commissioned as a lieutenant on the first of October, just a few days after Jack first arrived at Kirk's house in Surrey. On November 4 Jack wrote to Arthur, "Great Bookham and the present arrangement continue to give every satisfaction which is possible." That very day Warnie crossed the English Channel to join the British Expeditionary Force in France.

Jack was still three weeks shy of his sixteenth birthday, so war was not on his immediate horizon. And indeed he did not have to go to war at all, because Irish nationals were exempt from service unless they volunteered. (Warnie, having chosen the Army as a career, was beyond such considerations.) And why *should* Jack volunteer? He could have made a good case that neither by nationality nor by temperament was he suited for the Army. It is true that there was great social pressure on men to enlist: the writer G. K. Chesterton, though he was forty years old and weighed well over three hundred pounds, during the war was accosted on a London street by a woman who asked, "Why aren't you out at the front?" (Chesterton replied, "My dear madam, if you will step round this way a little, you will see that I am.") Yet Jack was spared much of this pressure by his private and reclusive life in Great Bookham. More than most young men of his age, he could think the matter through—and he had some time to do it, since only at age eighteen would he be eligible to serve in any case.

Writing to his father in June 1915, when the heavy fighting had been going on only about six months, Jack offered a judgment: "I think we may reasonably hope that the war will be over before it begins to concern me personally." A year later—when everyone understood that tens of thousands of men could die, on a single day, to gain a hundred yards of territory, territory that they would give up, at equal cost, a few weeks or months later—that was no longer a reasonable hope. For a time, during the first half of 1916, it appeared that the Military Service Act might indeed be understood to require Jack to serve. Kirk, writing to Albert Lewis in May, did not think that likely, though continuing to stay in England to study increased Jack's chance of being conscripted. But even if he were not conscripted, wrote Kirk, "at any rate we may give up the idea that the war may be over before Jany. 1917"—that is, when the eighteen-year-old Jack would be ready for university. "What is to become of the Eng. Universities under this new Conscription Act? I cannot say; but I do not see how they are to go on." In other words, even if Jack managed to avoid conscription, where would this brilliant young scholar go if the halls of Oxford and Cambridge were emptied of their young men?

Uncertainty reigned, then, on many levels, but Jack at least reduced his uncertainty by making for himself the most important decision of all. In May, Albert wrote back to Kirk saying, "Clive has decided to serve." (No hint of his thinking appears in his letters of the time.) But he would spend the remainder of that year preparing for Oxford's entrance examination. If the Oxford colleges continued to receive students, and if he were not called to the front, or if he were called to the front but returned alive—then, if Oxford would have him, an Oxford scholar he would eventually be.

One of the strangest periods of Jack's life now commenced—his own private version of the "Phony War" or "bore war" that all of England would have to endure two decades later, when the country was officially at war with Germany but very little was happening. Jack knew that when the time came he would enlist, and once enlisted would doubtless be sent to the front, but he continued to prepare for his Oxford entrance examinations as if peace reigned throughout Europe.

I did feel that the decision absolved me from taking any further notice of the war. . . . Accordingly I put the war on one side to a degree which some will think shameful and some incredible. Others will call it a flight from reality. I maintain that it was rather a treaty with reality, the fixing of a frontier. I said to my country, in effect, "You shall have me on a certain date, not before. I will die in your wars if need be, but till then I shall live my own life. You may have my body, but not my mind. I will take part in battles but not read about them."

(It is curious that he refers here to "my country," especially in light of the Irishness in which he reveled when at school. Perhaps he has come to accept the idea of the United Kingdom, but in that case it is odd that he uses the term "country." Had his time in Surrey made him English already?) When Lewis wrote *Surprised by Joy* in the late 1940s and early 1950s, he had almost all the letters that we now possess available to him, thanks to Warnie's years of labor in assembling the family's letters and other documents, typing them, and binding them into eleven volumes with the collective title "Memoirs of the Lewis Family: 1850–1930." These papers enabled Jack to be more factually accurate than autobiographers usually are, and no doubt when he was writing this section of *Surprised by Joy* he noted with interest the nearly complete absence of any reference to the war in his letters. There are only occasional mentions in them of "the colonel," which had become his nickname for Warnie—though in fact Warnie would never rise higher than the rank of major—but the uninformed reader would struggle to guess that "the colonel" was at war, or for that matter that anyone else was.

One of the rare occasions on which the reality breaks in is when, in early 1917, speculation is raging in Britain about the possibility of the United States's entering the war. Jack writes to his father, "Kirk says it will be a great disadvantage if she comes in, tho' I don't quite understand how; he also assures us that we shall be starving before next summer, which indeed (unless you are right in hoping to see it over before then) is like to be." But immediately after this rather laconic statement he signs off ("your loving son Jack") and in future letters falls back upon his usual topics of conversation. Three-fourths of his correspondence at this time is about his reading; the remainder describes walks in the Surrey countryside or the rare social occasion, or occupies itself with attempts to correct Arthur's sadly immature belief in Christianity ("the man Yeshua or Jesus did actually exist ... but all the other tomfoolery about virgin birth, magic healings, apparitions and so forth is on exactly the same footing as any other mythology") and indeed in any sort of religion at all ("strange as it may appear I am quite content to live without believing in a bogey who is prepared to torture me forever and ever if I should fail in coming up to an almost impossible ideal"). Any concerns about the war are forcibly suppressed; he does not even say whether he shares his father's hope that the war will end before the summer of 1917, nor does he mention that the question concerns him quite directly.

"I am very well pleased with life and have a very happy time on the whole"; so he tells Arthur, and truthfully no doubt, as long as he managed to fix his attention on his reading. It was very wide at this point: works of popular fiction, classic English novels, all of his classical, Italian, and German literature with Kirk, and deeper and deeper explorations of the greatest English poets. Spenser's *Faerie Queene*—for most young scholars of literature an acquired taste at best—was his particular delight at this time, but he was also devoted to the prose romances and verse narratives of William Morris, the many-minded genius—architect, furniture designer, bookmaker, poet, novelist, and socialist pamphleteer—who was perhaps the key figure in late-Victorian medievalism. And he was reading everything he could find by Yeats. (The dominance of Faery is clear.) Most important of all, there was a book that he picked up in the railway station at Leatherhead. In *Surprised by Joy* he says it happened on a chill October day, but a letter to Arthur suggests it was actually around the first of March in 1916:

> I have had a great literary experience this week. I have discovered yet another author to add to our circle—our very own set: never since I first read [Morris's] "The well at the world's end" have I enjoyed a book so much—and indeed I think my new "find" is quite as good as Malory or Morris himself. The book, to get to the point, is George MacDonald's "Faerie Romance," *Phantastes*. . . . Have you read it? I suppose not, as if you had, you could not have helped telling me about it. At any rate, whatever the book you are reading now, you simply MUST get this at once.

This book would, in significant ways, change Jack Lewis's life. Its author was a strange figure. Born into Scots Calvinism in 1824, MacDonald gradually veered away from that strict religious tradition—though into what is hard to say with any precision. If his mature theology was not unorthodox, it was certainly unusual—at least, so thought the deacons of the little chapel in Arundel where he was called as minister in 1850. Three years later they had forced him to resign, and for the remaining half-century of his life he would struggle to find any work at all; indeed, he and his family were at times in real danger of starvation. But despite his many afflictions, he wrote book after book: some of them "unspoken sermons," some rather realistic

novels (*Thomas Wingfold, Curate* and *What's Mine's Mine*), some
what we would call "fantasies" (*Phantastes* and *Lilith*), plus the novels for children (*The Princess and the Goblin* and *The Princess and
Curdie*) for which he is best known today. He also wrote many strange
tales that are the very epitome of Victorian fantasy: "The Golden
Key," for instance, and "At the Back of the North Wind." As a middle-aged man, Jack Lewis would call MacDonald his "master" and
make him a key character in one of his best books; he would go so far
as to say, "To speak plainly I know hardly any other writer who seems
to be closer, or more continually close, to the Spirit of Christ Himself." But he could not have discerned that "Spirit" at the time; had he
been able to do so, he would have thrown aside *Phantastes* in boredom or contempt. At this first reading, MacDonald was just another
author to add to the "circle" of fantasists whom Jack and Arthur
loved; the ways in which MacDonald differed from the others were
then invisible. It was only the strength of his appeal that set him apart.

In the meantime, Jack continued to prepare for his Oxford entrance
examinations. In December 1916 he made his first visit to Oxford and
was as taken by what are invariably referred to as its "dreaming
spires" as thousands of previous visitors had been: "The place has
surpassed my wildest dreams: I never saw anything so beautiful." A
few days later he received a letter from the master of University College announcing that he had been elected to a scholarship—that is, accepted as a student (and with what we would now call a "financial aid
package," though the Oxford term was "an Exhibition"). But Jack
would not be eligible to begin his studies until the spring of 1917, so it
was back to life with the Knock for a couple of months more, during
which he focused on modern languages, with the thought that if his
literary and academic dreams fell through, he could perhaps get a job
with the Foreign Office. His own private Phony War continued.

FOUR

"I never sank so low as to pray"

The Oxford to which Jack came in March 1917 was a strange place, simultaneously empty and full. Students had largely vacated the colleges, but soldiers were everywhere, many of them soldiers who had recently been undergraduates. At a time when the student population of Oxford was about 3,000, nearly 15,000 "members" of the university (which included both undergraduates and those who had left Oxford, with or without degrees) had joined the British Army. Many soldiers-in-training were billeted in the Oxford colleges—after all, so many of the beds were unused—before being sent off to the front. Young men still filled the streets of Oxford, but they wore the brown woolen uniforms of Tommies rather than flowing black silk gowns.

One 1915 honors graduate, a recently married young man named J. R. R. Tolkien, had gone off to the war in June 1916; when he kissed his wife, Edith, good-bye, he had reason to think that he would never see her again. "Junior officers were being killed off, a dozen a minute. Parting from my wife then ... it was like a death." Partly because he became a signal officer and was therefore rarely on the front lines, and partly because he contracted a severe and protracted case of trench fever just a few months after arriving at the Somme, he did survive and return to Edith, but, as he wrote many years later, "by 1918 all but one of my close friends were dead." Warnie Lewis, likewise, was spared the greatest dangers, in his case because he was a supply officer, charged with provisioning the troops. Though neither he nor Tolkien was ever safe, at least they were spared the daily horrors of trench warfare. Jack, however, would not be so fortunate.

But that was yet to come. Jack had arrived at Oxford in March 1917 to take a series of tests called Responsions. Though he had already been elected as a member of University College (or "Univ.") and therefore of the university itself, he had to take this preliminary examination in order to demonstrate that he had basic competence in the academic skills necessary for success at university. Unfortunately for Jack, one of these academic skills was mathematics, in which he was thoroughly, even flamboyantly, incompetent. (All his life he would struggle even to make change in shops.) In the exam he was, as he later put it, "handsomely ploughed"—that is, he simply flunked. He would spend the latter part of March and early April cramming for a retake. In the end he never managed to pass Responsions and, if he had not been exempted from it as a returning serviceman, would perhaps have been unable to attend a university at all.

After the ploughing he returned to Belfast for a holiday, but at the end of April he was back in Oxford, where he got rooms in his college and enrolled in the Officers' Training Corps. Because everyone knew he would soon be going to war, he lived in college without doing any organized academic work. "I have been to see the Dean ... and also my tutor," he told his father, "but they don't appear to suggest any real reading while I am in the Corps." So for a little more than a month he enjoyed a leisurely life in college, assigned spacious rooms that "really belong to a tremendous blood who is at the front—at least the furniture is his." With only twelve undergraduates at Univ., the collegiate authorities thought it pointless to have dinners in the old Great Hall, so the young men ate in a lecture room; none of the dons (that is, the faculty) bothered to show up. During the day, when he was theoretically supposed to be studying to retake Responsions, Jack browsed Oxford's bookstores or went swimming in the river. He quickly picked up items of the distinctive Oxford slang of the period—referring to breakfast as "brekker," for instance—and discovered how learned his companions were: one of them, a fellow Irishman named Butler, informed him that if he really wanted to learn more about spanking he should consult the writings of a certain "Visconte de sade." Once he went to a party and got sufficiently drunk that he offered to pay a shilling to anyone who would let him whip them—a shilling a lash, that is, which could have exhausted his allowance rather quickly. Reading stories like this, one imagines that Jack had managed to transport himself to the Aesthetes' Oxford of the 1890s, not a university barely functioning because so many of its members were fighting the bloodiest war thus far in human history.

On the seventh of June he was called to join a battalion of army cadets; so ended, for the time being, his odd half-life as a student of Oxford University. However, the cadets were billeted at Keble College, just a few hundred yards up Parks Road from Univ., so geographically his situation was almost unchanged. But only geographically. His bed was now an army cot, his uniform that of a Tommy, and his companions of a very different, and broader, social range than his fellow members of Univ. No wonder he tried to keep, as long as he could, his college rooms for use in his free time—an arrangement the dean eventually put a stop to. But Jack quickly came to like his fellow cadets, especially his roommate, a young man named Paddy Moore—Irish like Jack, though he had been raised in Bristol since age nine (where his mother had moved after the collapse of her marriage) and had attended a minor public school there, Clifton College. He was perhaps not university material, and at first Jack found him too "childish" for regular company. But soon, and unexpectedly, they grew close.

Paddy's mother, Janie Moore, was deeply attached to her son, so much so that when he moved from Bristol to Oxford to join his battalion, she and her daughter, Maureen, came along, taking rooms a few blocks from Keble. It was a natural thing for Paddy to invite his new friend home with him, and equally natural for Jack to return the hospitality, especially when he had lovely rooms at Univ. in which to entertain the Moore family. Soon they were all going on brief holidays together, and on August 27 Jack was writing to his father that he had spent an entire week "with Moore at the digs of his mother who, as I mentioned, is staying at Oxford. I like her immensely and thoroughly enjoyed myself."

Near the end of September Jack received his formal commission as an army officer, beginning with a month's leave—it was understood that at the end of that time he would be sent to France. But rather than heading straight for Belfast, as his anxious father expected him to do, he went with the Moores to Bristol and stayed there for two weeks. It appears that during this visit, as he and Paddy contemplated the unlikelihood that both of them would survive, they made a pact: if Paddy alone made it through, he would look after Albert; if Jack alone did, he would look after Mrs. Moore. This was a more significant commitment for Jack than for Paddy, because Albert, as a man of independent means and with another adult son, was less likely to need looking after than Janie Moore, whose only son was Paddy and whose husband (though they would never divorce) was out of the picture. And soon enough, Jack would need to uphold his end of the bargain.

In the meantime, though, Albert was waiting at home in Belfast. Jack finally arrived on October 12, but just four days later he received word that he was to report to Devonshire to train with his regiment, the Somerset Light Infantry. Presumably his leave had been shortened. On the eighteenth he was gone. And the acceleration continued: his training in Devonshire lasted less than a month, and on November 15 he received word that in two days he would be sent to the front. (One reason for the urgency was the recent collapse of the Tszarist government in Russia and its imminent replacement by the Bolsheviks; soon the Germans would be free from the obligation of fighting a war on two major fronts and could turn nearly their full attention to western Europe.)

Traveling quickly to Mrs. Moore's house in nearby Bristol—Paddy had already gone to the front—he sent an urgent telegram to his father: "HAVE ARRIVED BRISTOL ON 48 HOURS LEAVE. REPORT SOUTHAMPTON SATURDAY. CAN YOU COME BRISTOL. IF SO MEET AT STATION. REPLY MRS MOORE'S ADDRESS 56 RAVENSWOOD ROAD, REDLANDS, BRISTOL. JACK." Obviously Jack realized that as difficult as his father's company could be, and as strained as their relationship had become, this was no time to hold grudges: it was vital to see his father and say farewell before he was shipped across the Channel into what he would later call the "unskilled butchery" of the war. And there was no time for him to cross the Irish Sea and return to Southampton—it would be far better for his father to cross over and then return to Belfast at his leisure after Jack had been seen off.

Inexplicably, Albert wired back: "DON'T UNDERSTAND TELEGRAM, PLEASE WRITE." Jack could never figure out what prevented Albert's comprehension of what was, after all, a very straightforward message— Albert knew perfectly well that Southampton was one of the main points of departure for soldiers going to the Continent, and there could be only one reason for "reporting" there. As Warnie would write later, "anyone in England" (or for that matter Ireland) would have understood Jack's message immediately—but not Albert. When he finally received Jack's explanatory letter he wrote, "It has shaken me to pieces."

This miscommunication did nothing to aid an already troubled relationship, but Jack had more pressing concerns. On November 29 he reported for duty to a series of trenches on the front lines of the war, near the northern French town of Arras, a few miles from the Belgian border. It was his nineteenth birthday.

There had been a battle for Arras in April 1917, but it had been, like most battles in the Great War, both extremely bloody and utterly inconclusive. For the rest of the year, as John Keegan explains in his magisterial history *The First World War,* the armies had settled into a period of relative quiet, establishing themselves ever more securely in their intricate networks of trenches. The French and Germans pursued what Keegan calls a "live and let live" policy. This was hardly a matter of choice on the part of the French commanders: their soldiers were simply refusing to make any more pointless assaults on impregnable German positions. (They were not abandoning their posts or overthrowing their officers; they were just saying that enough was enough.) The Germans were not inclined to take the offensive either and instead focused their attention on the more active battlefields of the East—at least until the Tsar fell and peace could be concluded with Lenin and his crew. Only the British commanders, discontented with inactivity, conducted frequent trench raids and other such small-scale operations, but they no more than the others saw any point in another big battle. The simple fact of the situation was that neither side had the forces capable of overrunning the entrenched defenses of the other, and everyone knew it.

Indeed, the Western front had scarcely moved since the first trenches were dug in the late summer of 1914; this stability had resulted in a very strange environment for a young, freshly minted officer such as Jack Lewis to enter. Keegan sketches the scene with customary mastery:

> The chief effect of two years of bombardment and trench-to-trench fighting was to have created a zone of devastation of immense length, more than four hundred miles between the North Sea and Switzerland, but of narrow depth: defoliation for a mile or two on each side of no man's land, heavy destruction of buildings for a mile or two more, scattered destruction beyond that.... Beyond the range of heavy artillery, 10,000 yards at most, town and countryside lay untouched.

(One hears always, in soldiers' accounts of the Great War, about the overwhelming quantities of mud, which were a result of two years or more of shelling that had not only killed every living thing in the "zone of devastation" but also pulverized the soil into mush: this is what Keegan means by "defoliation.") But within easy walking distance from that zone were towns that, in spite of damage to some of them, not only survived but flourished in the war, economically at least, by serving the desires of soldiers getting their brief breaks from the trenches. (In Jack's first letter from France to his father he says, "I am present[ly] in billets in a certain rather battered town somewhere behind the line"—presumably Arras itself, which had indeed been battered but still functioned almost normally.) The difference between the towns and the trenches must have been utterly surreal to those who experienced it.

Once Jack got to the front itself, in the first days of 1918, he was able to explain to his father just how extensive and formidable the trenches were, at least on that part of the line: "They are very deep, you go down to them by a shaft of about 20 steps: they have wire bunks where a man can sleep quite snugly, and brasiers for warmth and cooking."

He would not be there for long; by the first of February he had contracted "trench fever" and had been shipped to a military hospital in Le Tréport, on the English Channel about fifty miles almost due west of his frontline position. He would take about a month to recuperate before being sent back to the trenches. It could not have been an unpleasant time for him, given his lifelong love for being "convalescent from some small illness" and having time to read; even if his time in the hospital at Le Tréport was not so pleasant, he was at least on the coast, "always seated in a window that overlooked the sea." As he told his father, "There are cliffs and a grey sea beyond—which one is very glad to see again—and from my own window pleasant wooded country," in which he would later take walks. And he could not but remember the last time he had been in that part of the world: in 1907, at Dieppe, with Warnie and his mother, just a few months before her death fissured his world. "They tell me Dieppe is about eighteen miles away: and that makes one remember. . . ."

Soon after his return to the trenches, on March 21, the Germans ended the "live and let live" policy once and for all by launching their largest offensive of the latter part of the war. It would be the first of five great assaults they mounted that spring and summer, trying to force a sudden and violent end to the war before they were starved into submission. Though the Germans had been able to bring hundreds of thousands of troops from the Eastern Front when the Russians collapsed, those were more than counterbalanced by the throngs of fresh American soldiers arriving almost daily. The American presence, in such great numbers, withered the morale of the long-suffering German troops, and it was now clear to the German leadership that the Allies were going to be able to keep their armies and their civilians well fed, while their own forces were rapidly running out of food. The German assaults, arising from pure desperation, were powerful, and they gained (by the standards of this static conflict) enormous chunks of territory—but not enough to bring about an immediate end to the war, which was the Germans' only hope. When the assaults failed the ultimate outcome was settled.

But meanwhile, during the first of those offensives, which the Germans called Michael, Second Lieutenant C. S. Lewis was wounded. It is not clear precisely what he was doing or where he was at the time, but he was with his sergeant, a man named Ayres, whom he revered: "I was a futile officer (they gave commissions too easily then), a puppet moved about by him, and he turned this ridiculous and painful relation into something beautiful, became to me almost like a father." (Heartfelt as this tribute is, I believe it is the only time, in books or letters, that Jack mentions Sergeant Ayres. One hears of relationships forged in battle that are too intimate for words; it is hard not to suspect that this was one such.) It was an English shell, meant for the German lines but fallen woefully short, that exploded behind the men; Ayres was killed, apparently instantly, as was Laurence Johnson, a fellow officer whom Jack later said "would have been a life-long friend if he had not been killed." (Some months later he wrote to his father about Johnson: "I had had him so often in my thoughts, had so often hit on some new point in one of our arguments, and made a note of things to tell him when we met again, that I can hardly believe he is dead.")

Jack was hit by three pieces of shrapnel—one in the hand, one in the upper leg, and one under the arm that broke a rib and entered his left lung—but was able to crawl out of danger. He was soon found by stretcher-bearers and quickly taken to a mobile army hospital in Étaples, which, like Le Tréport, was on the English Channel, but farther north. He wrote to his father that he had been "slightly wounded," but apparently Albert had already received a telegram from the War Office that declined to use the adjective "slightly." Albert therefore mentally added his own adjective—"severely"—and communicated the news to Warnie. Warnie managed to borrow a motorcycle and ride the fifty miles from his station to Étaples, where he was relieved to discover that Jack was "not much the worse, and . . . in better spirits than I have seen him in a long time." One can easily register the tone of reproach in his report to Albert: "I don't know who was responsible for the phrase 'severely wounded,' but it gave me a desperately bad fright."

There is a cemetery in Étaples, Le Mémorial Britannique, where 11,000 British soldiers from the Great War are buried. Jack Lewis would not be one of them; after three and a half months at the front, he was out of the war for good.

The Chronicles of Narnia are full of battles but, of course, bear no resemblance to the war Jack experienced. It is always fashionable to decry literary or cinematic depictions of battles as sentimental or romanticizing, unless they are so violent as to induce vomiting, in which case they are praised as "realistic depictions of the horror of war." But war does not consist only of battles; the memoirs of soldiers suggest that boredom is the most common problem (if not the most fearsome) in those long periods of waiting and watching and preparing that separate one battle from another. And not all battles are the same, nor does every soldier in the same battle have the same experience. The battles in Narnia are actually quite varied—and some of them far more sobering than one would expect in books for children.

It is true that the Narnian warriors have some lighthearted moments, but these are never in true battles: when, at the end of *The Silver Chair,* King Caspian and Eustace and Jill terrify the bullies of Experiment House—"Murder! Fascists! Lions! It isn't *fair*"—no one is in serious physical danger; the same is true when Bacchus sends the schoolgirls scattering near the end of *Prince Caspian.* When lives are actually at stake Lewis's descriptions are quite serious, though not always overly specific: for instance, when Aslan's army fights the army of the White Witch in the concluding pages of *The Lion, the Witch, and the Wardrobe,* we learn that "horrible things were happening everywhere [Lucy] looked," but not what the horrible things are.

However, elsewhere even in the same book the narration is more vivid:

Peter did not feel very brave; indeed, he felt he was going to be sick. But that made no difference to what he had to do. He rushed straight up to the monster and aimed a slash of his sword at its side. That stroke never reached the Wolf. Quick as lightning it turned round, its eyes flaming, and its mouth wide open in a howl of anger. If it had not been so angry that it simply had to howl it would have got him by the throat at once. As it was—though all this happened too quickly for Peter to think at all—he had just time to duck down and plunge his sword, as hard as he could, between the brute's forelegs into its heart. Then came a horrible, confused moment like something in a nightmare. He was tugging and pulling and the Wolf seemed neither alive nor dead, and its bared teeth knocked against his forehead, and everything was blood and heat and hair. A moment later he found that the monster lay dead and he had drawn his sword out of it and was straightening his back and rubbing the sweat off his face and out of his eyes. He felt tired all over.

Vivid indeed, and more blunt and brutal than most writers for children would risk. What seems particularly noteworthy is Peter's lack of conscious bravery—instead, he does what it seems he cannot help doing (the Wolf was threatening his sister Susan)—and the dense fog of confusion.

Confusion is also the chief note struck in the decisive struggle of *The Last Battle:* "The Fox lay dead at [Eustace's] own feet, and he wondered if it was he who had killed it." And somewhat later, when the Narnians are being overwhelmed by the Calormenes,

Tirian knew he could do nothing for the others now; they were all doomed together. He vaguely saw the Boar go down on one side of him, and Jewel [the Unicorn] fighting fiercely on the other. Out of the corner of one eye he saw, but only just saw, a big Calormene pulling Jill away somewhere by her hair. But he hardly thought about any of these things. . . . Tirian soon found that he was getting further and further to the right, nearer to the Stable. He had a vague idea in his mind that there was some good reason for keeping away from it. But he couldn't now remember what the reason was. And anyway, he couldn't help it.

But the confusion does not mask the brutality. Knowing, surely, that for many children the suffering of animals (perhaps especially sentient animals) is more agonizing that the suffering of humans, he does not spare Narnia's Talking Beasts: "Three dogs were killed and a fourth was hobbling behind the line on three legs and whimpering. The Bear lay on the ground, moving feebly. Then it mumbled in its throaty voice, bewildered to the last, 'I—I don't—understand,' laid its big head down on the grass as quietly as a child going to sleep, and never moved again."

These passages comprise some of the most powerful writing in the Narnia books, and I suspect Lewis risked the forthrightness because in just a few pages he would have Aslan call all the humans and other creatures into the New Narnia, his everlasting kingdom. Their suffering, then, is brief, and their reward immediate—but it is strong stuff all the same.

It is hard to know how much these descriptions owe to Jack's own experience as a soldier, but certainly they mesh with what many soldiers of the Great War said or wrote about their time at the front. It was the most brutal war ever fought, and one of the more pointless ones. In his letters Jack wrote very little about his battlefield experience: in the rougher periods there was no time, and all he could manage were scrawled notes telling his father that he was alive; in freer times—most of which were spent in the military hospitals at Le Tréport and Étaples—he chose to describe primarily whatever he was reading, as he had always done before, in letters to his father and Arthur alike. (He went on a George Eliot binge, reading *Adam Bede* and *The Mill on the Floss*.) In *Surprised by Joy,* he spends almost the whole chapter about the war describing people he met on the front—including one reacquaintance, his former teacher Pogo, whom he encountered to his surprise and Pogo's evident discomfiture. (Pogo appears to have been reluctant to admit that he had once been a schoolmaster.) Only about a page goes to the details of trench warfare, and there he is at pains to say that he and his troops didn't get the worst of it. Even about the darkest and most grievous memories he is strangely dismissive, confining them to a single interjection within a sentence, though a long and horrible interjection:

> But for the rest, the war—the frights, the cold, the smell of H.E. [High Explosive], the horribly smashed men still moving like half-crushed beetles, the sitting or standing corpses, the landscape of sheer earth without a blade of grass, the boots worn day and night until they seemed to grow to your feet—all this shows rarely and faintly in memory. It is too cut off from the rest of my experience and often seems to have happened to someone else. It is even in a way unimportant.

One senses in this rhetorical waving-away of the horrors of war a critique of the massive literature by his fellow soldiers: Robert Graves, Siegfried Sassoon, Wilfred Owen, and many more transformed these terrors into powerful words that will forever shape history's understanding of that war. It is with good reason that one chapter of Paul Fussell's classic *The Great War and Modern Memory* is titled "Oh What a Literary War." If Lewis is not critiquing that literature, he is at least declining to add to it.

But his dismissive account—"all this shows rarely and faintly in memory"—is either something less than fully honest or something less than fully self-knowing. At the end of the war, recovering from his wounds, he offered his father a "health report." Physically, he says he is doing well, though often tired and prone to headaches. But "on the nerves there are two effects which will probably go with quiet and rest." The first of these we will probably never know about, because Jack and Warnie excised the passage describing it when Warnie was typing up all the family letters for the Lewis Papers. (What it could have been I cannot imagine—Jack was thoroughly disinclined to reveal intimate or otherwise embarrassing details to his father—though of course I am deeply curious.) But the second effect is "nightmares—or rather the same nightmare over and over again. Nearly everyone has it, and though very unpleasant, it is passing and will do no harm."

Apparently, though, it did *not* pass. In 1939, when war returned to Europe, he wrote to a friend, "No, I haven't joined the Territorials" (a kind of volunteer reserve army, created in preparation for a possible German invasion of England, in which case local defense forces would be needed). "I am too old. It wd. be hypocrisy to say that I regret this. My memories of the last war haunted my dreams for years." Who knows, then, what long-term effects his wartime misery had on Jack? Clearly those effects were greater than he was willing to let on, except in rare unguarded moments, but it seems to have been part of his character to minimize his own suffering. (Perhaps what he discerned in much of the literature produced by the Great War was a tendency for the authors to *over*emphasize their misery.) Even as a young man with, at least according to his own later self-description, no principles or morals to speak of, he knew that he had little right to complain. In September 1918, still convalescing from his wounds, he learned that Mrs. Moore had finally received official word of her son Paddy's death. Jack wrote to his father, "Never a day passes but I thankfully realize my great good fortune in getting wounded when I did and thus being spared the very deadly months that followed."

During any downtime he had on the battlefield, and throughout his convalescence, Jack devoted the best of his thought and energy not to reading but to writing: a sequence, or "cycle," of lyric poems that he would later call *Spirits in Bondage*. They are not very good poems, but they are not very good in some interesting ways, for they reveal a young man very much in mental and emotional flux, subject to varied and even contradictory influences.

Though the poems vary in form and diction, they are always derivative of other poets, sometimes in obvious ways. One poem goes like this:

> For these decay: but not for that decays
> The yearning, high, rebellious spirit of man . . .

From this we can see how carefully Jack had already read Milton, whom he calls in one poem of the sequence his "Master." From Book III of *Paradise Lost:*

> Thus with the Year
> Seasons return, but not to me returns
> Day, or the sweet approach of Ev'n or Morn . . .

But the ideas expressed in these poems ("The yearning, high, rebellious spirit of man") are more reminiscent of Milton's Satan than of Milton himself; intellectually, the young Lewis strongly recalls A. E. Housman, whose likeness to the Great Knock I mentioned in the previous chapter. Here is Professor Housman:

> We for a certainty are not the first
> Have sat in taverns while the tempest hurled
> Their hopeful plans to emptiness, and cursed
> Whatever brute and blackguard made the world.

And here is Second Lieutenant Lewis:

> The ancient songs they wither as the grass
> And waste as doth a garment waxen old,
> All poets have been fools who thought to mould
> A monument more durable than brass.

The difference is in quality, not theme; Lewis's archaisms creak, and he cannot match Housman's masterful handling of strong rhythm. But we can already see here a trait that Lewis would possess for the rest of his life: a kind of literary ventriloquism, a facility for assimilating and regurgitating influences. (We return to this important topic later in our story.) His abilities as a translator—which Kirk noted and which would only grow as his scholarship grew—are one aspect of this facility; the channeling of Housman in these poems is another. He mentions Housman rarely in his letters, but in a 1929 letter to Arthur he gives some indication of how well he knew the poems: "I also glanced through A. E. Housman's *Shropshire Lad* for the hundredth time. What a terrible little book it is—perfect and deadly, the beauty of the gorgon." It is difficult to overstress the centrality of Housman for young men of Lewis's generation. George Orwell, less than five years younger than Jack Lewis, once wrote, "Among people who were adolescent in the years 1910–25, Housman had an influence which was enormous and is now not at all easy to understand. In 1920, when I was about seventeen, I probably knew the whole of the *Shropshire Lad* by heart." Given Lewis's extraordinarily retentive memory and the frequency with which he picked up the book, it is almost certain that he knew it as well as Orwell did. (Though he had clearly become wary of it by the time he wrote that letter to Arthur—thus "the beauty of the gorgon," fascinating but "deadly"—he had scarcely rejected the book. When he was about sixty he and his wife were found—by her son—weeping in the common room of their house. "Nothing's wrong, Doug," Lewis said. "We're reading the poems of A. E. Housman and they always do this to us.")

Although the metaphysical pessimism of these poems is Housman's (and Kirk's), they are filled with themes and personages that Housman would have found ludicrous: faeries, druids, and gods of various characters, sacred valleys, inspiring vistas of sea—in short, the whole varied apparatus of fantasy. William Morris and the early Yeats are here as surely as Housman, though often what the poems express is a dark sense of loss; what is being invoked is the absence of the faeries, the departure of the gods:

> Is it good to tell old tales of Troynovant
>   Or praises of dead heroes, tried and sage,
>   Or sing the queens of unforgotten age,
>   Brynhild and Maeve and virgin Bradamant?
>
> How should I sing of them? Can it be good
>   To think of glory now, when all is done,
>   And all our labour underneath the sun
>   Has brought us this—and not the thing we would?

All these were rosy visions of the night,
    The loveliness and wisdom feigned of old.
    But now we wake. The East is pale and cold,
    No hope is in the dawn, and no delight.

There is also great anger in these laments—anger against the faeries and heroes for their departure, or, more often, anger against a singular God for either withdrawing or not existing. The oddest thing of all about these poems, coming from a young man so vociferously atheist, is this constant and wrathful invoking of the very Being in whom Jack Lewis claimed not to believe at all:

It's truth they tell, Despoina, none hears the heart's complaining
For Nature will not pity, nor the red God lend an ear.
Yet I too have been mad in the hour of bitter paining
And lifted up my voice to God, thinking that he could hear
The curse wherewith I cursed Him because the Good was dead.

Or this:

And if some tears be shed,
Some evil God have power,
Some crown of sorrow sit
Upon a little world for a little hour—
Who shall remember? Who shall care for it?

Or, above all, this:

Come let us curse our Master ere we die,
For all our hopes in endless ruin lie.
The good is dead. Let us curse God most High.

Beneath the Schopenhauerian pessimism that Jack learned from Kirk lies this rather different strain, and the cycle's occasional references to Satan—two of the poems are called "Satan Speaks"—tell us what it is: not unbelief as such, but rebellion against "whatever brute and blackguard made the world." (In phrases like that Housman shows himself to be less than fully atheistic too.) Clearly the proud and powerful spirit of Milton's Satan has captured Jack's imagination, as indeed it had captured so many before him.

William Blake famously said that "Milton was of the Devil's party without knowing it," and the generation that succeeded him—the Romantics—were very much taken with the force of that infernal personality. Satan's refusal to bend the knee to the God he calls a tyrant resonated powerfully in that age of political revolution and transformation; one hears echoes of Milton's "great adventurer" (so his fellow rebel angels call him) throughout the literature of the period, perhaps nowhere more powerfully than in the Prometheus of Shelley's verse tragedy *Prometheus Unbound*. The cruel gods have chained him everlastingly to a rock and commanded vultures to come daily to eat his entrails, and he replies to them, not with pleas for mercy or repentance, but with sardonic defiance: "Pain is my element as hate is thine. Ye rend me now: I care not." And, "Ay, do thy worst. Thou art omnipotent."

Jack would have imbibed this ethos, or something very like it, more directly from his beloved Wagner than from Shelley: the gods of Asgard, in their "twilight," fight on bravely against dark forces they know will overwhelm them. But Shelley's Prometheanism is a real ancestor of Wagner, and Jack no doubt recognized it as such, and welcomed it.*

Jack's cycle of poems, then, adopts the heroic language of Milton's Satan and Shelley's Prometheus—imagine those words set to Wagner's

---

* Shelley, like Jack, had been a man of Univ., but either for writing a pamphlet called "The Necessity of Atheism" or for denying having written it, he was sent down in 1811, to his great grief. Some years after his untimely death at sea in 1822—he was not yet thirty—his widow commissioned a great statue of his drowned body to adorn his grave in the Cimitero Acattolico, or Protestant Cemetery, in Rome. Unfortunately for Lady Shelley, the cemetery refused to allow the massive sculpture, and it remained homeless until 1894, when Univ., having somewhat reconsidered its attitude toward the poet, agreed to take it. However, the college had not reached the point of full acceptance of its wayward son, so the big thing was stashed in an out-of-the-way location where an undergraduate such as Jack Lewis could see it every morning on his way to the bathroom. As he wrote to Arthur, "On a slab of black marble, carved underneath with weeping muses, lies in white stone the nude figure of Shelley, as he was cast up by the sea—all tossed into curious attitudes with lovely ripples of muscles and strained limbs. He is lovely." Loveliness notwithstanding, the college has been trying to get rid of the statue almost since first acquiring it; Oxford's Ashmolean Museum has declined to receive it in part because generations of undergraduates have occasionally defaced it with paint that now cannot be cleaned out of the cracks and dimples in the marble. On the other hand, the visitor to Oxford can purchase a lovely little facsimile edition of "The Necessity of Atheism" at the Bodleian Library Shop.

music—but adds a strain of peevishness and resentment generally absent from the sources. Though Albert Lewis was disturbed (and with good reason) by the apparent atheism of Jack's poems, what is more likely to strike the twenty-first-century reader is how *religious* the poems are. Nothing could be clearer than this young poet's attraction to the transcendent, his desire to believe—if he can but find something worthy of his belief. (His original title for the cycle, "Spirits in Prison," is a quotation, though significantly truncated, from the Bible: in 1 Peter 3:19 the apostle says that Jesus "went and preached unto the spirits in prison," a statement that in the Middle Ages helped to found the doctrine of Purgatory.) If in *Surprised by Joy* Lewis wants to portray himself as a cold-eyed proponent of philosophical pessimism—and if the young adult Jack Lewis wanted to present himself in the same way to his friends—the poems tell a different story. After returning to Oxford, he was asked by a friend, "Were you much frightened in France?" His answer: "All the time, but I never sank so low as to pray." But the God he would not pray to he nevertheless deigned to curse.

In the previous chapter I spoke of Lewis's sense that throughout his adolescence the two halves of his mind—the analytical and the imaginative—were completely divorced from each other. "Nearly all that I loved I believed to be imaginary; nearly all that I believed to be real I thought grim and meaningless." Reading *Spirits in Bondage,* one can see not only that the two halves are separate, but also, and more disturbingly, that the imaginative half is dying, unable to resist the combined forces of philosophical pessimism and the horrors of the Great War. The poems' laments for gods and faeries who fade are also laments for that part of Jack that loved them. The anger that suffuses the poems is anger not only at losing the gods but also at losing the love of them—losing Joy itself. It is rage against the diminishment of his very self. The poems are therefore the story of a kind of war—a war that the deeper part of Jack was losing. Balder is once more slain by Loki, and Jack is both the victim and the killer.

Spirits in Bondage does not neglect the evils of that other war, the one in France; one could even argue that it is the experience of battle that thematically binds the poems and gives them unity. It is occasionally a soldier who laments the loss or absence of the blessed realms, and the last poem in the sequence is called "Death in Battle." Jack had worked on some of the poems even while on the front—sending drafts sometimes to Arthur—and revising and polishing the manuscript had been his chief occupation since his wounding.

In late May he was transferred from Étaples to the Endsleigh Palace Hospital in London, and then, a month later, to a convalescent home in Bristol. London had its charms—for instance, he was able to see a performance of Wagner (*Die Valküre*) for the first time, which overjoyed him, as he told Arthur at great length—but no doubt the prospect of being near to Mrs. Moore was more attractive still. The liking that he had felt when he first met her had intensified into something deeper—something, as we shall see, evidently romantic. And whatever he felt was apparently fully reciprocated by her: she had visited him in London, and while he had told his father that she was there to visit her sister, and while that may have been true, it seems likely that Jack was the main object of her attention. In a letter to Albert he claimed that he had asked to be sent to Ireland to convalesce, but this was almost certainly untrue. In Bristol he could see all he wanted of Mrs. Moore but also have many free hours to read and to write. And perhaps there was another factor in his mind as well: when Jack had been in the London hospital, he had begged his father to visit him, but Albert had prevaricated and, in the end, refused to come. "One would have thought it impossible for any father to resist an appeal of this kind, coming at such a moment," Warnie later wrote, but Albert did resist it. Warnie attributed the resistance to Albert's "almost pathological hatred of taking any step which involved a break in the dull routine of his daily existence," but he knows that this is no excuse; "Jack remained unvisited, and was deeply hurt at a neglect which he considered inexcusable."

Lewis's recent and sometimes error-prone biographer Michael White insists that the real culprit here was Albert's increasingly serious alcoholism. His evidence is this June 1919 letter from Jack to Warnie:

Arthur managed to drift into the study unannounced one day. There he found our revered parent sprawling in an arm chair, very red in the face and drowsy. For some time he merely stared and refused to give any answer to any remark. Poor Arthur wondered what to do, till his host finally solved the question by saying in a husky voice, "I'm in great trouble, you'd better go away." No evidence as to what this "great trouble" was has ever been forthcoming, so I think we may with probability, if not quite certainty, breathe the magic word of AL-COHOL, "the subtle alchemist who in a trice" etc.! Of course no one objects to a man getting blind occasionally—although it is interesting to remember his merciless tirades on drink—but there is something unpleasant about this solitary tippling. He might have gathered some of his friends to share the fun.

(White claims that "Arthur mentioned nothing of this incident in [his] letters and only told his friend many years later, long after Albert had died"—but how can that be, given the letter I have just quoted, in which all of Jack's information about Albert's condition comes from Arthur, and given that Albert would live another decade?) It seems likely that Albert was drunk when Arthur visited him, but it's impossible to say how habitual his drinking had become. What's more noteworthy, it seems to me, is Jack's callousness: a drunk man who mutters that he's "in great trouble" is quite obviously not having "fun," and one wonders why Jack was determined to find humor in what was obviously a very sad event. If we are to guess anything from Arthur's encounter with Albert, it should probably be that alcohol was less a cause of Albert's problems than a symptom of them: surely this highly emotional and sociable man was immensely lonely, with his wife dead and his sons gone, and possibly in a state of depression—a situation that to untold millions has been an irresistible invitation to drink. And if Albert was indeed depressed, that in itself—given the overwhelming inertia that habitually accompanies depression—would be sufficient explanation for his failure to visit his son. But Jack makes light of it all, perhaps because by doing so he can maintain the shape of a narrative in which he is the victim and Albert the careless victimizer.

Warnie suspects that it was this apparent rejection by Albert that drove Jack to seek comfort from Mrs. Moore. But Jack was already in love with her, though he confessed this only to Arthur: "Perhaps you don't believe that I want all that [their friendship] again, because other things more important have come in: but after all there is room for other things besides love in a man's life," he wrote from France. And later: "However, we may have good times yet, although I have been at a war and although I love someone." (Even this discreet admission of affection he would later regret; secrecy about his relationship with Mrs. Moore set in very early, and the habit never left him.) Still, his father's attitude must have confirmed him in his determination to throw in his lot with the woman he loved.

The situation Jack discovered in Bristol was immensely frustrating to many other soldiers—"all the 'gilded youth' among the patients, who have no interests in themselves, of course grow more troublesome being confined"—but for him it would have been close to ideal, were it not for the constant presence of the "gilded youth" themselves. He worked hard on his poems and in early summer submitted them to one of the best of London's publishing houses, Macmillan, but he soon received a polite letter of rejection. He then turned to another highly reputable firm, Heinemann—which, to his great surprise, accepted the manuscript. On the ninth of September he wrote to Arthur with the "the best of news"; three days later he wrote, from Mrs. Moore's house, to his father. (It seems likely, then, that Mrs. Moore heard the good tidings first, then Arthur, then his father—an accurate reflection of Jack's personal priorities at that time.)

One gets a sense of the young man's naïveté in a comment to his father: "After keeping my MS. for ages Heinemann has actually accepted it." For "ages"? This letter was written on September 12, and in an August 7 letter to Arthur, Jack made it clear that he had yet to send the manuscript to Heinemann. In other words, the firm probably made its decision within two weeks of receiving the poems, something impossible to imagine today and probably extraordinary even at the time. Clearly Mr. Heinemann saw something that he liked very much, and given the generally mediocre quality of the poems, one wonders if it wasn't the soldier-poet angle that drew his attention. It was only at that point just becoming evident that this would indeed be a "literary war"—the outpouring of novels, memoirs, and poems (which had long been completed when *Surprised by Joy* was written) had scarcely begun then—but already Heinemann had published Siegfried Sassoon's book of poems *Counter-Attack*. (Sassoon was a friend of Wilfred Owen's. They had met when both, having been wounded on the front, were convalescing at a hospital near Edinburgh. Later, Sassoon would arrange for the publication of Owen's poems. In the letter to Arthur in which he mentions seeing Sassoon's book, Jack refers to him as "a horrid man." I don't know why.)

I have said that the poems are not very good, but all judgments are relative to some standard. In comparison with the notable poets of the period—Yeats, Housman, Thomas Hardy, Owen, and even Sassoon, not to mention the up-and-coming modernists, who wrote a very different kind of verse—and with the excellence that Lewis would later achieve as a writer of prose, not much can be said for *Spirits in Bondage*. But when one considers that those poems were written by a young man between the ages of sixteen and nineteen—a young man who had not yet studied at a university (though he had been briefly resident in one)—and that they had been revised largely while their author was recovering from significant war wounds and were accepted for publication by a major London publisher before his twentieth birthday . . . well, in that light they become rather more impressive. Jack Lewis (or "Clive Hamilton," since it was under that pseudonym that he decided to publish his book) was not nearly as accomplished a poet as Sassoon, but then Sassoon was twelve years older, and Owen was five years older. (Jack was also thirty-three years younger than Yeats, thirty-nine years younger than Housman, and fifty-eight years younger than Hardy, but perhaps those comparisons are not so relevant.) Clearly this was a poet of real gift and promise; surely he was one of the brightest young men of his generation. At least among those who survived the war.

On November 3 Jack wrote to his father from Bristol: "Indeed my life is rapidly becoming divided into two periods, one including all the time before we got into the battle of Arras, the other ever since. Already last year seems a long, long way off. However, there appears to be some prospect of the whole beastly business coming to an end fairly soon." The following day the finest poet of the war, twenty-five-year-old Wilfred Owen, was killed by German machine-gun fire on the Oise-Sambre Canal, not far to the east of Arras. One week later the armistice was signed that brought an end to the fighting. Warnie Lewis wrote in his diary: "It seems wonderful to think that the war is really over at last. Thank God Jacks has come through it safely, and that nightmare is finally lifted from my mind." On that very day, while celebration bells were ringing over much of Europe, Owen's parents received a telegram announcing their son's death in battle.

Among Owen's papers were found drafts of poems and a brief account of the poet's purpose in writing them. When the poems were published, a few months after *Spirits in Bondage,* that account served as a preface.

> This book is not about heroes. English Poetry is not yet fit to speak of them. Nor is it about deeds or lands, nor anything about glory, honour, dominion or power,
>> except War.
>> Above all, this book is not concerned with Poetry.
>> The subject of it is War, and the pity of War.
>> The Poetry is in the pity.

"A real home somewhere else"

T hanks primarily to Evelyn Waugh's *Brideshead Revisited,* we have a vivid picture of Oxford in the 1920s: a place of elegant, debauched young men, tuxedos and white silk scarves, excellent French wine and lots of cigarettes, aestheticism and homosexuality, the billowy pleated trousers called "Oxford bags." Harold Acton—who claimed to be the originator of the "bags"—became the undergraduate champion of a Victorian revival in furniture and decoration but also was known to lean out of his window in Christ Church and recite passages from T. S. Eliot's *The Waste Land* through a megaphone. Or perhaps Waugh just made that up; Acton at least read his own poems that way. The flamboyantly gay and extremely wealthy Brian Howard responded to ill treatment by some "Hearties" by declaring, "We shall tell our fathers to raise your rents and evict you." Waugh himself was once heard wandering about a quadrangle in the middle of the night and chanting, "The Dean of Balliol sleeps with men."

He was referring to F. F. Urquhart, universally called "Sligger," who every summer took groups of undergraduates to Switzerland for "reading parties," and this invocation reminds us that it was not just the undergraduates of Oxford who were the "characters." In addition to Sligger there was the inimitable William Spooner, Warden of New College, whose peculiarity of switching the initial consonants of words —"You have tasted a whole worm," "You have hissed my mystery lectures"—gave us the term "Spoonerism," which showed up in the *Oxford English Dictionary* while Spooner was still alive. George Alfred Kolkhorst, a don of Exeter College nicknamed "the Colonel," wore a lump of sugar on a string around his neck "to sweeten his conversation," but he was also once caught at the top of the Magdalen College tower spitting on people walking below him on the High Street.

Such was the Oxford of the 1920s, as we have come to know it. It was not Jack Lewis's Oxford.

Partly this was because he was a returning soldier; it was also partly because there was a brief period of sobriety that preceded the bright young things of the "Brideshead generation." Robert Graves—friend of Sassoon and Owen, later an acclaimed poet and novelist—had won a fellowship to St. John's College, Oxford, before the war but enlisted and fought instead. In his classic memoir *Good-Bye to All That,* he wrote about finally coming to Oxford in the autumn of 1919:

> We found the University remarkably quiet. The returned soldiers did not feel tempted to rag about, break windows, get drunk, or have tussles with the police and races with the Proctors' "bull-dogs," as in the old days. The boys straight from the public schools kept quiet too, having had war preached at them continually for four years, with orders to carry on loyally at home while their brothers served in the trenches, and make themselves worthy of such sacrifices.... G. N. Clarke, a history don at Oriel, who had got his degree just before the War and meanwhile been an infantryman in France and a prisoner in Germany, told me: "I can't make out my pupils at all. They are all 'Yes, Sir' and 'No, Sir.' They seem positively to thirst for knowledge and scribble away in their note-books like lunatics."

There seems to have been, at least briefly, a widely shared sense that a great price had been paid so that students could study at Oxford—a price paid by some of the students themselves, the ultimate price by some of their friends. Harold Macmillan, a future prime minister of England, had been a brilliant student at Balliol College before the war but had enlisted in the Army before taking a degree. Demobilized from the Army—that is, released from all duties (the last step before formal discharge)—and free to return to finish his education, he made his choice: "I did not go back to Oxford after the war. It was not just that I was still a cripple. There were plenty of cripples. But I could not face it. To me it was a city of ghosts. Of our eight scholars and exhibitioners who came up in 1912, Humphrey Sumner and I alone were alive. It was too much."

Jack Lewis returned, of course, though his thoughts were not unlike Macmillan's: "I remember five of us at Keble," he told his father, "and I am the only survivor. . . . One cannot help wondering why. Let us be silent and thankful." But immediately after this moment of silence he considers the possible circumstances in which he might return to Oxford—the sooner the better.

This letter (it is the one in which he mentions his nightmares and the other now-unknown "effect" of the war on his nerves) was written on November 17, six days after the armistice. At the time of writing he was in a camp in Eastbourne, Sussex—along with many other officers, most of whom were, like him, recovering from war wounds—waiting to see if and when he would be demobilized. Despite the armistice, no one could be certain that the war was really over for good, since no treaty had yet been signed to conclude the peace. He had been sent from Bristol to a "Command Depot" on Salisbury Plain and from there to Eastbourne; while he was still considered a convalescent, his moves had taken him progressively closer to the English Channel and therefore closer to the former scenes of battle. His future was quite uncertain, yet his clear and only purpose was to find a way back to Oxford as soon as he could manage it.

He had been told that he would not get leave until early January, which meant that he would be unable to spend Christmas with his father and Warnie, who had managed to get leave for the holidays. But suddenly and unexpectedly, on Christmas Eve, he was simultaneously discharged from his convalescent status and demobilized; his life as a soldier was over. He set off for Belfast immediately, and as a result Warnie's diary for December 27 reads like this:

A red letter day today. We were sitting in the study about 11 o'clock this morning when we saw a cab coming up the avenue. It was Jacks! He has been demobilized thank God. Needless to say there were great doings. He is looking pretty fit. We had lunch and then all three went for a walk. It was as if the evil dream of four years had passed away and we were still in the year 1915. In the evening there was bubbly for dinner in honour of the event. The first time I have ever had champagne at home. Had the usual long conversation with Jacks after going to bed.

Especially touching, I think, is the use in that last sentence of the word *usual:* it had been quite a long time since Warnie and Jack had been at home together, yet they immediately resumed their oldest habits. Any tensions between them from Jack's Malvern debacle must have been evaporated, at least temporarily, by the fearfulness of the war and the joy of its ending.

Jack stayed at Little Lea for another two weeks and then, at last, returned to Oxford, where he found that Univ. had given him the same rooms he had had previously. Apparently their previous occupant—as he had written twenty-one months earlier, they "really belong to a tremendous blood who is at the front"—did not make it back. And at the first meeting that autumn of the members of Univ.'s Junior Common Room (that is, the undergraduates), the first item on the agenda was the reading out of the minutes of the previous JCR meeting. It had been held in 1914. Jack wrote to his father, "I don't know any little thing that has made me realize the absolute suspension and waste of these years more thoroughly."

Later in life, C. S. Lewis would place great emphasis on the joys and benefits of friendship. We have already heard his claim, in the little potted autobiography he produced for his American publisher, that "there's no sound I like better than adult male laughter," and in one of his last (and best) books, *The Four Loves*, he insists that friendship is just as true a form of love as erotic passion or family attachment.

> Those who cannot conceive Friendship as a substantive love but only as a disguise or elaboration of Eros betray the fact that they have never had a friend. . . . In some ways nothing is less like a Friendship than a love-affair. Lovers are always talking to one another about their love; Friends hardly ever about their friendship. Lovers are normally face to face, absorbed in each other; Friends, side by side, absorbed in some common interest.

The Narnia books are often concerned with just such themes. One of the most important things that happens in *The Voyage of the "Dawn Treader"* is Eustace Scrubb's embrace—after his dragonish transformation—as a full member of a community of friends. And nothing is more important to *The Silver Chair* than the growth of the friendship between Eustace and Jill Pole, a growth that is mirrored in the relationship between Shasta and Aravis in *The Horse and His Boy*. (For someone who liked *male* laughter so much, and who is sometimes accused of misogyny, Lewis seems to have made a lot of room for male-female friendships.)

But the Jack Lewis we have so far seen in this book seems an unlikely proponent of such a high view of friendship. He and Arthur were very close, to be sure—or as close as friends can be who can go (even in peacetime) many months without seeing each other—but there seem to have been no other significant friends in his life. And he seems not to have minded; indeed, one would think that if he could have been left alone to read, he would not have needed any friends at all, not even Arthur. Thus my characterization of him, in the introduction to this book, as someone shaped by "a kind of personal and intellectual independence forged in solitude." But at Oxford he discovered the blessings of, not just a single friend, but a company of them. And the habits of friendship that he formed as an undergraduate would stay with him for the rest of his life.

Though perhaps it is wrong to say that Jack formed these habits as an undergraduate: it may be that the real turning point was his relationship with Laurence Johnson, the friend who was killed by the same shell that wounded him. The bond the two young men had formed was very different from Jack's friendship with Arthur. With Arthur, Jack could be sure of a commonality of aesthetic response—a love of the same books, the same music, the same walks in the hills—and he could also be sure of no threat to his intellectual superiority. He had learned the skills of dialectic and debate from Kirk but had chiefly exercised them in that pedagogical environment, where his arguments were being evaluated by a teacher. His friendship with Johnson—who possessed "dialectical sharpness such as I had hitherto known only in Kirk, but coupled with youth and whim and poetry"—had ushered him into a realm where argument between two young men could be a source of delight and a cement of affection. "He was moving toward Theism and we had endless arguments on that and every other topic whenever we were out of the line." Moreover, Johnson was "a man of conscience," someone willing to consider that it was worthwhile not only to *argue* about "strict veracity, chastity, or devotion to duty" but also, perhaps, to *practice* those virtues.

In the letter to his father in which he wrote of Johnson, "I can hardly believe he is dead," Jack also wrote. "I had hoped to meet him at Oxford some day"—Johnson was, at the time of his enlistment, a scholar of Queen's College—"and renew the endless talks that we had out there." But that renewal being impossible, it was people *like* Johnson whom Jack sought out when he returned to his university: smart people who loved to argue and debate, but who also knew that argument and debate were not just exercises, but ways of trying to figure out how to live. In his own college, Univ., he did not find many like-minded people, but he cast his net broadly. For instance, he joined an old Oxford literary club, the Martlets—a move rather surprising, one would think, for a young man so addicted to solitude. Perhaps this is an indication of the impact that Johnson's friendship made upon Jack.

The exception to his general verdict about his own college was one Ronald Pasley—or "Paisley," as Jack called him before learning to spell his name. Their point of connection was a love of poetry, though, having inspected Pasley's verse, he declared that "the thing rather sniffs of modernism"—"modernism" being a strongly pejorative term in Jack's lexicon, then and ever after. Pasley introduced Jack to Leo Baker, another poetry lover, and this developed into a real friendship, though one not without its limitations and difficulties, as Baker recalled many years later:

> One day over the tea cups in my room, Lewis cried out in an angry crescendo, "You take too many things for granted. You can't start with God. *I don't accept God!*" I was surprised into silence. As a subject, religion was out. So was German philosophy, a necessary subject for him, a blank of ignorance for me. He was impatient with my lack of logic and of rationalism. He profoundly distrusted my interest in mysticism. Under the circumstances one can well be amazed that our friendship matured so quickly.

One sees the two sides of Lewis at odds with each other here: the imaginative lover of poetry is taken with Baker, but the dialectician is frustrated by Baker's incapacity. Fortunately, Baker would do Jack the great service of introducing him to someone who would share Jack's love of poetry but who would also be his match—and indeed more than his match—in dialectics: Owen Barfield, who was, like Baker, a fellow of Wadham College.

Barfield would become one of the most important people in Jack's life. He was certainly the most intellectually gifted of Jack's friends: though he would never take an academic position, instead choosing to work for his family's law firm in London, the thesis he wrote for his *bachelor's* degree in English literature was published in 1928 under the title *Poetic Diction* and became a classic of linguistic literary criticism. (And that was his *second* book.) Barfield was quirkily brilliant; he was not nearly as widely read as Lewis, but perhaps in part because he did not seek academic preferment, was more original and speculative in his thinking. Almost as soon as the two young men met they began what they came to call their "Great War." The problem was that, though they admired each other greatly, they could agree about almost nothing. Lewis would come to see Barfield as the prototypical Second Friend (Arthur being the First): "He is not so much the *alter ego* as the antiself. Of course he shares your interests; otherwise he would not become your friend at all. But he has approached them all at a different angle. He has read all the right books but has got the wrong thing out of every one. It is as if he spoke your language but mispronounced it. How can he be so nearly right and yet, invariably, just not right?" Some years later, when their Great War was raging at its fiercest, Jack would write to his friend, with what I think is unintentional comedy, "In vain do I tell myself that you have a right to think what you please! I am often surprised at the extent to which your views occupy my mind when I am not with you and the animosity I feel towards them."

For both of them the Great War, however infuriating, would be immensely productive. Barfield dedicated *Poetic Diction* to Lewis—adding a tag from Blake, "Opposition is true friendship"—and Lewis would reciprocate eight years later, dedicating *The Allegory of Love* "To Owen Barfield, wisest and best of my unofficial teachers." The Great War also spawned, for a few years anyway, an enormous philosophical correspondence, Lewis's side of which is left out of the three-volume *Collected Letters of C. S. Lewis*. Apparently Walter Hooper, the editor of the volume, found the letters too technical for public consumption, an opinion that Warnie Lewis likely would have shared, since he was wont to complain about Barfield's tendency to launch into "some withering discourse on the nothingness of the utterness or some similar topic." But these discourses were not "withering" to Jack; instead, they pressed him to think harder and more clearly about what he believed and why he believed it—and this thinking would eventually have important consequences.

Barfield was not the only significant friend that Lewis made at the time: several others—including A. C. Harwood and A. E. Hamilton Jenkin—would become lifelong friends and later be part of the crowd called "the Inklings." But it is Barfield, and Barfield alone, without whom we could not imagine C. S. Lewis as we now know him. He became for Jack everything that Laurence Johnson could have been, and perhaps even more.

• • •

That Jack was able to make friends at all seems rather remarkable in light of his shadowy presence at Univ. When Ronald Pasley sought to introduce Leo Baker to Jack, he told Baker that this Lewis was "a strange fellow who seemed to live an almost secret life and took no part in the social life of the college." In a very short time Jack had become the object of joking attention from other Univ. men: "He has been noticed coming into college and going out," Pasley told Baker, "and opinion varies as to whether he is a college messenger or a don in some obscure subject." He could have been a don because he was older than most of the other undergraduates; he could have been a college messenger because he was often seen on his bicycle. The bicycle was necessary to get to and from Mrs. Moore's place.

Apparently Mrs. Moore and twelve-year-old Maureen had moved from Bristol to Oxford at about the time that Jack resumed his studies. In a letter to Arthur written ten days after his arrival, he describes his typical day: "After breakfast I work (in the library or in a lecture-room which are both warm) or attend lectures until 1 o'clock when I bicycle out to Mrs. Moore's.... After lunch I work until tea, then work again until dinner. After that a little more work, talk and laziness & sometimes bridge then bicycle back to College at 11. I then light my fire and work or read till 12 o'clock when I retire to sleep the sleep of the just." No wonder his fellow undergraduates thought him secretive or wondered who he was: if they did not happen to attend the same lectures he did, it was unlikely that they would see him except at breakfast. (However, he did benefit from a brief flurry of celebrity when *Spirits in Bondage* came out in March: of the "current literary set" in Oxford, he was pleased to say that "many of them have kindly bought copies of the book." But "their tastes run rather to modernism, 'vers libre' and that sort of thing," and "as nearly everyone here is a poet himself, they have naturally no time left for lionizing others." That last line sounds rather bitter; the flurry, obviously, had quickly passed, leaving the skies blank once more.)

The Moores' lodging was on Warneford Road. To get there he would have had to ride a mile or so: east on High Street, across Magdalen Bridge onto the Cowley Road, left on Divinity Road, right on Warneford. He called it "our" house, but he couldn't really live there because university regulations required undergraduates to live in their college: thus his need to return to his rooms before curfew. A. N.

Wilson argues that "it would have put his entire career in jeopardy had the authorities known about" Mrs. Moore, and this may well be true. "To have slept out of college was a very serious offense. To be shown to have associated with a member of the opposite sex was yet more serious." But the period just after 1918 was an unusual time at Oxford: the university became overcrowded as returning soldiers were added to the usual undergraduate population. Robert Graves tells us that Keble built a whole row of huts to house its surplus students and that he himself got permission from St. John's to live on Boar's Hill, five miles outside of town. Jack's situation was indeed highly irregular, but perhaps less likely to be noticed by the people in charge than it would have been at other periods in the university's history.

It was, nevertheless, awkward in a variety of ways. The liaison had to be hidden from Albert Lewis, but Albert had a pretty good idea of what was going on and discussed the topic repeatedly with Warnie. In a letter from May 1919 he fretted,

> I confess I do not know what to do or say about Jack's affair. It worries and depresses me greatly. All I know about the lady is that she is old enough to be his mother—that she is separated from her husband and that she is in poor circumstances.... If Jacks were not an impetuous, kind hearted creature who could be cajoled by any woman who has been through the mill, I should not be uneasy. Then there is the husband whom I have always been told is a scoundrel—but the absent are always to blame—somewhere in the background, who some of these days might try a little amiable blackmailing.

Warnie, rather more levelheaded than his father, replied that he was glad to hear that there *was* a husband—he had thought Mrs. Moore a widow—because this meant that Jack would never have to marry her. And he reminded Albert that Mrs. Moore certainly knew that Jack did not have enough money to make blackmail worthwhile.

Neither Albert nor Warnie would ever have their puzzlement eased or their curiosity satisfied. When Janie Moore died, in January 1951, Warnie Lewis would write in his diary, "And so ends the mysterious self imposed slavery in which J[ack] has lived for at least thirty years. How it began, I suppose I shall never know." Indeed, this is the great mystery of C. S. Lewis's life, about which he never spoke and from the meaning of which, it seems, everyone he knew was permanently excluded. Much

of the endless speculation the relationship has prompted revolves, naturally enough, around the question of sex. I once heard a longtime
friend of Lewis's give a lecture, at the end of which a member of the audience flatly asked whether Lewis and Mrs. Moore had a sexual relationship. The lecturer's face assumed a pained look, and he hesitated—
but then the elegant voice of his wife piped up from the back of the
room: "Oh, *of course* they did, dear—go ahead and say it!"*

Lewis's chief biographers, Green and Hooper, seem likewise embarrassed by the whole situation: they venture to suggest that the
connection "may have started with that incomprehensible passion
which attractive middle-aged women seem occasionally able to in-
spire in susceptible youths"—as though they have perhaps heard *ru-
mors* of this strange phenomenon but could not possibly say whether
there is anything to it. But they hurry on to claim that "it very soon
turned from the desire for a mistress into the creation of a mother-
substitute." And perhaps that is indeed what happened, but Green
and Hooper don't *know,* any more than you or I do, whether their
statement is true. Indeed, their judgment was shared by Warnie, but
Warnie also confessed that Jack flatly cut off any and every attempt
by Warnie to discuss the matter. Jack never kept any of Mrs. Moore's
letters to him, and she burned his to her in 1945, when she thought
she was dying, but no one knows why she burned them. So even
those closest to Jack were and are reduced to speculation: the idea
of Mrs. Moore being simply a "mother-substitute" is among the more
comforting (as well as one of the more plausible) of the options. But
let us remember that at the beginning, before the permanent wall of
secrecy had been completed, he could tell Arthur what he felt for
Janie Moore: "love."

Mrs. Moore was anything but an intellectual. Warnie would write,
long after her death and for public consumption, "In twenty years I

---

* Maureen Moore recalled, late in her life, that Jack and her mother used to insist that
she go to church every Sunday morning. (She also said that otherwise Jack paid no attention to her in those days, being thoroughly uninterested in children.) Both of them
were strict atheists, of course, and after Jack became a Christian Mrs. Moore would
denounce his participation in "blood feasts," as she called Communion services. It is
therefore not likely that they had Maureen's spiritual nurturing in mind but rather were
taking advantage of the only hour in the week when they could be sure to be alone. If
their relationship had been strictly that of mother and son, this would not have been
necessary.

never saw a book in her hands; her conversation was chiefly about herself, and was otherwise a matter of ill-informed dogmatism"—for instance, about the absurdity of Christianity. "The thing most puzzling to myself and to Jack's friends," Warnie continued, was Mrs. Moore's "extreme unsuitability as a companion for him. She was a woman of very limited mind, and notably domineering and possessive by temperament." I do not know that anyone who knew her ever denied this. Although some would contend that she was affectionate toward Jack and supportive of him, clearly she grew increasingly difficult to live with as ill health and old age came to afflict her. (She was forty-five when she and Jack met, seventy-eight at her death.) One of his first Oxford friends, Leo Baker, spoke warmly of her "ebullient temperament," and Jack's dear friend Owen Barfield and his wife were both shocked by the harshness of Warnie's picture of her—they thought she was solicitous of Jack to the point of "spoiling" him. This lack of consensus about the core features of her character adds greatly to the mysteriousness of the whole affair.

In any case, in those early years of the liaison, tensions in the Lewis family continued to rise. Even if there had been some healing in the brothers' relationship, they were not nearly as close as they had been: "I have heard from Jacks *once* since January of this year," Warnie told his father around the first of June 1919. His father replied, "It is sometimes difficult to keep one's temper with Jacks. . . . Always Mrs. Moore first. On one occasion he had six weeks leave and he spent five of them with her." Certainly Jack did not want to leave Mrs. Moore in order to spend the Long Vacation (essentially, July through September) in Belfast. He tried to convince his father to come and visit him in Oxford—to no avail. Warnie did come for a short visit, however, and after a triumphant visit to the Great Knock, around the first of August they crossed the Irish Sea together, as they had done so often in the past. But this visit would be a momentous one, in the worst way. Albert decided to give Jack a lecture about money: he knew, though apparently he did not say, that much of the allowance he was giving Jack was going to support Mrs. Moore and Maureen. When Jack told him that he had about £15 in the bank—perhaps $500 in today's money (currency equivalents are a tricky matter)—Albert produced a bank statement confirming that Jack was £12 overdrawn. Jack had unwisely left the statement in the Little End Room, and while he admitted that he had lied to his father, he was furious at Albert's snooping, and exploded.

It is not clear precisely how the argument progressed, but repeatedly in his diary Albert recalled Jack's most hurtful words: "He said he had no respect for me—nor confidence in me. . . . That all my love and devotion and self-sacrifice should have come to this—that he doesn't respect me. That he doesn't trust me, and cares for me in a way." The ellipses above represent a month's passage of time: Albert returned obsessively in his mind to the quarrel. "I have during the past four weeks passed through one of the most miserable periods of my life—in many respects the most miserable." (A strong statement from a man who had lost a beloved wife.) Albert knew that he was not faultless: "He has one cause of complaint against me I admit—that I did not visit him while he was in hospital." But he succumbed to self-justification nonetheless: "I should have sacrificed everything to do so and had he not been comfortable and making good progress I should have done so." Even so, it is impossible not to sympathize with Albert's pain: "The loss of Jacks' affection, if it be permanent, is irreparable and leaves me very miserable and heart sore."

When Jack got back to Oxford he resumed his regular letters to Albert. They began, as they always had, with "My dear Papy," and closed, as they always had, with "your loving son, Jack," but their coldness is palpable. He was absolutely without remorse. Once, in October, Albert dared to mention his pain, only to get this response:

> As regards the other matter of which you spoke in your letters, I must ask you to believe that it would have been much easier for me to have left those things unsaid. They were as painful to me as they were for you. Yet, though I have many things to blame myself for, I should blame myself still more if I had tried to establish the relations you refer to by any other means than that of saying frankly what I thought. I did not speak in anger; still less for the purpose of giving pain. But I am sure you will agree with me that the confidence and affection which we both desire are more likely to be restored by honest effort on both sides and toleration—such as is always necessary between imperfect human creatures—than by any answer of mine which was not perfectly sincere.

This, I think, speaks for itself. After all the years of silently tolerating Albert's eccentricities—surely even his "unjust" words and actions after Flora's death were remembered in this conflict—Jack's resentment overflowed, and kept on overflowing, though his epistolary tone remained almost unfailingly polite. When Warnie heard about the quarrel he wrote in his diary, "I am sure that the old conventional fiction of the happy family was the best arrangement for everyone." In his letters Jack resumed that "fiction," but now everyone was forced to recognize it for what it was—a consoling tale rather than the truth about their relations with one another.

During this period Jack complained to Arthur about having to write letters to his father and for a while referred to Albert only mockingly, as "Excellenz," but since Albert continued to send Jack the money he needed to live on, silence was not an option. It is telling, however, that he ended one letter to Arthur, written probably from the lodging he shared with Mrs. Moore, with the words "the family sends their love." Though he spent the Christmas season in Belfast, he wrote to Leo Baker that "being at home . . . to me is a synonym for busy triviality, continual interruption and a complete lack of privacy." And in April 1920 he told Arthur, "I am writing to my father on Monday to tell him that I shall not be home this Vac.—I really can't face him on top of everything else." Six months later he returned to the same theme—announcing, with something like despair, "I shall have to spend Christmas in Ireland"—and then added a note about the difficulties that are created "when you have a nominal home in one place & a real home somewhere else." The transfer of affection and loyalty was, it seems, complete.

Between his falling-out with his father and his new domestic life with Mrs. Moore, Jack's emotional life during his Oxford years was, to say the very least, complex. Yet he excelled in his studies. All his life he had the faculty of concentrating powerfully on intellectual work whatever the circumstances. This had first become evident when he took the entrance examination for Malvern College while suffering from a serious case of the flu—a feat that Warnie would later recall, with an awe undiminished by the passing of years: "I am inclined to rate the winning of a scholarship under these circumstances the greatest academic triumph of his career." Later, when Mrs. Moore had become increasingly infirm and increasingly demanding, Warnie and Jack's friends were amazed at how productive he managed to be while dealing with nearly constant interruptions. On the day of her death Warnie wrote in his diary:

In the last fifteen years of her reign, I don't think I ever saw J
work more than half an hour without the cry of "Baw-boys!"
[her nickname for Jack]—"COMING, dear!", down would go
the pen, and he would be away perhaps five minutes, perhaps
half an hour: possibly to do nothing more important than stand
by the kitchen range as scullery maid. Then another spell of
work, then the same thing all over again: and these were the conditions under which . . . all his books were produced.

Moreover, Maureen would later recall that during almost the whole
time that they lived in the same house Jack had to write in the room
where she practiced her music—and she would practice some five or
six hours a day. Between the music and the constant interruptions, it is
almost miraculous that Jack ever got anything done. But from their
first acquaintance Kirk had noted the young man's diligence and sin-
gleness of purpose; decades later a former pupil of his would write
that "Lewis valued time as few men I have met, before or since, have
done. . . . No man was better equipped for silent industry, hour upon
hour." It appears that he learned these skills early; it appears that he
had to.

In these early years it is likely that Mrs. Moore was more supportive and less demanding than she later became, but still, she had her expectations for Jack. Barfield—the same Barfield who felt that she
"spoiled" Jack—remembers visiting Jack at one of the houses where
he and Mrs. Moore lived and having Jack suddenly interrupt a conversation with the announcement that he had to "go and do Mrs.
Moore's jars." Barfield was puzzled by the phrase, but he later figured
out that the "jars" were hot-water bottles, which Mrs. Moore insisted
that Jack provide for her before bedtime.

A curious side note to this story is Barfield's implication that Jack
never introduced him to Mrs. Moore, even though, it would appear,
she was often just a room away as the friends conversed. He and
his friend Harwood had to concoct a scheme so that they could "try
and meet this mysterious Mrs. Moore." Eventually their scheme succeeded, and "before very long it was very much like coming to an ordinary house and meeting a man's family." But it would appear that
Jack was not eager—or perhaps Mrs. Moore was not eager—for these
two parts of Jack's life to be joined.

A complex situation indeed; yet, again, Jack succeeded brilliantly in
the third part of his life, that involving scholarship. On his return to

Oxford he had been exempted from Responsions—he was thus freed from the terrors of algebra—and also from the examination in Divinity, that is, basic theology. (It had long been perfunctory anyway.) It was also possible for him to skip the coursework in Greek and Latin literature that went by the strange name of "Honours Moderations," or "Honour Mods" for short. But he had told his tutor, A. B. Poynton, that he hoped for an academic career, and Poynton had advised him that in that case it was best for him to go ahead and take Honour Mods before proceeding to *Literae Humaniores,* the intensive program in ancient history and philosophy that went by the simple name "Greats."

(In the Oxford system an undergraduate's tutor was, and to some degree still is, the central figure in his or her academic life. A student would meet the tutor weekly to read an essay and have it critiqued, and this meeting would also provide an opportunity for general conversation, advice, and counsel. Since other duties were effectively optional—students were expected to attend lectures relevant to their course of study, but no one ever monitored their attendance—the success or failure of one's academic life could be largely determined by the competence of one's tutor. Pity the student who, for instance, had been assigned to William Spooner. Once Victor Gollancz, a London publisher, came to New College to have dinner with Spooner and found him in his room dressing. As they chatted Gollancz noticed a droning voice coming from the next room, behind a half-closed door. Then, when they were about to leave, Spooner exclaimed, "I'd almost forgotten," then put his head through the door to say, "Very bad, very bad indeed. Write for next week on the Epistle of St. Paul to the Ephesians." By contrast, Poynton was kind to Jack and gave him good advice; Jack was always grateful, knowing that things could have been almost infinitely worse. "After Smugy and Kirk I must be rather spoiled in the way of tutors," he told his father, "but this man comes up to either of them.")

In March 1920 Jack received a First—a first-class degree, the highest possible—in Honour Mods. (He wrote to tell his father the news, but only at leisure, and by the time the letter arrived Albert had already seen it announced in the *Times* of London, where such academic victories were faithfully registered, which of course made him feel very neglected.) The achievement was scarcely surprising, not just because of Jack's intelligence, but also because he had already read almost everything in the curriculum while studying under Kirk. Honour Mods was but a refresher course for him; when he attended the lectures of the great classical scholar Gilbert Murray he had already read not only the tragedies on which Murray was lecturing but Murray's own books. After Honour Mods, one might reasonably expect that he would have gone on to study (in Oxford parlance, to "read") English language and literature or perhaps do further work in classical literature. It was, after all, as a student of Homer and Greek tragedy that he had particularly excelled when at Kirk's, and it was that literature that he had particularly reveled in ("Homer whom I worship"). He not only attended meetings of the Martlets but within his first two months at Oxford read a paper to them—on William Morris, that great fantasist. All of his university friends were poets or lovers of poetry; Barfield himself was reading English. Yet Jack chose philosophy. Indeed, he told his father that he had chosen philosophy in part because he thought it less challenging even than Honour Mods: "'Greats,' being more philosophical and less strictly Classical, would be really rather easier to me as I am at present."

It is hard to believe that this was true. Certainly Kirk, while admiring Jack's dialectical abilities highly, thought him best suited to study classical literature. And we already know what Jack truly loved. It would seem that he was striving to make himself into a different sort of person than, by natural inclination, he truly was. I have already noted that his education and his experience had combined to stifle his imaginative side; he seems to have been determined, at this stage of his life, to extinguish it altogether—as though (again) he would be Loki's accomplice in the slaying of Balder. And he fully knew that Balder was moribund at best. Writing to Leo Baker in September 1920, he said, "I am more worried by what goes on inside me: my imagination seems to have died: where there used to be pictures that were bright, at least to me, there is now nothing but the trivialities and worries of the outer life—I go round and round on the same subjects which are always those I least want to think about." And yet it does not seem to occur to him that his imagination may have been suffering as a result of choices that he himself was making.

(It is also possible that the near-silence that greeted the publication of *Spirits in Bondage* was discouraging to him: in the reference to the imaginative "pictures that were bright, at least to me," there is an implicit recognition that others did not necessarily find them so luminous. Though the book did get a brief notice in the *Times Literary Supplement,* and though the reviewer did admit that the poems "are always graceful and polished," the review concluded by asserting that the sequence's "thought, when closed with, is found rather often not to rise above the commonplace." Perhaps Jack decided that if his imagination had to die, at least he could improve his "thought"; in any case, he seems at this point, though he worked intermittently on a long narrative poem, to have put aside the writing of lyric poetry. Indeed, he would never resume it as a central activity, though it had been the focus of his ambitions throughout much of his adolescence.)

I do not mean to say that the study of philosophy is necessarily, or even naturally, anti-imaginative. But *for Jack* it very well may have been just that. In *Surprised by Joy,* he looks back at his younger self and sees someone whose interest in philosophy was less than serious— indeed, less than truly philosophical. Even some years later, when he was actually *teaching* philosophy, he was having lunch with Barfield and a pupil named Griffiths when he casually referred to philosophy as a "subject." "'It wasn't a *subject* to Plato,' said Barfield, 'it was a way.' The quiet but fervent agreement of Griffiths, and the quick glance of understanding between these two, revealed to me my own frivolity." But in 1920 he was far from such self-knowledge. There is a telling passage, in the letter to Baker cited earlier, in which he laments the loss of his imagination. (Recall that Baker was a theist of some sort—it was to him that Jack had shouted, *"I don't accept God!"*)

You will be interested to hear that in the course of my philoso-phy—on the existence of matter—I have had to postulate some sort of God as the least objectionable theory: but of course we know nothing. At any rate we don't know what the real Good is, and consequently I have stopped defying heaven: it can't know less than I, so perhaps things really are alright. This, to you, will be old news but perhaps you will see it in me as a sign of grace. Don't mistake the position: its no cry of "all's well with the world": its only a sense that I have no business to object to the universe as long as I have nothing to offer myself—and in that respect we are all bankrupt.

Though Jack now "postulates some sort of God," it would be a mistake to see this move away from the rebellious, Promethean pessimism of *Spirits in Bondage* as a move toward Christianity. God is not encountered, believed in, or even raged against or defied—He, or rather It, is merely "postulated." It is an aridly intellectual comment by someone who is simply defeated—or "bankrupt," as he puts it. He has "nothing to offer," which makes him just like everybody else. God is merely to be assumed because that is the "least objectionable" assumption with which to begin addressing the philosophical problems that, at the moment, confronted him. Any confirmation, or refutation, of that assumption is simply ruled out. Another way to put this is that philosophy itself, in its original sense of loving wisdom and pursuing truth, is ruled out. Jack simply needs a "position" from which to pursue a certain set of wholly academic questions—this is the way he describes his twentysomething self in *Surprised by Joy*. A vague theism (or really just a belief in some undefined and undefinable Absolute) seems at the moment to work best, so he tries it on. Not for nothing did he later call it his "New Look": it was a recently discovered fashion, a momentarily attractive garment. Unwittingly, and sadly, Jack had become a practitioner of the "clothes philosophy" satirized a hundred years earlier by Thomas Carlyle in *Sartor Resartus*. The energy that had driven the poems of *Spirits in Bondage*— the poems in which he was "defying heaven," hurling contempt at the Jailer-God—had run out, and in the process his imagination had been starved.

He soon enough came even to welcome the starvation: "Now what, I asked myself, were all my delectable mountains and western gardens but sheer Fantasies? . . . With the confidence of a boy I decided I had done with all that. No more Avalon, no more Hesperides. . . . I was never going to be taken in again." This is why there are so few references to the Narnia books in this chapter: at this stage in his life, Jack had gone a long way toward turning himself into someone who wouldn't even *read* books such as the Narnia stories, much less write them.

He threw himself into his philosophical studies and strove to win the Chancellor's Prize, given annually to the best essay by an undergraduate—he mentions his determination often in letters to his father. The topic for that year was, ironically enough, "Optimism." In May 1921 he discovered that his essay had indeed won. His academic triumphs continued, and from his letters one might conclude that little else occupied him. Though his native country was about to achieve Home Rule, with resulting chaos in northern Ireland, where Protestants did not want union with the Catholic south of the country, Jack seems hardly able even to feign interest, addressing only occasional questions to his father about "what is going on" in Belfast. He inquires dutifully about his father's health and dutifully reports the events of his own public life, but shows no real interest in anything or anyone. He is at once very successful and increasingly apathetic.

In this frame of mind—largely without imaginative life, yet no longer passionately opposed to the idea of some Absolute—Jack may have been particularly susceptible to his old "passion for the Occult." And indeed, during his undergraduate years several events in his life prompted a return of that passion.

In 1921 William Butler Yeats came to stay for a while in Oxford. At age fifty-six, he was at the height of his powers. That year he published one of his finest books of poetry, *Michael Robartes and the Dancer*. Though in 1922 he would be elected to the new Irish Senate, and for a time would turn much of his attention to politics, in those poems and in every aspect of his life he was more fascinated than ever with magic and occult power. Even during and just after the Great War he had been suggesting that the vital things lay beyond this world: his mystical treatise *Per Amica Silentia Lunae* had appeared in 1918. A year earlier he had married, and soon thereafter his wife had begun to receive visions in trances—she had begun to practice "automatic writing." Yeats scoured the words that the "spirits" dictated through her pen; his comprehensive theory of history, *A Vision*, the first (privately distributed) edition of which would be published in 1926, was, he said, essentially the product of her trance-writing.

Jack had two opportunities to meet Yeats in the rooms the great poet occupied in Broad Street. The second one was largely occupied with literary conversation, but the first was about magic. The account of the event Jack gave to Albert was confident in its critical assessment:

> I have been taken recently to see the mighty Yeats. It was the weirdest show you ever saw.... You sit on hard antique chairs by candlelight in an oriental looking room and listen in silence while the great man talks about magic and ghosts and mystics: I should have loved to have had Kirk there. What fluttering of the dovecote! It is a pity that the real romance of meeting a man who has written great poetry and who had known William Morris and Tagore and Symons should be so overlaid with the sham romance of flame coloured curtains and mumbo-jumbo.

An orthodox response. But to Arthur he was more honest: "That room and that voice would make you believe anything." (And in 1950 his account of those meetings admitted that "I was overawed by his personality, and by his doctrine half fascinated and half repelled because of the fascination.") Years later he would realize that he was not at his best in such situations. In 1940 a friend visited him, and "we listened to Hitler's speech together. I don't know if I'm weaker than other people: but it's a positive revelation to me how *while the speech lasts* it is impossible not to waver just a little. I should be useless as a schoolmaster or a policeman. Statements which I *know* to be untrue all but convince me, at any rate for the moment, if only the man says them unflinchingly." But in 1921 he had neither self-knowledge nor a strong position of his own from which to respond to Yeats. Perhaps he wished Kirk had been there because Kirk would have known, as Jack did not, what to say in refutation of the "mumbo-jumbo." It is clear that Jack was taken aback by the easy complacency with which Yeats and his crowd held their beliefs in the supernatural, but it is not clear that he could any longer answer them. He told Arthur, "The last two or three years have taught me that all the things we used to like as mere fantasy are held as facts at this moment by lots of people in Europe." This statement is not followed by any profession of disbelief. Incredulity is implied but, perhaps significantly, never stated. (However, it is telling and sad that he thinks of the magic of fantasy as something he "used to like.")

In *Surprised by Joy,* Lewis says that during these years he came to know "an old, dirty, gabbling, tragic Irish parson who had long since lost his faith but retained his living." (In other words, he continued to serve as the pastor of an Anglican church.) "By the time I met him," Lewis continues, "his only interest was the search for evidence of 'human survival'"—that is, life after death. "On this he read and talked incessantly, and, having a highly critical mind, could never satisfy himself." What especially struck the young Jack about this man— his name was Frederick Macran, though he seems to have been called "Cranny" by his friends, among whom were Mrs. Moore and her brother—was the complete absence of any *reason* for wanting to live on after death. He didn't even want to be reunited with loved ones; Jack couldn't see that he loved anybody, alive or dead. "His state of mind appeared to me the most contemptible I had ever encountered. . . . The whole question of immortality became rather disgusting to me. I shut it out."

It is not clear when this "shutting out" happened—not, I think, near the beginning of his acquaintance with Cranny, which probably would have been in 1921. (In May of that year Cranny is mentioned for the first time in a letter to Warnie.) Under the influence of Yeats, and perhaps under the influence of his own temperament as well, the prospect of immortality was not yet "disgusting" to him. In April 1923 Kirk had died, and Albert simply could not reconcile himself to the funerary arrangements, even though they had surely been dictated by Kirk himself: "There was not to be a funeral—no service, no ceremony, no flowers, and he was to be cremated. My whole soul arose in revolt at the thought. The dear old man to be spirited away furtively—like an unclean thing—and burned!" (Clearly Albert, now nearing sixty, was losing none of his rhetorical verve.) Jack's reply began with words of sympathy, but he then reminded Albert of the need to be respectful of Kirk's unbelief: "At the same time, while this is sad, it would have been not only sad but shocking to have pronounced over Kirk words that he did not believe and performed ceremonies that he himself would have denounced as meaningless." But then, having thus stood on principle, he seems to open up a bit. I say "seems" because Jack is always calculating in his letters to his father, especially about matters of belief—he knew his father had been upset about the apparent atheism, or rebellion, of *Spirits in Bondage*—but his usual strategy was evasion rather than straightforward lying. In any case the next sentences of the letter are noteworthy:

> Yet, as you say, he is so indelibly stamped on one's mind once known, so often present in thought, that he makes his own acceptance of annihilation the more unthinkable. I have seen death fairly often and never yet been able to find it anything but extraordinary and rather incredible. The real person is so very real, so obviously living and different from what is left that one cannot believe something has just turned into nothing. It is not faith, it is not reason—just a "feeling." Feelings are in the long run a pretty good match for what we call our beliefs.

(It is hard not to think that Jack has his friend Laurence Johnson in mind also as he writes these words.) He says that he has a feeling about Kirk's ongoing life, and that our feelings are close to our beliefs; this is a very short step from saying that he believes that Kirk lived on after the death of his body.

Three months later he would write to Leo Baker about the negative theology of Buddhism and say, "Though I sometimes feel that complete abnegation is the only real refuge, in my healthier moments I hope that there is something better. This minute I can pine for Nirvana, but when the sky clears I shall prefer something with more positive joy." If indeed he was as revolted as he claims by Cranny's obsession with the afterlife, then at the very time that the possibility of life after death began to seem more real to him, the *desire* for such continued existence was revealed to him as futile and even repulsive. To judge by Cranny's miserable craving for mere existence, desiring "something better" than the nothingness of Nirvana might not be so healthy after all. Another door closed, then—another avenue of possibility was blocked and sealed off. The spiritual room he lived in was getting smaller and smaller.

After getting his First in Honour Mods, Jack went on to Greats under the tutelage of George Hope Stevenson (for history) and E. F. Carritt (for philosophy). Since Jack had settled on the idea of being a philosopher, Carritt was the tutor he was closest to and from whom he learned the most. He worked away with the energy and discipline that by now were almost second nature to him and continued his double life between college and the "digs" he shared with Mrs. Moore and Maureen. There were occasional interruptions—like the July 1921 automobile tour of southern England with Albert and some of his family (the "hardly precedented migration of the P'daytabird," Jack called it)—and there were "family" holidays with his "real" as opposed to his biological family. Moreover, he and Warnie, to judge by the letters, were gradually resuming their intimacy. Certainly his tone toward his father improved markedly in this period. But overshadowing all was the dark question: what to do after graduation?

Albert had continued his allowance to Jack, in spite of any concerns about the ménage with Mrs. Moore, and Jack was truly grateful—but worried about what he would or could do when the time for an allowance was over. In October 1922 he wrote:

I am very grateful for the slow period of incubation you have made possible.... I very often regret having chosen a career which makes me so slow in paying my way: and, on your account, would be glad of a more lucrative line. But I think I know my own limitations and am quite sure that an academic or literary career is the only one in which I can ever hope to go beyond the meanest mediocrity.... In business, of course, I should be bankrupt or in jail very soon.

Since, after the critical silence and lack of sales generated by *Spirits in Bondage,* literary life seemed unlikely to offer a living wage, the academic path seemed the only viable one. He had been awarded a First in Greats in July, and a Double First, such as he now had, was a classic mark of the true academic. Yet there were few jobs available. He had applied for a Fellowship in Philosophy—that is, a teaching job with tutorial and lecturing responsibilities—at Magdalen College, but it had gone to someone whom Jack recognized as being "the better man." It is unclear how thoroughly he looked for jobs outside of Oxford—in the letters there are few references to anything but the Oxford colleges, even though it was common for even the brightest Oxford and Cambridge graduates to have to start their academic careers elsewhere. (At this time Tolkien, for instance, was in the midst of a five-year stint at the University of Leeds; he would not return to Oxford until 1926. Even a titan of scholarship such as Gilbert Murray had started his career at Glasgow before returning in triumph to Oxford. So Jack may have had a somewhat unrealistic sense of the options available to him.) But he had been encouraged by one of his tutors—he does not say which one—to stay off the general job market and look for an opening at one of the Oxford colleges at some point in the next year. Clearly he was well thought of indeed.

So even before he learned that he had gotten a First in Greats, he had decided to get another BA degree, this time in English. Albert agreed to continue his allowance for the extra year this would take. The idea was presented to Albert as simply a practical one: Jack was getting, as he later put it, a "second string to [his] bow." And I believe it was, to Jack, a wholly pragmatic decision. Oxford was in the throes of a curricular revision: there had recently been a royal commission on Oxford to evaluate the university, and its commentary had been reported in the newspaper. It was not clear that classical education, of the sort represented preeminently by Greats, would continue to be as central to an Oxford education as it had been, and if its place was reduced, there would be less call for tutors with Jack's expertise. English, by contrast, was, as Jack put it to Albert, a "rising" subject—it had been taught at Oxford for only thirty years or so, and there was ongoing debate about how to make it academically rigorous, but it was popular and not likely to go away. So since Jack—given his extraordinarily wide reading, his analytical ability, and his skills as a writer—was likely to be good at it, it seemed a natural practical choice.

But the decision was more important, and more fateful, than he knew. As prudent as it surely was for him to get a second string to his bow, by choosing *this* string, he was opening himself up to the very world of literary experience—the "delectable mountains and western gardens"—that philosophically he was in the process of rejecting, all the more so because from the first he inclined toward medieval and Renaissance literature, where the mountains were especially delectable and the gardens profusive, where a path to Faery lay always nearby. At this point in his life, Jack was managing to keep the tension between the two sides of his nature under control chiefly by feeding one and starving the other; now, whether he intended to or not, he would be feeding his imagination too. Of course, he would be doing so under the guise of rigorous, analytical, academic study—but he would still be reading the kinds of books that had always brought him delight. And for a young man trying to protect himself—trying to disenchant himself—this flirting with delight was a dangerous thing.

He got another First, of course. His tutor, F. P. Wilson, thought as highly of him as Poynton and Carritt and Stevenson had, so when he applied for the next round of positions he had an impressive cadre of supporters. But in 1923 he was passed over for a philosophy position at St. John's and an English one at Exeter. He did some private tutoring and seems to have tried his hand at writing book reviews. (If he did, none was published.) He kept hearing of opportunities—one at Trinity College that Carritt mentioned to him looked especially attractive—but they seemed never to pan out. And he was not even sure that he wanted them to. Interestingly, his mixed feelings had something to do with the love of poetry that seemed suddenly to be rising again—revived in part, perhaps, by his study of English.

I have said that Jack began a diary in 1922. For the most part it is an extraordinarily boring document, a mere chronicle of the minutiae of daily life. (We learn in it that he read the diary aloud to Mrs. Moore, and it may be that it was for her, simply to keep a record of their life together, that he wrote it. This might explain its pedestrian character.) But there are occasional moments of illumination. Part of the entry for February 29, 1924, goes like this:

I walked home, looking at the details of the Trinity fellowship as I passed the lamps. For some reason the possibility of getting it and all that would follow if I did came before my mind with unusual vividness. I saw that it would entail living in [that is, living in College rooms] and what a break up of our present life that would mean, and also how the extra money would lift terrible loads off us all. I saw that it would mean pretty full work and that I might become submerged and poetry crushed out.

With deep conviction I suddenly had an image of myself, God knows when or where, looking back on these years since the war as the happiest or the only really valuable part of my life, in spite of all their disappointments and fears. Yet the longing for an income that wd. free us from anxiety was stronger than all these feelings. I was in a strange state of excitement—and all on the mere hundredth chance of getting it.

This is an extraordinary document—almost unique in Lewis's life. He stopped keeping the diary in 1927 and never resumed it; otherwise, we have only his letters, which are rarely (and even then only with Arthur) fully self-revelatory, and I have said that the diary as a whole lacks substance. This entry, though, seems to be a true opening into Jack's heart. And what it reveals first of all is the incompleteness of the picture I have been giving of him: for all that he did indeed stifle his own imagination (though half-wittingly or unwittingly), for all that he did shut himself into an ever-closer intellectual and spiritual prison, it remained the case that his life with Mrs. Moore gave him enough satisfaction that the very thought of losing its comforts—whatever they were—was enough to make him think that they were "the only really valuable part" of his life.

The entry also reveals that Jack was still afraid, four years after the letter to Leo Baker in which he first mentioned this fear, of losing "poetry"—his imaginative life. (In this context it matters that the Trinity fellowship was in philosophy—would he have had the same fear of the workload had it been an English position?) But clearly what occupied his mind above all was his own poverty and, subterraneanly, his dependence on his father's allowance, which may have been adequate for a solitary undergraduate but could scarcely be so for a young family man (Jack was now twenty-five), and in any case it could not be counted on forever. Being able to pay the bills without anxious sweat: that was what put him "in a strange state of excitement," even as he contemplated the possible "break up" of his true home.

He did not get the Trinity job, but his old tutor Carritt was going to America for a year, and Univ. needed a substitute. Jack was offered the job; though the money was less than half what the Trinity fellowship would have brought, it was the best opportunity he had yet seen. Of course he accepted. In the autumn of 1924, then, C. S. Lewis became a don; he would remain one to the end of his days.

SIX

"I gave in"

I n April 1935 Lewis—we had best call him Lewis now that he is a householder and a man fully employed in his chosen profession—wrote a letter to Leo Baker, with whom he had not been in touch for a long time. According to Baker, at some point in the 1920s Lewis had abruptly and inexplicably cut off their friendship, and he did not expect to hear from his university pal again. Here is how Lewis got Baker caught up on what had happened in the intervening years:

> My father is dead and my brother has retired from the army and now lives with us. I have deep regrets about all my relations with my father (but thank God they were best at the end). I am going bald. I am a Christian. Professionally I am chiefly a medievalist. I think that is all my news up to date.

Yes, that pretty much covered it. It had been an eventful decade.

Back to 1924. Though Lewis was now a don—giving lectures on "Moral Good"—his audiences were so small that he sometimes brought them to his rooms for discussion rather than letting them rattle around in a lecture hall. (Interestingly, given his later reputation as perhaps Oxford's best lecturer, he determined from the start never to read his lectures but to deliver them extemporaneously, and as vividly as possible, from notes rather than a complete text.) And his anxieties were scarcely over. The position at Univ. was for one year only, and as that year moved along no plausible positions for him at

Oxford came open. During this period his letters to his father—who had continued to supplement his income with an allowance—refer constantly to the uncertainty of his future.

Living with Mrs. Moore—whom he now called "Minto"*—kept him busy, as we have seen, and surely this was a distraction from worry, but he had some free time, mainly in the afternoons. Many of his diary entries in this period are devoted to descriptions of scenery he encountered when on walks with friends or alone. When alone he made himself attentive to any signs of Joy, but they were rare and fleeting. "The stone seemed softer everywhere, the birds were singing, the air was deliciously cold and rare. I got a sort of eerie unrest and dropped into the real joy." But far more common would be this experience: "I turned up to the left and so through the bracken to my favorite fir grove where I sat down for a long time and had the 'joy'—or rather came just within sight of it but didn't arrive." (It is obvious to the reader, as it would later become obvious to Lewis, that he was watching himself too closely—no wonder Joy so rarely appeared.) He enjoyed taking motorcycle rides in the countryside with Warnie, who for a time was posted in Colchester in Essex. (Since the end of the war he had served chiefly in Sierra Leone, but his traveling days were nearly done.) Once they even took bus and train to revisit Wynyard School: it had been transformed into a school for girls, and they had a tour.

Lewis also suffered, if that is the word, periodic bouts of minor illness, which he complained about to his father: "I spent the first fortnight of the term in bed with flu. I am very much afraid my organism is acquiring the HABIT of getting this troublesome complaint every time it becomes prevalent." But given the busyness of his life as household servant and new don (having to write all his lectures for the first time and from scratch), it's likely that he enjoyed these periods of convalescence even more than usual.

And he worked on a poem—not a short lyric poem (though he did write one or two of those also), but a long allegorical poem. He called it *Dymer*. The idea of the poem had been with him for a long time; he would write much later: "What I 'found,' what simply 'came to me,' was the story of a man who, on some mysterious bride, begets a mon-

---

* Previous biographers have usually speculated that this name was taken from a candy that Mrs. Moore liked, but it seems more likely that it derived from what Maureen called her, "Minnie."

ster: which monster, as soon as it has killed its father, becomes a god. This story arrived, complete, in my mind sometime about my seventeenth year." He mentions it to Arthur in a 1917 letter that assumes Arthur's familiarity with the story; at this point it was a prose tale, and it remained so until he set it aside. But in the diary entry for April 2, 1922, he wrote: "I sat in my own bedroom by an open window in bright sunshine and started a poem on 'Dymer' in rhyme royal." Rhyme royal was used often by Chaucer (in *Troilus and Criseyde* most famously), but Lewis probably associated it more closely with William Morris, who used it in his sequence of poems *The Earthly Paradise:*

> Of Heaven or Hell I have no power to sing,
> I cannot ease the burden of your fears,
> Or make quick-coming death a little thing,
> Or bring again the pleasure of past years,
> Nor for my words shall ye forget your tears,
> Or hope again for aught that I can say,
> The idle singer of an empty day.

(The rhyme scheme, obviously, is *ababbcc.*) Lewis also would have come across rhyme royal in the work of John Masefield, who lived near Oxford and represented, like A. E. Housman and Thomas Hardy, a staunch holdout for traditional verse forms against the modernist free-verse tide. For this Lewis respected him and would defend him against attacks, though in one undergraduate letter he admitted that some of Masefield's verse is "execrably bad." But it was with Masefield and the traditionalists that Lewis as a poet had cast his lot.

If Morris's rhyme royal depicts "the earthly paradise," *Dymer* begins in a false paradise: a Platonic "Perfect City" whose perfection is guaranteed by rigidly maintained uniformity. It is a city that combines, as Lewis would later say, everything he hated about school with everything he hated about the army:

> At Dymer's birth no comets scared the nation,
> The public créche engulfed him with the rest,
> And twenty separate Boards of Education
> Closed round him. He passed through every test,
> Was vaccinated, numbered, washed and dressed,
> Proctored, inspected, whipt, examined weekly,
> And for some nineteen years he bore it meekly.

But we see little of this *polis,* because very early in the poem the nineteen-year-old Dymer strikes and kills his schoolmaster, then flees into what immediately becomes a bizarre allegorical landscape—reminiscent in many respects of the world through which Anodos, the protagonist of MacDonald's *Phantastes,* wanders, but with darker and more disturbing imagery.

Dymer is a strange poem, and of all Lewis's work the one book least likely to find defenders, even among his most devoted fans. Yet it has its virtues. His command of poetic diction has clearly grown since the lyrics of *Spirits in Bondage,* and in a passage like the one cited earlier he shows a certain flare for satire. Unfortunately, he quickly abandons the satire and plunges into an apparently symbolic but ultimately meaningless story. The well-managed rhyme royal keeps the narrative moving along, but to no evident point or purpose. Dymer somehow meets a woman—who turns out to be a spirit—and impregnates her; she gives birth to a monstrous child. It is not clear what makes the child monstrous. Did it have something to do with Dymer's rebellion against the Perfect City? Perhaps: we discover about halfway through the poem that his act of rebellion brought disorder and ultimately destruction to the whole city, though why and how that could be is never explained either. And in any case, Lewis obviously did not believe that the Perfect City really was perfect or deserved Dymer's allegiance.

Moreover, why, when Dymer dies, does he ascend into a Heaven? Why does the heavenly sentry let Dymer wear his armor? Why does the monster come there? Why does it turn into a god when it has killed Dymer? And how can he die a second time? Why does Dymer's second death restore the whole world to wholeness?

> And from the distant corner of day's birth
> He [the sentry] heard clear trumpets blowing and bells ring
> A noise of great good coming into earth
> And such a music as the dumb would sing
> If Balder had led back the blameless spring
> With victory, with the voice of charging spears,
> And in the white lands the long-lost Saturnian years.

(So the poem concludes.) It is impossible to answer any of these questions—or rather, it is all too easy to answer them: the story allows a vast plurality of interpretations, no one of which is clearly superior to a dozen others. Someone once said that the writings of the mystic

Jakob Boehme are like a picnic to which the author brings the words and the reader the meaning. So too with *Dymer*.

Autobiography is, of course, often suspected, but Lewis insisted to friends that he was *not* Dymer, and there is little about Dymer that resembles him. Given his difficult relations with Albert, a more plausible—and stereotypically Oedipal—view would be that he is the monster who becomes a god after slaying his father. But there is one personal link. In a 1950 preface to a reissue of the poem, Lewis wrote of his twentysomething self and his friends:

> We felt ourselves (as young men always do) to be escaping from the illusions of adolescence, and as a result we were much exercised about the problem of fantasy or wishful thinking. The "Christina Dream," as we called it (after Christina Pontifex in Butler's novel), was the hidden enemy whom we were all determined to unmask and defeat. My hero, therefore, had to be a man who had succumbed to its allurements and finally got the better of them.

In one sense this is an odd passage: it is completely unclear why he would associate youthful wishful thinking with Christina Pontifex, whom we meet in Samuel Butler's *The Way of All Flesh* (1903) only when she is in her late twenties and who has a rather soberly realistic outlook on her possibilities in life. There is only one passage in the book in which she engages in anything like fantasy, and that is in a delightfully wicked scene in which she imagines the possibility of herself and her new husband as Christian missionaries: "'We, dearest Theobald,' she exclaimed, 'will be ever faithful. We will stand firm and support one another even in the hour of death itself. God in his mercy may spare us from being burnt alive. He may or may not do so. Oh, Lord' (and she turned her eyes prayerfully to heaven), 'spare my Theobald, or grant that he may be beheaded.'" This is very funny, but it's hard to see how a devout Christian woman recently rescued from a life of spinsterhood—she and her sisters had been instructed by their clergyman father to "play at cards" for the chance to hook Theobald—exemplifies the dangers of adolescent fantasy.

Nevertheless, what *does* become clear from this explanation is that *Dymer* constitutes the strangest episode in the long war between the two sides of Lewis's being. For, on the one hand, the poem is an attack on the deceits of imagination, the emptiness of envisioned "delectable mountains and western gardens"—but it is an attack conducted in verse, narrative, and metaphor. It is a disenchanting enchantment. If Lewis's own later account of it is at all correct, the poem is meant to suggest that the destruction of romantic illusions can (somehow, inexplicably) restore romanticism. If the poem is really about "getting the better of" the "allurements" of wishful thinking, how bizarre that it ends with a vision of Balder the Beautiful, the dying god come back to life again.

In April 1925 Lewis wrote to his father, "A Fellowship in English is announced at Magdalen and of course I am applying for it, but without any serious hopes as I believe much senior people including my own old English tutor are in for it. . . . These continued hopes deferred are trying, and I'm afraid trying for you too." As it turned out, F. P. Wilson was not a candidate for the position, the news of which suddenly buoyed Lewis's hopes, since he knew that he could then count on Wilson for a strong recommendation. But when he wrote to Wilson asking for a supportive letter, Wilson replied, with some chagrin and puzzlement, that he had been under the impression that Lewis had settled on philosophy; consequently, he had already recommended another candidate, Nevill Coghill—who happened to be a recently acquired friend of Lewis's. "This was enough to make anyone despair," Jack wrote to Albert.

But the story wasn't over. Coghill was offered a Fellowship by his own college, Exeter, and withdrew his name from consideration for the Magdalen job. Wilson and George Gordon, the Merton Professor of Literature at Oxford, wrote strong letters for Lewis. And he did not have to wait long for a decision. On the twentieth of May, in Belfast, Albert Lewis received a telegram that said, simply, "ELECTED FELLOW MAGDALEN. JACK." In his diary Albert records what he did then: "I went up to his room and burst into tears of joy. I knelt down and thanked God with a full heart. My prayers had been heard and answered." It is touching, somehow, that when Albert got this long-awaited good news his first action was to go to Jack's bedroom there in Little Lea—the house empty then except for the servants, with Flora dead and the boys grown and moved away—to kneel and offer thanksgiving. And it seems clear that he was so moved, not because Jack had finally become self-supporting, or finally become fully certified as an English gentleman, but because his younger son had achieved the only career he ever seemed suited for—"the only one in which" (as Jack himself had put it three years earlier) "I can ever hope to go beyond the meanest mediocrity."

The letter that the new Fellow of Magdalen wrote a few days later
to offer the details begins with these words:

My dear Papy,
    First, let me thank you from the bottom of my heart for the gen-
erous support, extended over six years, which alone has enabled
me to hang on till this. In the long course I have seen men at least
my equals in ability and qualifications fall out for the lack of it.
"How long can I afford to wait" was everybody's question: and
few had those at their back who were both able and willing to
keep them in the field so long. You have waited, not only without
complaint but full of encouragement, while chance after chance
slipped away and when the goal receded furthest from sight.
    Thank you again and again.

It is a gracious letter indeed, and one that indicates a considerable
healing in the relationship between father and son. A son as embittered as Jack had been several years earlier could certainly have
thanked Albert with sincerity, but he would not have been likely to ac-
knowledge Albert's real and rare virtues: it is the recognition that
Albert continued to support him "not only without complaint but full
of encouragement" that is most telling. Albert and Jack had turned a
corner, and they would get along well for the remainder of Albert's
life. One should not make too much of this: Jack had not come to love
or even feel affection for his father, but his now-complete independence seems to have relaxed the tension for them both. At least the old
consoling fiction of a happy family had been restored. At the beginning of October, when Jack visited Belfast, Albert wrote of the visit in
his diary: "Very pleasant, not a cloud."

To my eyes, beyond compare the most beautiful of the Oxford colleges
is Magdalen.* The college's tower, completed in 1509, is one of the more
elegant buildings in Oxford—the first King James, who would rather
have been an Oxford scholar than a king, adored it—and what is still
called the New Building is a model of eighteenth-century neoclassical

---

* The name is pronounced "Maudlin"; it is named after Mary Magdalene, from whom
Jesus cast out seven demons and who then followed him up to and after his crucifixion.
Legend has it that the unnamed woman "who was a sinner" and, in Luke 7, washes
Jesus's feet with her tears is also Mary Magdalene. She became therefore an image of
repentance and conversion.

elegance and simplicity. But more striking still, the college sits among a hundred acres of grounds, much of which is occupied by a deer park, and a river runs through it—the River Cherwell, which not far south of Magdalen joins the Thames. A path along the river is called "Addison's Walk" because it was much favored by Joseph Addison, a poet, essayist, and politician who was a fellow of Magdalen in the last years of the seventeenth century and the early years of the next. (Perhaps attracted by the nearness of the river, and perhaps by other things, a nineteenth-century Magdalen undergraduate named Oscar Wilde went out for crew but was soon dismissed from the team because he would only row slowly. He did not much mind being sacked: "I don't see the use of going down backwards to Iffley every evening," he said.) To a select group of readers it will be important to know that Magdalen was also the college of P. G. Wodehouse's Bertie Wooster—which suggests, perhaps, that when Lewis came there it was more noted for its social status than its intellectual rigor.

In October Lewis would write his first letter to his father from his rooms in New Building (or, as it was more commonly said in those days, New Buildings):

> My external surroundings are beautiful beyond expectation and beyond hope. To live in the Bishop's Palace at Wells would be good but could hardly be better than this. My big sitting room looks north and from it I see nothing, not even a gable or spire, to remind me that I am in a town. I look down on a stretch of level grass which passes into a grove of immemorial forest trees, at present coloured with autumn red. Over this stray the deer. They are erratic in their habits. Some mornings when I look out there will be half a dozen chewing the cud just underneath me, and on others there will be none in sight—or one little stag (not much bigger than a calf and looking too slender for the weight of its own antlers) standing still and sending through the fog that queer little bark or hoot that is these beasts' "moo." It is a sound that will soon be as familiar to me as the cough of the cows in the field at home, for I hear it day and night. On my right hand as I look from these windows is "his favourite walk" [Addison's Walk]. My smaller sitting room and bedroom look out southward across a broad lawn to the main buildings of Magdalen with the tower beyond it.

For the next thirty years Lewis would work and sleep in these rooms—at least during term time. When school was in session he would visit Minto in the afternoons and sleep in their house on the weekends. (During this period they were living in a house in Headington, east of central Oxford, called Hillsboro—or so read the name over the door.) During the vacations he would work in the house—thus the incessant interruptions ("Baw-boys!") that Warnie noted in his diary—and go into College only occasionally. Many things would change—and change dramatically—in his life before there was any alteration in this pattern of daily living.

Intellectually, he had established a new and lasting pattern as well. Though for a few years to come he would continue to take the occasional philosophy student—indeed, his having two strings to his bow may well have gotten him the Magdalen job—his career as a philosopher was essentially over: it was as a tutor in English that he had been hired, and he understood perfectly well that that was the field in which he would labor, not only as a teacher but also as a scholar. He had mixed feelings about this. "Indeed in turning from [philosophy] to literary history and criticism, I am conscious of a descent"—a descent from the highest and most demanding of intellectual callings. Lewis seems be confessing here a sense of his own intrinsic weakness, and it is fascinating that he does so in a letter to his father in which he associates himself with Albert by virtue of temperament and ethnicity:

> I have come to think that if I had the mind, I have not the brain and nerves for a life of pure philosophy. A continued search among the abstract roots of things, a perpetual questioning of all that plain men take for granted, a chewing the cud for fifty years over inevitable ignorance and a constant frontier watch on the little tidy lighted conventional world of science and daily life—is this the best life for temperaments such as ours? Is it the way of health or even of sanity? There is a certain type of man, bull necked and self satisfied in his "pot bellied equanimity" who urgently needs that bleak and questioning atmosphere. But what is a tonic to the Saxon may be a debauch to us Celts.

There is an odd alternation of self-judgment and self-congratulation here. On the one hand, Lewis seems to be deploring his lack of fitness ("I have not the brain and nerves") for serious philosophical work; on the other hand, he seems to say that he and his fellow Celts lack that

fitness because they are already excessively thoughtful and introspec-
tive—as opposed to the "bull necked and self satisfied" Saxon who
needs to be jolted out of his false "equanimity." But all this tends to
evade the fact that the decision was not really Lewis's own: had he
gotten a philosophy position, it would have been a very different letter
that he wrote to his father.

And a very different C. S. Lewis would surely have emerged. It is
true that in this same letter to Albert, Lewis depicts himself as having been liberated, *by philosophy*, from a cheap philosophical materialism:

> If the air on the heights did not suit me, still I have brought back
> something of value. It will be a comfort to me all my life to know
> that the scientist and the materialist have not the last word: that
> Darwin and Spencer undermining ancestral beliefs stand them-
> selves on a foundation of sand; of gigantic assumptions and ir-
> reconcilable contradictions an inch below the surface. It leaves
> the whole thing rich in possibilities: and if it dashes the shallow
> optimisms it does the same for the shallow pessimisms.

This is extremely subtle. He does not exactly endorse "ancestral beliefs"—for instance, his father's Christianity—but he admits that the
standard late-Victorian case against them is much weaker than he had
previously thought. He does not commit himself to anything, but he
acknowledges that his current intellectual situation is one that is "rich
in possibilities." He makes it clear that he owes a debt to philosophy
for guiding him to this new personal landscape. But he also insist that
philosophy cannot do any more, at least not for him: "It is perhaps
best to shut the trap door and come back to ordinary life: unless you
are one of the really great who can see into [the darkness] a little
way—and I was not." Philosophy had gotten Lewis to Mount Pisgah,
from which (like Moses) he could look out across the Promised Land.
But it would be literature—*story*—that would take him into that land
so that he could taste its milk and honey.

In September 1926, at the beginning of his second year at Magdalen, *Dymer* was published by the London firm of Dent. Once again
he used the pseudonym Clive Hamilton. The poem's publication is
mentioned but once in his letters, and not at all in his diary—which
for reasons unknown he had put aside in the second half of 1926. (He
would resume it briefly in 1927 and then cease diary-writing perma-

nently.) It is hard not to think that by the time *Dymer* was published Lewis had left it and its concerns far behind.

One of Lewis's favorite writers in these days was G. K. Chesterton, that indefinable man. Chesterton enjoyed a career to describe which the phrase "burst upon the scene" is unavoidable. In the first decade of the twentieth century (he had been born in 1874 and had studied art at the Slade School in London, where Arthur Greeves would also study for a while during Lewis's undergraduate years), words started exploding from him like firecrackers. He wrote weekly essays for the *Illustrated London News,* he wrote poems of all sizes and kinds, he wrote strange fantastic fiction, he wrote detective stories, he wrote biographies, he wrote political manifestos—and that was just between 1903 and 1910. Chesterton was an enormous man, weighing well over three hundred pounds, and claimed to be suspicious of "hard, cold, thin people." He loved nothing better than arguing, and Chesterton's public debates with a wide range of opponents were one of the great spectator sports of early-twentieth-century England. One of his opponents, a dramatist and (later) screenwriter with the delightful name of Cosmo Hamilton, was, like most people who knew him, simply overwhelmed: "To hear Chesterton's howl of joy ... to see him double himself up in an agony of laughter at my personal insults, to watch the effect of his sportsmanship on a shocked audience who were won to mirth by his intense and pea-hen-like quarks of joy was a sight and a sound for the gods.... It was monstrous, gigantic, amazing, deadly, delicious. Nothing like it has ever been done before or will ever be seen, heard and felt like it again."

Cosmo seems to exhaust his supply of superlatives in this passage, but if we rightly suspect his stylistic judgment, we must also note the impact of Chesterton's personality. It was indeed, repeatedly for many years, the sort of concussion that might register on the Richter scale. There were few public figures more recognizable in Lewis's young manhood: that vast bulk enclosed in a still vaster cape, those pince-nez, that disordered mop of curly hair—all evoked in the English mind by the initials GKC, which were universally seen to stand in opposition to the spare, bearded figure of the equally famous GBS. George Bernard Shaw, with his cool, witty, ironic, rational socialism, was GKC's proper opposite and his most frequent and most famous debating partner. What shows they put on! They were wonderful together because they shared certain virtues—above all, quickness of tongue

and brilliance of image—while representing wildly divergent under-
standings of what the Good Life was. (Shaw's biographer Michael
Holroyd has described these "spectacular tournaments between puritan and cavalier": "Their jousting over the years had developed into
an aesthetic performance, a perfect balance of contrasting styles, romantic and idealistic, with breathtaking displays of analogy and tricks
of paradox in which the chivalric ideal was central.") For GKC, who
looked around and saw a world wildly prolific in its richness and diversity, GBS's moralistic socialism was as narrow as his waistline.
"Shaw is like the Venus de Milo," Chesterton once said; "all that there
is of him is admirable."

GKC was just the sort of writer that Lewis was bound to love, even
if he had to step gingerly around the fact that at some point in that
great prolific first decade of his writing career Chesterton had become
a Christian—a movement he recounts in his 1909 book *Orthodoxy*.
There is no mention of reading Chesterton in Lewis's early letters, and
the man himself gets but passing mention. Instead, it is Lewis's diary
that is revealing. In 1922 and again in 1924 he is reading Chesterton's
biography of Robert Browning; he thinks it "a thoroughly bad book,
full of silly generalisations," which in truth it is. But on the same page
of his 1924 diary there is a commendation of the biography of St.
Francis of Assisi, even if Lewis is unwilling to give Christianity the
same credit for moral good that GKC gives it. In 1926 Lewis is reading
a novel (*The Club of Queer Trades*), a biography (*George Bernard
Shaw*), and a collection of moral essays (*Eugenics and Other Evils*). Perhaps most noteworthy of all is the diary's first mention of Chesterton's
writing: his 1913 play *Magic,* which is about, among other things,
skeptical naturalism's skill at exposing the tricks of magicians, but its
incompetence to refute the supernaturalism of Christian belief. Lewis
mentions it in his entry for May 14, 1922—just six weeks after beginning *Dymer.* One cannot help wondering if that play had any effect on
the shaping of the character of the magician, who is quite evidently
based in some ways on Yeats and who plays a major role in the later
stages of Lewis's poem. It is interesting that as shrewd a reader as
Lewis, faced with this skillful but not especially subtle drama, professes incomprehension: "a pleasant little play—I am not sure that I
understand it." (Incidentally, it was GBS who demanded that GKC
write a play in the first place: "I shall repeat my public challenge to
you; vaunt my superiority; insult your corpulence; torture [Chesterton's
friend Hillaire] Belloc; if necessary, call on you and steal your wife's af-

fections by intellectual and athletic displays, until you contribute
something to British drama.")

One of Chesterton's most famous essays is an early one (1901)
called "In Defense of Penny Dreadfuls"—"penny dreadfuls" being
what we might call "pulp fiction," but for adolescents. Apparently
many cultural pedagogues of the time were exercised by the popularity
of such "vulgar" stories and wished them to be replaced by genuine
literature. GKC is half-puzzled and half-offended by this alarm. He
has no wish to defend the "dreadfuls" as literature, but he does want
to defend them as "the actual centre of a million flaming imaginations." To Chesterton, "the simple need for some kind of ideal world
in which fictitious persons play an unhampered part is infinitely deeper
and older than the rules of good art, and much more important. Every
one of us in childhood has constructed such an invisible dramatis per-
sonae, but it never occurred to our nurses to correct the composition
by careful comparison with Balzac." In fact, he continues, "literature
is a luxury; fiction is a necessity." That is, while we can live without
Balzac, brilliant though he may be, the penny dreadfuls are truly vital
to human well-being.

Chesterton believes that the popular novel for boys, while often
poorly written, nevertheless operates in the same moral world as
many works considered to be literary classics: "That is to say, they do
precisely the same thing as Scott's *Ivanhoe,* Scott's *Rob Roy,* Scott's
Lady of the Lake, Byron's *Corsair,* Wordsworth's "Rob Roy's
Grave," Stevenson's *Macaire,* Mr. Max Pemberton's *Iron Pirate,* and
a thousand more works distributed systematically as prizes and
Christmas presents." It is modern writing—the same writing in comparison to which the moral world of the penny dreadfuls is condemned—that has lost its way:

> It is the modern literature of the educated, not of the uneducated,
> which is avowedly and aggressively criminal. . . . The vast mass of
> humanity, with their vast mass of idle books and idle words,
> have never doubted and never will doubt that courage is splen-
> did, that fidelity is noble, that distressed ladies should be rescued,
> and vanquished enemies spared. There are a large number of cul-
> tivated persons who doubt these maxims of daily life.

The real importance of this insight can be seen better if we note
something that Chesterton wrote in another essay of the same period

called "A Defence of Nonsense": "The 'Iliad' is only great because all life is a battle, the 'Odyssey' because all life is a journey, the Book of Job because all life is a riddle." That is, the stories most greatly treasured, and treasured for the longest periods, are those that trace, in bold lines, the outlines of our deepest experiences. And if it is *stories*, among all the things we make and do, that mean the most to us as we face our own battles, journeys, and riddles, what does that suggest? Chesterton would only figure that out a few years later, when he wrote *Orthodoxy*:

> All Christianity concentrates on the man at the cross-roads. The vast and shallow philosophies, the huge syntheses of humbug, all talk about ages and evolution and ultimate developments. The true philosophy is concerned with the instant. Will a man take this road or that?—that is the only thing to think about, if you enjoy thinking. The aeons are easy enough to think about, any one can think about them. The instant is really awful: and it is because our religion has intensely felt the instant, that it has in literature dealt much with battle and in theology dealt much with hell. It is full of *danger*, like a boy's book: it is at an immortal crisis. There is a great deal of similarity between popular fiction and the religion of the western people.

Christianity, then, *is* a penny dreadful—or perhaps the seed from which all penny dreadfuls grow. The story of each human life, in the account given by Christianity, is filled with the suspense and tension of a "boy's book"—that is, with just the vital decisions and dramatic consequences that were banished from much modern literature. Sixteen years later—in a book published the same year Jack Lewis assumed his duties at Magdalen College—Chesterton would return to the same point: "The life of man is a story; an adventure story; and in our vision the same is true even of the story of God."

In studying philosophy—philosophy, let me hasten to say, as he conceived of it, not as it necessarily is—Lewis had tried to turn himself into something like Shaw, an analytical creature capable of sharp-edged distinctions and clearly delineated, if dark, pictures—someone impervious to the mystifications of fantasy and Faery, of battles and journeys and riddles. Yet when given free time to read, it was just such stories that he invariably chose, completely ignoring and even despising the modern literature that fit his professed opinions more closely.

(Thus the strangeness of *Dymer*, which clothes the thoughts of Schopenhauer and Nietzsche in the language of William Morris.) And even in philosophy itself he had never managed to achieve anything like clarity: he tended to think of "ages and evolution and ultimate developments" in what even at the time he knew to be a vague and watered-down variant of Hegel's philosophy of *Geist*—that is, "Spirit," or what Lewis called "the Absolute" without having any real sense of what that Absolute might be. As he put it in *Surprised by Joy*:

> The Absolute Mind—better still, the Absolute—was impersonal, or it knew itself (but not us?) only in us, and it was so absolute that it wasn't really much more like a mind than anything else. And anyway, the more muddled one got about it and the more contradictions one committed, the more this proved that our distinctive thought moved only on the level of "Appearance," and "Reality" must be somewhere else. And where else but, of course, in the Absolute?

Incoherent though it be, this is pretty much Shaw's philosophy. As Shaw wrote in a 1907 essay called "The New Theology: A Lay Sermon": "In a sense there is no God as yet achieved, but there is that force at work making God, struggling through us to become an actual organised existence, enjoying what to many of us is the greatest conceivable ecstasy, the ecstasy of a brain, an intelligence, actually conscious of the whole, and with executive force capable of guiding it to a perfectly benevolent and harmonious end." But Lewis was not like Shaw. A man who from early boyhood had been repeatedly pierced by the "stab" of Joy was not the sort of man to believe that the "greatest conceivable ecstasy" is "the ecstasy of a brain." He was, like his father—and as we have seen, he had recently recognized just how much like his father he was—"sentimental, rhetorical, and passionate," and thus far more like GKC than GBS. "Like all us Celts," he told Albert, "I am a born rhetorician, one who finds pleasure in the forcible emotions."

In becoming a literary historian and critic—and moreover, in focusing his attention on medieval and Renaissance literature, where the major works almost all had the quality of dynamic adventurousness that Chesterton so loved—Lewis was, whether he knew it or not, and for good or for ill, opening himself to the side of his nature that he shared with his father. "Now that I was reading more English, the paradox"—of loving what he did not believe in while getting no nour-ishment from authors who shared his convictions—"began to be ag-gravated." Much of what he read, or rather what most moved him in his reading, turned out to be built on a foundation of Christian belief.

> Most alarming of all was [the seventeenth-century poet and priest] George Herbert. Here was a man who seemed to me to excel all the authors I had ever read in conveying the quality of life as we actually live it from moment to moment, but the wretched fellow, instead of doing it all directly, insisted on medi-ating it through what I still would have called "the Christian mythology." On the other hand most of the authors who might be claimed as precursors of modern enlightenment seemed to me very small beer and bored me cruelly.

That he was reading Chesterton at the same time—and thus en-countering a persistent argument that the love of story is intimately connected with the Christian faith—made it all the more likely that his defenses against religious belief were going to crumble. And at about this time they started crumbling quickly. The realm he had en-tered was truly "rich with possibilities," in ways that he was only be-ginning to imagine: he could at this point just intuit that the unbelief that he had always thought his protection was in fact his prison. As Chesterton wrote in *Orthodoxy,* "The man of the nineteenth century did not disbelieve in the Resurrection because his liberal Christianity allowed him to doubt it. He disbelieved in it because his very strict materialism did not allow him to believe it." Lewis was no longer for-bidden to believe.

About these changes Lewis's diary, while it lasts, is silent—unsurpris-ingly, given that it was written largely for the benefit of a woman (Mrs. Moore) who was a convinced and passionate atheist. The letters tell little more, at least until the change is nearly complete. He writes relatively rarely to Arthur during this period, but often to Barfield, and Barfield was a theist. Not an orthodox Christian, by any means—he was already an adherent of the strange Germanic synthesis of various religious and philosophical traditions called Anthroposophy—but he was firmly convinced of supernatural reality. The same was true of Cecil Harwood, Barfield's fellow Anthroposophist, and also of Lewis's now good friend Nevill Coghill. Though he would not have come across believers often in college, his correspondents during this period are almost all theists of one kind or another. But no major change in thinking is discernible in the letters until the last months of 1929—and then only after a momentous event had run its course.

Near the end of July 1929 Lewis got a letter from his uncle Dick, Albert's brother, expressing concern over Albert's health: he had been losing weight and (as his diary records) suffering from frequent and intense intestinal pains. A letter from a cousin, soon afterward, confirmed that there was cause for concern. "Poor, poor old Pdaitabird," he wrote to Arthur. "I cd. cry over the whole thing." Warnie's most recent tour of duty had taken him to Shanghai, so he could not help, and it was only after Lewis had been home caring for Albert for two weeks that he found time to inform Warnie of the situation. At that time (late August) it was thought that Albert was suffering from "a narrowing of the passage in one of his bowels," but when the doctors operated in September, they discovered cancer of the colon—something very like what had killed Flora.

From about the twelfth of August to the twenty-second of September, Lewis stayed at Little Lea nursing Albert. It was a miserable time for him, though in his letters to Warnie—which Warnie did not receive until October—he tried to keep his account as lighthearted as possible: "Things are no better since I last wrote, and I am really very despondent about him. Yet it would be an offense against Pigiebotian ethics to seal ourselves up therefore in perpetual solemnity: and, however you may feel in China, I on the spot can only get through my days and nights by allowing myself an enjoyment of the old humours, which, needless to say, show through even this situation." But it was not just pity for his father that Lewis suffered from. Being constantly in Albert's presence for the first time in years brought back all the old frustrations and resentments—and they must have been all the more maddening with no Warnie there to maintain the common Pigiebotian front. To Barfield, Lewis described Albert as "one for whom I have little affection and whose society has for many years given me much discomfort and no pleasure." Little Lea itself contributed to the misery: "I have never been able to resist the retrogressive influence of this house which always plunges me back into the pleasures and pains of a boy.... Every room is soaked with the bogeys of childhood, the awful 'rows' with my father, the awful returnings to school: and also with the old pleasures of an unusually ignoble adolescence." The adult Lewis—in two months he would turn thirty-one—found himself transformed by a kind of dark magic into the adolescent whose life he had largely hated at the time and hated still more in retrospect.

When the doctors discovered Albert's cancer they told Jack that he was in no immediate danger—"They said he might live a few years"—and encouraged Jack to return to Oxford, where the work of the new term was already stacking up quite alarmingly. So Jack left on September 21, only to get a cable two days later saying that Albert was much worse. Immediately he returned to Belfast, but his arrival on the evening of the twenty-fifth was too late: Albert had died that afternoon, of cardiac arrest rather than the cancer itself.

When Warnie got the telegram from Jack announcing their father's death—and since Jack's letters would not arrive for another two weeks, he did not even know that Albert had been ill—he was devastated, though perhaps more by the imminent loss of his childhood home than by the loss of his father. As he wrote in his diary,

> Mixed, perhaps rather callously, with my feelings about P., is the wrench of losing Leeborough, the Leeborough of the little end room and the attics, and of our room, and rare warm summer afternoons in the garden with the gramophone. And worst of all, being pulled up by the roots.... The thought that there will never be any "going home" for me, is hard to bear. I'd give a lot at this minute for a talk with J.

How much "J." would have shared Warnie's nostalgia is hard to say, but in any case he had little time for it. To him fell the whole responsibility of disposing of his father's estate and selling the house. He had to do much of this work from Oxford, since the demands of teaching (not to mention the demands of Minto) would not wait, and the details occupied much of his mind for the next few months. But also, strangely, it is during just this time that Lewis's letters begin to scatter references to his new religious beliefs—new because he is no longer talking just of an abstract Absolute but rather of more concrete and more traditional belief, belief in Someone called God.

It is impossible to know whether he had shared any of these internal developments with Albert—impossible, even, to know precisely when the decisive moment occurred. But if his later account is to be trusted, it had happened *before* Albert's death, even if he did not mention it in his letters "in the Trinity term of 1929," that is, in the springtime. ("Trinity term," in Oxford parlance, is the term during which Trinity

Sunday, or Pentecost Sunday, falls, and that is always fifty days after Easter.) In the most famous passage from *Surprised by Joy* he writes:

> You must picture me alone in that room in Magdalen, night after night, feeling, whenever my mind lifted even for a second from my work, the steady, unrelenting approach of Him Whom I so earnestly desired not to meet. That which I greatly feared had come upon me. In the Trinity Term of 1929 I gave in, and admitted that God was God, and knelt and prayed: perhaps, that night, the most dejected and reluctant convert in all England. I did not then see what is now the most shining and obvious thing; the Divine humility which will accept a convert even on such terms. The Prodigal Son at least walked home on his own feet. But who can duly adore that Love which will open the high gates to a prodigal who is brought in kicking, struggling, resentful, and darting his eyes in every direction for a chance of escape? The words *compelle intrare,* compel them to come in, have been so abused by wicked men that we shudder at them; but, properly understood, they plumb the depth of the Divine mercy. The hardness of God is kinder than the softness of men, and His compulsion is our liberation.

C. S. Lewis never wrote anything more magnificent, and yet, in the context of the story I have been telling, it is puzzling. Surely I have left something out: how did he get so quickly from the Absolute to this forthright Christian belief?

The answer is, first, that in 1929 he had *not* come to Christian belief—a point that he insists on in *Surprised by Joy* but that is obscured by the language of this passage, dominated as it is by references to two of Jesus's greatest parables: that of the Prodigal Son (from Luke 15) and that of the wedding feast (from Luke 14). But when he "admitted that God was God" in his Magdalen rooms, he was admitting nothing about Jesus. It was, rather, simply the move from a belief in something Absolute to a belief in a personal God. He can describe the moment in Christian terms only because what happened that night later developed into a straightforward embrace of Christianity. To what extent the God he prayed to then resembled the God of Christianity is impossible to tell from his autobiography.

But how, then, did he get from his vague Hegelian Absolute Spirit to a personal God? This too is hard to understand. In *Surprised by Joy* he traces the purely intellectual steps that broke down his resistance to belief in a personal God, but one would never know from his diary or his letters—except, perhaps, for a few of the technical philosophical ones he wrote to Barfield—that he was moving in that direction. One gets the impression from the autobiography that he was hiding even from himself how close he was to theism, at least until it was too late to prevent the wave from crashing over him.

One thing does seem clear: he was right to describe his conversion as an almost purely intellectual one. Again and again in *Surprised by Joy* he emphasizes his dread of "admitting that God was God," his desire to be "left alone." Insofar as he was attracted by the supernatural, it was the occult that drew him, as a vision of power without responsibility—a theme in Lewis's work we explore in some detail later. Certainly the Christian ideal of obedience to the commandments of Jesus could scarcely have been less attractive to him. I mentioned in the previous chapter his statement to Baker about his philosophical stance: "I have had to postulate some sort of God as the least objectionable theory." Even from the tone of this one sentence it is obvious that here is a young man whose interest in God is strictly as a postulate of a theory, not as a living Being. If it was only through the world of stories that God took on something like real life for him, it was through philosophy that the movement toward belief began.

We are accustomed to thinking of unbelief as something that is achieved through the intellect, and belief through emotion or will, but does that custom have any real warrant? A. N. Wilson, writing not about Lewis but about the agnosticism and atheism of the Victorian period—the kind of intellectual culture that produced the Great Knock— claims that "when the human race in Western Europe began to discard Christianity, the loss was not merely an intellectual change, the discarding of one proposition in favour of another. Indeed, though many intellectual justifications were offered by those who lost faith, the process would seem to have been, in many cases, just as emotional as religious conversion; and its roots were often quite as irrational." I would amend this to say that such losses of faith were often *more* emotional and irrational than many conversions to belief, Lewis's included.

It cannot have been long after this conversion—if it is rightly called a conversion—that Lewis learned of Albert's illness. Then there was the period of nursing, Albert's sudden decline and death, and the tedious accumulation of estate settlement details. But by the end of 1929 he was beginning to give an account of himself to Arthur, with whom his correspondence had taken on a new life. (It is interesting that Arthur, who had been for some time displaced by Barfield at the center of Lewis's network of friendships, was the person with whom, at least in letters, he was most open about the changes in himself.) He praises George MacDonald's collection of Christian poems for every day in the year, *The Diary of an Old Soul.* "How I would have scorned it once!" On the day after Christmas he writes, again to Arthur, of the Absolute—but the Absolute as the "maker" of their Irish homeland, "desolate and keen" County Antrim and "all the sleepy Cumnor country." On January 2, 1930, he reports that Dante's *Paradiso*—that greatest of all depictions of the Christian idea of heavenly blessedness—"has really opened a new world to me." He is clearly reading the New Testament also, and he suspects that Arthur's gentle, Quakerish Jesus is something less than the full picture: "I am still inclined to think that you can get only what *you* call 'Christ' out of the Gospels by picking & choosing, & slurring over a good deal." And then on January 30: "Things are going very, very well with me (spiritually)."

But actually he does not quite say that things are going well with him spiritually. Instead, he says that he is *tempted* to say that, but knows that there is danger in such a claim: "One knows from bitter experience that he who standeth should take heed lest he fall, and that anything remotely like pride is certain to bring an awful crash. The old doctrine is quite true you know—that one must attribute everything to the grace of God, and nothing to oneself. Yet as long as one *is* a conceited ass, there is no good pretending not to be."

I first read a book by C. S. Lewis twenty-five years ago, and I have been reading his work consistently since then. I know his writerly voice quite well, as well as I know anyone's; it is utterly distinctive. And the most dominant feeling I get when I read his early letters—that is, those written in his first thirty years of life—is that in none of them does he sound like *himself.* The pre-conversion Lewis is, though obviously highly intelligent, neither a particularly likable nor a particularly interesting person—at least in his letters. He may have been delightful to know, though I doubt it. But once he "admitted that God was God," it is as though the key to his own hidden and locked-away personality was given to him. What appears almost immediately is a kind of gusto (sheer, bold enthusiasm for what he loves) that is characteristic of him ever after. One sees this on the intellectual plane: after reading the mystic Jakob Boehme, he writes, "It's not like a book at all, but like a thunderclap. Heaven defend us—what things there are knocking about the world!" His responses to the natural world are intensified as well: "I think almost more every year in autumn I get the sense, just as the mere nature and voluptuous life of the world is dying, of something else coming awake. . . . Does the death of the natural always mean the birth of the spiritual? Does one thing never sleep except to let something else wake?"

During the fall of 1929 and winter of 1930 his sense of a dramatic energy and tension in the observable world—something very like what the poet Gerard Manley Hopkins means when he talks about the "instress" and "inscape" of Creation—escalates to the point of eroticism: "To-day I got such a sudden intense feeling of delight that it sort of stopped me in my walk and spun me round. Indeed the sweetness was so great, & seemed so to affect the whole body as well as the mind, that it gave me pause—it was so very like sex." With this intensity of experience, this gusto, comes also an enlivening of his critical intelligence. He knows perfectly well that someone of Freudian inclinations would say that such an experience "is sublimated lust, a kind of defeated masturbation which fancy gives one to compensate for external chastity. Yet after all, why should that be the right way of looking at it? If he can say that It ['It' being what he and Arthur call Joy] is sublimated sex, why is it not open to me to say that sex is undeveloped *It?*—as Plato would have said." This turning of the tables on conventional wisdom, this paradoxical inquiry into the legitimacy of what "everyone knows," is very Chestertonian—and, Chesterton would insist, very Christian, Christianity comprising largely paradoxes, starting with "God became human." (This very argument against the Freudian emphasis on the universal centrality of sexual experience would be used by Lewis throughout his career, even thirty years later in one of his last books, *The Four Loves.*)

If both intellectually and sensually Lewis was growing in enthusiasm and delight, about himself he was becoming more wryly critical. Some years later he reflected on the response to the first book that made him truly famous, *The Screwtape Letters:* "Some have paid me an undeserved compliment by supposing that my *Letters* were the ripe fruit of many years' study in moral and ascetic theology. They forget that there is an equally reliable, though less credible, way of learning how temptation works. 'My heart'—I need no other's—'showeth me the wickedness of the ungodly.'" (That is Psalm 36:1, in the *Book of*

Common Prayer's version.) It is clear that he began seriously to consult this source of knowledge about temptation in the winter of 1930, and it is remarkable how quickly he got to what he would soon see as the heart of the matter. This is from the same letter to Arthur that I have been quoting:

> During my afternoon "meditations,"—which I at least *attempt* quite regularly now—I have found out ludicrous and terrible things about my own character. Sitting by, watching the rising thoughts to break their necks as they pop up, one learns to know the sort of thoughts that do come. And, will you believe it, one out of every three is a thought of self-admiration: when everything else fails, having had its neck broken, up comes the thought "What an admirable fellow I am to have broken their necks!" I catch myself posturing before the mirror, so to speak, all day long. I pretend I am carefully thinking out what to say to the next pupil (for *his* good, of course) and then suddenly realise I am really thinking how frightfully clever I'm going to be and how he will admire me. . . . And then when you force yourself to stop it, you admire yourself for doing *that*. It is like fighting the hydra. . . . There seems to be no end to it. Depth under depth of self-love and self-admiration.

Already, then, at the very beginning of Lewis's life as a believer, we see an insight that would dominate his thinking ever after: that our inner lives are *simultaneously* "ludicrous and terrible": dark, evil, rebellious, and yet in our self-flattery always rather comic too—just as, after his conversion, his earlier attempts to avoid God ("a prodigal who is brought in kicking, struggling, resentful, and darting his eyes in every direction for a chance of escape") assume a humorous aspect. All those years of fleeing from God!—and therefore from the romantic hopes of blessedness, the idealistic "Christina dreams." And then in the end it turned out that the richness that awaited him was more than he had even hoped for—though there was the constant painful discovery of how far short he fell of being worthy to inherit such a world of delight.

The Lewis of these last years of unbelief and first years of belief receives his proper fictional description in the character of Eustace Scrubb—at least, the Eustace of *The Voyage of the "Dawn Treader."* Eustace does not choose to enter Narnia, and when he gets there he constantly complains about its difficulties, about all the ways it differs from his own world—a world in which, he manages to forget, he was never happy. He too is "kicking, struggling, resentful, and darting his eyes in every direction for a chance of escape"; had he remained in that state his ultimate fate would have been that of the Dwarfs at the end of *The Last Battle,* who in the midst of a glorious landscape huddle together and face each other, insisting that "rich red wine" is but "dirty water out of a trough" and a magnificent feast no more than an old turnip and a raw cabbage leaf. When the children beg Aslan to help them, he tries—the wine and the feast are his effort— but must conclude, "They will not let us help them. They have chosen cunning instead of belief. Their prison is only in their own minds, yet they are in that prison; and so afraid of being taken in that they cannot be taken out."

Something like this could very well have happened to Eustace: he could have continued believing that Edmund and Caspian are prigs, the crew incompetent, and everyone preoccupied with plans to make him miserable. The diary that he keeps indicates that he had gone a long way toward constructing a rock-solid narrative of superiority and paranoia—had he not been transformed into a dragon. It was only the good fortune, or good grace, of that dreadful metamorphosis by which Eustace was saved: becoming a dragon, he completes the alienation from the human world that he has been trying to achieve by his own efforts. And once that alienation is complete he sees how little he likes it. He becomes ready to give up the story he has been telling in his diary, as well as his opinions of himself and of the others, but the process by which he is remade into a boy is hideously painful.

It is especially noteworthy that Eustace's own attempts to remove his scaly skin are ineffectual. To peel off his skin is "a most lovely feeling," but he is just the same after doing so—just as Lewis himself had been exactly the same after "breaking the neck" of a prideful thought, or several prideful thoughts. Eustace skins himself three times before realizing that his best efforts are inadequate. It is only Aslan who has the strength (and the love) to do the job properly—that is, to turn Eustace back into a boy again—and Eustace welcomes the gift, even if "the very first tear he made was so deep that I thought it had gone right into my heart."

But then it is characteristic of Aslan, as Lord of Narnia, to do for his people what they cannot do for themselves. He heals, he saves—he even dies for them when there is no other remedy. But it is not clear that when Lewis was discovering his "depth under depth of self-love and self-admiration" he yet understood the deepest character of the God in whom he now believed. He was still trying to strip away his own skin, but every day, whether he knew it or not, he was moving closer to the recognition that it was not just any God but the God of Jesus Christ into whose hands he had fallen, and that if any radical change in him were ever to happen, his own powers of insight and determination would not be adequate to the task. Only the claws of that God could penetrate to his very heart.

SEVEN

"Definitely believing in Christ"

I n the greatest of George MacDonald's books, the children's story *The Princess and the Goblin,* Princess Irene helps the young miner Curdie to escape from the goblins who have imprisoned him in their caves. She does so by virtue of the magical thread her grandmother gave her, which infallibly leads her (and therefore also Curdie) back home. But Curdie cannot see the thread and calls Irene's story "nonsense," which, understandably, upsets her very much. When she sees her grandmother again and gives her a full account, her grandmother says,

> "He is a good boy, Curdie, and a brave boy. Aren't you glad you've got him out?"
>
> "Yes, grandmother. But it wasn't very good of him not to believe me when I was telling him the truth."
>
> "People must believe what they can, and those who believe more must not be hard upon those who believe less. I doubt if you would have believed it all yourself if you hadn't seen some of it."

And when Curdie gets to *his* home, in a conversation with his mother he is unapologetic about his attitude toward Irene:

> "It's no explanation at all, mother; and I can't believe it."
>
> "That may be only because you do not understand it. If you did, you would probably find that it was an explanation, and believe it thoroughly. I don't blame you for not being able to believe it, but I do blame you for fancying such a child would try

to deceive you. Why should she? Depend upon it, she told you all she knew. Until you had found a better way of accounting for it all, you might at least have been more sparing of your judgment."

Embedded in these passages is a deep meditation on the puzzle of belief, and the relationship between belief and trust. In the narrative world MacDonald is weaving here, belief is neither a virtue nor an obligation, but a gift—and those who have received the gift should not be unduly critical of those who have not. Conversely, those who do not believe can't just decide whether what someone else believes seems plausible to them or not: they must also consider the character of the believing person. So the believing Irene must remember that she has been blessed with the opportunity of seeing *some* marvelous things, primarily in her grandmother's room, which makes it much easier for her to believe in the *other* marvelous things her grandmother tells her—whereas Curdie has seen no such marvels. And for his part, Curdie needs to temper his skepticism with reflection on the kind of person he knows the princess to be: she certainly has no motive to lie to him, and besides, she managed to save his life when he could do nothing to save himself, by means that he cannot "account for" at all.*

Jack Lewis knew, by 1930, that he had been given that gift of faith. He entered a new world—or, to be more precise, he recognized that he had already entered a strange and delightful new land. (This is, after all, what habitually happens to the visitors to Narnia: they must come to see that they are in a new world, a different world than the one they were born in. People do not really *discover* Narnia; more accurately, they are *converted* to it.) But if he now knew that he was living in a new world, he did not know who the Lord of that world was. He did not know where his adventure would take him next, though he did understand that it was a voyage over which he had no control. As he wrote to a friend, A. K. Hamilton Jenkin, in March 1930, what he

---

* It is just this part of *The Princess and the Goblin* that Lewis drew upon in writing the scene from *The Lion, the Witch, and the Wardrobe* in which Professor Kirke chastises Peter and Susan for their too-easy dismissal of Lucy's tale of the world beyond the wardrobe. Indeed, the substance of Professor Kirke's lecture to the Pevensie children is identical to that of the smaller lectures given by Irene's grandmother and Curdie's mother.

then believed was "not precisely Christianity, tho' it may turn out that way in the end." But if it did "turn out that way," it would not be because he chose to "adopt Christianity"—to "postulate" it in the way that he had earlier postulated a God for philosophical purposes: "I now wait to see if it will adopt me: i.e. I now know there is another Party in the affair—that I'm playing poker, not Patience, as I once supposed." Like Jill Pole when she first enters Narnia near the beginning of *The Silver Chair,* he finds himself borne aloft, floating on the breath of Someone he does not know, moving slowly but inexorably toward an equally unknown destination.

This was still anything but a comfortable experience for him: the prodigal was still struggling to escape. As he wrote in a poem of the time, a poem addressed to God, "Round about, / Beating my wings, all ways, within your cage, / I flutter, but not out." But such a poem is an acknowledgment that his imprisonment was necessary; he could do little but wait. And as he waited, the task of teaching him Whose cage he was in (Whose breath he was riding on), and what destination he was headed for, fell primarily to some friends, chief among them a fellow don named Tolkien.

Again, Tolkien had left Leeds University at the end of 1925 to return to Oxford as the Rawlinson and Bosworth Professor of Anglo-Saxon. It is important to understand that in the English academic setting the title of "Professor" is given only to a few distinguished scholars—Lewis would actually never be named to a professorial position at Oxford, remaining instead a "Fellow and Tutor," like most of his colleagues, for nearly thirty years. (It turned out to be Cambridge that elected him to the professoriate.) Tolkien had been named Professor of English Language at Leeds in 1924 when he was only thirty-one—an extraordinarily early age—and his appointment at Oxford was, given the prestige of the university, even more remarkable. Unlike Lewis, he had established himself as a major figure in his field almost from the beginning of his career.

That field was somewhat different from Lewis's. Though both were members of Oxford's English faculty, Tolkien was on the "language side," while Lewis was on the "literature side." Between the two sides there was some rivalry, largely because Oxford (like Cambridge) was slow to recognize the study of English literature as a proper academic pursuit. Throughout the nineteenth century and well into the twentieth, it was widely thought that the study of English literature was to be expected of all well-bred persons—it was even considered accessible to mere women—but that it lacked the rigor of "real" scholarly disciplines, chief among which were Latin and Greek. Because the language side of the English curriculum focused on Anglo-Saxon ("Old English") and Middle English—including various regional dialects—even more rigorous scholars deemed it a worthy academic pursuit: after all, Anglo-Saxon was as "dead" a language as Latin or classical Greek, and nearly as hard to learn. Anglo-Saxon philology (that is, the study of the history of that language) was therefore on an equal footing, at Oxford, with classical philology. Strange though it may seem to us, when Lewis began his career as an English *literature* don he was entering a field that was quite popular among students but highly suspect among other dons—almost like pop culture programs in today's universities.

In *Surprised by Joy,* Lewis writes, "At my first coming into the world, I had been (implicitly) warned never to trust a Papist, and at my first coming into the English Faculty (explicitly) never to trust a philologist. Tolkien was both." At their first meeting Lewis seemed determined to heed that advice. It happened in May 1926, when the whole of England was convulsed by a great general strike that almost shut down the country and greatly occupied the Oxford students, many of whom fled to London to join the strikers on the picket lines. (There is a nice treatment of this momentous event—and the mixed motives of the students who participated in it—in Waugh's *Brideshead Revisited.*) Despite the uproar, the English faculty held its monthly meeting on May 11, and there the two young dons talked for the first time. In his diary entry—it is worth remembering that this is well before the transformation in his character explored in the previous chapter—Lewis contrives to condescend to a man who, though just six years his senior, had achieved far more and whose career seemed at that time far more promising: "He is a smooth, pale, fluent little chap. . . . No harm in him: only needs a smack or so."

But perhaps there was some justification for annoyance, since Tolkien had apparently expressed some of the skepticism about academic literary study that I have just sketched: "Thinks language is the real thing in the school—thinks all literature is written for the amusement of *men* between thirty and forty—we ought to vote ourselves out of existence if we were honest." Presumably the "we" in that last phrase refers to the literature dons, though perhaps Tolkien thought *he* had no business in the university either. It is not clear whether Tolkien was unaware that Lewis was on the literature side or did not care;

both stances would be characteristic of him, but the latter a little more so. Tact was not a virtue Tolkien cultivated with much enthusiasm, then or ever.

Certainly it was not a meeting that heralded future friendship. But, though neither of them knew it at the time, they had much in common. For one thing, Lewis was himself the product of an education—especially under Kirk—that treated English literature as a delightful holiday from the rigor of classical languages. Moreover, he knew that, though his literary interests lay largely in the medieval and Renaissance periods, he did not have the linguistic equipment that he needed. And perhaps most important of all, though he had been deeply attracted to the Norse myths since childhood, he knew almost no Old Norse (or Old Icelandic), the language in which many of the great myths and legends were written; so when Tolkien started a club for his fellow dons to study that tongue, Lewis was quick to sign up. Tolkien called the club the Kolbitar—in Norse, the "Coal-biters," that is, people who sit so close to the fire that they are virtually gnawing the coals—and Lewis not only threw himself into the linguistic study but continued gnawing the coals with Tolkien long after everyone else had gone home. In 1929 he wrote to Arthur of one December evening in which "Tolkien ... came back with me to college and sat discoursing of the gods and giants and Asgard for three hours"—which made it a relatively short night. Tolkien's wife, Edith, quickly had to learn not to expect her husband to be home before bedtime on those evenings he spent with Jack Lewis. (Since Lewis was sleeping in College during the week anyway, Minto was not similarly affected.)

Though their conversations began in Asgard, they eventually migrated, for at least part of the time, to Jerusalem, for Lewis, given the systematic dismantling of his unbelief, could scarcely be uninterested in Tolkien's deep commitment to Catholic Christianity. Yes, Tolkien was a "Papist"—and thus someone highly untrustworthy in the Ulster Protestant world in which Lewis had been raised. But then Flora Lewis had always been exceptionally tolerant of Catholics, hiring several to work in her home and help raise her boys, and in any case, at this point in his life Lewis was far more taken with the fact that Tolkien was a Christian than concerned with the particular variety of Christianity his new friend professed. As Lewis moved from philosophical idealism to theism—from the Absolute to God—his talks with Tolkien grew deeper, longer, and more impassioned.

Though Lewis had largely rejected the anthropological pessimism he had imbibed from Kirk, there was one aspect of it that still dogged him. It was the resemblance of the story of Jesus—especially his crucifixion and resurrection—to the crowd of pagan myths about dying gods. What, after all, made the story of Christ any different than the story of Balder? How were those who wept at the tomb of Jesus of Nazareth any different than those who cried, "Balder the Beautiful is dead, is dead"? Were these not all figures in the same kind of story—indeed, in one sense, the very same story? The questions, as Lewis worked through them in his own mind and in conversations with Tolkien and others, boiled down to two central ones. First, what is *myth*? And second, what relation does the Christian story have to myth?

We have already seen the answer to the first question that Lewis—and thousands upon thousands of other European and North American intellectuals of his generation—had been taught: that the myths of various cultures resemble one another so much because they arise from common material (especially agricultural) conditions—the changes of the seasons, the ceaseless alternation of seedtime and harvest, the fears of bad harvests and hopes for good ones. Those students who came up to university after the Great War were perhaps more likely to hear a variant account, perhaps that of Freud, for whom stories have the shapes they do because we inherit violent tendencies from our primitive ancestors, along with the desire to be delivered from that violence. (As Freud put it in *Civilization and its Discontents,* "Men are . . . creatures among whose instinctual endowments is to be reckoned a powerful share of aggressiveness. As a result, their neighbor is for them not only a potential helper or sexual object, but also someone who tempts them to satisfy their aggressiveness on him, to exploit his capacity for work without compensation, to use him sexually without his consent, to seize his possessions, to humiliate him, to cause him pain, to torture and to kill him.") Then would come the arguments of Freud's onetime collaborator, Carl Jung, for whom the shared features of the world's myths are testimony to the "collective unconscious," the one mind in which all of our minds participate and from which well up the "archetypes" or common images of humanity. Lewis would not have been influenced by Jung—whose chief works on this subject were yet to be written in 1930—but he would have seen very similar arguments in the prose and poetry of Yeats. As early as 1911 Yeats had written "that the borders of our mind are ever shifting, and that many minds flow into one another, as it were, and create or reveal a single mind, a single energy. . . . This great mind and great memory can be evoked by symbols."

Though Yeats (and possibly Jung) believed in supernaturalism while Frazer and Freud disbelieved in it and gave materialist explanations for the world of myth, all with equal force ruled out the historical validity of the Gospel story and, just as important, its uniqueness. The Christian narrative, all the critics agreed, was just another dying-god story. They might have disagreed about what the typical dying-god story *was,* but not that the Gospel narratives were exemplary of that form.

As we have seen, Yeats's frank occultism both frightened Lewis and struck him as a kind of wishful thinking (offering as it does, as he would later put it in a comment about similar views, "all the thrills of religion and none of the cost"). And the positions taken by Frazer and Freud now felt reductive to him: they were of the "X is *only* Y" form, and as we have seen, he had already come to mistrust that kind of argument. Recall his comment to Arthur: "Yet after all, why should that be the right way of looking at it? If he can say that It is sublimated sex, why is it not open to me to say that sex is undeveloped *It?*—as Plato would have said." Thus, twenty years later, he would write this exchange in *The Voyage of the "Dawn Treader"* between a boy of our world and a star in human form named Ramandu:

> "In our world," said Eustace, "a star is a huge ball of flaming gas."
>
> "Even in your world, my son, that is not what a star is but only what it is made of."

Not long after he wrote these words, Lewis wrote a preface to a book called *Smoke on the Mountain* by a woman named Joy Davidman, and he quoted with great approval her account of the beliefs into which she had been educated as a young woman: "Life is only an electrochemical reaction. Love, art, and altruism are only sex. The universe is only matter. Matter is only energy. I forget what I said energy is only." (The wit of that last sentence provides a partial explanation of Lewis's ultimate decision to marry Joy. But that story will have to wait.) What alternative was there to the materialists' suspicious undermining of all myth and the supernaturalists' universalizing of the Christian story?

The question of myth was one that had much occupied Tolkien for many years, and his thinking on the subject was therefore considerably more sophisticated than Lewis's. For Tolkien the problem had several dimensions. In part he wanted simply to understand his own deep attraction to myth, especially the whole apparatus of Norse mythology. He also found it curious and rather sad that England had no body of mythology to compare with those of Scandinavia, Greece, or India. But the issue was complicated for him by his desire not merely to *read* myths but to *make* myths. Since his teen years he had been constructing an ever more elaborate network of mythological stories and poems, but these works arose first as a way to use languages he had invented, the "Elvish tongues" called Quenya and Sindharin (inspired by, respectively, Finnish and Welsh). Only as these writings grew in complexity and came to mean more to him did he have to think about *why* they meant so much to him and what he would be communicating through them if (as seemed highly unlikely) anyone ever read what he wrote. And of course, the whole business was rendered yet more problematic by Tolkien's commitment to a Catholic Christianity that presented itself as a clear alternative to pagan myths. As a great scholar of the Anglo-Saxon world, he doubtless would have encountered many times the great question of the eighth-century monk Alcuin, "What has Ingeld to do with Christ?" (Ingeld was a legendary Danish king who appears in *Beowulf,* and Alcuin was exasperated at the popularity of such pagan stories among his fellow monks.) What indeed?

The two young dons spent hundreds of hours in those last years of the 1920s meditating on these questions as they bit the coals in Lewis's Magdalen rooms. And what emerged was a clear difference of opinion: Lewis firmly insisted that myths were "lies"—even if they were beautiful, "breathed through silver"—but Tolkien defended them passionately as vehicles for moral and spiritual truth. Eventually he wrote a long poem "for C. S. L." called "Mythopoeia," that is, "mythmaking." He gave the poem the subtitle "Philomythus to Misomythus": myth-lover to myth-hater. And he began it with the very question of what the natural world *is:*

You look at trees and label them just so,
(for trees are "trees," and growing is "to grow");
you walk the earth and tread with solemn pace
one of the many minor globes of Space:
a star's a star, some matter in a ball
compelled to courses mathematical

amid the regimented, cold, Inane,
where destined atoms are each moment slain.

(That matter of the stars again! But also trees, for which Tolkien had a particular fascination, as can be seen in the Ents of *The Lord of the Rings*.) What is immediately striking about this beginning is the characterization of Lewis as a despiser of myths who looks upon the world with a cold materialist eye. We know that not to have been the case at this stage in his life; we know the violent blows his earlier strict atheism had already taken. But we also know that Lewis was a man who loved the give-and-take of argument, and it is not hard to guess that in debating these matters with Tolkien he put up more resistance than he really felt. It was a way of putting the supernatural beliefs to which he was drawn to a real test. In his poem Tolkien attempts to meet that challenge—and it is interesting that he chooses to do so in a poem. Though the two men argued endlessly, then and later, dialectic was Lewis's native ground, not Tolkien's. "*Distinguo*, Tollers, *distinguo!*" Lewis was known to shout, and probably Tollers was less capable—at least in the heat of the moment—of making shrewd philosophical distinctions than Lewis was. For the fullest expression of his deepest convictions he turned, then and always, to literary means: verse and story.

Later in the poem Tolkien invokes the story from Genesis of Adam's naming of the animals and extends it to a naming of all Creation:

Yet trees are not "trees," until so named and seen
and never were so named, till those had been
who speech's involuted breath unfurled,
faint echo and dim picture of the world,
but neither record nor a photograph,
being divination, judgement, and a laugh,
response of those that felt astir within
by deep monition movements that were kin
to life and death of trees, of beasts, of stars:
free captives undermining shadowy bars,
digging the foreknown from experience
and panning the vein of spirit out of sense.

The argument here is that when imagined unfallen beings—Tolkien does not speak directly of Adam, that was not his way—first named the things of this world, they did so by means of an instinctive insight into (a "divination," a "deep monition" of) their natures. And the natures of things are primarily defined, always, by their having been *created*, made by the commanding Word of God. (Likewise, in his *Confessions* Saint Augustine looks around at the world and asks what it can tell him about God, and everything "shouts aloud, 'He made us!'") Therefore,

He sees no stars who does not see them first
of living silver made that sudden burst
to flame like flowers beneath an ancient song.

Tolkien is arguing here that anyone who, like Eustace, sees a star as "a huge ball of flaming gas" is not really *seeing*: to perceive the Creation truly we must move beyond knowing what stars are "made of," and because we are fallen and finite creatures, this we can do only by image, metaphor, and myth. To be sure, we lack the direct, immediate power of "divination" that Adam had; nevertheless,

The heart of man is not compound of lies,
but draws some wisdom from the only Wise,
and still recalls him. Though now long estranged,
man is not wholly lost nor wholly changed.
Dis-graced he may be, yet is not dethroned,
and keeps the rags of lordship once he owned,
his world-dominion by creative act.

To this argument Lewis posed a question: are these not mere "Christina dreams," wish-fulfillment fantasies? We know he posed that question because the poem addresses it directly: "Yes! 'wish-fulfilment dreams' we spin to cheat / our timid hearts and ugly Fact defeat!" But Tolkien goes on to ask a countering question: "Whence came the wish, and whence the power to dream"? That is, if the materialist philosophy is true, why do we even have such dreams and desires? What planted in us this longing, this *Sehnsucht*, Joy itself?

Here Tolkien was reaching to the heart of his friend. Lewis had focused all his attention either on what Joy was or how to get it, but Tolkien was forcing him to consider the matter in a wholly different light. It was not Joy itself but its presence in a biological organism comprising largely water, nitrogen and carbon that constituted the greatest puzzle. That we dream and wish *at all* is a powerful element of the case for belief that myths communicate some truth that cannot be communicated in any other way. Lewis would use this argument repeatedly for the rest of his life: as he would write years later:

> Do what they will, then, we remain conscious of a desire which no natural happiness will satisfy. But is there any reason to suppose that reality offers any satisfaction to it? Nor does the being hungry prove that we have bread. But I think it may be urged that this misses the point. A man's physical hunger does not prove that that man will get any bread; he may die of starvation on a raft in the Atlantic. But surely a man's hunger does prove that he comes of a race which repairs its body by eating, and inhabits a world where eatable substances exist.

So too the craving for myths (hearing them, reading them, making them) suggests the presence of a nonphysiological need that they satisfy—or, more accurately, *try* to satisfy. Because they reach something deep within us, we return to them repeatedly, but because they do not and cannot meet the need they invoke, our experience with them is characterized by longing.

But surely not *all* desires are meant to be fulfilled? Indeed, says Philomythus, they are not, and he suggests to Misomythus that he knows—perhaps we all know—what is to be rejected as wishful thinking and what is to be embraced as the courage to believe what we cannot see:

> Blessed are the men of Noah's race that build
> their little arks, though frail and poorly filled,
> and steer through winds contrary towards a wraith,
> a rumour of a harbour guessed by faith.
>
> Blessed are the legend-makers with their rhyme
> of things not found within recorded time.

It is with these people that Philomythus casts his lot, and he encourages Misomythus to do the same. In the end Tolkien does not offer certainty of reward for the voyagers and mythmakers, but rather faith and hope:

> In Paradise perchance the eye may stray
> from gazing upon everlasting Day

to see the day-illumined, and renew
from mirrored truth the likeness of the True.

And he encourages Lewis to take the same chance he is taking, to count on the "perchance." And Lewis did. For the rest of his life he was a champion of the knowledge-giving power of myth, fantasy, Faery.

But "Mythopoeia" did not solve all his problems. Still he had to ask, what *is* the truth that myth communicates? And what relationship does that truth have to Christianity—the Christianity that still might "adopt" him? One could say that, for Lewis, the Christ-and-Ingeld question remained. On what grounds could he say that the Christian myth was fundamentally different from all other myths, such that it deserved unique allegiance?

The groundwork for an answer to this question had actually been laid even before Lewis met Tolkien, and by someone who would surely have been dismayed to learn the effect he had. As Lewis would tell the story in *Surprised by Joy*:

> Early in 1926 the hardest boiled of all atheists I ever knew sat in my room on the other side of the fire and remarked that the evidence for the historicity of the Gospels was really surprisingly good. "Rum thing," he went on. "All that stuff of Frazer's about the Dying God. Rum thing. It almost looks as if it had really happened once."
>
> To understand the shattering impact of it, you would need to know the man (who has certainly never since shown any interest in Christianity). If he, the cynic of cynics, the toughest of the toughs, were not—as I would still have put it—"safe," where could I turn? Was there then no escape?

So perhaps this story was indeed different from all the other myths—different because it happened, because it was a historical event rather than an imagined story. (Lewis's reading in Chesterton—especially *The Everlasting Man*—was helpful to him in this regard.) But even so, there remained a still deeper problem: So what if it happened? So what if Jesus of Nazareth died on a cross? So what if he even rose from the dead? "What I couldn't understand," he wrote to Arthur, "was how the life and death of Someone Else (whoever he was) 2000 years ago could help us here and now—except in so far as his *example* helped us. And the example business, tho' true and important, is not Christianity: right in the centre of Christianity, in the Gospels and St. Paul, you keep on getting something quite different and very mysterious." That "something" was the idea of Atonement: that the death of Jesus on that cross was sacrificial; that it was somehow a death on our behalf; and that it therefore, again somehow, put us right with God—or at least made it possible for us to be put right with God. The problem for Lewis was the "somehow": he just could not figure out how the thing was supposed to *work,* and until he did figure it out, he did not see how he could embrace Christianity. On this shoal he ran aground and was stranded; it did not seem that from there he could go anywhere.

On September 19, 1931, Lewis invited Tolkien and Hugo Dyson—an English don at the University of Reading whom Lewis had met through Nevill Coghill, and a Christian—to dinner at Magdalen. "It was really a memorable talk," Lewis told Arthur. "We began (in Addison's Walk just after dinner) on metaphor and myth—interrupted by a rush of wind which came so suddenly on the still warm evening and sent so many leaves pattering down that we thought it was raining. We all held our breath, the other two appreciating the ecstasy of such a thing almost as you would. We continued (in my room) on Christianity: a good long satisfying talk in which I learned a lot." It is worth noting that by this time Lewis had already explained to Tolkien an argument made by Barfield in *Poetic Diction:* that in ancient languages that have a single word for "wind," "breath," and "spirit," or "Spirit" (Hebrew *ruach*, Greek *pneuma*, Latin *spiritus*), the meaning of such words originally comprised all three of our meanings *at once*—or, more precisely, formed a single, unified meaning that we have since broken into shards. Lewis knew what he was intimating when he spoke of the rushing wind and how they held their breath.

Tolkien finally excused himself at 3:00 a.m., but Lewis and Dyson (who was spending the night at Magdalen) returned to Addison's Walk and continued talking for another hour. Almost a month later Lewis wrote again to Arthur to explain what he had learned that night—especially about the vexed problem of the Atonement:

> Now what Dyson and Tolkien showed me was this: that if I met the idea of sacrifice in a Pagan story I didn't mind it at all: and again, that if I met the idea of god sacrificing himself to himself ... I liked it very much and was mysteriously moved by it: again,

that the idea of the dying and reviving God (Balder, Adonis, Bacchus) similarly moved me provided I met it anywhere *except* in the Gospels. The reason was that in Pagan stories I was prepared to feel the myth as profound and suggestive of meanings beyond my grasp even tho' I could not say in cold prose "what it meant."

Now the story of Christ is simply a true myth: a myth working on us in the same way as the others, but with tremendous difference that *it really happened:* and one must be content to accept it in the same way, remembering that it is God's myth where the others are men's myths: i.e. the Pagan stories are God expressing himself through the minds of poets, using such images as He found there, while Christianity is God expressing himself through "real things."

The extent to which he had made Tolkien's ideas about myth and truth his own can be seen in the claim, later in the same letter, that "the 'doctrines' we get *out of* the true myth are of course *less* true: they are translations into our *concepts* and *ideas* of that wh. God has already expressed in a language more adequate, namely the actual incarnation, crucifixion, and resurrection." That is, the language of actual historical event, such as can be narrated in mythical form, is a *more* truthful language than the language of "concepts and ideas."

In *The Lion, the Witch, and the Wardrobe,* when Aslan has been slain on the Stone Table—taking the place of Edmund—and Susan and Lucy are wandering about in the field, not knowing what to do next, the girls hear a sudden crack ("as if a giant had broken a giant's plate"). It is the Table, broken in half. "What does it mean?" Susan cries out. "Is it more magic?" And then the girls hear, from behind them, the voice of the risen Lion: "Yes! It is more magic." He gives an explanation, of sorts: if the Witch had been able to look back before the dawn of time, "she would have known that when a willing victim who had committed no treachery was killed in the traitor's stead, the Table would crack and Death itself would start working backwards." But really, what sort of explanation is that? Why should things be this way? *How* does the death of the "willing victim" take the traitor from the clutches of the Witch? And how can the magic that frees the traitor be older than the magic that condemns him?

It is highly significant, I think, that Susan and Lucy ignore the explanation. They neither comment on it nor ask questions about it, so absorbed are they in the joy of being once more in Aslan's presence. (It is Lucy who always understands, better than any of the other children, the infinite value of the mere presence of Aslan. At the end of *The Voyage of the "Dawn Treader,"* when Aslan tells her and Edmund that they will not be able to return to Narnia but must stay in their home world, she weeps, and says, "It isn't Narnia, you know. . . . It's *you*. We shan't meet *you* there. And how can we live, never meeting you?") Later, when the great battle for Narnia is over and the Witch is dead, Lucy tells Susan that she thinks Edmund "ought to know . . . what Aslan did for him," but "at that moment they were interrupted," and if Edmund ever did hear the explanation, we do not learn of it. Because it is not the explanation that matters: it is the sacrifice itself— and the new life it brings even to those who have been turned into statues—and the victory over the forces of evil that really matter. And these are best communicated through the story—the one that begins with Lucy's opening a door into the snowy Lantern Waste and ends with the Kings and Queens following the white stag back to that very spot, where there still remains that door that joins Narnia to our world.

So all of Lewis's major obstacles to specifically Christian belief had been cleared away. When, then, did he actually *become* a Christian? It turns out that this is difficult to say: as wonderful as the evening with Tolkien and Dyson was, and as beautiful as is the image of the wind blowing through the trees above Addison's Walk, he did not have an immediate and permanent conversion, like Saul on the Damascus Road. On the first of October, less than two weeks after that "memorable talk," he would write to Arthur, "I have just passed on from believing in God to definitely believing in Christ—in Christianity. I will try to explain this another time. My long night talk with Dyson and Tolkien had a good deal to do with it." But when he gets around to the promised explanation—the long letter of October 18 from which I have largely been quoting on the preceding pages—he can no longer put the matter so definitively. After having described his new understanding of myth, he asks the question he knows he must confront: "Does this amount to a belief in Christianity? At any rate I am now certain (a) That this Christian story is to be approached, in a sense, as I approach the other myths; (b) That it is the most important and full of meaning. I am also *nearly* certain that it really happened." This is hardly a direct answer to the question and surely constitutes a step back from the straightforwardness of his October 1 letter. Maybe he had not yet "passed on" to Christianity after all.

But in a larger sense that didn't matter, for he was now committed to *living* as a Christian. He had already, some months earlier, begun regular attendance at his local parish church, Holy Trinity Heading-ton, and similarly, he had begun daily attendance at Matins (morning prayer) in Magdalen College Chapel. Clearly, Christianity had indeed adopted him, regardless of his views-of-the-moment on the subject. Tolkien, in the midst of overwork, the complications of life with four children, and frustration at being able to write so little that he really cared about, confided to his diary: "Friendship with Lewis compen-sates for much, and besides giving constant pleasure and comfort has done me much good from the contact with a man at once honest, brave, intellectual—a scholar, a poet, and a philosopher—and a lover, at least after a long pilgrimage, of Our Lord."

On the home front there were also great changes afoot. The sale of Little Lea, in the aftermath of Albert Lewis's death, had made it possi-ble for Lewis and Mrs. Moore to consider buying their own house. Though they had now been at "Hillsboro" for several years, the ac-commodations there were cramped, and of course a certain tentative-ness always accompanies the life of a renter. But they were by no means well off, even with Albert's inheritance, and through late 1929 and early 1930 they struggled to (as the lingo of real estate has it) find anything suitable in their price range. One thing could open new pos-sibilities to them, though, and that was the participation of Warnie in the scheme. His possible retirement from the Army was approaching, and if that happened he would need a home. The addition of his share of the estate could make a much nicer house possible than Lewis and Mrs. Moore by themselves could ever consider.

The prospect excited Warnie, though for an odd reason: he saw it as the opportunity to reconstitute the lost world of Leeborough, Little End Room and all. Indeed, it was his hope—and let us pause to re-member that Warnie was now thirty-five years old—to resurrect the world of Boxen and perhaps resume, with Lewis, the work of chroni-cling its labyrinthine history. Lewis chose to deal with these ideas gently but firmly, in a long letter of January 1930 that shows every sign of having been drafted with the utmost care. (It is stylistically far more precise than almost any of his letters.) On the question of what to do with the various Boxen toys that they had made, he insisted that they be burned, since God "has long since announced his intention of ending the universe with a general conflagration, we will follow suit.... No, Brother. The toys in the trunk are quite plainly corpses. We will resolve them into their elements, as nature will do to us." It seems that Warnie was amenable to this. But more alarming to Jack was the notion of a "new little end room," as Warnie had described it: "a place where we can always meet on the common ground of the past and *ipso facto* a museum of the Leeborough we want to preserve." Jack did not say to Warnie what he very likely was thinking—that there *was* no Leeborough he wanted to preserve—but instead questioned the "museum" idea: "a *museum* is preciously like a *mausoleum*." Underlying Warnie's suggestion, Jack saw, was the belief that their "common ground" could *only* be their shared boyhood past, and this belief Jack wished to challenge.

At this point the delicacy of the letter becomes positively surgical, because Jack knows perfectly well that his relationship with Minto— or, if not the relationship itself, then his refusal ever to explain it or even discuss it with his brother—has been the prime cause of Warnie's sense that they can fully share only their past. Here we find ourselves face-to-face with that black curtain that Lewis always lowered, in the presence (as far as we know) of everyone he knew, when the subject of Mrs. Moore arose. For at the very time when, in his letters to Arthur, Jack is full of new critical self-understanding and new remorse, to Warnie and on the issue of his life with Minto he is both stubborn and uncommunicative:

> I have no doubt that there have been times when you have felt that, shall we call it, Pigiebotianism was in danger of being swallowed up by, shall we say, Hillsborovianism.... I am very sorry to have been the cause of such a period (this is not an apology but a statement)—but isn't that period itself passed? We have both changed since the real old days, but, on the whole, we have changed in the same direction.

Two things are noteworthy here: first, the evasiveness of the term "Hillsborovianism," that is, naming his commitment to Minto and Maureen as a principle, summed up impersonally in the name of a rented house, rather than acknowledging that personal relationships are the heart of the matter and also the source of his conflict with Warnie. (Indeed, the terms Jack uses to represent his two conflicting commitments are intensely awkward, even ridiculous; that as gifted a writer as Jack could do no better suggests the difficulties with which he was faced in writing this letter.) Second, there is the refusal to apologize: he wishes he had not been the cause of Warnie's discomfort, but he does not repent of anything he did. Perhaps indeed he has nothing to apologize for, but at this point in his life, when his letters are so full of regrets about his relationship with his father and about the sins of his youth, it is odd to hear him take such an intransigent stance with his brother. He even concludes the letter by giving Warnie a kind of ultimatum—though it comes in language that at least acknowledges the real issues (the real *people*) at stake:

> I spoke above of Pigiebotianism and Hillsborovianism. I presume that if you join us you are prepared for a certain amount of compromise in this matter. I shall never be prepared to abandon Pigiebotianism to Hillsborovianism. On the other hand there are the others to whom I have given the right to expect that I shall not abandon Hillsborovianism to Pigiebotianism. Whether I was right or wrong, wise or foolish, to have done so originally, is now only an historical question: once having created expectations, one naturally fulfills them.

This was, as far as I know, as close as Jack ever got to telling Warnie anything substantial about his feelings for Mrs. Moore. And it seems noteworthy that he puts the matter in terms of duty: if one "naturally" fulfills the expectations one has created, that can only be because it is one's "natural" duty to do so. There is no talk here of love—as he had once talked to Arthur of being in love—nor even of pleasure. This does not mean that love and pleasure were absent from his life with Minto, any more than his raising the possibility that he was "wrong" or "foolish" to live with Minto means that he convicts himself of either sin. But when the curtain of intense privacy lifts so rarely, and so briefly, it is hard not to interpret what one sees carefully—and therefore, possibly, to overinterpret it.

What Warnie thought about this letter we do not know. In the selection of his brother's letters that he edited, he presents it without comment, and he does not mention it in his diary, though he does consider the implications, for him and for the others, of his joining the ménage. After much thought, he chooses to pitch in with them rather than strike out on his own.

In May 1930 Warnie was posted to Bulford, in Wiltshire, and got weekend leaves to participate in the house-hunting. In early July they finally found something to be excited about: a house near Headington Quarry—not far from Hillsboro—called the Kilns (from the kilns for brick-making that lay next to the house). Though the house was indeed larger than Hillsboro and attractive on that account, what caught the imagination of the Lewis men was the property: eight full acres, with a pond surrounded by woods. The grounds, wrote Warnie in his diary, are "such stuff as dreams are made on. I never imagined that for us any such garden would ever come within the sphere of discussion." Within weeks it was theirs. The house would eventually become almost as famous as its principal owner; today it is the site of many pilgrimages, but the Kilns one may now visit is considerably more elegant and better kept up than it was in Lewis's lifetime, when it often tended toward the ramshackle. On the other hand, it was much more secluded then—that part of Headington was semirural—whereas today it feels like it is right in the middle of town. Whatever its virtues or vices, it was home, and for the three adults—Jack, Warnie, and Minto—it would be home for most or all of the rest of their lives.

With the purchase of the Kilns, and the commitment to Christianity, a certain stability had come to reign in Lewis's life. He had a profession, a house, a family (of sorts), and a clear set of religious commitments. For the next seventeen years or so—until Minto's physical and psychological condition began seriously to deteriorate—the outward circumstances of his life would change little. He would continue to live in College through the working week and return to the Kilns for weekends and holidays (and many afternoons, when he loved to dig in his garden and the surrounding woods). He would faithfully attend chapel and church, usually accompanied to the latter by Warnie, who had shared his brother's skepticism about religion until his own return to Christianity (almost simultaneous with Jack's). After his formal retirement from the Army at the end of 1932, Warnie would spend his days in one of Jack's Magdalen rooms, occupying himself for several years with organizing and typing copies of what the brothers came to call the Lewis Papers—the letters and other documents of the family, going back several generations, which had been collected and rescued from Little Lea. (Generations of Lewis's pupils, reading their weekly essays to their tutor, would grow familiar with the sound of typing from the next room and the occasional glimpse of a bald, bespectacled man drifting in and out.) This would be the frame of Lewis's life for almost two decades: even the Second World War would bring little change to it, though the war would certainly bring other changes.

Internally, however, the going, especially in the early 1930s, was not so smooth. I have already mentioned Lewis's reconsideration—especially in his letters to Arthur—of the picture he had built up over the years of his pre-Christian life. This reconsideration extended to his whole life—not just his "moral" or "spiritual" condition, but everything about himself, including his aesthetic and intellectual ambitions. In August 1930 he found himself needing to respond to a request from Arthur for advice: a friend had told Arthur that he should abandon the novel he was working on, and Arthur thought that Lewis, as the author of two collections of poems, should be able to give him good advice. But Lewis replied:

> I am *still* as disappointed an author as you. From the age of sixteen onwards I had one single ambition, from which I never wavered, in the prosecution of which I spent every ounce I could, on which I really and deliberately staked my whole contentment: and I recognize myself as having unmistakably failed in it.

That ambition, the letter makes clear, was not so much to write great poetry as to be *recognized* as a major poet, to be "approved as a writer ... distinguished beyond our fellows." And he confesses that there is "rest" to be had in giving up all such hopes—and that in that rest he can at last say, "Thy will be done." (But what *is* "Thy will"? That question always remained.)

In any event, he kept writing. He started a philosophical novel that he called *The Moving Image,* but soon abandoned it; he continued to work on narrative and lyric poems. But he lacked clear direction, at least in his nonscholarly work. He did not know what *difference* being a Christian was supposed to make, or could make, in his life as a literary writer. He needed clarification—he needed a better grasp of the intellectual landscape through which he was moving. In August 1932, when he was taking an Irish holiday at Arthur's house, he found himself sketching that landscape and forming the story of a man's travels through it. In two weeks he had written his first book of prose, an allegorical narrative called *The Pilgrim's Regress.*

It is worth taking a moment to reflect on this achievement. As we have just seen, all of Lewis's literary ambitions to this point in his life had revolved around poetry. His prose publications at this point consisted of a mere handful of book reviews and brief academic articles, though he had been working (fitfully) on a scholarly book for several years. This burst of fluency had therefore to be completely unexpected to Lewis—unexpected, but also gratifying, for he learned, in that fortnight with Arthur, that he could write vivid prose and write it quickly, with minimal revision. And so he would write prose for the rest of his life: with a nib pen flowing across page after page of paper with few pauses—except to dip the pen in the inkwell—and still fewer corrections or crossings-out. (He never learned to type.) After *The Pilgrim's Regress* he would produce thirty-five more books of prose—slightly more than one a year—and hundreds of articles and essays on an astonishingly wide range of subjects. And during his most productive years he was not only working as a tutor but caring for an increasingly infirm Mrs. Moore. He *had* to be fluent, else he would have gotten nothing done.

To be sure, fluency did not always serve him well: the sloppiness of many of Lewis's books was immensely annoying to Tolkien (than whom a more obsessively careful writer never existed) and actually became a cause of significant tension in their friendship. Probably all his books—with the signal exception of the long-labored-over history of sixteenth-century English literature—would have benefited from at least one more good revision before being sent to the publisher. The inconsistencies in the Narnia books troubled Lewis, and had he lived longer, or been in better health in his final years, it is likely that he would have cleaned those up. But in general he seems not to have worried much about the flaws in his books—nor could he have, since by the time he sent one to the publisher he was halfway through the next. He felt he had work to do, a calling to fulfill, and given the limited time and difficult circumstances in which for most of his life he had to write, surely he would have appreciated that great maxim of Chesterton's, "Anything worth doing is worth doing badly."

When he started the story that became *The Pilgrim's Regress*, Lewis lacked that sense of calling—he had nothing yet to drive him forward, to give him a sense of purpose as a writer. But the writing of that book was a key step in the process of discovering the direction that he would take. This does not mean that *The Pilgrim's Regress* itself is the kind of thing that he would later write, nor does it mean that the book is a success. *The Pilgrim's Regress* is C. S. Lewis's least successful book, as he himself knew—he was a shrewd discerner of its faults. In a 1943 preface to a new edition of the book, he wrote, "On re-reading this book ten years after I wrote it, I find its chief faults to be those two which I myself least easily forgive in the books of other men: needless obscurity, and an uncharitable temper." It is indeed rather uncharitable, and certainly very obscure—but then Lewis was not really writing it for others so much as for himself. For the second (1935) edition of the book, Lewis wrote an "Argument"—a brief summary—of each chapter, just as John Milton had been asked to do for *Paradise Lost,* whose publisher thought no one would understand it if it lacked its own internal *Cliffs Notes.* For the 1943 edition Lewis abandoned those "Arguments" in favor of ongoing marginal commentary exactly like that found in the book's most direct model, Bunyan's *The Pilgrim's Progress.* And even the very first edition contained—because friends who had seen the story in manuscript form requested it—a *Mappa Mundi,* a map of the world through which John, the protagonist, travels.

But for Lewis the story itself simply *was* a *Mappa Mundi,* a detailed sketch of the intellectual and moral world through which he had passed on his way to Christian belief. He needed this exercise in narrative cartography to establish his coordinates, to see where he had started, what dangers he had passed through, and what brave new world he was now living in. It is the story of voyage and return, very like the patterns sketched by Chesterton in two books that were especially important to Lewis, *Orthodoxy* and *The Everlasting Man.* At the beginning of *Orthodoxy* Chesterton imagines writing the story of "an English yachtsman who slightly miscalculated his course and discovered England under the impression that it was a new island in the South Seas." At the beginning of *The Everlasting Man* he imagines a boy who leaves his hillside home to go on an adventure in search of a giant's grave, "and when he was far enough from home he looked back and saw that his own farm and kitchen-garden . . . were but parts of some such gigantic figure, on which he had always lived, but which was too large and too close to be seen." John, the protagonist of *The Pilgrim's Regress,* enacts both of these stories: he leaves his home in Puritania in fear of that realm's Landlord, only to make an ultimate return, when he sees his homeland with new eyes—in one sense rediscovering it, in another discovering it for the first time. Puritania under an imagined tyrant is a very different land from Puritania under the benevolent guidance of the Landlord who, as John tells his friend Vertue, "has knit our hearts so closely to time and place—to one friend rather than another and one shire more than all the land."

The chief figure who guides John to this renewed understanding of his homeland is "Mother Kirk," and clearly Lewis meant for her to represent orthodox Christianity in any or all of its forms. Many readers, however, thought of the classic Roman Catholic formulation "Holy Mother Church" and assumed that Lewis was (as he would have put it) a "Papist." Perhaps they should have attended more closely to the word "Kirk"—the Kirk (Church) of Scotland has historically been defiantly Presbyterian—and to the fact that John *returns* to Puritania. But what is really noteworthy here is that Lewis is already groping toward an understanding of the importance of a transdenominational orthodoxy—the kind of thing that he would later call, borrowing a phrase from the seventeenth-century preacher and writer Richard Baxter, "mere Christianity."

This taking hold of simple orthodoxy as a standard and guide is important, because otherwise *The Pilgrim's Regress* is an overwhelmingly negative book. In submitting the manuscript to Dent, the publishers of *Dymer,* he wrote that the book "is a kind of Bunyan up to date. It is serious in intention but has a good many more comic passages than I originally intended, and also a fair controversial interest (the things chiefly ridiculed are Anglo Catholicism, Materialism, Sitwellism, Psychoanalysis, and T. S. Elliot)." The Sitwells were a family of writers and artists who lived near Oxford and who represented, for Lewis, decadent aestheticism; the early career of T. S. Eliot (not "Elliot") would have been, for Lewis, a variety of Sitwellism, though his more recent embrace of "Anglo Catholicism" would have made him a target on those grounds instead. Lewis's dislike of Eliot verged on the pathological and seems to have been based largely on misunderstanding: until late in his life he did not grasp the depth and seriousness of Eliot's conversion to Christianity, which occurred several years before Lewis's own, nor did he see how many of his beliefs about culture and ethics Eliot shared. (Lewis's *The Abolition of Man* and Eliot's *Notes Toward the Definition of Culture* and *The Idea of a Christian Society* are nearly contemporaneous works of cultural criticism that walk a long, long way along the same road.) Almost certainly these misunderstandings were based on sheer ignorance: though Lewis read and responded quite negatively to some of Eliot's literary criticism, it is not clear that he knew any of the poetry—though he makes contemptuous reference to "The Love Song of J. Alfred Prufrock" in books and letters and calls *The Waste Land* an "infernal" poem in a 1935 letter. Lewis was utterly unaware of Eliot's purposes in writing the poem, nor did he know that, in the succeeding fifteen years, Eliot had become a strong critic of his earlier work and had set a completely new poetic and direction for himself. For Lewis to pronounce such harsh judgments based on so little evidence—and to dismiss Eliot's conversion to Christianity because the *kind* of Christianity he embraced was "Anglo Catholicism"—is really rather troubling.

Indeed, much of *The Pilgrim's Regress* is devoted to rejecting ideas Lewis really doesn't know much about—or elevating the importance of ones he does know. From reading John's adventures one would think that followers of the German philosopher Hegel constituted the leading philosophical tradition at the time the book was written. In fact, the "dynasty of Green, Bradley, and Bosanquet," as Lewis calls it—the "British Hegelians," as the histories of philosophy call them—was strictly an Oxford dynasty, and even there had already fallen (in the eyes of many) by the time Lewis arrived as an undergraduate. Meanwhile, in Cambridge truly major figures such as Bertrand Russell, Alfred North Whitehead, and Ludwig Wittgenstein dominated the scene—but there is no place for them on John's *Mappa Mundi*.

All (or most) of this Lewis later understood, which is why his 1943 preface to the book is so apologetic. But at the time of writing he was trying to clear a path for himself, a path for his thinking and writing. Through all the negativity some positive commitments shine through—products of his recent experience that would continue to be important for his future thinking. One I have already noted, and that is the grasping for the general Christian orthodoxy represented by Mother Kirk. But perhaps even more important to the narrative is the centrality of the experience of Joy. John's pilgrimage begins with his attempts to satisfy a longing that comes upon him when he looks out at a beautiful island. Most of his struggles thereafter arise because he is pursuing some false means of fulfilling the desire aroused in him by that sight. It is especially significant that moral and intellectual errors alike arise from misunderstandings of this desire and of how to respond to it.

Much of this is revealed to John by History, who explains to him the great value, and great danger, of coming to know the truth (especially about the Landlord) through pictures and images—through stories. Pictures are dangerous without "the Rules," that is, the moral Law, which teaches us how to interpret those pictures. Without the Rules to guide us, when given a glimpse of an attractive picture—like John's glimpse of the beautiful island—we "keep on trying to get the same picture again," and when that does not work we go on "making up more stories for [ourselves] about the pictures, and then pretending the stories are true." Of course, History explains, even if we possess both the Rules and the pictures—and are therefore much better off than people who have only one or the other, or neither—we can remain ignorant of "a third thing which is neither the Rules nor the pictures and was brought into the country by the Landlord's Son." That third thing, the Gospel, is now in the charge of Mother Kirk: "That is why the best thing of all is to find Mother Kirk at the very beginning." But that was not John's, or Lewis's, good fortune, so we see throughout the narrative both the power of "pictures" and their limitations. For the rest of his life Lewis would write books about the Rules and books of pictures—but both kinds of books were intended to draw people to the "third thing": the Gospel that he had finally received from the Landlord's Son.

Also crucial to the narrative is the passage—modeled on the chapter of *Pilgrim's Progress* in which Christian is imprisoned in the dungeon of Doubting Castle, the home of the giant Despair—in which John is taken captive by the Spirit of the Age. In his captivity John is told that the presence of a desire indicates not the existence but the nonexistence of the thing desired. (Neither islands nor mountains are real, he is told.) More terrifyingly, he is granted a kind of X-ray vision that allows him to see through people and things—or, in the terms of the star Ramandu, to see "what they are made of"—and is encouraged to believe that that is what things really *are*. To "see through" something is often not to see at all—what is required is a restoration of the innocent eye, the eye that can see wonderingly.

John learns his lessons well and ends his story by coming back home—but now he leaves there not in fear of the Landlord, but in humble obedience to the teachings of Mother Kirk. John's story ends with his "crossing the brook"—that is, with his death. And here is where his tale diverges from that of his author. For Lewis had many years left to live. What would he do with them?

Well, some things—many things—demanded his attention and his energy regardless of what he might have preferred to do. There were Minto and Maureen, and in a sense Warnie, to care for. (Though Maureen was by now in her twenties and working as a music teacher, she still lived at the Kilns and would do so until her marriage to a fellow music teacher named Leonard Blake in 1940.) There were pupils to supervise and friends to meet. And above all there were books to write. After spending so much time and energy trying to establish a literary career for himself, in the late 1930s Lewis found a career emerging almost without his willing it. *The Pilgrim's Regress* was not really the start of it, though it had slightly more success than his poems had had. Rather, it was his first scholarly book, *The Allegory of Love,* published by Oxford University Press in 1936, that opened to him an audience that he had never really sought or imagined.

For a first scholarly book it is remarkably bold—but perhaps that is because it was a decade in the making. (Lewis was thirty-eight in the year it was published.) By considering allegory both theoretically and historically, and by comparing traditions of love poetry from ancient Rome to medieval France and then on to early Renaissance Italy and England at the turn of the seventeenth century, it took on an enormous intellectual territory and did so with what those Italians would have called *sprezzatura*—the performing of an extraordinarily difficult task as though it were easy. The American scholar Norman F. Cantor, in surveying the achievement of medievalists throughout the twentieth century, ranks *The Allegory of Love* very highly indeed: it was a "bold, original, seminal" book that "rocked the transatlantic Anglophone world of medieval studies and did a great deal of good."

We consider some of the content of this book later on, but for now I merely want to point out that this one book established C. S. Lewis as a significant figure in the British intellectual world. Even before it was published, scholars who had read it in draft begged Lewis to write a volume in the ongoing *Oxford History of English Literature,* and the early success of *Allegory* led the press to publish a collection of his scholarly essays, *Rehabilitations.* It is likely that his scholarly reputation—and his particular reputation as a remarkable stylist as well as a deeply learned man—got him a better hearing from publishers for his first novel, *Out of the Silent Planet* (1938), though the vocal support of Tolkien, who had recently had a surprise success with *The Hobbit,* helped too. A publisher named Ashley Sampson put together the Lewis who was a rising Oxford don with the Lewis who had written *Out of the Silent Planet* and invited him to write a book for a series he was developing called "The Christian Challenge." This proved to be Lewis's first work of apologetics, *The Problem of Pain* (1940). Almost immediately thereafter came Lewis's first truly popular book, *The Screwtape Letters* (1941), the correspondence of a fictional devil, and then—because J. W. Welch, the director of the BBC's Religious Broadcasting Department, had been touched and impressed by *The Problem of Pain*—the radio broadcasts that made him truly famous and were later collected as *Mere Christianity.*

Lewis would never again have to worry about getting anything published; his future concern would rather be deciding which of the many demands on his time and skill he could meet. Being an exceptionally fluid writer who rarely revised, he could meet more of those demands than most writers could have. In the two decades from 1936 to 1956, he published at least twenty-four books (counting *Mere Christianity* as one book rather than the three short volumes of its original publication). Burdened by overwork in his job and at home, occupied for some years with the task of reinventing his inner life and recharging his imagination, Lewis in the late 1930s began making up for lost time at an extraordinary rate. He seems to have entered his maturity as a Christian and as a thinker almost overnight and immediately to have begun putting a set of core ideas into various forms and genres. It was common for him to develop an idea in one way in a science fiction novel, another way in a scholarly book, yet another way in a work of Christian apologetics, and in even a different way in one of the Narnia tales. These echoes yield not mere repetition but rather a set of powerful insights or concerns being refracted through different facets of experience.

This is the point in Lewis's life when a strong unity of consciousness, or single-mindedness—or what Owen Barfield called his "presence of mind" ("somehow what he thought about everything was secretly present in what he said about anything")—became notably characteristic of the man, so that to describe his books one at a time is to court the very repetition that the books themselves manage to avoid. A more organic treatment of his thought and work is called for. Fortunately, though his physical life was oddly compartmentalized— many college and university colleagues who knew him quite well had no idea of his life with Minto—his intellectual life was anything but. He was blessed to live much of his daily life in environments where his various interests and passions could blend and merge and illuminate one another. Lewis was, after all, a *teacher:* the lecture hall and the tutorial session were the environments in which many of his most deeply held convictions were brewed. So it is in seeing his life as a don that we can best discern how that distinctive "presence of mind" took form and took flight.

EIGHT

"Do you think I am trying to weave a spell?"

"The plain fact is," wrote one of Lewis's friends, "he hated teaching." There can be little surprise in this, considering how deeply he hated his own schooling: there is a certain irony in reflecting that this young man, whose second book's plot begins when a student slays his teacher in front of the classroom, would end up being a teacher himself. It is true, of course, that he found university life far less onerous than his earlier schooling, but for Jack Lewis even good tutors and good lectures were little more than necessary evils, in that they prevented him from doing what he always preferred to do: reading and writing.

Even his devoted biographers, Roger Lancelyn Green and Walter Hooper, do not deny Lewis's dislike for his job but simply point out that he fulfilled his obligations faithfully. It was the tutorials that he most loathed: the endless series of pupils droning through shabby and half-baked or simply unimaginative essays. Many of Lewis's former pupils have paid great tribute to his skill and dedication as a tutor— indeed, one of them, Derek Brewer, later a distinguished medievalist, said that "many of his pupils became teachers of one sort or another and all, or most of them, became his friends"—and that is all the more remarkable given that tutoring was drudgery in which he could take no pleasure. Still less could he abide serving as an external examiner for other institutions, since this involved marking endless piles of paper written by people he had never met, but for many summers he did it to supplement his relatively meager don's income. (Tolkien did the same.)

The giving of lectures Lewis seems to have taken at least some pleasure in; certainly he put a great deal of effort into making himself the most stimulating lecturer possible. I mentioned earlier his plan, right from the beginning of his career, to deliver lectures from notes rather than reading them, which was the practice of most dons. Tolkien, for instance, was notorious for reading his lectures in a rapid mumble directed usually toward the floor, only raising his voice and speaking clearly when he was reciting Anglo-Saxon poetry. By contrast, Lewis had a booming voice—the "hroom, hroom" of Treebeard in *The Lord of the Rings* is an echo of him—and used it well. His students were usually struck first by his appearance: he wore old tweed jackets until they fell apart, kept well into his fifties overcoats that he had inherited from Albert, and, with his ruddy complexion and hearty manner, reminded many students of a grocer or a butcher. But the voice soon captivated them. Little of Ulster remained in it—in 1928 he would write casually to his father of his "southern English" accent, and by 1944 he could say that he had tried to keep his northern Ireland accent but failed—except, perhaps, for a delight in rolling his r's; as I listen to the recording made late in his life of his book *The Four Loves*, the accent sounds really quite plummy. But it was a deep voice and an exceptionally strong voice, and it mesmerized his audiences, whether in lecture halls, churches, or living rooms when his "broadcast talks" came over the radio.

(When *Time* magazine published an article about Lewis in 1947—we consider in a later chapter the fame that led to that article—he was initially described as "a short, thickset man with a ruddy face and a big voice," but his friends habitually described him as a "big" man and even a "tall" man. And in a letter he wrote in 1954 to some American schoolchildren he described himself as "tall, fat, rather bald, red-faced, double-chinned, black-haired," and added that he had a deep voice and wore reading glasses. All that noted, a less detailed but more scientific item may resolve this perplexity: in April 1917, when Lewis joined the Oxford University Officers' Training Corps, he had a physical examination, and the records say that he measured just shy of five feet eleven inches and weighed thirteen stone, or about 182 pounds. So he was indeed, if not unusually large, taller and heavier than the average man in America and Europe alike. *Time* got it wrong.)

As the popularity of his lectures grew (and the rate at which it grew accelerated when he became a well-known spokesman for Christianity), undergraduates would not only flock to his lectures but seek every opportunity to talk with him before or after. Therefore Lewis—who hated answering questions anyway—developed the strategy of arriving at the last minute, sometimes even beginning his lecture while he was still in the hallway so that he was in full flight by the time he entered the room, and then, as the period drew to a close, while still talking, gathering his notes and walking out of the room, declaiming his last sentence as he departed the premises. He would be long gone before his dutiful audience had finished scribbling the great man's pearls of wisdom.

As he told Leo Baker, at this point he was "chiefly a medievalist," and the lectures he was best known for were called "Prolegomena to Medieval Literature" and "Prolegomena to Renaissance Literature." Long before he ever thought of defending Christianity, he defended—in articles, lectures, and a book—the beauty and wisdom of the premodern literature of Europe. Such a defense required that he root out what he called "chronological snobbery": "the uncritical acceptance of the intellectual climate common to our own age and the assumption that whatever has gone out of date is on that account discredited." He knew that this tendency was strong among undergraduates, because it had been a key feature of his own intellectual makeup in his undergraduate days; only through his friendship with Barfield had he been shown how unforgivably lazy such "snobbery" really is. Barfield taught him a new catechism: "You must find out why [a belief held commonly in the past] went out of date. Was it ever refuted (and if so by whom, where, and how conclusively) or did it merely die away as fashions do? If the latter, this tells us nothing about its truth or falsehood." And if an undergraduate as well read as Jack Lewis, and as temperamentally disposed to love what he simply called "old books," required that catechism, the average Oxford student would have been in far more desperate need of it. Lewis never forgot this.

The first obstacle to a proper appreciation for "old books" is this common failure to understand that our own world is also merely a "period" in intellectual history, with many unquestioned assumptions that later generations will find absurd. It is certain that those later generations will look back at the ancestors that we despise or mock and conclude that they got many things right that we got wrong. (And after all, do we not sometimes say that there was wisdom in ancient Greece or Rome or China or India that the modern Western world has neglected or forgotten?) But this is a very hard lesson to learn in an age that believes that its rapid technological development must be

accompanied by like progress in morality and wisdom. Lewis was not
even convinced that technological changes should regularly earn the
label of "progress"—he thought that buttons served far better than
zippers to keep the fly of his trousers closed, and he dipped a pen in an
inkwell to the end of his days—and was thoroughly skeptical of any
claim that we morally exceed our ancestors. In his first book of Christian apologetics, *The Problem of Pain,* he argues that human cultures
are prone to "lopsided ethical developments": they have their "pet
virtues" but also their "curious insensibilities" to other virtues. Why
should our time be any different? Or perhaps we believe that the "pet
virtue" of our time—which in this book Lewis identifies as "humane-
ness," though soon afterward he settles on "unselfishness" as the better word for it—is *such* a great virtue that "God might be content
with us on that ground." If you are inclined so to think, then Lewis
suggests that you "ask yourself whether you think God ought to have
been content with the cruelty of cruel ages because they excelled in
courage or chastity. . . . From considering how the cruelty of our ancestors looks to us, you may get some inkling of how our softness,
worldliness, and timidity would have looked to them, and hence how
both must look to God."

(Looking at the previous paragraph, one may easily see that the defense of old *books* and old *ideas* was, for Lewis, bound up quite
tightly with some old *beliefs*—especially beliefs about God and the
character of God's Creation. His students would invariably say that he
never made any attempt to impose or even "push" his Christian beliefs
in lectures or tutorials, but it could not have escaped Lewis's notice—
or that of the more attentive students—that in laying the groundwork
for an appreciation of medieval and Renaissance literature, he was
also silently removing some of the impediments to an appreciation of
the *religion* of those eras—which happened to be Christianity. Granted,
The Problem of Pain is an openly Christian book rather than a university lecture, but Lewis employed the same rhetorical techniques in
many different settings.)

The great books of the past, then, if we read them properly and
carefully, can be mirrors in which we see the sins and limitations of
our own period. And perhaps once we see them we can begin to remedy them. In *The Discarded Image,* a book not published until after
Lewis's death but largely transcribed from the "Prolegomena" lectures, he describes the outlines of the medieval "Model" of the universe—its structure, its inhabitants, its history—and then writes in an
epilogue:

Flora Lewis during her university years

"Jacksie"

Warnie, Albert, Jack (probably taken not long after
Flora's death)

Albert and Jack, when Jack was studying with Kirk

Jack and Paddy Moor on an army training exercise

Jack, Maureen, and Minto at the seaside

The Kilns (taken near the time that the Lewises purchased it)

Jack and Warnie on a walking tour

Joy Lewis in the garden at the Kilns

Jack at his desk

I have made no serious effort to hide the fact that the old Model delights me as I believe it delighted our ancestors. Few constructions of the imagination seem to me to have combined splendour, sobriety, and coherence in the same degree. It is possible that some readers have long been itching to remind me that it had a serious defect; it was not true.

I agree. It was not true.

But having acknowledged this point, Lewis insists that we are still not free to dismiss the Model altogether. For we now know—thanks in part to the development of quantum physics, which reveals that the Newtonian laws that apply uniformly in the world visible to us do not apply at all on the subatomic level—that our own Model is not simply and straightforwardly "true" either: our understanding of the natural world remains a "Model," not simply a collection of Facts. "We can no longer dismiss the change of Models as a simple progress from error to truth. No Model is a catalogue of ultimate realities, and none is a mere fantasy."

Lewis is certainly not saying here that the shift from believing that the Sun revolves around the Earth to the belief that the Earth revolves around the Sun is a mere social construct, subject to revision when intellectual fashions change. Rather, he is saying that when we rejected geocentrism we rejected a lot of other beliefs as well because they were part of that Model—but not all of those beliefs had been disproven in the way that geocentrism was. We tend to assume that if our ancestors were so wrong about that, they must have been equally wrong about everything else, and we go on to assume that anything we believe they must have disbelieved. So we hear that someone we call "Medieval Man" thought that the world was flat (which is untrue). Or we say that our ancestors believed that the sun revolved around the earth because they naively and arrogantly assumed that they were the most important beings in the universe (which is also untrue*). It turns out that

---

* "The central position had not implied pre-eminence," Lewis writes in his history of English literature in the sixteenth century. "On the contrary, it had implied . . . 'the lowest story in the house,' the point at which all the light, heat and movement descending from the nobler spheres finally died out into darkness, coldness, and passivity." Therefore when the people of this period came to accept the alternative Copernican model, they were less likely to feel embarrassment or a sense of demotion than "exhilaration"—we're not as blighted as we had thought.

it is a lot easier to keep believing what everyone around us believes if we ignore or misrepresent the beliefs of our ancestors.

In 1940 Lewis started writing a series of fictional letters from a demon named Screwtape to his pupil, a tempter-in-training named Wormwood. Does this Infernal setting tell us what Lewis really thought about being a tutor? At the least it tells us that the didactic role was one that came easily to him—even if he was turning it upside down for the purposes of this book, with good becoming bad and bad good, "Our Heavenly Father" replaced by "Our Father Below," and the "Beatific Vision" that Christian mystics seek giving way to a "Miserific Vision" of the depths of Hell and its devilish Proprietor. (Not all of the readers of the *Guardian*—the Anglican weekly in which the letters were originally published—got the joke: one clergyman wrote in to cancel his subscription to the magazine on the grounds that the advice given by Wormwood was "not only erroneous but positively diabolical.")

Demons themselves are teachers, of a sort, and in Screwtape's view they have been very successful ones. He is especially proud of their ability to instruct their "patients"—as he calls the humans they are charged with tempting—in a system of thought whose prevalence made Lewis's job much harder. Screwtape calls this system "the Historical Point of View." "Only the learned read old books," he boasts to Wormwood, "and we have now so dealt with the learned that they are of all men the least likely to acquire wisdom by doing so. We have done this by inculcating the Historical Point of View, [which,] put briefly, means that when a learned man is presented with any statement in an ancient author, the one question he never asks is whether it is true." Instead, the scholar asks about who influenced this ancient writer or whom this writer influenced, describes how "the learned man's own colleagues" have misunderstood the author, and so on. "To regard the ancient writer as a possible source of knowledge—to anticipate that what he said could possibly modify your thoughts or your behavior—this would be rejected as unutterably simple-minded."

The Historical Point of View is one of the chief means by which we insulate ourselves from the possible wisdom of our ancestors. Another is the mode of thought that Lewis humorously calls "Bulverism," after its imaginary founder, Ezekiel Bulver,

whose destiny was determined at the age of five when he heard his mother say to his father—who had been maintaining that

two sides of a triangle were together greater than the third—"Oh
you say that *because you are a man.*" "At that moment," E.
Bulver assures us, "there flashed across my opening mind the
great truth that refutation is no necessary part of argument. Assume that your opponent is wrong, and then explain his error,
and the world will be at your feet. Attempt to prove that he is
wrong or (worse still) try to find out whether he is wrong or
right, and the national dynamism of our age will thrust you to
the wall." That is how Bulver became one of the makers of the
Twentieth Century.

In writings of this kind, Lewis produces an incisive critique of what
Marxists call "ideology," that is, the system of beliefs that are so taken
for granted in a given culture that hardly anyone even notices that
they *are* beliefs—they are treated as unquestioned facts. Lewis was an
exceptionally skillful exposer of ideological forces and their titanic influence over us, but he rarely gets credit for this from contemporary
intellectuals because it is *their* most treasured beliefs that, more often
than not, he is exposing. So instead of praising him for the acuity of
his insights, they call him "reactionary" or "Victorian"—precisely the
sorts of things that Bulverists and chronological snobs are bound to
call him, given their premises.

For to say that someone is "reactionary" or "Victorian" is to say
nothing at all about the validity (the truthfulness) of the positions he
or she takes. And indeed, this is the diabolical purpose of Bulverism
and the Historical Point of View: to remove questions of truth and
falsehood from the mind's life. In his very first letter to his nephew,
Screwtape reminds Wormwood that his patient "doesn't think of
doctrines as primarily 'true' or 'false,' but as 'academic' or 'practical,' 'outworn' or 'contemporary,' 'conventional' or 'ruthless.' Jargon,
not argument, is your best ally in keeping him from the Church.
Don't waste time trying to make him think that materialism is *true!*
Make him think that it is strong, or stark, or courageous—that it is
the philosophy of the future. That's the sort of thing he cares about."
And the sort of thing, Screwtape insists, he *needs* to think about.
Screwtape is proud of the inroads this indifference to truth has made
into the Church itself: "Only today I have found a passage in a Christian writer where he recommends his own version of Christianity
on the ground that 'only such a faith can outlast the death of old
cultures and the birth of new civilisations.' You see the little rift?

'Believe this, not because it is true, but for some other reason.' That's the game."

And it is a game that Screwtape and his colleagues have played well. What seems to concern Lewis more than any other aspect of this situation is the way that, after being indoctrinated into a systematic disregard of truth and falsehood, people can find themselves unable to recognize the difference even when it is put before them plainly: they come to possess an *invincible* ignorance, or nearly so. Thus, in *That Hideous Strength*—a novel that Lewis began soon after completing *The Screwtape Letters*—Mark Studdock, when presented with a dense fog of "progressive" and technocratic rhetoric from the leaders of NICE, has no means of resistance:

> It must be remembered that in Mark's mind hardly one rag of noble thought, either Christian or Pagan, had a secure lodging. His education had been neither scientific nor classical—merely "Modern." The severities both of abstraction and of high human tradition had passed him by: and he had neither peasant shrewdness nor aristocratic honour to help him. He was a man of straw, a glib examinee in subjects that require no exact knowledge (he had always done well on Essays and General Papers).

We can learn a lot about the force and point of Lewis's critique by noting these two small facts: (1) Mark is by profession a sociologist, and (2) NICE puts him to work writing newspaper editorials. Where do rhetorical flourishes inattentive to truth or falsehood find a happy home? In the "soft" social sciences and in journalism (or so thinks Lewis).

Note that Lewis's quarrel here is clearly not with science itself, but with pseudo-science: a "Modern" education that clothes itself in scientific language without undergoing the "severities" of scientific method.* A rather comical—though in the end nearly tragic—version of this

---

* Having said that Lewis was against pseudo-science rather than science, I nevertheless find myself recalling a scene from Tom Stoppard's great play *Arcadia* (London: Faber, 1995) in which an English don, Bernard Nightingale, unleashes a tirade on an unsuspecting scientist: "How did you people con us out of all that status? All that money? And why are you so pleased with yourselves?" One suspects that similar questions at least hover in the back of Lewis's mind, since he lived through the very period in which scientists seized "all that status" and "all that money" from the defenders of classical education.

rhetoric is spouted by Uncle Andrew in *The Magician's Nephew*. Though Andrew is the "magician" of the title, he is more of a mad scientist: though he has inherited rings with magical powers and knows a bit of the history of magic, he calls his work with the rings "experiments" and speaks of "testing" his ideas. He even has guinea pigs. This conflation of magic and science is central to Lewis's thinking, as we will soon discover, but for now I want to emphasize what Uncle Andrew's years as a magician mean to him when he is faced with *real* Magic.

First, the magical (if infernal) power of the Empress Jadis, when Digory and Polly accidentally bring her to our world, is invisible to him. Though when Digory sees the two of them together he immediately recognizes what's what—"*Him* a magician? Not much. Now *she's* the real thing"—Uncle Andrew never gets past a kind of bewildered and frightened infatuation. She is to him a "very distinguished person" and, of course, in the last words of the book, a "dem fine woman." Not only does her gigantic physical size seem to escape him, but he is (if possible) still more blind to her *libido dominandi*, her overwhelming will to power: it is as though he cannot even hear her when she speaks of her determination to rule our world or, failing that, destroy it altogether, as she destroyed her own world, Charn. To Uncle Andrew this terrifying giant, who, even in our world with her powers greatly diminished, can make animals run mad and break iron lampposts with her bare hands, is but a "dem fine woman"—a little frightening, perhaps, but in a sexy kind of way. The worst he can say to her is that, when they were in the restaurant together, her "behavior and conversation attracted the unfavorable attention of everyone present."

And if he is blind to her presence and deaf to her words, what hope is there for him to understand what happens when he finds himself in Narnia at the moment of its creation? In fact, he utters the words of reproach I have just quoted at the very moment that Aslan is singing Narnia into being, and though the cabby tells him that "watchin' and listenin's the thing at present; not talking," Uncle Andrew can neither see nor hear. When the fragment of the London lamppost roots itself in Narnian soil and begins to grow, he does not see Aslan's creative Magic—his "Model" really is, in the end, more pseudo-scientific than magical—but instead merely exclaims, "The commercial possibilities of this country are unbounded." And since it is manifestly impossible for lions to sing, the longer and the more beautiful the Lion sang, the harder Uncle Andrew tried to make himself believe that he could hear nothing but roaring. Now the trouble about trying to make yourself stupider than you really are is that you very often succeed. Uncle Andrew did. He soon did hear nothing but roaring in Aslan's song. Soon he couldn't have heard anything else even if he had wanted to. And when at last the Lion spoke and said, "Narnia awake," he didn't hear any words: he heard only a snarl.

Soon he couldn't have heard anything else even if he had wanted to. This is the tragedy of Uncle Andrew, as it is the tragedy of Weston and Devine in Lewis's first science fiction novel, *Out of the Silent Planet*. These two scientists, having gone to all the trouble of traveling to Mars—whose true name, Lewis tells us, is Malacandra—simply cannot grasp that the creatures they find there are fully sentient, indeed, far more sentient than Weston and Devine themselves. They are incapable of the careful looking and attentive listening that would alert them to the presence of *eldila* (angel-like spirits) and the Oyarsa (governing spirit of the planet) himself. They just hop around the Malacandrians like fools, shouting in pidgin English like Victorian explorers in solar topees hectoring the savages. The satire gets rather too broad here, but its point is more than valid.

Likewise, as we have already seen, in *The Last Battle* the Dwarfs proclaim so insistently and repeatedly that "the Dwarfs are for the Dwarfs"—they teach themselves so well—that they make themselves incapable not only of receiving Aslan's gifts but even of recognizing that anyone is giving them anything:

> "Well, at any rate there's no Humbug here. We haven't let anyone take us in. The Dwarfs are for the Dwarfs."
>
> "You see," said Aslan. "They will not let us help them. They have chosen cunning instead of belief. Their prison is only in their own minds, yet they are in that prison; and so afraid of being taken in that they cannot be taken out."

If we are tempted to think the Dwarfs comical, we might consider their exact analogues, the terrible Ghosts of *The Great Divorce*. This book—which Lewis began immediately after completing *That Hideous Strength*, though he had been thinking over its topic for more than a decade—is, like *Screwtape*, a "theological fantasy." In it Lewis envisions a modern retelling of a curious but ancient idea that Christians have sometimes considered: the *refrigerium*, a kind of holiday for the damned. The idea seems to have originated in the thought that through the power of his Resurrection Jesus earns an annual Easter "day off" for the denizens of Hell. In Lewis's imagination, however, the people (or rather, the Ghosts) who leave a dingy, dark city and take a flying bus to a much brighter land have the chance to remain there, to become something more real than Ghosts—to learn, eventually and with great difficulty, how to live in Heaven.

Most of them, though, will not relinquish their ghostliness. They insist on being themselves—or what they call themselves—even in Hell rather than giving up their identities—or what they call their identities—to gain Heaven. Coupling this story with the previous reference to *The Last Battle,* one can see that for Lewis, this is what our age, our "period," characteristically produces: Ghosts and Dwarfs. They may take the form of decayed Victorian gentlemen such as Uncle Andrew or bright young sociologists such as Mark Studdock, but ultimately (morally and spiritually) they are tiny and spectral, far smaller and more constricted than they were made to be and far less substantial. Indeed, their perfect representative may be found in *The Great Divorce* in one of the Ghosts who is also a Dwarf: he has projected a false image of himself, a sadly comical figure the narrator calls the Tragedian, who has outgrown him and even displaced him. On earth the Dwarf was not a Dwarf at all but a man named Frank Smith; now he is a tiny creature at the end of a chain, silent and vague: it is the Tragedian he has projected as his fictional self-image who speaks, the Tragedian who is large and *seems* real. (But when they meet the Lady—a great saint who was once known as Sarah Smith and was married to Frank Smith—she ignores the Tragedian and always speaks to the Dwarf.)

Standing before his eager listeners in the lecture rooms of Oxford, his cheerful butcher's face suspended over his black robes, Lewis would hammer home his message: our Model—the model of Modernity—makes the universe silent and vague, so we come to resemble it. It shrinks the scope of human action, mistrusting or debunking the heroic and the noble; we shrink correspondingly. Yes, we project forward a great image of Progress to console ourselves, but it is only an image. Nevertheless, by investing so much in it and so little in ourselves, we make it more and more real, ourselves less and less so, until we confront the possibility that, in the end, it will replace us: all that will be left is a fiction, and though human beings will *physically* continue, humanity itself will have been abolished.

In Lewis's view, the chief blame for this state of affairs should be laid squarely at the door of his own class and his own profession: the intellectuals, the educators. "Bless me, what *do* they teach them at these schools!" cries Professor Kirke in *The Last Battle,* but the real question is, "What *don't* they teach?" Teachers who should be inculcating in their students a passion for truth teach them instead skepticism or indifference. Though perhaps in many cases they market their message as humility, it is in fact a false humility, and Lewis rails against it, because he believes that in the long run this abdication of responsibility—the responsibility to seek knowledge—will lead to the "abolition of man," our transformation into a species unable ever to hear the music that Creation really *does* make.

The Abolition of Man, another document from this same period, the years of the Second World War, began life as a series of lectures in 1943, not at Oxford but at the University of Durham. It remains the most profound of Lewis's cultural critiques. The first chapter, which concerns high-school-level textbooks in English, is prefaced with a quotation:

So he gave the word to slay,
And slew the little childer.

These words come from an old English Christmas carol, "Unto us is born a son," and they refer to the "massacre of the innocents"—King Herod's order that all the male children of Bethlehem under the age of two be killed. Surely it must have been a kind of macabre joke on Lewis's part to preface a critique of *textbooks* with these lines? But no: Herod could but kill the body; our teachers (he thinks) are killing our children's souls, and this is the more grievous sin.

The target of Lewis's critique becomes evident in the book's first pages, when he looks at a textbook he calls *The Green Book,* written by two schoolmasters he calls Gaius and Titius. (He wishes, he says, to spare them embarrassment; thus the pseudonyms.) The book's real authors are Alec King and Martin Ketley, and its real title is *The Control of Language.* That title is telling. For the key assumption of King and Ketley is that we are all under the subtle control of a certain kind of language: words that treat our personal feelings as though they correspond to something objective in the world. King and Ketley believe value judgments in particular to be the former disguised as the latter. Therefore, they see the prime task of a teacher to be disenchantment: unweaving the spell of value-laden language so that children control it rather than being controlled by it. (The book's title thus has a double meaning.)

To illustrate their conviction that judgments of value are "mere" preferences, King and Ketley look at an account by the poet Samuel Taylor Coleridge of a visit to a waterfall in England's Lake District. Two other tourists are present, and one of them says that the waterfall is "sublime," but the second calls it "pretty." It is not likely that the second tourist thought she was disagreeing with the first one; she was simply adding another word of commendation or approval. But Coleridge, listening to them, thought the second tourist ("poor woman") did not understand what she was seeing at all, while the first one did. To understand Coleridge's thought, one must recognize that the concept of "the sublime" was extremely important in Romantic thought: it had been defined most clearly only a few decades earlier by the philosopher Immanuel Kant, who said that the sublime "is that in comparison to which everything else is small." For Coleridge, the woman who called the great and powerful waterfall "pretty" was not really paying attention, neither to her experience nor to her language; only the one who called it "sublime" got it right.

King and Ketley, remarkably enough, draw exactly the opposite conclusion from this scene than the one Coleridge drew—without appearing to be aware that they disagree with the poet. They write, "When the man said *This is sublime,* he appeared to be making a remark about the waterfall.... Actually ... he was not making a remark about the waterfall, but a remark about his own feelings.... This confusion is continually present in language as we use it. We appear to be saying something very important about something: and actually we are only saying something about our own feelings." But Lewis insists that the whole point of the story, at least from Coleridge's point of view, is that it is something in the nature of the waterfall *itself* that quite properly calls forth the judgment that it is sublime. When King and Ketley consider what Coleridge himself might have been thinking, they somehow miss this: "Why did Coleridge think the one word was exactly right, and the other exactly wrong? Obviously not because the one adjective described correctly, as it were, a quality of the water or the rocks or the landscape, and the other adjective described this quality incorrectly.... No, Coleridge thought 'sublime' exactly the right word, because it was associated in his mind with the emotion he was himself feeling as he looked at the waterfall." Obviously!*

For Lewis, the first problem here is that it turns every statement into a value judgment. He deals with this problem in *Mere Christianity*—another work written in these war years—when he imagines that some will object to his giving the name "Christian" only to people who believe in the Christian doctrine: "May not a man who cannot believe these doctrines be far more truly a Christian, far closer to the spirit of Christ, than some who do?" Lewis acknowledges that indeed this may sometimes happen, but he insists that that should not affect our use of the *word* "Christian." He explains his point by considering the development of the word "gentleman," which at one time had a very specific meaning: "one who has a coat of arms and some landed property." When people started saying, "Surely he is the true gentleman who behaves as a gentleman should," and altered the meaning of the word so that what was once a simple descriptive term became a value judgment—meaning "hardly more than a man the speaker likes"—then "gentleman" became a "useless word": "When a word ceases to be a term of description and becomes merely a term of praise, it no longer tells you facts about the object: it only tells you about the speaker's attitude toward that object." His point is that we do not have to allow that to happen to language, and we would do well to keep descriptive terms free from this particular kind of corruption. "When a man who accepts the Christian doctrine lives unworthily of it, it is much clearer to say that he is a bad Christian than to say that he is not a Christian." Not all statements need to be reduced to value judgments, but the counsel of King and Ketley makes us more prone to that error.

But more important is the insistence by King and Ketley that value

---

* It is pleasurable to visit the Marion Wade Center at Wheaton College, consult Lewis's own copy of *The Control of Language,* and see his dialogue, via marginal annotation, with its authors. At one point they write, "To the eighteenth century, 'vulgar' simply meant, 'belonging to low life,' as opposed to the life of 'polished society.'" To which Lewis wrote in the margin: "Wrong." And indeed, they are wrong: in the eighteenth century "vulgar" still primarily meant the ordinary or common people—it was not a belittling term. They continue, "If you wished properly to understand [the reference of such words] you would need to read fairly widely in the critical writings of the eighteenth century." Lewis: "You would."

judgments are "only" or "merely" statements of personal *feelings.* In making this claim, our schoolmasters believe that they are helping to remove illusions that control us. They want to teach young people to "see through" the rhetoric of value that, in our politics and our mass media and our religion, is used to control us. They consider themselves liberators who enable young people to make their own judgments of value in independence from the reigning social authorities. But, for several reasons, Lewis sees them as tyrants who "slay the little childer." First, King and Ketley are not debunking *all* values as mere preferences, only the ones they disagree with: that young people should make their own decisions independent of the political or social or familial or religious authorities is, after all, itself a value judgment—even if it is correct—and they don't debunk *that.* "Their scepticism about values is on the surface: it is for use on other people's values; about the values current in their own set they are not nearly sceptical enough."

But closer still to the heart of the problem, for Lewis, is a particular consequence of King and Ketley's argument: what it implies about the scope and purpose of education itself. In the educational theory implied by King and Ketley, only the mind can be educated and not the heart. If value judgments are merely preferences, then there is no moral education to be done: "The heart wants what it wants," as Woody Allen once said. But from the time of Plato and Aristotle, Lewis is quick to point out, philosophers and educators have agreed that it is not just the minds of young people that need to be trained but also their responses, their judgments—even their emotions:

> St. Augustine defines virtue as the *ordo amoris,* the ordinate condition of the affections in which every object is accorded that kind or degree of love which is appropriate to it. Aristotle says that the aim of education is to make the pupil like and dislike what he ought. . . . Plato before him had said the same. The little human animal will not at first have the right responses. It must be trained to feel pleasure, liking, disgust, and hatred at those things which really are pleasant, likeable, disgusting, and hateful.

Lewis's experiences as a student *and* a teacher speak through such a passage. Throughout his childhood he was told that he was supposed to like activities—games, clubs, social activities—that he could take no pleasure in, preferring always the company of good books and challenging ideas. But his Oxford students were by and large people who either liked sports and games and social activities naturally or had learned to do so through their school years. Trying to teach his twenty-year-old pupils that Spenser or Milton or Chaucer could give *delight*—well, that was a nearly superhuman task. It would have been far better if someone had captured their imaginations a decade earlier, as some of his teachers had captured his; twenty-year-olds are already too fully formed, though (alas) usually formed in bad mental and emotional habits.

This theme runs throughout Lewis's work, and especially his fiction. Again and again we see people who are imperfectly educated—and who, like the best educated among us, are of course also fallen, flawed persons—and who struggle with their mixed responses when presented with either virtue or vice. We have already noted that in *That Hideous Strength* Mark Studdock's education has made him into a "man of straw" who, though he experiences real discomfort when in the company of the officials of NICE, does not know what that discomfort means and cannot act in proper response to it. There's a telling moment when he is sitting in a lovely little pub in a pleasant village that NICE is planning to destroy, and he even dares to say to his ruthless companion, "On a fine morning there is something rather attractive about a place like this, in spite of all its obvious absurdities." When this comment is met with contempt, Mark immediately backs off: "Of course, you're quite right: that sort of thing has to go. But it had its pleasant side." The use of the past tense in that last sentence is key: it *had* its pleasant side. In the space of a minute or two, Mark goes from a warm commendation of the village and its pub to the simple consignment of the whole thing to history's rubbish bin. He has no resources with which to evaluate—to recognize the importance of—his feelings about the village, so they are immediately overcome by his stronger feelings: the ones that make him want to be accepted at NICE. Augustine and Aristotle and Plato would say that Mark's feelings are *inordinate:* he feels the wrong ones more than he should, and the good ones less than he should. But Mark has been educated to be blind to his own condition.

Mark's wife Jane, by contrast—perhaps in part because her education has been in the literature of the seventeenth century, during which virtue, and the need for training in it, were still taken seriously—is properly drawn into the homey circle of the Director (aka Mr. Fisher-

King, though his real name is Ransom). She feels at first a certain dis-comfort in the presence of the company gathered around the Director; she is indeed fearful of being "taken in" and of losing her individuality in their fellowship. She is actually of *four* minds, Lewis says. But the "fourth and supreme Jane was simply in the state of joy. The other three had no power over her," because, though indeed these other feel-ings are in her—it is only human to have mixed feelings and to be pulled in different directions—they are properly subordinated to the most important thing, which is that in the presence of goodness and holiness she feels joy. During the course of the book, because she fol-lows her strongest inclinations, Jane is drawn deeper and deeper into a community of virtue; conversely, Mark, because he follows *his* deepest inclinations, is drawn deeper and deeper into a nightmare of evil.

Ultimately Mark escapes, but only barely, and many others do not. In Lewis's understanding, it is the work of the Evil One and his slaves—Satan and his devils, like Screwtape—to provide a *negative,* topsy-turvy moral education, gradually diminishing and in the end ex-tinguishing whatever draws us to the Good and magnifying and inten-sifying our inordinate desires: to make us all into Ghosts and Dwarfs. We see this not only in the advice Screwtape gives to Wormwood but also in the way the White Witch deals with Edmund in *The Lion, the Witch, and the Wardrobe.* She preys incessantly on his inordinate de-sires, and not simply his passion for Turkish delight: far more useful to her, and far more important in Edmund's heart, is his resentment of Peter. Edmund would give up candy forever if that would win him a victory over his hated elder brother. Turkish Delight is just the begin-ning, the first enticement of the Witch; soon enough that temptation is put aside, once she learns what he *really* cares about. When he cannot be convinced to bring his brother and sisters back to Narnia by the promise of more treats, the Witch strikes the effective chord when she tells him, "You are to be the Prince and—later on—the King." For the pleasures of candy pale in comparison to the pleasures of Power: this is what the Witch teaches (or rather, discovers in) Edmund—this is the heart of *her* "moral education." And once Edmund has, in effect, sold his soul for the promise of such Power, only the greatest of sacrifices can win back his life.

Ultimately, though unwittingly, the authors of *The Green Book* co-operate in this infernal pedagogy: by insisting that our feelings are mere preferences—none of which can be greater or more valuable than another—they open the way for dark forces to conduct their own campaign of education in the values of Hell. Again, in *That Hideous Strength,* Professor Frost serves as a representative of the logical extension of the teachings of King and Ketley about judgments and feelings. When Mark says a few kind words about "the elimination of war and poverty" and "the preservation and extension of our species," Frost replies that even such elementary and utilitarian values "are mere generalisations from affectional feelings." He has gotten "beyond" even the assumption that health is better than disease, life than death, continuation than destruction. It is because their model of education, fully implemented, would *make* people like Frost that King and Ketley, despite their no doubt "good intentions," are like King Herod, giving the word that "slays the little childer."

But why do the children fall so easily into grave danger? If we all have mixed feelings—if even a "man of straw" such as Mark Studdock still has some remnants of proper response, some residual ability to "feel pleasure, liking, disgust, and hatred at those things which really are pleasant, likeable, disgusting, and hateful"—why don't more people find the path to virtue? There are, of course, many answers to this question: we do not all share the same motives or vices. But there is one motive that Lewis finds especially interesting—and very much underestimated. We have had a sight of it already, in chapter 2—the description of the scene from *The Silver Chair* when Eustace and Jill talk about how Eustace had once "curried favor" with "Them"—and we can readily suspect that when Lucy remembers "that horrid school which was where [Edmund] began to go wrong," she knows that *They* had a lot to do with it. *They* are the Inner Ring.

In December 1944, almost exactly a year after completing *That Hideous Strength,* Lewis gave what was called the Commemoration Oration at King's College in London, a public lecture largely attended by students. These were not Lewis's own students, but he took the opportunity of this "oration" to produce something like a commencement address—full of the sort of advice that he would have wanted to give his students if the protocols of the Oxford lecture had allowed so directly moralistic a form of address. (Only to his tutorial pupils, and then only if they asked for his counsel, could he speak in such a way.) He calls his audience's attention to the presence, in schools and businesses and governments and armies and indeed in every human institution, of a "second or unwritten system" that stands next to the formal organization.

You discover gradually, in almost indefinable ways, that it exists and that you are outside it, and then later, perhaps, that you are inside it. . . . It is not easy, even at a given moment, to say who is inside and who is outside. . . . People think they are in it after they have in fact been pushed out of it, or before they have been allowed in; this provides great amusement for those who are really inside.

Lewis does not think that any of his audience will be surprised to hear of this phenomenon of the Inner Ring, but he thinks that some may be surprised when he goes on to argue that, "in all men's lives at certain periods, and in many men's lives at all periods between infancy and extreme old age, one of the most dominant elements is the desire to be inside the local Ring and the terror of being left outside." And later in the talk he asserts the point even more strongly: "This desire is one of the great permanent mainsprings of human action. . . . Unless you take measures to prevent it, this desire is going to be one of the chief motives of your life, from the first day on which you enter your profession until the day when you are too old to care." It is important for young people to know of the force of this desire, he believes, because "of all passions the passion for the Inner Ring is most skillful in making a man who is not yet a very bad man do very bad things."

The draw of the Inner Ring has such profound corrupting power because it never announces itself as evil—indeed, it never announces itself at all. On these grounds Lewis makes a "prophecy" to his audience at King's College: "To nine out of ten of you the choice which could lead to scoundrelism will come, when it does come, in no very dramatic colours. . . . Over a drink or a cup of coffee, disguised as a triviality and sandwiched between two jokes . . . the hint will come." And when it does come, "you will be drawn in, if you are drawn in, not by desire for gain or ease, but simply because at that moment, when the cup was so near your lips, you cannot bear to be thrust back again into the cold outer world."

It is by these subtle means that people who are "not yet very bad" can be drawn to "do very bad things"—by which actions they *become,* in the end, very bad. The method of temptation is outlined by Screwtape: "Indeed the safest road to Hell is the gradual one—the gentle slope, soft underfoot, without sudden turnings, without milestones, without signposts." And this is managed, in our time, by the devils hiding their existence from us (as Screwtape also tells Wormwood) and therefore hiding the true spiritual and moral significance of the temptations they present to us. That "hint" over drinks or coffee points to such a *small* thing, such an insignificant alteration in our principles—or what we thought were our principles—but "next week it will be something a little further from the rules, and next year something further still, but all in the jolliest, friendliest spirit. It may end in a crash, a scandal, and penal servitude; it may end in millions, a peerage, and giving the prizes at your old school. But you will be a scoundrel."

What Lewis is trying to show us here is that the Inner Ring offers *power*—more specifically, the kind of power that comes through knowledge. What many young people, and especially the intellectuals and artists, want is not "an invitation from a duchess," that is, social success, but "the sacred little attic or studio, the heads bent together, the fog of tobacco smoke, and the delicious knowledge that we—we four or five all huddled beside this stove—are the people who *know*." (Recall that, for the young Jack Lewis, "'we few' ... was an evocative expression.") What Frost offers Mark Studdock, when he lays out a plan that would involve the destruction of almost the whole human race and the gross disfigurement of the whole planet, is "an invitation that beckoned you right across the frontiers of human life ... into something that people had been trying to find since the beginning of the world ... a touch on that infinitely secret cord which was the real nerve of all history." In short, what the Inner Ring—in its deepest and truest form—offers is precisely what the serpent offered Eve at "the beginning of the world": the Knowledge that makes mere people into Gods.

But of course, one of the greatest pleasures of such Knowledge—the reason why people will go through dreadful rigors of initiation to become members of secret societies—is the exclusion of others from the charmed circle of those Inside. "Your genuine Inner Ring exists for exclusion." When we grasp this point, we will also grasp why the Director's little community, into which Jane Studdock is absorbed, is *not* an Inner Ring, but rather in fact its opposite. People are scarcely even invited there; rather, they come only if they are attracted to it. No one is excluded: the aim is to bring more and more—indeed, in the end, everyone—into the fellowship. If Inner Rings shun the person who is "not one of us," the Director's party glories in its social and intellectual diversity. The members of this community are indeed many members or organs of one body (this is how Saint Paul describes the church, a matter we explore later) with widely varying functions but a common love of their leader and of one another.

The failure to recognize the difference between this kind of community and an Inner Ring is what dooms the Hard-Bitten Ghost in *The Great Divorce:* standing in the midst of the glories of Heaven he is full of suspicion: "Of course they'll play the old game here if anyone's fool enough to listen.... It's *never* a new management. You'll always find the same old Ring." Like the Dwarfs in *The Last Battle,* he will not be "taken in." Fearing rejection by an imagined Inner Ring, he rejects them first and thereby consigns himself to Hell, where he can congratulate himself on having the shrewdness to discern "the old game" and the courage to refuse it.

In my judgment the greatest of all of Lewis's books is the one with the least resonant title: *English Literature in the Sixteenth Century (Excluding Drama).** It is also the one that took him the longest to write and that gave him the greatest misery: it is part of the Oxford History of English Literature (OHEL) series, which just gave him an excuse to call it his "O Hell" book. He signed on to write it in 1935; he finished it in 1953. His frustration with the interminable labor of it is an occasional feature of his correspondence, but in the end he produced a great masterpiece of literary and intellectual history. He wrote it in a very odd way: assembling it from a series of essays about individual authors that he wrote, he then graded them, as he graded his pupils' weekly essays—perhaps it was his way of finally getting to read some essays that he could enjoy. This odd method lends a certain ease and charm to what is, after all, an immense feat of scholarship. (Here is yet another example of how he turned the very teaching environment he despised to good use for himself and his readers.) The book not only surveys the whole territory of English Renaissance but transforms the survey into a grand and compelling narrative. The best part of the book is its long introduction, "New Learning and New Ignorance," which is as learned and wide-ranging an account of the intellectual history of the period as one could imagine. And surely few books so learned have also been so witty. Only a man very secure in the depths

---

* Oxford University Press has recently given the book a new title, *Poetry and Prose in the Sixteenth Century,* but for simplicity's sake, and also for fun, we will just call it "the OHEL book."

of his learning—and Lewis read *every single sixteenth-century book* in Duke Humfrey's Library, the oldest part of Oxford's great Bodleian Library, in preparation for writing this history—can risk such an exhibition of panache: he obviously knows too much to be accused of frivolity.

One of the most brilliant passages in the book concerns the rise of experimental science. It was a topic he also treated in his lectures—yes, the English don talking about science again, but in this case not to lament the cultural dominance of modern pseudo-science but to launch another attack on the cheap and easy distinctions that strengthen our "chronological snobbery." We all know that science is rational and magic superstitious, do we not? But it turns out that, like many other things that everybody knows, this is untrue. In this passage Lewis is writing about *magia*—high magic, that is, or what we might call white magic, as opposed to the dark magic that the Renaissance called *goetia:*

> The new *magia* ... falls into place among the other dreams of power which then haunted the European mind. Most obviously it falls into place beside the thought of [Sir Francis] Bacon. His endeavour is no doubt contrasted in our minds with that of the magicians: but contrasted only in light of the event, only because we know that science succeeded and magic failed. That event was then still uncertain. Stripping off our knowledge of it, we see at once that Bacon and the magicians have the closest possible affinity. Both seek knowledge for the sake of power (in Bacon's words, as a 'spouse for fruit' not a 'curtesan for pleasure'), both move in a grandiose dream of days when Man shall have been raised to the performance of 'all things possible.'... Nor would Bacon have denied the affinity: he thought the aim of the magicians was 'noble.'

This historical argument proves to be crucial to the critique of modern culture that we have been tracing throughout this chapter. Lewis makes this clear when he pursues exactly the same point in *The Abolition of Man:* "The serious magical endeavour and the serious scientific endeavour are twins: one was sickly and died, the other was strong and throve. But they were twins. They were born of the same impulse." But what is that impulse?

There is something which unites magic and applied science while separating both from the "wisdom" of earlier ages. For the wise men of old the cardinal problem had been how to conform the soul to reality, and the solution had been knowledge, self-discipline, and virtue. For magic and applied science alike the problem is how to subdue reality to the wishes of men: the solution is a technique; and both, in the practice of this technique, are ready to do things hitherto regarded as disgusting and impious.

The "impulse" that magic and "applied science" share, then, is *control*—and at this point we must remember that the real title of Gaius and Titius's *Green Book* is *The Control of Language*. Though they are educators, they do not believe that they are in the business of "conforming the soul to reality" through "knowledge, self-discipline, and virtue"; instead, they want to liberate young people from the control that language has over them. For them language is but an instrument by which some people control and others are controlled. As Humpty Dumpty once said, in a very similar context, "The question is which is to be master, that's all." As Lewis emphasizes with great force in *The Abolition of Man*, Humpty Dumpty's view of things is deeply embedded in all the projects and hopes of modernity, even (or especially) when we talk about achieving human power over Nature: "What we call Man's power over Nature turns out to be a power exercised by some men over other men with Nature as its instrument."

This view was shared exactly by Tolkien, who wrote in a letter that his work—especially but not only *The Lord of the Rings*—"is concerned with Fall, Mortality, and the Machine," and who links the Machine directly with Magic. The most corrupted of beings—first the Adversary Morgoth, then his lieutenant Sauron, and ultimately the wizard Saruman—seek to remedy all ills (or what they think of as ills) by the Machine. In Tolkien's understanding, the Rings of Power are simply the most subtle and advanced of machines. Saruman treats with contempt Gandalf's pursuit of wisdom even in such unlikely corners of Middle-Earth as the Shire, but that is because, as Treebeard the Ent says, "He has a mind of metal and wheels; and he does not care for growing things, except as far as they serve him for the moment." By contrast, Gandalf, who cares nothing for machines and among the Wise is "the only one that goes in for hobbit-lore," is the one who finds the way to defeat the evils of the great Technocrats of

Middle-Earth. For Saruman such "lore" is deeply impractical, and one of the key traits that scientists and magicians have in common is practicality. Lewis writes of Jadis, as she waits in Uncle Andrew's laboratory for him to do some service for her, "Now that she was left alone with the children, she took no notice of them.... I expect most witches are like that. They are not interested in things or people unless they can use them; they are terribly practical."

Modern humanists, like the scientists and magicians of the Renaissance, seek power and control rather than wisdom. That is how they have cut themselves off from the moral law—what Lewis calls the Tao*—and are contributing, not to the enrichment of humanity, but to its abolition. (Lewis takes great pains to insist that his quarrel is not with science itself, though he is aware that some will not be able to get the distinction: "Nothing I can say will prevent some people from describing this lecture as an attack on science." Science as such—scientific method, scientific practice—is for Lewis morally neutral. But science also has a history, and as we have seen, it arose in a time when the European mind was "haunted" by "dreams of power." As he puts it in *The Abolition of Man*, science "was born in an unhealthy neighbourhood and at an inauspicious hour.")

Having thus been led back to *The Magician's Nephew*, we can now discern the real character of that apparently comical figure, Uncle Andrew. I have already noted the way he conflates the language of the scientist with the practices of the magician, and now we can see why Lewis brings those two worlds together. Uncle Andrew is the descendent of magicians, but he appropriates the language of science because, in his dim way, he recognizes the affinity that Francis Bacon recognized: he sees that his scientific contemporaries have the same goals as his magical forebears. I have already noted his guinea pigs, and I find that whenever I think of him I picture him, though without any warrant, in a white lab coat: that garb of authority, recognizable in our time as having the same meaning that the wizard's cloak had for an earlier age.

---

* *Tao* is a Chinese word meaning "the Way"—Lewis takes it from the ancient philosophical treatise called the *Tao te Ching*, traditionally attributed to a philosopher of the sixth century b.c. named Lao Tze. Lewis adopts the term in order to indicate that there is a large agreement among all the world's great religions and philosophical traditions about what the virtuous life is.

Uncle Andrew *recognizes* ordinary morality and is willing to use it to motivate Digory. When the boy shows reluctance to take a magical ring and go in search of Polly, whom Uncle Andrew has just made to disappear, the old man says he would be disappointed if the boy "shows the white feather"—he sounds at those moments like a Victorian schoolmaster, the very embodiment of the principles of Thomas Arnold—but he has no intention of practicing any of those virtues himself. Mere morality is beneath him. When Digory points out that he broke a promise to his dying godmother, Uncle Andrew replies:

Oh, I see. You mean that little boys ought to keep their promises. Very true: most right and proper, I'm sure, and I'm very glad you have been taught to do it. But of course you must understand that rules of that sort, however excellent they may be for little boys— and servants—and women—and even people in general, can't possibly be expected to apply to profound students and great thinkers and sages. No, Digory. Men like me, who possess hidden wisdom, are freed from common rules, just as we are cut off from common pleasures. Ours, my boy, is a high and lonely destiny.

Though "he looked so grave and noble and mysterious" as he said these words that for a moment Digory was almost fooled by them, the boy quickly translates Uncle Andrew's rhetoric into the terms of the ordinary moral law, the Tao: "All it means . . . is that he thinks he can do anything he likes to get anything he wants." And of course, Digory is right.

To complete our picture of Uncle Andrew, and of what Lewis thinks of him, we merely need to note this: later in the book, when Digory suggests to the Empress Jadis that it is really rather regrettable that she spoke the Deplorable Word and destroyed all life in her world, Charn, she replies: "You must learn, child, that what would be wrong for you or any of the common people is not wrong in a great Queen such as I. The weight of the world is on our shoulders. We must be freed from all rules. Ours is a high and lonely destiny." But this time Digory fails immediately to grasp what the words mean: "They sounded much grander when Queen Jadis said them; perhaps because Uncle Andrew was not seven feet tall and dazzlingly beautiful." Eventually Digory comes to understand what Jadis is really like and to realize that those words coming from her, far from being *less* objectionable than they were in the mouth of Uncle Andrew, are infinitely *more* objectionable because she has the power that Uncle Andrew can merely dream of. It is Jadis who will become the White Witch, the Adversary (which is what the Hebrew word *Satan* means) of Aslan, the would-be enslaver of Narnia, and, ultimately, if she had her way, its Destroyer.

Is it silly to think of Uncle Andrew as a Satanic figure? Yes and no. Certainly he lacks the stature of Jadis or Satan himself, not to mention their vast powers and iron resolution to undermine and destroy, but for Lewis that is not really the point. He is as evil as he can be, given his limitations of intelligence and commitment. As Lewis writes in *Mere Christianity,* "The better stuff a creature is made of—the cleverer and stronger and freer it is—then the better it will be if it goes right, but also the worse it will be if it goes wrong. A cow cannot be very good or very bad; a dog can be both better and worse; a child better and worse still; an ordinary man, still more so; a man of genius, still more so; a superhuman spirit best—or worst—of all." It is because Uncle Andrew is lazy and frivolous that in the end he does not do much harm; conversely, it is the greatness of Jadis that enables her to destroy one world and threaten another. Their powers are drastically different, but their orientation to the moral law is precisely the same. And it is in this direction that Gaius and Titius are drawing their students; it is in just this way that they assume their place among the Herods of our time. Digory is young enough, untrained enough, to see Uncle Andrew and, eventually, Jadis for what they really are, but those throngs of undergraduates in C. S. Lewis's lectures on medieval and Renaissance literature were probably, by and large, too far gone to reclaim. Still, against his preferences and inclinations, he continued to teach: to persuade, to plead, to encourage. That was his job.

At the outset of this book I said that the work of C. S. Lewis is largely a response to—and an attempt to reverse—what the sociologist Max Weber called "the disenchantment of the world." And indeed this is true. But one can profitably describe his goals in another way, reversing the terms of the equation. In his great sermon "The Weight of Glory," he makes a case for Joy (though he does not there use that word): he describes—in words we will later have cause to reflect on—the most piercing of pleasures known to us and contends that even the greatest of them are but "the scent of a flower we have not found, the echo of a tune we have not heard, news from a country we have never yet visited." And then he pauses for a moment and asks his audience a question:

Do you think I am trying to weave a spell? Perhaps I am; but remember your fairy tales. Spells are used for breaking enchantments as well as for inducing them. And you and I have need of the strongest spell that can be found to wake us from the evil enchantment of worldliness which has been laid upon us for nearly a hundred years.

Who laid this spell upon us? The answer, for Lewis, is clear: those scientists and magicians who told us that they have the power to make heaven on earth and can give it to us; those educators who promise us "the control of language." "Almost our whole education has been directed to silencing this shy, persistent, inner voice" that tells us that true Joy lies beyond this world. How can we be released from the evil enchantment that threatens to abolish humanity itself?

Perhaps the greatest resource on which he draws—and it is a mighty one—is, simply, *delight*. He calls us to take note of what gives us pleasure, for, though our pleasures can indeed lead us astray, they are in their proper form great gifts from God. Screwtape is painfully aware of this:

Never forget that when we are dealing with any pleasure in its healthy and satisfying form, we are, in a sense, on the Enemy's ground. I know we have won many a soul through pleasure. All the same, it is His invention, not ours. He made the pleasures: all our research so far has not enabled us to produce one. All we can do is encourage the humans to take the pleasures which our Enemy has produced, at times, or in ways, or in degrees, which He has forbidden.... An ever increasing craving for an ever diminishing pleasure is the formula.... To get a man's soul and give him *nothing* in return—that's what really gladdens Our Father's heart.

So Lewis begins his disenchanting spell in this surprising way: by calling us back to our pleasures, to the things in life that we enjoy, and not the things that we think we ought to like, or that some Inner Ring hints to us we should like, but what really and truly delights us. Writes Screwtape, "The man who truly and disinterestedly enjoys any one thing in the world, for its own sake, and without caring two-pence what other people say about it, is by that very fact forearmed against some of our subtlest modes of attack"—among them, surely, the lure of the Inner Ring. And Lewis himself was a man to take the greatest possible delight in the pleasures put before him. How he loved "adult male laughter"; how he loved his pipe and (perhaps above all) his books. When the London newspaper the *Daily Telegraph* did a story on him in 1944, the writer referred to him at one point as "ascetic Mr. Lewis," a description that made Tolkien splutter with incredulity and indignation. He wrote to his son, "'Ascetic Mr. Lewis'—!!! I ask you! He put away three pints in a very short session we had this morning, and said he was 'going short for Lent.'" To any who might criticize such gusto as unseemly for a Christian, Lewis could reply, "There is no good trying to be more spiritual than God. God never meant man to be a purely spiritual creature. That is why He uses material things like bread and wine to put the new life into us. We may think this rather crude and unspiritual. God does not: He invented eating. He likes matter. He invented it."

Armed with this sound theology of pleasure, Lewis's perpetual task both as a defender of Christianity and as an advocate of medieval literature is to call people to delight—and delight even in old books. Yes, those were written by people different than ourselves—but not radically different. They are still recognizably human; they inhabit a world that is sometimes strange to us but not wholly alien. In fact, they are just different *enough* to be valuable to us as instructors in virtues we have neglected. We cannot go back in time and teach them to be more compassionate, but if we read them with care and sympathy they can instruct us in courage and chastity. We will not, however, read them with care and sympathy unless there is some reward for us in it: it is for this reason that Lewis emphasizes the delight that can come from them. He wants us to know that it is indeed possible for a twentieth-century man to enjoy reading four-hundred-year-old books just for the sheer pleasure of it. And any book that delights us may more readily teach us its wisdom.

In *The Lord of the Rings*, the wise and ancient Elf Celeborn counsels the Company, in response to a gibe from Boromir about "old wives' tales," "Do not despise the lore that has come down from distant years; for oft it may chance that old wives keep in memory word of things that were once needful for the wise to know." Several of the plots of the Narnia books turn on the forgetting of old lore by some and its remembering by others. In *Prince Caspian*, Doctor Cornelius, Caspian's tutor, is primarily a historian, and his passionate remembrance of "Old Narnia"—"my old heart has carried these secret memories so long that it aches with them"—is key to the return of the Talking Beasts and the restoration of the great kingdom that Caspian's

Telmarine ancestors ruined. The confusion and discord sown by Shift the Ape in *The Last Battle* is possible because Aslan is only a name to the people of Narnia: they know nothing of his history, or of his character, so they can easily be made to believe that he has commanded deeds (for instance, the destruction of the forests) that are incompatible with his care for Narnia.

Among the "old lore" of *our* world there is one tradition that Lewis found especially fascinating, and that turns up repeatedly in his fiction. Most of us have heard the phrase "the music of the spheres"—the spheres being, in medieval astronomy, the abodes of the planets. These spheres surround the earth, moving outward from us in concentric circles; beyond them is the Empyrean, the Heaven of Heavens, where God's presence dwells most fully. But what is their "music"? That music is made by the friction of their contact as they ceremoniously rotate at their various speeds: it is of extraordinary beauty, and the contrasting stillness of the Earth is one of the chief reasons why medieval astronomers said that the Earth is "the point at which all the light, heat and movement descending from the nobler spheres finally died out into darkness, coldness, and passivity." But what makes the spheres move? That is the task of their governing spirits: "Each sphere, or something resident in each sphere, is a conscious and intellectual being, moved by the 'intellectual love' of God. . . . These lofty creatures are called Intelligences." It was usually thought that an Intelligence was a very particular kind of angel—a "creature," but not embodied, and with the single function of being the mover of its sphere.

These are the Oyarsa of Lewis's space trilogy. In *Out of the Silent Planet,* Ransom learns early on that the name of the planet he is on is Malacandra, but he does not yet understand that when he meets the Oyarsa of that planet he is meeting Malacandra itself. What Ransom calls the "planet" is in a sense the body, and just as you would not say that you know someone when you see their body, but rather only when you converse with them, so Ransom must know the Oyarsa in order to know the world. Malacandra is the Intelligence that moves the planetary body, just as Perelandra is the Intelligence that moves the planet we call Venus. But who is the Intelligence of *our* world, of Earth—Thulcandra, as it is known to the Oyarsa? Well, it helps to know that Thulcandra means something like "the silent planet"—the planet that is cut off from the others, whose Intelligence has removed himself from communication with the other Intelligences, or has been removed by Maleldil (that is, God). Thulcandra, the Intelligence of our world, is "the Bent One": that is, Satan.

In imagining these mighty creatures, Lewis is not asking his students, or us, to reconsider the *mechanical* errors of the Medieval Model—indeed, the Earth is not *literally* at the dead, cold center of the universe. But he *is* asking us to imagine at the very least a mythological truth in that Model: it serves to teach us that we are unlike the rest of the Universe, that something dark and horrible has happened here that has not happened, or at least need not have happened, elsewhere. (It almost happens on Perelandra—Ransom is sent there to prevent it from happening, to struggle with the evil forces that want to make the lords of that planet fall and corrupt themselves.) In the same way, the linkage, in Greek and Roman mythology, of the planets with gods can be seen as a memory or intuition of something actually Christian: the idea that God put his angels, or celestial beings like angels, in charge of different territories of his Creation. It is not impossible or even unlikely for a Christian to think so; what, after all, *was* the original job description of Lucifer, son of the morning?*

---

* If a Lewis scholar named Michael Ward is right, each of the Narnia stories is associated with one of the planets, starting with the festal Jovian character of Aslan's saving of Narnia. Then:

The Silver Chair: the Moon
The Horse and His Boy: Mercury
The Magician's Nephew: Venus
The Voyage of the "Dawn Treader": the Sun
Prince Caspian: Mars
The Last Battle: Saturn

It is hard not to be skeptical of Ward's argument, because Lewis flatly told a young reader that the series was unplanned: "When I wrote *The Lion* I did not know I was going to write any more. Then I wrote *P. Caspian* as a sequel and still didn't think there would be any more, and when I had done *The Voyage* I felt quite sure it would be the last. But I found I was wrong." Nevertheless, it is difficult to deny that a strong Martial character dominates *Prince Caspian* (in the overall plot and in the strong figure of that warlike mouse Reepicheep), or that *The Voyage of the "Dawn Treader"* moves toward the light of the Sun, or that the Time-Giant who brings the history of Narnia to a close in *The Last Battle* is a version of Saturn, old Kronos. And there are other resonances that Ward does not mention in his short article, for instance, the farcical infatuation of Uncle Andrew with that "dem fine woman," the Empress Jadis, in the book Ward associates with the Goddess of Love, as well as the greater Love that moves Aslan to speak Narnia into being. Though the Intelligences are not presented directly, as they are in the space trilogy, perhaps they are hidden there and provide an emotional foundation for each of the Narnian chronicles.

Why is this aspect of the Medieval Model so deeply and consistently appealing to Lewis, so compelling that he would passionately commend it to students who must have found the arguments odd indeed? Because the universe conceived by our ancestors was "tingling with anthropomorphic life, a festival not a machine," and this festival took place in a space perceived as vast, "towering," and even "vertiginous," so that looking up into the night sky was like looking up into the great central dome of St. Paul's Cathedral—only magnified a thousand times. And yet this space was orderly and secure: "overwhelming in its greatness but satisfying in its harmony." In this world the Divine Reason and Divine Love manifested themselves everywhere, despite the spiteful attempts of sinful humans to destroy all signs of them. And when we look at the Medieval Model in this way, do we have real reason to think that it was *wrong?* Or is there not in Scripture and Christian tradition, and even in the pangs of desire that strike us when we look at the world, plenty of evidence that that Model got something right that, in our cold Sarumanian cosmos of metal and wheels, we have forgotten?

These are the questions that, term after term and year after year, Lewis put before the audiences of his lectures. Then, leaving the possibilities hanging in the air, he would return the watch he had borrowed from someone in the front row—he never wore one himself, but had no intention of exceeding his allotted time—and strode back to his rooms. Dropping into the chair at his desk, he fished a pipe from the pocket of his jacket, scanned the half-finished page before him, picked up his pen, took a deep breath, and began to write.

NINE

"What I owe to them all is incalculable"

When the lectures and tutorials were finished for the day, and when it was time to take a break from the writing, Lewis habitually turned to one of the greatest of his life's pleasures: time with his friends. As we have already heard him say, "My happiest hours are spent with three or four old friends in old clothes tramping together and putting up in small pubs—or else sitting up till the small hours in someone's college rooms talking nonsense, poetry, theology, metaphysics over beer, tea, and pipes. There's no sound I like better than adult male laughter."

If many of the ideas discussed in the previous chapter found their first audiences in the lecture halls, Lewis's actual books—the forms into which he poured those ideas—had trial runs in "someone's college rooms" in weekly meetings with his friends that began around 1933 and continued for twenty years. These were almost always Lewis's own rooms in Magdalen. The Kolbitar, having ceased to bite the coals, had bitten the dust, but soon thereafter Lewis and Tolkien were invited by an undergraduate named Edward Tangye Lean to participate in an informal literary club whose members would read drafts of writings to one another and receive criticism, ideally of the constructive variety. It was apparently Lean who named the club the Inklings; though the club would fade away after his graduation, Lewis took over the name when he started inviting friends to Magdalen for similar sessions.

Reading aloud was the main thing. As Tolkien would write many years later, "C.S.L. had a passion for hearing things read aloud, a power of memory for things received in that way, and also a facility in extempore criticism, none of which were shared (especially not the last) in anything like the same degree by his friends." One important point that emerges from this letter is Tolkien's relative lack of enthusiasm for the whole project of the Inklings. He was a regular attender, and he was gratified especially that the non-academic Inklings, like Warnie Lewis and the physician Humphrey Havard,* enjoyed the work-in-progress that became *The Lord of the Rings*—when he thought that he might never finish the book their general enthusiasm was encouraging—but it was Lewis's opinion that he truly craved. (However, Tolkien could be quite fierce in rejecting even Lewis's criticisms when they touched on some matter he thought, for his own peculiar reasons, especially important. "No one ever influenced Tolkien," Lewis once wrote. "You might as well try to influence a bandersnatch. . . . He has only two reactions to criticism: either he begins the whole work over again from the beginning or else he takes no notice at all.") No doubt Tolkien would have been happy to continue meeting just with Lewis on Mondays, as he had been doing since the late twenties, without bringing anyone else into the mix. In short, the Inklings was Lewis's club: he was the heart of it, and the members gathered primarily because of him, and when he could no longer be regularly involved the Inklings faded away.

I have referred to a "club" and its "members," but that terminology is inappropriate: there was nothing so formal about it, and if Lewis had not adopted Lean's clever name for the gatherings, future generations would not have been misled on this point. Lewis started asking friends to his rooms for readings and conversations; this became a regular Thursday evening practice, and eventually it became equally common for some of them to meet on Tuesday mornings around eleven at a pub called the Eagle and Child (more familiarly, the Bird and Baby). It appears—especially from Warnie's diaries, the chief source of information about the meetings—that the readings happened usually during the more private evening sessions, while the Bird and Baby meetings were typically devoted just to "talking nonsense, poetry, theology, metaphysics" over beer, hard cider rather than tea (Lewis chose that

---

* Havard's real name was Robert, but once Hugo Dyson forgot that and called him Humphrey—and Humphrey he remained to all the Inklings forever after.

pub because he liked the cider), and pipes or cigarettes. Perhaps Hugo Dyson could come up from Reading for Thursday dinner and an Inklings session, then stay the night in Lewis's rooms; perhaps on a given Tuesday Barfield could get the day off from his London law firm and take the train up. And Oxford locals such as Nevill Coghill, Adam Fox (the Dean of Divinity—that is, the chaplain—at Magdalen), and, after the Second World War, Tolkien's son Christopher could show up at either locale or both. The various "meetings" were just ways for Lewis's increasingly far-flung acquaintance to find ways to get together.

Perhaps the most interesting person among the Inklings was one of the temporary members of the party: Charles Williams, an odd and charismatic man about whom it is difficult to write with justice or even clarity. He was unlike the other Inklings socially and educationally, and though he shared with them Christian belief and literary interests, he would never have been one of them had it not been for a series of odd accidents. He was older than the others (born five years before Tolkien, a dozen before Lewis) and a lifelong Londoner. Far from being an Oxford man, Williams lacked any university degree, though he had attended University College, London, for a while. Before the Great War he had landed a job with the London office of Oxford University Press and would work there for the rest of his life. He wrote plays, poems short and long (including a sequence based in Arthurian legend), works of literary criticism, and theological treatises, but Williams was chiefly known for his novels, which he did not begin writing until he was in his forties. Often referred to as "supernatural thrillers," they include among their various furniture a lion escaped from captivity, Black Masses, magical Tarot Cards, the crown of King Solomon, an Antichrist, and dead people who can speak with the living.

A reader of Williams's biography is likely to come to the conclusion that he was rather creepy. His "romantic theology"—which understands erotic love not so much as a path or ladder to the love of God but as a *form* of the love of God—encouraged him to flirtations, at the very least, with young women (Williams was married and had a son). He seems to have had the same sadomasochistic tendencies as the young Jack Lewis, though without ever escaping them. His fascination with the occult exceeded what most Christians think of as appropriate bounds. Yet few who knew him saw him in this light. Lewis adored him, finding him chivalrous, generous, even selfless, as well as a major thinker and a brilliant (though often too obscure) writer. "I begin to suspect that we are living in the 'age of Williams,'" he once wrote in a letter to his friend, "and our friendship with you will be our only passport to fame." T. S. Eliot wrote, "I think he was a man of unusual genius, and I regard his work as important." The poet W. H. Auden, who worked with Williams on a collection of poetry he edited for Oxford University Press, had perhaps a stronger response still, though he never knew Williams as well as the others. Many years after first meeting Williams, he would recall that interview in surprising terms and mark it as one of the events that led him to embrace the Christian faith:

> For the first time in my life, [I] felt myself in the presence of personal sanctity. . . . I had met many good people before who made me feel ashamed of my own shortcomings, but in the presence of this man—we never discussed anything but literary business—I did not feel ashamed. I felt transformed into a person who was incapable of doing or thinking anything base or unloving. (I later discovered that he had had a similar effect on many other people.)

Yet in all this praise there remains—and all the praisers are well aware of this—an element of the inexplicable. How could a conversation about "literary business" generate such an aura of "personal sanctity"? Likewise, Eliot, after having affirmed the value of Williams's work, goes on to say, "It has an importance of a kind not easy to explain." And Lewis has to agree with a colleague—probably Tolkien—who says that Williams was "one in whom, after years of friendship, there remained something elusive and incalculable." Williams simply made an exceptionally powerful impression on almost all who knew him, and his work similarly affects people, though in more variable ways: for some, like me, his books, especially his novels, are disturbing. (Tolkien, though he liked Williams personally very much, found his writing "wholly alien, and sometimes very distasteful, occasionally ridiculous.") I find that I do not *trust* Williams, though almost all who knew him trusted him implicitly.

Williams and Lewis met by exchanging fan letters. In 1936, on the advice of Nevill Coghill, Lewis had read Williams's novel *The Place of the Lion* and was so taken with it that ("for the first time in my life") he wrote a fan letter to the author; almost immediately he received a reply from Williams explaining that he had been just about to write a similar letter to Lewis after reading the proofs of *The Allegory of Love* (which OUP was about to publish). They would meet only occasionally, in London or Oxford, until 1939, when the outbreak of war and the beginning of the London Blitz caused OUP to move its staff to Oxford. There Williams would remain, continuing to work for the press but also giving occasional lecture series for the university, and of course meeting with the Inklings, until his sudden and unexpected death in May 1945, just a week after the surrender of the Germans ended the war in Europe.

Lewis was devastated by the loss, more than any of the other Inklings. Williams had, in the relatively short time he lived in Oxford, effectively displaced Tolkien from his place in Lewis's life—indeed, he called Williams, in a letter written soon after the man's death, "my dearest friend." The friendship between Lewis and Tolkien would never be restored. It is impossible, I think, to say whether the intimacy with Williams was the cause or the effect of the loss of intimacy with Tolkien. A thread of criticism of his friend appears in Tolkien's letters only after Williams's arrival in Oxford, but the critique has nothing to do with Williams. Tolkien was annoyed when Lewis used, in his science fiction novels, broken-off chunks of Tolkienian mythology; he thought Lewis wrote too much and too quickly. The Narnia books appalled him, probably because of their promiscuous mixing of mythological elements, and he would find Lewis's last book, *Letters to Malcolm*, "distressing and in parts horrifying." Some of Lewis's comments on marriage in *Mere Christianity* upset Tolkien so greatly that he could not even speak to Lewis about them: instead, he drafted a letter of protest, which in the end he never sent. In 1948 Tolkien wrote Lewis a long and tortured letter, hovering among several purposes and tones: it is apologetic, defensive, wounded, and complimentary by turns, but always inscrutable. A characteristic sentence looks like this: "And instead of confessing as sinful the natural and inevitable feeling of pain and its reactions (I am sure never unresisted, and immediately), do me the great generosity of making me a present of the pains I have caused, so that I may share in the good you have put them to." (And no, it does not become clearer in context.) It's impossible to tell what Tolkien hoped the letter would accomplish, or even what the cause of the letter was: it appears, as best one can tell, to have been prompted by criticism Tolkien made of Lewis's OHEL book when parts of it were read to the Inklings. (It is probably rash to guess what the problem was, but Tolkien was likely angered by Lewis's decision—which he claimed, absurdly, was driven by a desire to be evenhanded and impartial—to describe Catholics throughout the book as "Papists.") Was Lewis hurt by the criticism? Did Tolkien on reflection think he had gone too far? This remains unclear. But what virtually shouts from the letter is a profound discomfort, a simple inability to write directly to someone who had once been an intimate friend.

Perhaps deeper than anything else in Tolkien's mind was a simple and straightforward disagreement with the course his friend's career had taken. For more than he disagreed with any particular idea or element in Lewis's writings, he repudiated the very idea of a *layman* serving as a popular apologist for the Christian faith. This view stemmed from the insistence of Tolkien's Catholic tradition on the very different roles of clergy and laity. What Lewis took upon himself was, in Tolkien's judgment, none of Lewis's business: the defense of the Christian faith was the province of the ordained priesthood. Though Tolkien himself could perhaps have written a strong and appealing commendation of his own beliefs, he did not think that he had the right to do so, and in his view, neither did Lewis. (Lewis's own view was that he would have been happy to give up the job of defending the faith to the clergy had the clergy showed any inclination to take up the responsibility. In 1956 he wrote a letter to his friend Katherine Farrer, whose husband, Austin, an Anglican priest, had just written a book of popular spirituality. Lewis commented that if more priests had written such books, "the world might have been spared C.S.L."—that is, Lewis the all-purpose apologist.)

Of course, the firmness of Tolkien's judgment on these matters may well have been influenced by his own difficulties in writing, especially as compared to his friend. Tolkien was aware of this possibility. At the time of Williams's death, Tolkien had published nothing significant since *The Hobbit*—which had appeared in print in 1937, just after *The Allegory of Love*—and he was still struggling through drafts of the central sections of *The Lord of the Rings*, which he only rarely believed could be published even if he could complete it. Meanwhile, Lewis had written *Out of the Silent Planet*—the time-travel story that Tolkien had pledged to write to complement Lewis's space-travel one had never gotten off the ground—and the remaining two books in the Space Trilogy, plus *The Problem of Pain, The Screwtape Letters, A Preface to "Paradise Lost," The Abolition of Man,* and *The Great Divorce*—though not all those books had yet been published, the printers apparently being unable to keep up with the pace of Lewis's nib pen. Moreover, he had delivered the series of radio talks that would become *Mere Christianity* (about which more in the next chapter) and had already made him a kind of national celebrity. If all this fluency and success did not make Tolkien envious—even if he thought the fluency purchased at too high a price—then Tolkien was a saint indeed.

It does not seem that Lewis had any such mixed feelings about his friend. Though obviously he was taken aback by the intensity of Tolkien's responses to criticisms of *The Lord of the Rings*—speaking of how Tolkien rejected some of his criticisms, he adds, "*rejected* is perhaps too mild a word for your reaction on at least one occasion!"—he invariably spoke in the warmest and most commendatory terms about Tolkien's work, praising it publicly and privately at every opportunity. In the letter I have just quoted, which was written in October 1949 and contains Lewis's overwhelmed and grateful response to the final, or nearly final, draft of *The Lord of the Rings*, he concludes with a single unpunctuated sentence:

I miss you very much

But if Lewis missed the closeness of their old friendship and felt little or none of the disapproval toward Tolkien that Tolkien felt toward him, it nevertheless seems likely that the arrival of Charles Williams in Oxford offered to Lewis a friendship that lacked the tension and disease that was increasingly characterizing his relations with Tolkien. Though the friendship of Lewis and Tolkien would certainly have deteriorated in any case, the arrival of Williams accelerated the separation. Later events would only pull them further apart, as we shall see, though they would never cease to remember their earlier intimacy and be grateful for it, as we shall also see.

In any event, Williams was not just a friend to Lewis: his influence on Lewis's writing was great, especially after he came to Oxford. Almost every reader of the Space Trilogy notes the significant alteration in style and tone that appears in *That Hideous Strength*, and almost everyone who has read a Charles Williams novel can explain the change. Lewis himself, curiously, could never see that Williams had greatly influenced him, though he knew that each of them had affected the other. (I am not sure that Lewis ever understood just how extraordinarily receptive he was to the voices and styles of his favorite writers. He had an almost unmatched ability to absorb those styles and

voices; that is what made him, as his friends have all testified, a brilliant parodist. That receptiveness to other voices is also what makes
the Narnia books into a virtual encyclopedia of fairy-tale motifs, and
in a different aspect of his life, is what made Lewis susceptible to losing his Ulster accent and unable to get it back.) But perhaps the most
significant influence Williams had on Lewis would not appear until
more than a decade after his death; we will consider it in a later
chapter.

The Inklings have been written about so much, and so reverently, that
it has been hard for me to dismiss the temptation to ignore them altogether, as though I had never heard of them. (Imagine a book on
Shakespeare that never mentions a play called *Hamlet*.) But they had
an enormous influence on Lewis, as in a smaller way they helped
Tolkien: they provided an enthusiastic, but constructively critical, audience for all sorts of stories and arguments; they formed a society in
which formerly lonely and isolated men discovered that it was not necessarily so crazy to believe in God and miracles or to write stories
about Elves and Dwarfs and creatures called "hobbits." It must be remembered that these were highly unusual people, Lewis and Tolkien
perhaps above all. Lewis almost never read newspapers, professed
from an early age a dislike of what he knew about "the modern
world" and a lack of interest in learning much more, and did not even
follow, on a regular basis anyway, the academic gossip of his own college. (Adam Fox wrote of Lewis that "his innocence and ignorance
were unlimited. . . . Some current discussion about College or University affairs which had been in everybody's mind and on everybody
else's lips passed him by, though when at last he heard of it, he often
made a very sound observation slightly tinged with petulance.") The
tastes in literature shared by the Inklings were minority tastes indeed.
And it should be remembered that Lewis led, by his own desire and inclination, an isolated adolescence: as he writes to Arthur in the same
1914 letter in which he professes complete boredom with "this real,
hard, dirty Monday morning modern world," he also insists that "the
people whose society I prefer to my own are very few and far between." One would not have expected such a boy to develop the enormous gift for friendship that Lewis eventually possessed, such that as a
man in his fifties—when his friendship with Tolkien had cooled and
he was no longer a member of the Oxford faculty—he could write
these words:

In a perfect Friendship this Appreciative love is, I think, often so great and so firmly based that each member of the circle feels, in his secret heart, humbled before all the rest. Sometimes he wonders what he is doing there among his betters. He is lucky beyond desert to be in such company. Especially when the whole group is together, each bringing out all that is best, wisest, or funniest in all the others. Those are the golden sessions; when four or five of us after a hard day's walking have come to our inn; when our slippers are on, our feet spread out towards the blaze and our drinks at our elbows; when the whole world, and something beyond the world, opens itself to our minds as we talk; and no one has any claim on or any responsibility for another, but all are freemen and equals as if we had first met an hour ago, while at the same time an Affection mellowed by the years enfolds us. Life—natural life—has no better gift to give. Who could have deserved it?

These were the adult males whose laughter Lewis took particular pleasure in—and with whom he found another species of delight. And like the delight he took in myths, the cosmos of the medieval imagination, and old books generally, the pleasure of friendship pointed him toward truths and virtues of which our time knows little.

But at this point one might reasonably ask a question: hasn't Lewis simply sketched a picture of what an Inner Ring looks like to one within rather than one without? I am inclined to say, probably not. The Inner Ring is constructed around some hidden purpose or secret knowledge: the value of the members of the group is subordinated always to what they know or seek or desire. But the friends sitting around the fire value nothing, at that moment, but one another's company: "no one has any claim on or any responsibility for another." In the chapter from which this passage is drawn—it is the one on "Philia," or friendship, in *The Four Loves*—Lewis takes pains to explain that what differentiates friendship from erotic love, or familial affection, is complete disconnect from the world of biological need. There is a kind of *freedom* intrinsic to friendship, a freedom that can be better understood when one thinks of how accidental friendships are, how rarely they are looked for or chosen, and how inexplicably they develop over the years. Christians speak of their "brothers and sisters in Christ," because the relationship is indeed that of a family, and one has obligations to one's family members whether one happens to like them or not. Lewis's relationships with most of his friends were ones of "brotherhood in Christ" as well as friendship, but the freedom of friendship dominated, and this helped to make the gatherings of the Inklings a kind of informal school—the only kind of school Jack Lewis could ever like: a thoroughly informal training in living better and thinking more wisely.

Once Charles Williams was describing the "friends" of Job—the "comforters" who tell Job that all the horrific evils afflicting him must be his fault and the consequence of his sins—and casually noted ("immeasurably dropping his lower jaw") that they were surely "the sort of people who write books about the Problem of Pain." This was but gentle teasing of Lewis, of course, but it also contained a genuine warning, a reminder of the dangers of speaking too confidently about matters that, as Job himself ultimately came to admit, are too deep for us and beyond the scope of our powers. (Williams "used to say that if he were rich enough to build a church he would dedicate it to St. Thomas Didymus Skeptic"—that is, Doubting Thomas.) Beneath the bluff, hearty beer-and-pipes manner of the group a course of moral instruction, led by all and learned by all, was going on.

But the Inklings were something more even than that: they constituted a kind of tiny counterculture, an ongoing reminder to each member that there were possibilities for the human mind, heart, and spirit beyond what one might read in the newspapers, or in intellectual journals, or in textbooks such as Gaius and Titius's *Green Book*. Lewis, a shrewd analyst of the countercultural possibilities of true friendship, points out in *The Four Loves* the habitual hostility of all "Authority" to friendship. "Every real friendship is a sort of secession, even a rebellion. . . . In each knot of Friends there is a sectional 'public opinion' which fortifies its members against the public opinion of the community in general. Each therefore is a pocket of potential resistance." It is not surprising, then, that so many movements of resistance and rebellion over the centuries—"the Royal Society . . . the Romantic movement . . . Communism, Tractarianism, Methodism, the movement against slavery, the Reformation, the Renaissance"—had their origins in small groups of friends. Such a network can support radical ideas, whether innovations or recoveries, that even the most deeply committed individual would be hard-pressed to sustain on his or her own: "Alone among unsympathetic companions, I hold certain views and standards timidly, half ashamed to avow them and half doubtful if they can after all be right. Put me back among my Friends and in half an hour—in ten minutes—these same views and standards become once more indisputable."

This cultural "secessionist" movement was perhaps necessary in an Oxford that was rapidly modernizing itself, intellectually as well as economically and architecturally, but it had its dangers as well. Certainly the Inklings encouraged one another in their dislike of the twentieth century, and that was not always a good thing. Lewis would have been antimodern in any case, but no one among the Inklings was likely to challenge his view that the great German theologian Karl Barth was a "dreadful man"—even though Barth was, in his own way, as devoted an opponent of "liberal" Protestant theology as Lewis himself. And only Charles Williams was likely to have defended T. S. Eliot to Lewis, though it is not clear whether he actually did so. It is not always healthy to dwell in an environment where one's ideas become "once more indisputable." Lewis knew this perfectly well: "Friendship (as the ancients saw) can be a school of virtue; but also (as they did not see) a school of vice. It is ambivalent. It makes good men better and bad men worse." It is likely that he had his own early friendship with Arthur Greeves in mind when he wrote, "It was wonderful when we first met someone who cared for our favourite poet. . . . But it was no less delightful when we first met someone who shared with us a secret evil."

Clearly he did not believe that anything of the kind defaced the friendships between the Inklings. And perhaps it was only in their dogmatic antimodernism that the Inklings went slightly astray, resembling at times an Inner Ring. In his foreword to the second edition of *The Lord of the Rings,* Tolkien makes a statement that is characteristic of the Inkling position in matters of literary taste, and perhaps in other matters as well: "Some who have read the book, or at any rate have reviewed it, have found it boring, absurd, or contemptible; and I have no cause to complain, since I have similar opinions of their works, or of the kinds of writing they evidently prefer." As Tolkien's comment suggests, those of different tastes would not have been interested in joining the conversation anyway, but this blunt refusal of dialogue is not perfectly charitable.

Now, Tolkien was excessively hard to please, even by his friends. I have mentioned his distaste for Williams's writings and his frustration with much of Lewis's work. Dorothy Sayers's famed fictional detective Lord Peter Wimsey inspired in Tolkien "a loathing for him (and his creatrix) not surpassed by any other character in literature known to me, unless by his Harriet [Vane]." These views made Tolkien the odd man out in what was otherwise an extremely *simpatico* group—with one significant exception: Hugo Dyson hated Tolkien's stories so much that he would audibly groan and even swear as they were being read, whether by Tolkien himself in a mumble or by his son Christopher with eloquence; ultimately Dyson's objections led to Tolkien's fiction being taken permanently off the Inklings' menu. Perhaps this was not wholly to be regretted: as Lewis writes in *The Four Loves,* if friendship "is not full of mutual admiration, of Appreciative love, it is not Friendship at all." However, "it must not become what the people call a 'mutual admiration society'"—a group in which strong criticism is ruled out.

So there were limits to the Inklings' charity, both to one another and to outsiders, but consistently they were indeed a fellowship of friends whose pleasure was simply in the company of one another and who had no mutual obligations but in mutual love offered strength, encouragement, and sympathy. Once, when Warnie was away, Lewis wrote this account of a memorable evening in which any of the aforementioned tensions disappeared:

> On Thursday we had a meeting of the Inklings—you and Coghill both absented unfortunately. We dined at the Eastgate [Hotel, near Magdalen]. I have never in my life seen Dyson so exuberant—"a roaring cataract of nonsense." The bill of fare afterwards consisted of a section of the new Hobbit book [that is, *The Lord of the Rings*] from Tolkien, a nativity play from Williams (unusually intelligible for him, and approved by all) and a chapter out of the book on the Problem of Pain from me. It so happened—it would take too long to explain why—that the subject matter of the three readings formed almost a logical sequence, and produced a really first rate evening's talk of the usual wide-ranging kind—"from grave to gay, from lively to severe." I wished very much we could have had you with us.

And in a letter to a friend who wondered who were the Inklings to whom Lewis dedicated *The Problem of Pain,* after listing a few of the members he foreshadowed what he would write years later in *The Four Loves:* "We meet ... theoretically to talk about literature, but in fact nearly always to talk about something better. What I owe to them all is incalculable. Dyson and Tolkien were the immediate human causes of my own conversion. Is there any pleasure on earth as great as a circle of Christian friends by a good fire?"

Christian friends. Lewis believed that the Bible uses metaphors of erotic love and family attachment to depict Christian love but not metaphors of friendship: "Perhaps we may now hazard a guess why Scripture uses Friendship so rarely as an image of the highest love. It is already, in actual fact, too spiritual to be a good symbol of Spiritual things." But this spirituality is intensified when the friends are also fellow Christians. Less intense than friendship is something Lewis calls "companionship": a relationship based on "a common religion, common studies, a common profession, even a common recreation." But if companionship is "below" friendship, then above it, for Lewis, lies a love for one another "in Christ," that is, a love that is rooted in an *agreement* about the truth that friendship is not required to have. When mutual love, deep agreement, and common purpose all come together, we have something extraordinary and in the best sense supernatural: membership.

"Membership" is the title of a lecture Lewis gave in February 1945 to a group of Christians interested in building bridges between the Eastern (or Orthodox) and Western branches of the Church. This lecture is one of the deepest and wisest of his writings. He is first concerned to make sense of a phrase used on several occasions by Saint Paul, who speaks (for example, in Romans 12:5 or 1 Corinthians 6:15) of the Church as the "body of Christ" and says that this body has many "members." The most important thing one must keep in mind when seeing the English word "member" is that the everyday meaning of that word, "items or particulars included in a homogeneous class," like the members of a mathematical set, is "almost the reverse of what St. Paul meant by members. By members he meant what we should call organs, things essentially different from, and complementary to, one another."

Lewis insists that "true membership in a body differs from inclusion in a collective"—again he stresses the dangers of the structured, bureaucratic organization of modern society, in which communities have been replaced by "collectives." Our Authorities prefer us to belong to collectives; they suspect friendship and membership alike as being unpredictable, anarchic, and therefore indefensible. (On these very grounds Plato, like many later builders of Utopias, sought to have the State itself rather than parents charged with the raising of children.) To the State our affections are immature, *childish,* and therefore Lewis has hit upon a deep insight when he chooses characters from children's books to illustrate this theme. In *The Four Loves,* he writes, "The quaternion of Mole, Rat, Badger and Toad suggests the amazing heterogeneity possible between those who are bound by Affection," and in "Membership" he writes, "A trio such as Rat, Mole, and Badger symbolises the extreme differentiation of persons in harmonious union, which we know intuitively to be our true refuge both from solitude and from the collective." Toad is omitted from the second sentence because, as the resident Id of *The Wind in the Willows,* he is too utterly out of control to be in a state of "harmonious union" with anyone else, but the others have a deep affection for him all the same and extend to him a grace he does not deserve. This offer of "unmerited favor" happens often wherever Love reigns, but must always be anathema to the logical rigor of Authority or the collective: it will seem to express partiality as well as idiosyncrasy. What is Toad that his friends should be mindful of him? Considered as an "item or particular included in a homogeneous class," he is simply defective, because Toad is not homogeneous with anyone or anything else. But it is not as an item or particular that Toad is cared for, and his rescue sought; it is as Toad of Toad Hall, a unique personage in the community. And this kind of membership therefore echoes membership in the Body of Christ, for "it was not for societies or states that Christ died, but for men. In that sense Christianity must seem to secular collectivists to involve an almost frantic assertion of individuality."

But, Lewis wants to argue, it is not really an assertion of individuality at all. Rather, healthy communities (including families and churches) characteristically produce highly differentiated individuals, even the sorts of persons we call "characters." Lewis shares with several English writers—notably Charles Lamb, Dickens, Chesterton, Orwell, and today Roger Scruton—a deep love for the English propensity not only to tolerate but positively to encourage eccentricity. The English love their eccentrics not because the eccentricities themselves are necessarily delightful but because the mere presence of such odd folks among them is a testimony to the community's gentleness, tolerance, and humor. In the single most incisive essay on the English character I know, "England Your England"—written during the Second World War—Orwell asks why the Nazi goose-step, that terrifying image of "a boot crashing down on a face," is not used in England, and his answer is simple: "because the people in the street would laugh." (It is telling that in one of the greatest of P. G. Wodehouse's novels, *The Code of the Woosters,* the aspiring fascist dictator Roderick Spode—leader of the Black Shorts—is defeated and humiliated by the twit Bertie Wooster, though of course with the invaluable assistance of Jeeves, who discovers that Spode designs women's undergarments in his spare time. As Bertie sagely notes, one cannot be a dictator *and* design women's lingerie. "One or the other. Not both.") The society that encourages its eccentrics safeguards itself against the worst excesses of tyranny. A "rational" society would never tolerate Toad, but such a "rational" society would not be worth living in. The excesses of Toad are the price the community pays to make room for Badger to construct his snug underground estate and Rat and Mole to "mess about in boats."

That the four chief characters of *The Wind in the Willows* have such different interests but also (not excepting Toad, who knows that he is lamentably out of control and repents fervently of his foolishness, even if he never achieves the power of self-restraint) such commonality of morals—this is the chief sign, for Lewis, of the health of their world. Likewise, in a family

> the grandfather, the parents, the grown-up son, the child, the dog, and the cat are true members (in the organic sense), precisely because they are not members or units of a homogeneous class. They are not interchangeable. Each person is almost a species in himself.... If you subtract any one member, you have not simply reduced the family in number; you have inflicted an injury on its structure. Its unity is a unity of unlikes, almost of incommensurables.

The same is true in a fellowship of friends, as Lewis explains in a passage written in remembrance of the untimely death of Charles Williams ("Ronald" here is John Ronald Reuel Tolkien, though he and Lewis never used first names): "Now that Charles is dead, I shall never again see Ronald's reaction to a specifically Caroline joke. Far from having more of Ronald, having him 'to myself' now that Charles is away, I have less of Ronald. Hence true Friendship is the least jealous of loves." And of course this welcoming tendency is—or should be—still more characteristic of the Body of Christ: if "we possess each friend not less but more as the number of those with whom we share him increases," then "in this, Friendship exhibits a glorious 'nearness by resemblance' to Heaven itself where the very multitude of the blessed (which no man can number) increases the fruition which each has of God."

Point taken—but the people with whom we go to church, as opposed to our friends and family, may be people with whom we have no history, to whom we are not attracted, and with whom we have no other bond except church. Yet Christians believe that it is with just these people that we will form the strongest bonds, and ones that will last forever—even when the bonds that mean the most to us now have been, shockingly, dissolved: "For in the resurrection they neither marry nor are given in marriage, but are like the angels of God in heaven" (Matthew 22:30). How can this happen?

Lewis's most detailed and direct picture of it is *The Voyage of the "Dawn Treader,"* which I am tempted to call an allegory of the Church. After all, historically Christians have linked the Church with Noah's Ark: each boat is, in its time and place, a unique vessel of salvation. As the Church sails toward Heaven, so the *Dawn Treader* sails toward Aslan's country at the end of the world. And on this voyage Eustace's situation is the most significant one. He finds himself on this ship, knowing no one, comprehending nothing, and staying with the others only because he has no other option, as the slave trader Pug discovered when he "threw him in free with other lots and still no one would take him." He doesn't see that the *Dawn Treader* is his only hope of survival; he doesn't see that from the other members of that crew he could learn skills and virtues alike. Thanks to his parents and his school, he is a "boy without a chest" and is simply incapable of understanding what motivates the others, the martial Mouse Reepicheep above all.

And the only way for this to be remedied—as we saw in an earlier chapter—is for Eustace to undergo a kind of death: to have his very skin stripped away by Aslan, and only by Aslan, and to emerge newly born from the encounter. Moreover, the first part of what he must learn is simply that he is not a very good boy, that he is weak and cowardly—that, to put it bluntly, he is simply inferior to Caspian and Edmund and, yes, Reepicheep. It is noteworthy that after he becomes a boy again he tells Edmund, "You'd think me simply phony if I told you how I felt about my own arms. I know they've no muscle and are pretty mouldy compared with Caspian's, but I was so glad to see them." This is the first time that Eustace has considered himself anything but superior to everyone else, and if it seems obvious that Eustace's musculature would be dwarfed by that of the powerful young king, well, in the matter of self-knowledge everyone has to start somewhere. Only once he has acknowledged the "mouldiness" of his arms and the "beastliness" of his behavior is Eustace ready to begin the process of becoming a real member of the *Dawn Treader*'s crew. And it is but a beginning: "It would be nice, and fairly nearly true, to say that 'from that time forth Eustace was a different boy.' To be strictly accurate, he began to be a different boy. He had relapses. There were still many days when he could be very tiresome. But most of those I shall not notice. The cure had begun." And not only does the author politely refrain from noticing Eustace's shortcomings, but so too do the other members of the *Dawn Treader*'s crew. If Eustace is imperfect, he is growing, and we see him grow still further—though he never loses all his rough edges—in *The Silver Chair* and *The Last Battle*.

All of these themes are developed in theological language in the great lecture on "Membership." Thus: "I am going to venture to say that artificial equality is necessary in the life of the State, but in the Church we strip off this disguise, we recover our real inequalities, and are thereby refreshed and quickened." We cannot help but recall here how Eustace's disguise of self-importance is stripped off, revealing the real weakness and nastiness that must be recognized before it can be cured—but we are not accustomed, in our day and time, to hearing a frank disavowal of equality! Now Lewis passionately defends equality under the law. But he disavows equality of value in two senses: first, "if value is taken in a worldly sense—if we mean that all man are equally useful or beautiful or good or entertaining—then it is nonsense." Second, if we mean "that all are of equal value as immortal souls," then Lewis thinks we are close to a "dangerous error." Why? "God did not die for man because of some value He perceived in him.... He loved us not because we were lovable, but because He is Love." It is His love that *gives* value; we do not *possess* it.

When Aslan strips away Eustace's self-chosen disguise—when he rescues Eustace from the dragon-nature Eustace made for himself—it is a pure gift, and only as a result of that gift can Eustace start to become what he was made to be. In God's plan, "there is no question of finding for [a person] a place ... which will do justice to his inherent value and give scope to his natural idiosyncrasy. The place was there first. The man was created for it. He will not be himself until he is there." I think Lewis may have in mind here—as he does in several of his writings—the great vision of Paradise that Dante describes at the end of his *Divine Comedy*, when he looks back at the great vertical hierarchical universe through which he has been ascending and discovers all the saints arrayed in perfect order like the pieces of glass in a great cathedral's rose window. Though the vision of hierarchy is true, the vision of equality, in which what matters is that everyone holds his or her appointed place in the great scheme, is truer. "In His will is our peace," says one of the blessed to Dante. An unwillingness to accept an appointed place—the contrary determination to make a place for oneself—keeps more than one of the Ghosts in *The Great Divorce* from accepting Heaven. (Given Lewis's consistent critique of his own class, it is surely not accidental that among those Ghosts the two considered at the greatest length are a theologian and an artist, neither of whom will die to his ambition or self-regard.) Lewis was much taken with George MacDonald's great dictum: "The one principle of Hell is—'I am my own.'"

When Lewis writes that a man "will not be himself until he is there"—that is, in his appointed place in the cosmos—he is reminding us that the gift of new life begins with the gift of death. "You will be dead so long as you refuse to die," wrote MacDonald, and in Tolkien death is the "gift of Eru" (God) to humans: the Elves, as they grow weary of Middle Earth after their long ages of life, often envy it. The root of all this is in the Gospel: "Verily, verily I say unto you, except a corn of wheat fall into the ground and die, it abideth alone: But if it die it bringeth forth much fruit" (John 12:24.) As Lewis puts it in "Membership": "Nothing that has not died will be resurrected." And he goes on to say—unexpectedly in the context but perhaps fittingly in light of the path this chapter has followed—"That is just how Christianity cuts across the antithesis between individualism and collectivism." In other words, we die to ourselves so that we may live in the fellowship of the Body of Christ. It is precisely as "organs" of the body that we are resurrected, that we have eternal life, not as either individual entities or units in some homogeneous collective.

By contrast, the denizens of Hell come to have a dreadful, infinitely dull uniformity, something far less than humanity: "To enter hell, is to be banished from humanity. What is cast (or casts itself) into hell is not a man: it is 'remains' . . . to have been a man—to be an ex-man or 'damned ghost'—would presumably mean to consist of a will utterly centered in itself and passions utterly uncontrolled by the will." Thus the featureless, characterless, gray city of the damned in *The Great Divorce*. Likewise, though *Screwtape* portrays a bureaucratic Hell, it has the same motto—"Eat or be eaten"—and none in the Infernal Office can ever realize that the consumption of the damned never eases their ravenousness but only intensifies it.

It is the blessed in Heaven who continue to develop and grow in the knowledge and love of God, and each comes more and more fully to fulfill a unique place in the Divine design: again thinking of the images of bodily organs, Lewis writes, "Those who are members of one another become as diverse as the hand and the ear. That is why the worldlings are so monotonously alike compared with the almost fantastic variety of the saints." That variety is copied at the end of *The Last Battle* when all the major characters we have come to know from the earlier books begin to find their way into Aslan's country, the new and perfected Narnia, when the diversity of species (from Men to Badgers to Fauns to Centaurs to Marsh-wiggles) is exceeded only by the diversity of personalities. But much of this story we must save for later in our own tale. For now what matters is that the diversity-in-unity of these characters, who share no predicate except their devotion to Aslan, is modeled on the picture of the blessed in the seventh chapter of John's Revelation, when the apostle sees "a great multitude, which no man could number, of all nations, and kindreds, and people, and tongues"—yet this inconceivably various crowd all wear white robes, all hold palm branches aloft, all sing the same hymn. Their diversity is meaningful only because they are united in purpose and devotion, and their unity is given point and richness by their awesome variety.

The hymn this great assembly sings is a simple one: "Salvation to our God which sitteth upon the Throne, and unto the Lamb." (A clearer translation might be, "Salvation belongs to our God upon the Throne, and to the Lamb.") One of Scripture's names for Jesus Christ is the Lamb of God, and what all these people have in common is simply that they believe that this Lamb is the one who saves them. Every denomination, every variety of genuinely Christian belief, that the world has ever seen or will ever see is represented in this gathering: Orthodox, Catholic, Coptic, all the varieties of Protestantism (Anglican, Baptist, Congregationalist, Methodist, Presbyterian, and on and on). In this world such folks may well mistrust one another, each thinking the others misguided, prone to the wrong emphases, or perhaps even heretical, but around the Throne such distinctions have disappeared. They are indistinguishable because they are united in a common love and a common praise. They are merely Christians.

The term "mere Christianity" was coined by a seventeenth-century Anglican writer, Richard Baxter, who used to be famous: the piety of his work *The Saints' Everlasting Rest* was almost universally admired by our ancestors. But in his time Baxter was a rare voice of irenic tolerance. He lived through the English Civil War, which, though not strictly a religious war, was pretty close to it: rare was the Puritan who supported the King, and rarer still the higher-church Anglican who supported Parliament. Baxter, as a Puritan, backed Oliver Cromwell and the Parliamentary forces, but not without reservation and significant concern. Cromwell actually summoned Baxter from his church in Kidderminster, Worcestershire, to help establish the "fundamentals of religion" for the new postmonarchial government, but complained that Baxter's summary of Christianity could be affirmed by a Papist. "So much the better," replied Baxter, "and so much the fitter it is to be the matter of concord." This did not earn him Cromwell's trust, but his support for Cromwell, however qualified, earned him persecution after the restoration of the monarchy. Even a quarter-century later, during the "Bloody Assizes" of 1685, Baxter's books fell under the suspicious eye of the infamous Hanging Judge Jeffreys, who thought those writings seditious: the seventy-year-old Baxter had to spend two years in prison, which in the circumstances he probably thought of as getting off lightly.

Baxter's problem with the "Authorities" of his time, of whatever party, was that he refused to allow Christianity to succumb to the spirit of faction and sect. He believed that there was a core of orthodox Christianity that Puritans, Anglicans, and Catholics all affirmed and that should have been a source of peace among them. "Must you know what Sect or Party I am of?" he wrote in 1680. "I am against all Sects and dividing Parties: but if any will call Mere Christian by the name of a Party, ... I am of that Party which is so against Parties." For Cromwell and Judge Jeffreys alike this is a contemptible refusal to choose sides, but Baxter felt he *was* choosing his side: "I am a CHRISTIAN, a MERE CHRISTIAN, of no other religion."

One could, of course, point out that England in the middle of the twentieth century was a very different country than England in the middle of the seventeenth: if in that earlier time almost everyone in the country had been a Christian of one kind or another, by Lewis's time British Christianity was in a sad state. Churches throughout the island of Britain had lost many members in the period of the Great War and, after a slight recovery in the 1920s, resumed their decline during the Depression and have been declining ever since. If the danger in Baxter's time had been warfare among various kinds of Christians, the danger in Lewis's time was the evaporation of Christianity altogether. Yet

Lewis felt that the remedy for the first crisis was also the remedy for the second: if Christianity is embattled and declining, it is all the more important for Christians to put their differences aside and join to sing the One Hymn of the One Church. In Lewis's view, the hostility of Christians to one another had been the great affliction of Christ's Church at least since the Reformation. Describing in his book on English Renaissance literature the history that led to the idea that Protestants believe in "salvation by faith" while Catholics favor "salvation by works," he allows himself a rare expression of frustration, even anger:

> The process whereby "faith and works" became a stock gag in the commercial theatre is characteristic of that whole tragic farce which we call the history of the Reformation. The theological questions really at issue have no significance except on a certain level, a high level, of the spiritual life; they could have been fruitfully debated only between mature and saintly disputants in close privacy and at boundless leisure. Under those conditions formulae might possibly have been found which did justice to the Protestant . . . assertions without compromising other elements of the Christian faith. In fact, however, these questions were raised at a moment when they immediately became embittered and entangled with a whole complex of matters theologically irrelevant, and therefore attracted the fatal attention both of government and the mob. When once this had happened, Europe's chance to come through unscathed was lost.

Christians today are still living with the consequences—and often enough making those consequences worse.

The core of Lewis's position is his claim that "the theological questions really at issue have no significance except on a certain level, a high level, of the spiritual life." Again and again he reminds us that some of the questions most dear to our hearts are simply not within the scope of our knowledge. In several different contexts he invokes a peculiar passage from the last chapter of Saint John's Gospel. Jesus, speaking to his disciples after his Resurrection, prophesies the death of Peter, but Peter wants to know what will become of "the disciple whom Jesus loved," that is, John himself: "Lord, and what shall this man do?" It is Jesus's reply that Lewis often quotes: "What is that to thee? Follow thou me." Indeed, the scene is replayed quite exactly at the end of *The Voyage of the "Dawn Treader"* when Aslan tells Lucy that she will not return to Narnia. Lucy counters with a question: "And is Eustace never to come back here either?" But Aslan is firm, if gentle: "Child, . . . do you really need to know that?"

The suggestion that Lewis seems to be making in the passage I quoted from his OHEL book is that Christians create "Sects and dividing Parties" within the Church when they become overly fascinated with matters beyond the scope of human beings' proper concern— or, to put it another way, when their curiosity exceeds their faithfulness. Therefore, when it is necessary to approach difficult questions, one must, Lewis believes, stick as closely as possibly to "the belief that has been common to nearly all Christians at all times." This is especially important when such questions are raised in the presence of unbelievers, that is, in public: "I think we must admit that the discussion of these disputed points has no tendency at all to bring outsiders into the Christian fold. . . . Our divisions should never be discussed except in the presence of those who have already come to believe that there is one God and that Jesus Christ is His only Son." This is a very strict rule! *Never* discuss those divisions in public? But Christians' failure to obey it seems to have done Christianity little good and much harm.

Indeed, Lewis raises the bar extraordinarily high even for discussions of theological differences in "private," that is, among Christians only. When he writes that these disputed questions "could have been fruitfully debated only between mature and saintly disputants in close privacy and at boundless leisure," he implicitly encourages us to ask ourselves whether we are saintly enough, discreet enough, and patient enough to conduct such debates properly. Moreover, for Lewis there is no shame or even loss in simply sticking to "the belief that has been common to nearly all Christians at all times." Probably his best expression of this vital point is found, not in *Mere Christianity,* but in an introduction he wrote to someone else's book—a translation by one Sister Penelope of the great fourth-century Alexandrian theologian Athanasius's treatise *On the Incarnation.* (She was a nun at the Anglican Convent of St. Mary the Virgin in Wantage, near Oxford; Lewis enjoyed a long and meaningful correspondence with her and thought of her as his "elder sister" in the faith.) This is the essay in which he passionately defends the reading of "old books"; in the course of that defense he explains that it was scholarly reading that (among other things) led to his conversion:

I myself was first led into reading the Christian classics, almost accidentally, as a result of my English studies. Some, such as Hooker, Herbert, Traherne, Taylor and Bunyan, I read because they are themselves great English writers; others, such as Boethius, St. Augustine, Thomas Aquinas and Dante, because they were "influences." George Macdonald I had found for myself at the age of sixteen and never wavered in my allegiance, though I tried for a long time to ignore his Christianity. They are, you will note, a mixed bag, representative of many Churches, climates and ages. And that brings me to yet another reason for reading them. The divisions of Christendom are undeniable and are by some of these writers most fiercely expressed. But if any man is tempted to think—as one might be tempted who read only contemporaries—that "Christianity" is a word of so many meanings that it means nothing at all, he can learn beyond all doubt, by stepping out of his own century, that this is not so. Measured against the ages "mere Christianity" turns out to be no insipid interdenominational transparency, but something positive, self-consistent, and inexhaustible.

Because "mere Christianity" is positive, it provides direction for the spiritual inquirer; because it is self-consistent, it provides security; because it is inexhaustible, it provides delight. As young Jack Lewis the unbeliever discovered: "In the days when I still hated Christianity, I learned to recognise, like some all too familiar smell, that almost unvarying something which met me, now in Puritan Bunyan, now in Anglican Hooker, now in Thomist Dante.... It was, of course, varied; and yet—after all—so unmistakably the same." This testimony from a former unbeliever is important because it provides a necessary corrective of perception, a reminder that as grievous as divisions among Christians can be, they are not the whole story:

> Those who have always lived within the Christian fold may be too easily dispirited by them. They are bad, but such people do not know what it looks like from without. Seen from there, what is left intact despite all the divisions, still appears (as it truly is) an immensely formidable unity. I know, for I saw it; and well our enemies know it. That unity any of us can find by going out of his own age. It is not enough, but it is more than you had thought till then.

One of those "enemies," Screwtape, agrees:

> One of our great allies at present is the Church itself. Do not mis-
> understand me. I do not mean the Church as we see her spread
> out through all time and space and rooted in eternity, terrible
> as an army with banners. That, I confess, is a spectacle which
> makes our boldest tempters uneasy. But fortunately it is quite in-
> visible to these humans.

So in emphasizing this "positive, self-consistent, and inexhaustible"
mere Christianity, Lewis is not only—not primarily—calling Christians to a new commitment to unity, a new tolerance and patience;
rather, he is calling Christians to recognize what already is: a Church
of unity and power "spread out through all time and space and rooted
in eternity." Only by recognizing what the Church truly *is* can Christians begin to make it what it *should be.*

Armed with these convictions, Lewis dedicated himself to explaining and defending this "mere Christianity": even in the preface to his
first book of apologetics, *The Problem of Pain,* he writes, "I have believed myself to be restating ancient and orthodox doctrines.... I have
tried to assume nothing that is not professed by all baptised and communicating Christians." Concerned to do the same when he wrote
Mere Christianity, he had his work read by Christians of various de-
nominations to be sure he had not inadvertently made a claim distinctive to him or to Anglicanism. For the rest of his life he would
steadfastly refuse to enter into disputes among his fellow Christians—
though he did make clear again and again his disdain for all movements to "liberalize" or "demythologize" Christianity, which he
tended to place in the category of "Christianity-and-water." (It is
rather comical that when he discusses such compromises or rejections
of orthodoxy Lewis can assume the tone of the schoolmasters of his
youth: Christianity-and-water and atheism are "boys' philosophies";
"next to Christianity Dualism is the manliest and most sensible creed
on the market.") It is somewhat paradoxical, perhaps, that though one
of the chief purposes of Protestant liberalism was to strip away supposedly unnecessary supernatural accretions from Christianity, thereby
leaving a lowest common denominator of belief that all could agree to,
the result has been not to make Christians more tolerant of one another but to reduce the number of Christians—and to make the "lib-
erals" increasingly hostile to any reassertion of "ancient and orthodox

doctrines." As Lewis wrote after his *Mere Christianity* lectures had been around for a while:

> Certainly I have met with little of the fabled *odium theologicum* ["theological hatred"] from convinced members of communions different from my own. Hostility has come more from borderline people whether within the Church of England or without it: men not exactly obedient to any communion. This I find curiously consoling. It is at her centre, where her truest children dwell, that each communion is really closest to every other in spirit, if not in doctrine. And this suggests that at the centre of each there is a something, or a Someone, who against all divergencies of belief, all differences of temperament, all memories of mutual persecution, speaks with the same voice.

Conversely, he felt, "the liberal and 'broad-minded' people in each Body could never be united at all.... The world of ... watered-down 'religion' is a world where a small number of people (all of the same type) say totally different things and change their minds every few minutes. We shall never get re-union from them."*

In 1938, just as Lewis was beginning his career as a defender of Christianity, his near-contemporary, the American theologian Reinhold Niebuhr, came to Edinburgh to deliver the Gifford Lectures, and there he decried what he called "the easy conscience of modern man." An "easy conscience" is precisely the problem, Lewis felt, with the "liberal and 'broad-minded'" Christians of his or any other time: their self-satisfaction, their inability to sense that they need to be "obedient" to *any* particular teaching or set of beliefs. Feeling no need to obey, they never discover that they *cannot* obey, and therefore never discover the need for repentance, conversion, transformation—the kind of transformation that would make them fit participants in the

---

* More pointed still is this passage—nearly a tirade—from a 1945 letter to Sister Penelope: "The truth is we shall never get on till we have stamped out 'religion.' 'Religion' as it is called—the vague slush of humanitarian idealism, Emersonian Pantheism, democratic politics and material progressiveness with a few Christian names and formulae added to taste like pepper and salt—is almost the great enemy. If one can't talk to a Christian then give me a real believing member of some other religion or an honest clear-headed skeptic like J. S. Mill. One can at least get sense out of them."

great assembly of the redeemed that John envisioned in his Revelation. Though, like the Tragedian in *The Great Divorce,* they project a vast self-image, it is insubstantial: their real selves get ever smaller and ever ghostlier. But they never notice it.

Transformation is not optional but mandatory for Christians. This was Lewis's consistent position. After all, he had undergone his own transformation, discovering "depth under depth of self-love and self-admiration" (as he told Arthur right at the beginning of his Christian pilgrimage) and submitting to the lifelong discipline of being purged of such sin. We must die in order to live, lose our lives in order to find them, give up what we *think of* as ourselves in order to gain our true selves. And this is the most difficult of tasks: as Eustace discovers, our best efforts at self-understanding and self-correction are but feeble; the revelation of who we *really* are must come from without, and when it does come it devastates us. Then the sin and folly of even our noblest labors and wisest words appear before us with a heartbreaking clarity. For Lewis, Christian unity *begins* with the recognition that we have all, like Eustace, through our pride and selfishness, made ourselves into dragons. We must then understand that we cannot undragon ourselves—we lack the strength—and after that we must accept that God is ready and willing to undragon us, if we will but allow Him do to so. For Lewis, only those who share this picture of the human predicament and its cure can join together in true unity—can really, and not just nominally, become members of one another in a single Body.

TEN

"Nobody could put Lewis down"

If the arrival of Charles Williams in Oxford marked a significant development in the life of Jack Lewis, his life was changed in other ways by another by-product of the war: he became a famous radio personality. One of the books we have been discussing, *Mere Christianity*, began life not as a book but as a series of radio addresses; only much later did those addresses all go between two covers and assume their now-famous title. The consequences of this new fame would be great indeed, for Lewis and for many others.

The return of war to Europe, on September 1, 1939, though it had been foreseen as all but inevitable for some time, nevertheless brought terror to the whole continent and moved millions to question what they believed in and why. W. H. Auden, in New York City, condemned the Treaty of Versailles, which at the end of the Great War had imposed crushing sanctions on defeated Germany: "Those to whom evil is done / Do evil in return." Others blamed Germany for a long history of imperial ambition; still others focused on Adolf Hitler (a "psychopathic god," in Auden's phrase) as the locus and impetus of evil. Even Lewis was unsettled in a variety of ways. Warnie, who as a retired officer was technically in the reserve, was called up for duty, and Jack (who had not yet turned forty-one) was actually eligible to be drafted; moreover, he did not know what his university would do, though he remembered its emptiness during the previous war. Indeed, memory was Lewis's curse in those dark days. I mentioned in an earlier chapter his comment in a letter that "my memories of the last war haunted my dreams for years." Yet he knew how evil Hitler was and understood full well the scope of German ambition and the necessity of resisting it.*

"If its got to be, its got to be," Lewis wrote, with evident resignation. "But the flesh is weak and selfish and I think death wd. be much better than to live through another war." And he told Arthur, "As [Warnie] said in his last letter what makes it worse is the ghostly feeling that it has all happened before—that one fell asleep during the last war and had a delightful dream and has now waked up again." Indeed, the whole of Europe was experiencing this déjà vu—except, perhaps, for the young men who were poised to fight this new war and were too young to remember the horrors of the previous one. It is obvious from the comments I have just quoted that Lewis did not think of the onset of another vast conflict as anything *but* a horror, yet as a Christian he was bound to ask whether God might be able to bring *some* good from the misery. As he wrote to Arthur, "I daresay for me, personally, it has come in the nick of time: I was just beginning to get too well settled in my profession, too successful, and probably self-complacent." Without in any way minimizing the horror and tragedy of another vast war, Lewis had already begun to ask himself questions that put the war into both smaller and larger contexts: the smaller one of how he as one ordinary person might grow in virtue or fall into sin as a result of the wartime situation, and the larger one of what a war meant in light of eternity. *The Screwtape Letters,* which were written in the first years of the war and use the war consistently as a backdrop, are much concerned with these two contexts. When Wormwood expresses delight at the commencement of hostilities, Screwtape warns

---

* Interestingly, he and Tolkien alike were horrified by what had already been revealed about Nazi policy toward Germany's Jews—which, by the way, makes nonsense of the oft-heard claim that people outside Germany had no idea what Hitler was up to. Even in 1933, the year in which Hitler was first elected Germany's chancellor, Lewis wrote to Arthur that "the iniquity of Hitler's persecution of the Jews" was inexcusable. And in 1938, when the publication of a German edition of *The Hobbit* was being held up because of the publisher's doubt that Tolkien was an Aryan name, Tolkien drafted a reply stating that his name was a German one, but "if I am to understand that you are enquiring whether I am of *Jewish* origin, I can only reply that I regret that I appear to have *no* ancestors of that gifted people. . . . I cannot, however, forbear to comment that if impertinent and irrelevant inquiries of this sort are to become the rule in matters of literature, then the time is not far distant when a German name will no longer be a source of pride." It is not clear whether Tolkien actually sent this letter, but his position could not be clearer.

him "not to hope too much from a war." "Of course a war is enter-taining," he tells his nephew. "The immediate fear and suffering of the humans is a legitimate and pleasing refreshment for our myriads of toiling workers. But what permanent good does it do us unless we make use of it for bringing souls to Our Father Below?" Screwtape worries that people in mortal danger will prepare themselves spiritu-ally for death; he fears that even those who lack Christian belief will "have their attention diverted from themselves to values and causes which they believe to be higher than the self"—a very dangerous de-velopment from the Infernal point of view. Worst of all, "if we are not careful, we shall see thousands turning in this tribulation to the Enemy." And it was just this outcome, so feared by Screwtape, that Jack Lewis determined to do all he could to encourage.

His determination took several forms, but primarily he began a temporary career as an itinerant lecturer on Christian topics—not ex-actly a circuit-riding preacher, but something not far from it. In addi-tion to sermons preached in Oxford and London, during the war he wrote for Christian magazines and newspapers as well as newspapers of a general readership in London, Oxford, and Coventry. He spoke to countless student groups, to Anglican priests and youth leaders, to members of the Royal Air Force (including the Women's Auxiliary), even to the Electrical and Musical Industries Christian Fellowship. But above all, he spoke to the national radio audience of the British Broad-casting Company.

Britain was a different society in those days; the BBC understood that in time of war part of its mandate was to provide moral and spir-itual support for a beleaguered nation. (The story is told fully in a re-cent book by the late Justin Phillips, C. S. *Lewis at the BBC: Messages of Hope in the Darkness of War.*) The key figure in this project was James Welch, an Anglican priest who had left parish ministry and pas-toral education in 1939 to become the BBC's director of religious broadcasting. Early in 1941 he addressed a letter to Lewis: "I write to ask whether you would be willing to help us in our work of religious broadcasting." In making this request, which was also an offer, Welch was taking a chance: as someone who had been not only impressed but significantly helped by *The Problem of Pain,* he knew that Lewis was a vivid and fluent writer, but it is not clear whether he knew that Lewis was also a dynamic speaker. Perhaps Lewis's reputation as a lec-turer had spread even to the corridors of the BBC's London offices, but even if it had, no one could be sure that someone accustomed to the relatively free environment of the lecture hall could adapt to the strictures of radio broadcasting—especially since what Welch had in mind was *live* broadcasting.

In any event, with some caveats and conditions, Lewis agreed to speak. He was put in touch with a man named Eric Fenn, who would be his producer for all his talks, which began in August. Lewis's plan from the beginning was to make a case for simple right and wrong— for what he would soon come to call the Tao, the Moral Law—without invoking Christianity until a very late stage in the argument: "The first step is to create, or recover, the sense of guilt" for trespasses of that Law. "Hence if I give a series of talks I should mention Christianity only at the end." These talks—which, with limited revisions, may be found in *Mere Christianity* as book I, "Right and Wrong as a Clue to the Meaning of the Universe"—were sufficiently successful that Lewis gave a second series in January and February of 1942, now covering specifically Christian doctrine, especially regarding Jesus Christ himself. Series I and II were then almost immediately published in book form as *Broadcast Talks*—which gives some indication of their popularity, especially since the paper available to publishers was under pretty strict rationing. A third series ("Christian Behaviour") was given in the fall of 1942; after Lewis had refused several requests by Fenn, a fourth and final series was broadcast in early 1944.

Lewis found it frustrating to work with the BBC, especially since they wanted him to broadcast his talks at times that required him to take late-night trains back to Oxford and put him considerably behind on his rest. He was able to get them to record some of the talks rather than broadcast them live, but not enough to his taste: "If you know the address of any reliable firm of assassins, nose-slitters, garrotters and poisoners I should be grateful to have it," he wrote to Fenn, apparently blaming unspecified higher-ups rather than his poor producer, which must have been a relief to Fenn.

But such inconveniences were the least of Lewis's worries, because with the commencement of his career as a broadcaster there commenced also a problem that would afflict him to the end of his days: a daily cascade of letters from angry, worried, confused, bemused, curious, and grateful listeners. In February 1942, during the second series, he wrote to Fenn and noted, rather plaintively, "I'm still wading [through] the correspondence caused by the talks. . . . I wrote 35 letters yesterday: all out of working hours of course. It 'gets one down'—not to mention postage." (At this point in his career, when Lewis was not yet well off and in any case was giving away all the money he earned from these talks, as well as from *The Screwtape Letters,* to charity, the postage was a significant expense. Moreover, he did not realize that even when he gave the money away he was still expected to pay taxes on it, so when his tax bill came due he could barely pay it. After that shock, Barfield helped Lewis set up his own charity so he could practice his extraordinary generosity without bankrupting himself.) He got so much in the habit of writing these letters that he would sign notes to close friends "C. S. Lewis," then cross it out and add "Jack." He does this in a January 1943 letter to Arthur that also contains this bit of information: "As you will have noticed I've been having great luck with my books lately, and it wd. be affectation to pretend I hadn't got much pleasure out of it: but the catch is it increases the amount of letters one has to write almost beyond endurance."

Usually it was only to Arthur, in letters anyway, that he acknowledged the price he was paying for adding weekend lectures to the RAF, sermons, and broadcast talks—all of which generated correspondence—to his other duties as lecturer, tutor, writer, and general household servant. (And pray-er: his list of people to pray for had become so long, largely as a result of all his correspondence, that he was having trouble getting through it, and only on the advice of Father Walter Adams—whom he had chosen to be his spiritual director and, later, confessor—did he abbreviate it, at least sometimes.) Sadly, at just this point Minto began to become particularly burdensome to him. It is unlikely that she ever reconciled herself to his Christianity: remarkably often in his writings Lewis mentions the tension that can arise in a family when one member becomes a Christian. In an interview he commented, "It is extraordinary how inconvenient to your family it becomes for you to get up early to go to Church. It doesn't matter so much if you get up early for anything else, but if you get up early to go to Church it's very selfish of you and you upset the house." With something similar in mind, Screwtape sees the possibility of exploiting the conversion of Wormwood's patient to exacerbate conflict between the young man and his mother. In *The Four Loves,* Lewis writes, even more pointedly—perhaps because by this time Minto was dead—"Few things in the ordinary peacetime life of a civilised country are more nearly fiendish than the rancour with which a whole unbelieving family will turn on the one member of it who has become a Christian." One cannot imagine that these statements do not arise from harsh personal experience, so we can guess at least some of what Lewis had in mind

when he asked Sister Penelope, in November 1941, to "Pray for *Jane*....
She is the old lady I call my mother and live with (she is really the
mother of a friend)—an unbeliever, ill, old, frightened, full of charity
in the sense of alms, but full of uncharity in other senses. And I can do
so little for her."

So, "I'm pretty well," he tells Arthur, "sometimes sad, other times
not." And considering Lewis's lifelong preferences, the next bit of
news is not a good sign at all: "Except in bed and in trains I get v. little
reading done now.... it's a weary world, isn't it?" It is unsurprising
that in his very next surviving letter—to a woman named Mary Neylan,
a former pupil of his who wrote often for advice on all sorts of matters
—he writes wistfully of one of his favorite pleasures: the peaceful irre-
sponsibility of mild illness.

In these circumstances one would think that any old body who
happened to write Professor C. S. Lewis with a question about Christianity or morals or whatever would have to expect silence or, at
best, the briefest of replies—especially if, as was sometimes the case,
they "sign themselves 'Jehovah' or begin 'Dear Mr. Lewis, I was married at the age of 20 to a man I didn't love.'" So he told Arthur, and
perhaps indeed *those* correspondents got cursory replies. Or perhaps
not: throughout the decade of the 1950s he wrote 138 letters to an
American woman who did little other than complain to Lewis about
the sins and foibles of her family. Lewis knew, as he told a friend, that
she was "a very silly, tiresome, and probably disagreeable woman,"
but he also knew that she was "old, poor, sick, lonely, and miserable." So he replied unfailingly to her letters. And then, as he also
told Arthur, "it was a duty to answer fully" the letters he received
from "serious inquirers." And he meant *duty*: the refrain that recurs
in his comments on this subject is that a writer, by the very fact of
putting ideas before the public, contracts an unshirkable responsibility to that public—especially since readers can draw conclusions
or formulate interpretations at odds with the author's purposes. My
favorite letter along these lines (probably my favorite of all Lewis's
letters) was written in 1955 to the mother of a nine-year-old American boy who feared that he was sinning by loving Aslan more than
Jesus. Lewis suggests some words of reassurance as well as a prayer
the boy might pray; then he adds to the end of the prayer: "And if
Mr. Lewis has worried any other children by his books or done them
any harm, then please forgive him and help him never to do it
again."

When these letters started rolling in, Warnie's assistance, which had already been valuable to Lewis, now became invaluable. At the beginning of 1940 Warnie had been recommissioned at the rank of major and sent back to France, where he immediately fell ill and was deposited in a hospital. In May he was one of the thousands of British soldiers evacuated from Dunkirk in that great miracle, when fishing boats and pleasure yachts and fire-brigade boats sailed across the Channel to rescue troops pressed almost against the shore by the German Blitzkrieg through Belgium and France. By August he was, once and for all, back at the Kilns—just in time to offer aid to his beleaguered brother. (The timing was excellent on other grounds as well: Maureen got married in October, and if Warnie had not been around, the whole responsibility for caring for Minto would have fallen on Jack.)

During the war years, when paper was scarce, Lewis often wrote his responses on the blank portions of the letters addressed to him, or else used tiny scraps of paper, but in less stringent conditions he would dictate a response to his brother or sketch out (verbally or in writing) an answer that Warnie would develop into a full letter. I have mentioned that Lewis's pupils became very familiar with the sound of a typewriter knocking away in the next room as they read their essays; Warnie also developed a system for filing incoming letters and carbon copies of the replies. But the volume of correspondence was so great that Lewis still spent far more of every morning than he could comfortably spare answering the earnest questioners, lonely hearts, and megalomaniacs whose pleas the Royal Mail delivered so consistently to his door, day after day, season succeeding season, world without end, Amen.

There was a bright spot in the Lewis home during at least part of the war: her name was June Flewett, and she was one of the many thousands of children who were evacuated from London and housed elsewhere as soon as the war began. The Kilns had taken in four schoolgirls the day after the Germans invaded Poland; they and others would come and go throughout the war. But June, who came to live with the Lewises in the summer of 1943, was different. She was certainly a saint, perhaps an angel of mercy. Sixteen when she arrived, she was a devout Catholic and an aspiring actress, and her favorite writer was C. S. Lewis, but she had no idea that the "Jack" whose house she was living in was the same man. It is not even clear that she knew his last name was Lewis, since it was Mrs. Moore to whom she was first introduced, and Jack and Warnie, as far as June knew, were just Mrs. Moore's sons. Only after she had been around long enough to develop what she later called "a tremendous crush" on Lewis—"Of course I fell madly in love with him"—did she discover his identity. It was quite a shock. (Significantly, the first thing that attracted June to Lewis was his unfailing kindness to Minto, and she also saw very clearly that Minto nearly worshiped Lewis. The relationship had become very difficult, but much love was still in it—though obviously of a very different kind than that with which their relationship began.)

The two years that June lived at the Kilns were the best of the decade in that household. Everyone adored her, and she managed to keep Minto happier than anyone else could. There were, as I mentioned in the introduction, two maids working in the house at this time, but both of them were in their different ways mentally unstable, and in any case they could not achieve the standards of housekeeping that Minto thought necessary. Only June could mediate these conflicts, and when it became clear in late 1944 that at the turn of the new year she would be leaving—to study at the Royal Academy of Dramatic Art in London—the whole household was devastated. Warnie's tribute to her, in his diary, is really astonishing:

> I have met no one of any age further advanced in the Christian way of life. From seven in the morning till nine at night, shut off from people of her own age, almost grudged the time for her religious duties, she has slaved at the Kilns, for a fractional [wage]; I have never seen her other than gay, eager to anticipate exigent demands, never complaining, always self-accusing in the frequent crises of that dreary house. Her reaction to the meanest ingratitude was to seek its cause in her own faults. She is one of those rare people to whom one can venture to apply the word "saintly."

Lewis too—habitually more precise in his language than Warnie, who tended to exaggerate—called her "a perfectly saintly girl" in a letter to Sister Penelope, and to her parents said that "she is, without exception, the most selfless person I have ever known."

A difficult moment for Lewis had arisen when June's parents wrote to ask him whether she should leave the Kilns to enroll in the Royal Academy, where she had already been accepted. Though acting was her passion and lifelong dream, the difficulty had arisen because, as Lewis told her parents, "June's own view is simply and definitively that she won't leave here of her own free will." Lewis—and clearly this took an extraordinary effort of will—replied that "June ought, in her own best interests, to go to the Academy this coming term." The conventions of such a situation required that he go on to say how much they would all miss her, but he did not, and he told the Flewetts why: "I don't like thinking of it." However, he had already spilled the beans: earlier in the letter he had written that "when June goes the only bright spot in our prospect goes with her."

June left; that prospect darkened. I have outlined in the introduction the miseries of these years for Lewis, or rather the years immediately following her departure: the general overwork, the ongoing demands of Minto, the lunacy of the housemaids, Warnie's drinking—which may have accelerated as a more or less direct result of June's departure, since that left him with no barrier of protection from Minto, whom he obviously detested. And I have said that these were the circumstances in which he first contemplated the writing of a story for children. But another element of the situation—perhaps the most important of all—I have not yet mentioned.

In late 1941 a woman named Stella Aldwinckle, who had read theology at Oxford in the 1930s and then returned to work for St. Aldate's Church, enlisted Lewis's help in forming a debating society in which the claims of Christianity, and the objections to those claims, would be featured. They called it the Socratic Club, and Lewis remained its president (and Stella Aldwinckle its chairman) until Lewis's departure for Cambridge. The idea was that at one week's meeting— the club met weekly during term time—a Christian would give a paper to which an unbeliever would respond; the following week the roles would be reversed. And of course, there would be time for general questions and debate. From the beginning of the Socratic Club, Lewis was the dominant personality: though he did not often give a paper himself, he was almost always present and ready to contribute to the discussion. Austin Farrer—a priest and theologian who, along with his wife, Katherine, was a close friend of Lewis's and Tolkien's— wrote of how he feared situations when he, rather than Lewis, would be expected to stand up for the faith: "I went in fear and trembling, certain to be caught out in debate and to let down the side. But there Lewis would be, snuffing the imminent battle and saying 'Aha!' at the sound of the trumpet. My anxieties rolled away. Whatever ineptitude I might commit, he would maintain the cause; and nobody could put Lewis down."

"Nobody could put Lewis down"—this proved, for Lewis himself, to be just the problem. In writing an introduction to the first *Socratic Digest* (a gathering of the papers and responses from the club's meetings), he freely acknowledges that the founders of the club were not impartial or neutral on the matter of Christianity. But, he goes on to say, "argument . . . has a life of its own. No man can tell where it will go. We expose ourselves, and the weakest of our party, to your fire no less than you are exposed to ours. . . . The arena is common to both parties and cannot finally be cheated; in it you risk nothing, and we risk all." That is, the unbeliever whose case for unbelief seems weaker at the end of the day has not "lost" anything: at worst, he or she must do further thinking about the evidence for and against Christian belief. But the believer whose case for Christianity is undermined by such debates is in a much more vulnerable position. So much is clear, and the points are valid ones. But to this argument Lewis adds something unexpected:

> Worse still, we expose ourselves to recoil from our own shots; for if I may trust my personal experience no doctrine is, for the moment, dimmer to the eye of faith than that which a man has just *successfully* defended. [emphasis added]

Two years later Lewis concluded a talk on "Christian Apologetics" for a group of priests and youth leaders in Wales with a word of confession and warning:

> One last word. I have found that nothing is more dangerous to one's own faith than the work of an apologist. No doctrine of the Faith seems to me so spectral, so unreal as one that I have just *successfully* defended in a public debate. For a moment, you see, it has seemed to rest on oneself: as a result, when you go away from that debate, it seems no stronger than that weak pillar. That is why we apologists take our lives in our hands and can be saved only by falling back continually from the web of our own arguments . . . into the Reality—from Christian apologetics into Christ Himself. [emphasis added]

The remarkable thing about these two statements is the confession that Lewis's faith was more endangered by his skill in argument and flair for debate than it would have been by failure. "Nobody could put Lewis down," but this did not give Lewis confidence; rather, it made him question a faith that had to be upheld by his own dialectical efforts.

This curious phenomenon helps to explain something otherwise difficult to understand. I have already noted, again in the introduction, that in 1947 Lewis began to experience a terror of death—or more specifically, of ceasing to be. ("I have, almost all my life, been quite unable to feel that horror of nonentity, of annihilation, which, say, Dr. Johnson felt so strongly. I felt it for the first time only in 1947. But that was after I had long been reconverted and thus began to know what life really is and what would have been lost by missing it.") Yet in 1945 the conviction of life after death, of Christian immortality, had been particularly strong in him, and indeed in some of his friends, thanks to the death of Charles Williams. In a letter to Sister Penelope—the one in which he refers to Williams as "my dearest friend"—he writes that Williams's death

> has greatly increased my faith. Death has done nothing to my idea of him, but he has done—oh, I can't say what—to my idea of death. It has made the next world much more real and palpable. We all feel the same. How one lives and learns. I have often heard of widows and bereaved mothers who "felt that 'he' was now nearer to them than while in the body" and always thought it a sentimental hyperbole. I know better now.

And he then goes on to relate a remark of Hugo Dyson's—a remark he quotes in at least three other letters—to the effect that what was true of Jesus (he departed only to return in a new form) is also true, in a different and lesser degree, of our Christian friends.

Yet from this mood—sadness and loss overcome by exaltation and faith and confidence in "the next world"—Lewis moved in a relatively short time to an unprecedented fear of annihilation. How could this have happened?

It happened, I believe, because at the same time that he was experiencing the presence of his dead friend, he was also writing about life after death and the miracle of resurrection. Indeed, on the very day that Williams fell ill and was admitted to the hospital where, five days later, he died, Lewis wrote to another friend, "I . . . have been v. much occupied by the idea of the New Creation. . . . New heavens and new earth—the resurrection of the body—how we have neglected these doctrines.... I'm working on a book on Miracles at present in wh. this theme will play a large part." And he had just completed *The Great Divorce,* with its underlying idea that all people live forever, whether into increasing blessedness or increasing hellishness. Or as he had put it in his greatest sermon, "The Weight of Glory" (preached in June 1941), "There are no *ordinary* people. You have never talked to a mere mortal. Nations, cultures, arts, civilisations—these are mortal, and their life is to ours as the life of a gnat. But it is immortals whom we joke with, work with, marry, snub, and exploit—immortal horrors or everlasting splendours." During the year of his fear of annihilation, the same year that *Miracles* was published, Lewis was preparing that sermon for publication in a book. One wonders whether, at times, those powerful words rang hollow.

A. N. Wilson's biography of Lewis is a highly readable and thoughtful book, and about some aspects of Lewis's life and work he is more acute than any other biographer. But he also has some very odd ideas: that the Dwarf Ghost in *The Great Divorce* is Lewis's vicious portrait of Dante; that Jane Studdock's attraction to the sanctity of Ransom in *That Hideous Strength* is Lewis's portrait of June Flewett's crush on him*; that "the Second World War was one of the happiest periods of C. S. Lewis's life" (these all from a single chapter). But the oddest of them all is his insistence that Lewis was driven to abandon apologetics, and to turn to the making of Narnia, by being bested in a debate at the Socratic Club.

One of the key chapters in *Miracles* is the third one, which is devoted to clearing away some of the major objections to a belief in miracles. It is key because it shows, or attempts to show, that "naturalism"—which in this context is the belief that the processes of the human brain arose by pure, undesigned evolutionary contingency and that therefore our thoughts are "merely subjective events, not apprehensions of objective truth"—is "self-refuting." In other words, the claim that "Accidental Nature is all there is" is a claim that people

---

* To think that Jane is to Ransom as June is to Jack, one must assume that Jack had a very high view of his own holiness, for it is precisely the holiness, the sanctified serenity and spiritual power, of Ransom to which Jane responds so strongly.

who believe it have, according to their own position, no reason to trust, since that very claim is just the accidental product of random evolutionary developments. The details of the argument do not concern us here; what does concern us is the fact that in 1948, a year or so after the book came out, a young philosopher named Elizabeth Anscombe read a paper to the Socratic Club that claimed that Lewis's argument in that chapter was essentially flawed.

The only thing that the participants in, and the audience of, that evening seem to concur on was that the debate was vigorous, even exciting. Though not all philosophers agree with Anscombe's critique—not all philosophers agree about *anything*—Lewis came to believe that, at the least, he had phrased his argument poorly, and thus he revised it for a later edition of *Miracles*. But some of his friends thought that the critique had a far deeper effect on him. Derek Brewer, a friend and former student, met with Lewis two days afterward and said that he described the argument "with real horror" and was "deeply disturbed." George Sayer remembers Lewis's telling him that "his argument for the existence of God had been demolished," which makes no sense: the existence of God was not up for debate in that session. (And if it had been, Anscombe would not have been the atheist undermining it: whatever she thought about Lewis's arguments, she was herself a deep and thoughtful Catholic Christian. It is not clear that Sayer knows that.) According to Hugo Dyson—or so claims Wilson—the experience brought Lewis "to the foot of the Cross," but Humphrey Havard, who knew Lewis just as well and was as regular an Inkling, did not remember any such feelings. Anscombe herself is the source for that last comment: "Neither Dr. Havard (who had Lewis and me to dinner a few weeks later) nor Professor Lewis Bennett [a Magdalen colleague and friend] remembered any such feelings on Lewis's part.... My own recollection is that it was an occasion of sober discussion of certain quite definite criticisms, which Lewis's rethinking and rewriting showed he thought were accurate." (Havard would later offer an almost identical account of matters.) Wilson himself probably comes close to the truth when he puts the controversy in academic terms: "All that had happened, humiliating as it had been at the time, was that Lewis had been shown to have no competence to debate with a professional philosopher on her own terms." Even this is an exaggeration: Anscombe herself certainly did not think Lewis philosophically incompetent, just mistaken about one particular issue, which he then corrected to her satisfaction; in any case, she was one of the most formidable thinkers of her time, not just "a professional philosopher." To be bested by Elizabeth Anscombe in argument, or simply to have her reveal a weakness in one's argument, would be shameful to no one. Havard remembers Lewis's telling him, "Of course, she is far more intelligent than either of us."

One reason for excessive speculation about this debate is that both participants were legendary "characters"—not just major figures in their academic fields but also dominant personalities. Anscombe was, as noted, a devout Catholic who eventually had seven children; she also smoked cigars and invariably wore trousers at a time when skirts were *de rigeur* for Oxbridge women. She was just as much larger than life as Lewis himself. More spice was added to the mix by the fact that, in an environment in which "nobody could put Lewis down," he was "put down" by a woman—and a fellow Christian at that. There were just too many quirks and oddities and delightful ironies in the whole business for it *not* to attract a lot of attention. But Wilson's belief that this debate was the impetus for Lewis to abandon apologetics and turn to the making of Narnia—and that, most absurd of all, the White Witch is a demonized version of Elizabeth Anscombe!—just doesn't make sense. We already know that Lewis's interest in fairy tales and children's stories was lifelong; we further know that in 1947 he said that he had once tried to write a fairy tale, "but it was, by the unanimous verdict of my friends, so bad that I destroyed it."

It is at least possible that this was an early version of what would become *The Lion, the Witch, and the Wardrobe*. According to Walter Hooper, the manuscript of an unpublished story by Lewis called "The Dark Tower" has this paragraph written on the back of one page: "This book is about four children whose names were Ann, Martin, Rose and Peter. But it is mostly about Peter who was the youngest. They all had to go away from London suddenly because of the air raids, and because Father, who was in the army, had gone off to the war and Mother was doing some kind of war work. They were sent to stay with a relation of Mother's who was a very old Professor who lived by himself in the country." Hooper dates "The Dark Tower" around 1939, but this paragraph could not have been written before 1940, which is when the German air raids on London began. Moreover, many doubts have been raised about the authenticity of the manuscript containing "The Dark Tower." But the existence of this one paragraph does seem to fit with Lewis's claim that he had tried a children's story some time before completing the first Narnia story.*

The possibility fits with another piece of evidence too. June Flewett did not come to the Kilns until 1943, but the first evacuee children had arrived in the Lewis home immediately after the German invasion of Poland on September 1, 1939. (The government had assumed that German bombing of London would begin immediately.) Lewis—writing to Warnie during the latter's brief return to active duty—was struck by the children's lack of imagination and inability to entertain themselves: "Modern children are poor creatures. They keep on coming to Maureen and asking 'What shall we do now?' She tells them to play tennis, or mend their stockings, or write home: and when that is done they come and ask again. Shades of our own childhood!"—by which he means, not that he and Warnie were equally helpless, but that they were anything but. Looking at these "poor creatures," Lewis already had an explanation for their helplessness. He had formulated it in a letter to Arthur four years earlier, in 1935, in which he described the visit to the Kilns of a young boy named Michael, a distant relation of Mrs. Moore's:

> Minto reads him the Peter Rabbit books every evening, and it is a lovely sight. She reads very slowly and he gazes up into her eyes which look enormous through her spectacles—what a pity she has no grandchildren. Would you believe it, the child has never been read to nor told a story in his life? Not that he is neglected. He has a whole time Nurse (an insufferable semi-lady scientific woman with a diploma from some Tom-fool nursing college), a hundred patent foods, is spoiled, and far too expensively dressed: but his poor imagination has been left without any natural food at all. I often wonder what the present generation of children will grow up like.... They have been treated with so much indul-

---

* In an oral history interview in the Wade Center at Wheaton College, Maureen recalls a morning when Jack came down to breakfast and announced that he was going to write a children's book. This would certainly have been no later than 1940, because Maureen got married in that year and moved away. In any case, Maureen's account of her response, and Minto's, is noteworthy: "So my mother and I just laughed, because, I mean, he didn't understand children at all. Wasn't interested in them, and, well, it was astonishing that he really did write it, in a way, isn't it?"

gence yet so little affection, with so much science and so little mother-wit. Not a fairy tale nor a nursery rhyme.

Lacking the "natural food" of fairy tales and nursery rhymes, they were sure to grow up imaginatively malnourished—indeed, almost certain to become the "men without chests" whose cultural dominance Lewis laments in *The Abolition of Man.* By the time such young people got to university, they would be almost unreachable and uncorrectable (men of straw such as Mark Studdock); it is no wonder, then, given Lewis's deep concern for moral education, that he would consider writing stories for children—stories that would provide that imaginative nourishment at a time when they most needed it and lay the groundwork for further education in the "mother-wit" of the Tao, the moral law. It is worth remembering at this point that *The Green Book,* which prompted such harsh critique in *The Abolition of Man,* is a textbook for high school students.

So there were in Lewis's mind long-considered ideas about education and the nourishing of young imaginations that made it natural for him to think about writing children's stories, and those ideas would have been encouraged by the books he was writing during the war years whether he had had a debate with Elizabeth Anscombe or not. Moreover, the constant conflicts at the Kilns (especially after the departure of June), the immense pressures of correspondence, and other corollaries of his increasing fame were driving Lewis toward exhaustion and, a year after the Anscombe debate, complete collapse. These factors, which play such a large role in his letters of the time, in Warnie's diaries, and in the recollections of his friends, are almost completely ignored by Wilson. Whatever changes took place in Lewis's career at this time, the debate with Anscombe could have played but a minor part, if indeed it played any part at all, in their emergence.

For changes there certainly were. Wilson is right at least about this, that *Miracles* was the last of Lewis's straightforward polemical books of apologetics. Though he would write fifteen more books, none of them would be that sort of book. But even this point is less important than Wilson would have it. Among all Lewis's books, only *three* can plausibly be described as apologetics in the pure sense: *The Problem of Pain, Mere Christianity,* and *Miracles*—and even *Mere Christianity* contains about as much simple explanation as argument (just as later works that set out to exposit or present Christian belief about certain topics—*Reflections on the Psalms,* for instance, or *The Four Loves*—

also contain defenses of those beliefs). Theological argument plays a minor role in Lewis's body of work, if it plays a disproportionately large role in the memories of some of his admirers. But such arguments recede into the background, into supportive roles, in his writings from this time on. If we are seeking reasons for this, the most plausible are the ones I have suggested: exhaustion and fame. Exhaustion, because in illness—and in Lewis's life illness seems often to have been the direct product of fatigue—Lewis always turned for consolation to children's books and works of fantasy or romance: "For my own 'flu,'" he wrote in the fall of 1948, "I always go back to *The Wind in the Willows* while the temperature is really high, and progress to Scott or Wm. Morris (laced with Trollope) as I get sane." And for a man who by the late 1940s was so accustomed, if not addicted, to writing, what could be more natural than to *write* just the sort of books he loved to read? After all, *Out of the Silent Planet* came about because Lewis and Tolkien had agreed that, since there were not enough books of the kind they liked available, they would have to write some themselves. Even back in his days with Kirk he had written to Arthur, in the tones of a world-weary old man, "However, cheer up, and whenever you are fed up with life, start writing: ink is the great cure for all human ills, as I have found out long ago."

But I think the travails of fame were more important still as a reason for Lewis to turn to the making of what would become Narnia. As we have seen, apologetics had been hard on his own faith, and once the war ended he no longer had the obligation of offering moral and spiritual support to the country's servicemen. But insofar as apologetics were still required, he was increasingly frustrated with people's reliance on him as the one no one else could "put down." Just after the war's end he received a letter from a priest named John Beddow who wanted Lewis to write a book commending Christianity to the "workers"—as we might put it, the "blue-collar" workers—of England. Lewis demurred: "I can't write a book for workers. I know nothing at all of the realities of factory life." Perhaps, he suggested, he could help edit a book if it were written by someone who *did* know the lives of the workers—if indeed he was needed at all. And then suddenly, in the midst of these suggestions, comes a kind of *cri de coeur*:

> People praise me as a 'translator,' but what I want is to be the founder of a school of 'translation.'
> I am nearly forty-seven. Where are my successors? Anyone can

learn to do it if they wish.... I feel I'm talking rather like a tutor—forgive me. But it is just a technique and I'm desperately anxious to see it widely learned.

The "it" in that last sentence is, simply, the "translation" of Christian doctrine into vernacular terms that ordinary people can understand. Lewis is convinced that such translation requires no special abilities, that "anyone can do it if they wish," and that the reliance on *him* to do it has been bad for the cause of Christianity and bad for him. And we hear another note here, one that will creep with increasing frequency into his letters: a sense that he is getting *old,* that he does not know how much time he has left, that it is past time for someone to appear to whom he can pass the baton. In the 1956 letter to Katherine Farrer in which he thinks of how "the world could have been spared C.S.L.," there's a hint that he knows he has become a recognizable public figure—like GKC and GBS in the previous generation—and that there is something of caricature in that.

In the letter about his missing "successors" there is a hint of the panic that can accompany exhaustion ("I'm desperately anxious"), a sense that he does not know how much longer he can hold the fort against an endless wave of enemies, many of which he simply lacks the resources to fight. Surely that awareness that he was not omnicompetent, the "defender of the Faith" for all occasions, lay behind this statement from a 1951 letter to an American friend:

I am going to be (if I live long enough) one of those men who *was* a famous writer in his forties and dies unknown—like Christian [in *The Pilgrim's Progress*] going down into the green valley of humiliation. Which is the most beautiful thing in Bunyan and can be the most beautiful thing in life if a man takes it *quite* rightly—a matter I think and pray about a good deal. One thing is certain: much better to begin (at least) learning humility on this side of the grave than to have it all as a fresh problem on the other.

The problem of pride, and how to combat it, was one that had occupied Lewis since the earliest days of his Christian life: as he told Arthur even *before* he became a Christian, when he had first begun to practice self-examination, "Will you believe it, one out of every three is a thought of self-admiration.... Depth under depth of self-love and

self-admiration." Now, as *Time* wrote admiringly of him and put
him on its cover, hordes of people turned to him to solve their spiritual
and moral problems, and he routed the infidels who dared to show
their faces at the Socratic Club, he had far more objective cause for
self-admiration and far more reason to fear that he would come to
trust too much in his own powers of argument and persuasion. (In the
last months of his life, when Walter Hooper asked him whether he
thought of the praise and admiration he was winning through his
books, he replied in a quiet voice, "One cannot be too careful *not* to
think of it.") He was now in a double bind indeed: his humility endangered and his faith weakened by every successful foray into the
realm of apologetics.

I have said that all these concerns are important "insofar as apologetics were still required"—but *were* they still required? How important are arguments for the Christian faith? It seems almost certain that
at some point in these dark years Lewis remembered how he himself
had become a Christian. Argument played a role, to be sure, but a
largely preparatory one. Arguments had cleared away many of his
philosophical objections to Christianity, but even when those objections disappeared he could not move forward into actual belief—first
theistic and then specifically Christian belief—until he had acquired a
positive vision of a *story* that he could inhabit. It is vital to remember
that it was that long night's talk with Tolkien and Dyson that made all
the difference to him, the talk that revealed to him the true nature of
myth and the place of the Gospel narrative in the world of mythological stories. He became a Christian not through accepting a particular
set of arguments but through learning to read a story the right way.
And maybe others could move closer to Christian belief by the same
path.

Of course, we cannot know whether such thoughts were on Lewis's
mind as he began (or resumed) his story about the Pevensie children.
Perhaps it began as no more than an exercise in the E. Nesbit mold,
in which a family of children encounter unexpected supernatural
powers; or perhaps in that first imagined "picture of a Faun carrying an umbrella and parcels in a snowy wood," theological implications could already be discerned. No one now can say. But I think
we can begin to approach this question properly by taking a long
way around it—by considering some of the ideas that dominate the
one work of fiction that Lewis wrote after he finished the Narnia

books: *Till We Have Faces.* The novel is set in a pagan world, some obscure land at the edges of the influence of Greek culture, where the central god, Ungit, is a disturbing version of Aphrodite—not Aphrodite as a bright Olympian goddess, but Aphrodite as a "dark god of the blood." The theme is sexuality as compulsion, as force, as the power that brings forth our birth in blood and pain. There is also a god of the Grey Mountain overlooking the city of Glome, and the sacred stories say that that god is Ungit's son. The novel's protagonist, a woman named Orual, first a princess and then Queen of Glome, cherishes a long and detailed complaint against the gods—indeed, the first four-fifths of the book simply *are* that complaint, or at least what Orual thought her complaint was, until the gods grant her a vision in which (as we saw earlier) she recognizes her complaint for what it really is. She wishes to be heard; she desires to make her charge before competent Authorities; she wants Judgment.

Every day during term Lewis attended chapel at Magdalen, where the service of Morning Prayer was read from the *Book of Common Prayer*, and in that way he went through the whole of the Psalms many times—he certainly knew the entire Psalter by heart. One of the themes he noticed, and indeed found important enough to make the topic of the first chapter of his book *Reflections on the Psalms*, was the theme of desiring judgment. "Give sentence with me, O Lord, according to my righteousness and according to the innocency that is in me" (Psalm 7:8, in the translation by Miles Coverdale that is used in the *Prayer Book*). This is the plea of Orual. At other times she sounds like Jeremiah—"Righteous art thou, O Lord, when I plead with thee: yet let me talk with thee of thy judgments" (12:1)—but then, near her story's end, utterly embittered, she no longer acknowledges, even ritually, the justice or righteousness of her gods. She had begged them for a sign to tell her whether her sister, Psyche—who claimed to be the bride of the god of the Grey Mountain—was truthful or mad or deceived; they gave her no sign, or no unambiguous sign. And the lives of both sisters were, by Orual's actions, thereby destroyed. Thus the complaint: "I say, therefore, that there is no creature (toad, scorpion, or serpent) so noxious to man as the gods. Let them answer my charge if they can."

The gods hear her complaint, but—and this is the key moment of the story—Orual also hears her complaint. That is, she hears it for what it really is, a cry of frustrated possessive love, a cry of one who

wants to keep her beloved sister for herself. The details of her misbegotten, twisted love are not important here, though we will consider
them in the next chapter; what matters to us at this moment is the
light this scene sheds on the power and the poverty of *words*.

Orual spent a long time writing her book—and *Till We Have Faces*
is her book—detailing every last jot and tittle of her anti-theistic
tirade. She amassed the evidence with great care; she shaped her narrative with passionate skill. But what was revealed to her when she actually stood before the otherworldly Court, where she was constrained,
or empowered (depending on how you look at it), to deliver her *true*
complaint and her true complaint *only*—was that the greater purpose
of her word-shaping had been to hide the truth of her character from
herself. Even more than she wanted to accuse the gods she wanted to
excuse herself, and so, in that Court, she does precisely that. She is
shocked and appalled to discover on that stage what she had so carefully hidden behind the impressive edifice of her long-crafted prosecu-
torial address.

Remembering, later, that moment of revelation, she also remembers
her tutor, that philosophical Greek called the Fox, and that is what
leads her to the passage with which I ended the previous chapter:

> Lightly men talk of saying what they mean. Often when he was
> teaching me to write in Greek the Fox would say, "Child, to say
> the very thing you really mean, the whole of it, nothing more or
> less or other than what you really mean; that's the whole art and
> joy of words." A glib saying. When the time comes to you at
> which you will be forced at last to utter the speech which has lain
> at the center of your soul for years, which you have, all that time,
> idiot-like, been saying over and over, you'll not talk about joy of
> words. I saw well why the gods do not speak to us openly, nor let
> us answer. Till that word can be dug out of us, why should they
> hear the babble we think we mean?

The Fox, who is among the dead who thronged that dark courtroom,
does not hear her say this, but having heard her speech, he realizes
what he has done, and accuses himself more strongly than she could
accuse him: "Send me away, Minos, even to Tartarus, if Tartarus can
cure glibness. I made her think that a prattle of maxims could do, all
thin and clear as water. For of course water's good; and it didn't cost
much, not where I grew up. So I fed her on words."

Anyone who thinks this is merely a critique of Greek philosophy or cheap rationalism has, I believe, misunderstood the passage, for it is equally a critique of Christian apologetics. The emptiness of the Fox's words is scarcely greater than the emptiness of the apologist's words. No doubt, what Lewis had written and said as a defender of the Christian faith was truer than what the Fox had taught Orual—indeed, far truer—but it had the defect of being in words, and it is easy to forget that even true words bear the limitations of all language: they are, inevitably, "thin and clear as water." The gods demand more than water: indeed, they demand blood, for, as the author of the letter to the Hebrews writes in a passage at which the priests of Ungit would have nodded sagely, "without the shedding of blood there is no remission of sin" (9:22).

This is, of course, not an argument—by me or by Lewis—for a restoration of the practice of blood sacrifice! Christians believe that the death of Jesus Christ was the perfect, final, and efficacious sacrifice for the remission of everyone's sins. Moreover, even when sacrifices were offered at the Temple in Jerusalem, it was understood that they were but a sign of something greater, something that God truly desired for his people: "Thou delightest not in burnt offerings. The sacrifice of God is a troubled spirit: a broken and contrite heart, O God, thou shalt not despise" (Psalm 51:16f). The Fox, his eyes opened in the afterlife, sees this now: the gods, he says, "will have sacrifice—will have man. Yes, and the very heart, center, ground, roots of a man; dark and strong and costly as blood." That is, the gods will not be content with mere assent to propositions—with a "sacrifice" consisting of words. (In Matthew 15:8 Jesus quotes Isaiah: "This people draweth nigh unto me with their mouth, and honoureth me with their lips; but their heart is far from me.")

Nor is our complaint against the gods something that goes into words: it lies far deeper than that, in an outcry of the offended will, in a raw assertion and reassertion of pure want. Thus Orual: "While I was reading [my complaint], it had, once and again, seemed strange to me that the reading took so long; for the book was a small one. Now I knew that I had been reading it over and over—perhaps a dozen times. I would have read it forever, quick as I could, starting the first word again almost before the last was out of my mouth, if the judge had not stopped me." In the end, it almost does not matter what the words of complaint are: Orual does not want them understood or correctly interpreted; she wants to be heard—or rather, she wants to be *obeyed,* and if, time being what it is, obedience to her will is now impossible, then she wants to inflict some kind of vengeance on those who thwarted her desires. Words have nothing to do with it; they are merely the only instrument, the only tool, she has to hand.

Objections to Christianity—so we may extend the lesson of this story—are phrased in words, but that does not mean that they are really a matter of language and analysis and argument. Words are tokens of the will. If something stronger than language were available, then we would use it. But by the same token, words in *defense* of Christianity miss the mark as well: they are a translation into the dispassionate language of argument of something that resides far deeper in the caverns of volition, of commitment. Perhaps this is why Saint Francis, so the story goes, instructed his followers to "preach the Gospel always, using words if necessary." It is not simply and straightforwardly *wrong* to make arguments in defense of the Christian faith, but it is a relatively superficial activity: it fails to address the core issues. A Christian who participates in a Socratic "debate" about Christianity—one conducted at the level of argument and counterargument, as though what is at stake is simply figuring out what propositions to assent to—could be said to be falsifying the spiritual situation, or allowing it to be falsified. After all, an apologist for Christianity, to some degree at least, commits himself or herself to answering questions that Jesus himself consistently refused to answer. Here again we should recall Lewis's frequent emphasis on the problems that arise when, as I put it in the previous chapter, our curiosity exceeds our faithfulness; here again we should remember Jesus's reply to Peter's question about the fate of another disciple: "What is that to thee? Follow thou me" (John 21:22).

But strange to say, there is a kind of language that, if it does not avoid such superficiality, nevertheless shows an awareness of that danger and in a sense can point beyond itself. I refer to the language of stories—perhaps especially the language of fantasy and fairy tale. Sometimes fairy stories may say best what's to be said.

"I am not quite sure," Lewis wrote in 1952, when most of the Narnia books were done, "what made me, in a particular year of my life, feel that not only a fairy tale, but a fairy tale addressed to children, was exactly what I must write—or burst." But he has a guess:

> Partly, I think, [the reason is] that this form permits, or compels you to leave out things I wanted to leave out. It compels you to

throw all the force of a book into what was done and said. It checks what a kind, but discerning critic called "the expository demon" in me.

According to Green and Hooper, the "kind but discerning critic" was Barfield, but I do not know which of Lewis's books he would have been referring to. Presumably not the ones, such as *Mere Christianity*, which were *supposed* to be expository; more likely the fiction, which is indeed marred at times by a tendency to explain what should simply be shown. (I have always found the dominance of Lewis's "expository demon" to be the downfall of *Perelandra*; this was his favorite among his novels—at least until he wrote *Till We Have Faces*—and indeed is the favorite of many other readers, but I find it nearly unreadable because of its ceaseless exposition and explanation.) But the fairy tale for children simply will not allow that "demon" in the door: as Lewis puts it elsewhere, a list of that genre's features would include "its severe restraints on description, its flexible traditionalism, its inflexible hostility to all analysis, digression, reflections and 'gas.'" And what is the name of the demon that brings analysis, digression, reflections, and gas? Why, he is the Apologist—the one sometimes called Defender of the Faith.

The difference between the complaint that Orual wants to utter and the one that pours forth from her when she gets her day in court is simple: the former is a self-justifying fiction; the latter is her true *cri de coeur*, "the speech which has lain at the center of [her] soul for years." But if this sharp distinction reveals the real character of the unbeliever, the one trapped by a lifetime of self-deception, should not a similar difference—or rather a mirror-image of it—lie at the heart of the believer's life? I have noted in a previous chapter Lewis's insistence that God is about the transformation of the lives of his children: those who are "in Christ" are in the process of becoming "new creatures." Perhaps, if the Apologist could be silenced, could be driven from the room, Lewis could discover what difference Christ had made to his life —could discover whether he was indeed being transformed or instead had just learned to parrot certain words, words "thin and clear as water."

"Everything began with images," he wrote: "a faun carrying an umbrella, a queen on a sledge, a magnificent lion. At first there wasn't even anything Christian about them; that element pushed itself in of its own accord." There was not, he says over and over again, an evangelistic plan in the making of Narnia, no apologetic scheme:

Some people seem to think that I began by asking myself how I
could say something about Christianity to children; then fixed on
the fairy tale as an instrument; then collected information about
child-psychology and decided what age-group I'd write for; then
drew up a list of basic Christian truths and hammered out "allegories" to embody them. This is pure moonshine. I couldn't write
in that way at all.

Or perhaps he could have, but knows that it would have been a dreadful mistake, a giving over of his imaginative life to the "expository
demon." What he has to do instead is to *trust the images* that come
into his mind—or, more accurately, trust that he is being formed as a
Christian in such a way that the images that come to his mind are au-
thentic ones, ones that lie at, or at least near, the center of his soul. He
can do this only if he rejects not only the market-driven questions of
modern authors and publishers ("What do children want?") but even
the more morally sound question of the Christian apologist ("What do
children need?"): "It is better not to ask the questions at all. Let the
pictures tell you their own moral. For the moral inherent in them will
rise from whatever spiritual roots you have succeeded in striking during the whole course of your life."

*The moral inherent in them will rise from whatever spiritual roots
you have succeeded in striking during the whole course of your life.*
This is a terrifying, or liberating, word: liberating in that one need not
expose oneself to the sanctimonious drudgery of drawing up lists of
Christian truths and hammering out allegories that will meet the desires
or needs of children. But terrifying because as those images rise from
your mind you discover what you are really made of: you discover
whether you are one whose moral and aesthetic responses have been
shaped by the Christian narrative or whether you remain a person
"without a chest," lacking in true spiritual formation. Trusting the images, you find out who you are. Orual does not really have a choice—
images are granted her when she receives a vision—but most of us have
to choose whether to heed what rises up from our inner selves. For
Orual what the vision reveals is devastating, as it may be for us, but
even in her case the devastation is necessary, and the self-knowledge it
brings rights the ship of her life at the very last moment. "I was being
unmade; I was no one," she writes, but having been unmade, she then
receives her true face, her very self. She dies to live. It's an old story.

Stories that deal in such matters have various names. Scholars often call them what they used to be called long ago: romances. More often we call them fairy tales, or fantasies. They are associated with children now, though a little less exclusively than when Lewis and Tolkien were writing, but as Tolkien wrote in his great essay "On Fairy Stories," making a point that Lewis quoted often,

> the association of children and fairy-stories is an accident of our domestic history. Fairy-stories have in the modern lettered world been relegated to the "nursery," as shabby or old-fashioned furniture is relegated to the play-room, primarily because the adults do not want it, and do not mind if it is misused. It is not the choice of the children which decides this. Children as a class— except in a common lack of experience they are not one—neither like fairy-stories more, nor understand them better than adults do; and no more than they like many other things. . . . Fairy-stories banished in this way, cut off from a full adult art, would in the end be ruined; indeed in so far as they have been so banished, they have been ruined.

One of the writers most important to Lewis, and about whom he wrote as a scholar frequently, was Edmund Spenser, whose *Faerie Queene* almost creates the realm of Faery in the English literary imagination. Lewis likewise adored *Arcadia,* the pastoral romance of Spenser's contemporary Sir Philip Sidney, and saw in Sidney an imagination like his own, though he would never have said so for fear of seeming arrogant: few English writers are as great as Sidney. But in describing the world of *Arcadia,* Lewis notes that "theoretically we are all pagans in Arcadia. . . . Nevertheless, Christian theology is always breaking in." For Lewis this is not a flaw, though for Tolkien it would have been: as the latter wrote in a letter, "Myth and fairy-story must, as all art, reflect and contain in solution elements of moral and religious truth (or error), but not explicit, not in the known form of the primary 'real' world"—and in our "real" world Christianity is the "known form." The consistency and integrity that Tolkien believed necessary to all "sub-creation" demanded that the "real" world and the imaginary world of Faery be kept completely separate.

But such was not the view of Spenser and Sidney and other "romancers" of their time. That Christian theology should "break in" to Arcadia, or to Faery, was in that era a "convention . . . well understood, and very useful. In such works the gods are God *incognito* and everyone is in on the secret. Paganism is the religion of poetry through which the author can express, at any moment, just so much or so little of his real religion as his art requires." This is a very precise account of what Lewis himself does in *Till We Have Faces* and, in a different way, in Narnia. It is wrong, therefore, to suppose that the difference on this matter between Tolkien and Lewis can be described in terms of a careful, scrupulous Tolkien and a thoughtless, inattentive Lewis. Tolkien may have been a greater writer of fiction than Lewis—indeed, I feel sure that he was—but not because he had a sound theory of subcreation while Lewis was just playing with his toys. The approach Lewis took has deeper historical roots than Tolkien's, and in following it Lewis was walking in the footsteps of great predecessors indeed. It was also an approach that he felt was warranted on *theological* grounds—after all, key to his own conversion had been a wide range of stories and myths with no direct connection to Christianity. We should recall here what he wrote in the aftermath of his late-night conversation with Tolkien and Dyson: "The 'doctrines' we get *out of* the true myth are of course *less* true: they are translations into our *concepts* and *ideas* of that wh. God has already expressed in a language more adequate, namely the actual incarnation, crucifixion, and resurrection." And as he also realized then, the "more adequate" language of historical event is best approximated by story. Who taught Lewis that? Tolkien, of course.

But whatever the aesthetic and even theological issues at stake, it is more important, at least for the purposes of this biography, to understand that Lewis's determination to follow the Sidneyan or Spenserian "convention" was a form of self-testing, a means of discovering what "speech" indeed lay at the center of his soul. And the test reached its point of crisis when the great Lion appeared. He was not part of the plan, insofar as Lewis had a plan beyond connecting the various images into a story: why was the Faun carrying a package, and where was he taking it? Is it important that he carries it through snow? Why is the Queen on that sledge? How do all these images relate to the four children evacuated from London during the Blitz? Questions difficult enough without a great Lion turning up and demanding the center of the stage. Yet turn up he did, and once that happened the only question was whether to follow him. The Lion himself, as we have seen, is not much for answering questions, at least not the kinds of questions we tend to ask. Even when (in *The Horse and His Boy*) Shasta asks him, simply and straightforwardly, "Who are you?" the answer is but

a mysterious, threefold, amplifying word: "Myself. Myself. Myself."
Had he been asked anything more he would likely have said something like, "What is that to thee? Follow thou me."

Lewis followed. "At first I had very little idea how the story would
go. But then suddenly Aslan came bounding into it. I think I had been
having a good many dreams of lions about that time. Apart from that,
I don't know where the Lion came from or why He came. But once He
was there he pulled the whole story together, and soon He pulled the
six other Narnian stories in after Him."

ELEVEN

"We soon learn to love what we know we must lose"

Aslan pulled those stories in after him, and did so quickly. *The Lion, the Witch, and the Wardrobe* was finished in the spring of 1949, at about the same time that Lewis told Barfield that his day was chiefly occupied with "dog's stools and human vomit." By then he had already begun the story that would become *The Magician's Nephew*—having described the Redemption of Narnia, he sought to go back and tell its Creation—but the writing did not go well and he set it aside, whether before or after his collapse and hospitalization in June I do not know. After his recovery it was *Prince Caspian* that he turned to next, then *The Voyage of the "Dawn Treader,"* which was finished early in 1950. In the same year he wrote *The Horse and His Boy,* followed by *The Silver Chair;* he then returned to *The Magician's Nephew* but continued to struggle with it. *The Magician's Nephew* was actually the last of the stories to be finished, early in 1954; *The Last Battle* had been written the previous year. During this period he was also finishing up the OHEL book and writing *Surprised by Joy,* as well as producing essays on a range of topics.

By my unscientific estimate, during the period from 1949 to 1955 Lewis wrote, and published, about 600,000 words of prose—roughly four times the number of words in this book. The Narnia tales alone contain more than 400,000 words. (This is not counting the OHEL volume, because it is hard to know how much of it he had already written before 1949 rolled around, but given that he took a leave from his academic duties in 1951 and 1952 to finish the book, it is possible that we should add another 100,000 words or so to the stack. Nor have I counted the thousands of letters.) All this from a man who, at the beginning of 1949, had written to an Italian priest, Giovanni Calabria, "I feel my zeal for writing, and whatever talent I originally possessed, to be decreasing. Nor (I believe) do I please my readers as I used to." If we wish to understand how he could nonetheless have been so productive, we can begin by saying that, for Lewis, it was the best of times and the worst of times.

After his breakdown, major changes came upon him one after another. It was about this time that the Thursday evening meetings of the Inklings ceased—as Walter Hooper has pointed out, after a November entry reading "No Inklings tonight, so dined at home," Warnie's diary never again referred to the Inklings. The daytime sessions at the Bird and Baby continued, but thanks in large part to the ongoing tension between Lewis and Tolkien, exacerbated by Tolkien's thorough disapproval of the Narnia books, the era of "sitting up till the small hours in someone's college rooms talking nonsense, poetry, theology, metaphysics over beer, tea, and pipes" had ended, at least for Lewis. It is hard to know how much he regretted this change; a theme that creeps increasingly into his letters after his breakdown is that of the onset of old age. In an October letter to an American friend, Lewis says that old age is "the subject that is uppermost in my mind and has been for some days.... What has come lately is much harsher—the arctic wind of the future catching me, so to speak, at a corner."

He was fifty as he wrote these words, soon to be fifty-one—rather early in life to be talking like a senior citizen, we might think. But Humphrey Havard, his friend and physician, had told him that a breakdown as severe as the one he had just experienced was worrisome in a man his age; in any case, his father, Albert, had lived to only age sixty-five (and his mother, Flora, to forty-six). As Lewis wrote in a 1954 letter, "I come of a stock that grows early old." Lewis had no reason to believe that he had much more than a decade of life remaining to him, and indeed, his self-assessment on that point would be accurate.

In the midst of all this, the arrival of Don Giovanni Calabria in his life (if only through letters) was a gift, and one very much like the arrival of June Flewett several years earlier: a single bright spot in a dark prospect. Don Giovanni had written to Lewis in praise of *The Screwtape Letters*—then the only book of Lewis's translated into Italian (Don Giovanni knew no English)—and rightly discerned in Lewis a person who shared his deep concern for the reunification of the Christian churches. They corresponded in Latin, as learned men of Europe had done for centuries, and perhaps the unfamiliar discipline of writing in that language released Lewis from his usual reticence about himself. Certainly Don Giovanni's warm, paternal spirit—he was twenty-five years older than Lewis and had done great things for the poor and the orphaned in his home city of Verona—had a great deal to do with it. To Don Giovanni, Lewis confessed weakness, fear, and sadness that he rarely revealed to his other correspondents, and Don Giovanni replied with words of great encouragement. The priest believed that Lewis had a great deal to contribute to the Christian cause as an author; as he wrote in one letter, "I wish that for your love of me, you would see fit to write what you think about the moral state of our times. . . . I would like you to indicate saving remedies, so far as they seem opportune to you, for reparation and the removal of evil, for the renewal of courage, for advancing the unity of hearts in charity." It is likely that this conviction, coming from so unexpected a source, helped Lewis to recover his "zeal for writing." In any case, the knowledge that Don Giovanni would be regularly praying for him— Lewis habitually concludes his letters by writing *"Oremus pro invicem"* ("Let us pray for each other") or by asking for specific prayer, often for his "mother"—was a great comfort.

In September 1953 Don Giovanni wrote to Lewis, "Divine Providence binds us together with the sweet bonds of love, even if we have never known each other personally. But in love and in mutual prayer we know each other well." That was his last letter to Lewis; he died the next year. In 1988 Pope John Paul II came to Verona to proclaim Giovanni Calabria's beatification.

Whatever comfort Lewis had in the affection and encouragement of the great Italian priest, back at the Kilns he had the constant image of Minto's decline before him and the increasing unreliability of Warnie. (When Jack had been taken to the hospital, Warnie gave Minto a stern lecture, demanding that she release him from all domestic duties and allow him to go on a vacation. Apparently taken aback by Warnie's uncharacteristic boldness, she agreed, but immediately thereafter the prospect of being her chief caregiver, even for a short time, depressed Warnie so much that he went on a major bender. No holiday for Jack.) Minto had been a semi-invalid for several years, thanks to varicose ulcers in her legs, and she suffered from some degree of dementia: her obsession was her elderly dog, Bruce, whom she demanded be taken out a dozen times or more a day for his "little walks"—and of course, it was Lewis who had to walk him. When Bruce finally died, in January 1950, Warnie ran to his diary and wrote, "Joyful news"—and now that this "penultimate gate of J's prison" was down, he was openly hoping for the last one to fall, at Minto's death. Four months later her condition had so deteriorated—she was almost completely out of her mind now and repeatedly fell out of her bed—that she had to be taken to a nursing home. The doctors made it clear to Lewis that she would never return to the Kilns.

Though he visited her every day for the brief months that remained to her, even when she could no longer recognize him, the greater part of his domestic servitude had now ended. (As an old woman, Maureen gave an interview in which she described those days: "I remember coming over from Malvern"—where she and her husband, Leonard, then lived—"to visit my mother, in the nursing home, and Jack was there, sitting with her, talking to her. And her mind had completely gone with the stroke, which shows how good he was.") The long-deferred holiday was now at last possible, but the expense of the nursing home had emptied Lewis's bank account, and he gave away too much of his writing income for that to be much help. To Arthur, with whom he had planned to take that vacation, he wrote, "I hardly know how I feel. Relief, pity, hope, terror, and bewilderment have me in a whirl."

On January 12, 1951, Janie Moore died in the nursing home, with Lewis at her side. Warnie went again to his diary and wrote the words I have already quoted: "And so ends the mysterious self imposed slavery in which J[ack] has lived for at least thirty years. How it began, I suppose I shall never know." But what Jack thought no one then knew (unless he shared it with his confessor), or now knows, or will ever know. For Warnie, whose wrathful tirade against Minto, written on the day of her death, goes on for pages without remission or compassion, she stole much of his brother's life from him: that was the story in a nutshell. But others—characters as diverse as Owen Barfield and June Flewett—saw a depth of affection and tenderness on both sides from which Warnie was excluded and to which he was blind. There is no doubt that Mrs. Moore's death brought Lewis relief; he admitted as much, and a few months after her death would write to Sister Penelope, "I am (like the pilgrim in Bunyan) travelling across 'a plain called Ease.' Everything without, and many things within, are marvellously well at present." But how much he missed the first woman with whom he had fallen in love, the woman with whom he shared his life from

the age of nineteen to the age of fifty-two, and what he most missed—
these are secrets that none of us will ever penetrate. And about that relationship there is nothing more to be said.

Especially after the *Time* story in 1947, many of Lewis's admirers were
Americans, and they make up a good deal of his subsequent correspondence. This was not always a bad thing. In the years immediately
after the Second World War, when America was booming economically while Britain was afflicted by drastic rationing of all sorts of
goods, from nylon to potatoes, Lewis was the beneficiary of a great
deal of American generosity: "care packages" arrived on a regular
basis, mostly containing food but often enough writing paper and sta-
tionery, and in one case a tuxedo, of all things. (It was a little big for
Jack but fit the taller Warnie perfectly.) The most frequent giver was a
physician from Johns Hopkins Medical School named Warfield Firor:
one of his parcels contained a large ham, and Lewis was so vigorous in
expressing his awe of the thing (having almost forgotten what ham
tasted like) that Firor sent several more. Lewis and friends started calling him "Firor-of-the-Hams," and on one occasion a dozen or so of
the Inklings signed a collective letter of gratitude to him. Like a few
other American correspondents, Firor became a real friend: it was to
Firor that Lewis confessed his sense of encroaching old age. But the
good doctor could never convince Lewis to visit his ranch in Wyoming.

If Lewis's correspondents were often Americans, they were also disproportionately female. As he wrote in a 1952 letter, "It isn't chiefly
men I am kept in touch with by my huge mail: it is *women*. The female, happy or unhappy, agreeing or disagreeing, is by nature a much
more *epistolary* animal than the male." To such questioners he wrote
patiently and dutifully, almost without exception. I say "almost" because one woman, an antiques dealer in London named Kitty Martin,
had become interested in Lewis after hearing his radio talks and wrote
to him seeking advice. Lewis answered her letters until he discovered
that she had become convinced that his books were encoded love letters to herself. She wrote her own amorous treatises in reply, sometimes several per day, but Lewis threw them all away unopened,
burning them if he happened to have a fire going. Miss Martin also
told anyone who would listen that she and Lewis were engaged to be
married, and indeed, after some years of silence from him, she actually
scheduled a marriage in London in 1956 and announced it to the papers, saying that her plan was to "shock him into an answer."

Oddly, this was not the only experience of this kind that Lewis had. One day in April 1952 the proprietor of a hotel in Kent came to Magdalen and demanded that Lewis pay the bills for food and lodging that his wife had run up over the past few months. A certain Mrs. Hooker had been posing as the wife of C. S. Lewis and enjoying the hotel's bounty on the famous author's credit. Apparently Mrs. Hooker had done this before, using other authors' names, but on those occasions had escaped capture. Barfield advised Lewis that he would need to file charges against her to avoid having to pay the bills, which Lewis did, with a reluctance that deepened when he had to go to court to testify against her. "I never saw Justice at work before, and it is not a pretty sight," he wrote to the hotel's owners; "one felt one was committing a sort of indecency by being present." Mrs. Hooker was sent to Holloway Prison in North London, where she came to believe, like Kitty Martin, that if she and Lewis were not married they were at least engaged. A few months after she arrived at Holloway she told the prison chaplain that she was dying and wanted to see her beloved one last time. Astonishingly, Lewis went down to visit her. She was, of course, perfectly healthy.

A man of deeply ingrained daily habits who did not even drive a car but who would nevertheless find a way to go from Oxford to London to meet a deranged woman who thought she was engaged to him is surely the sort of man to be a faithful correspondent. But what did he *think* of these women whose questions he answered, whose anxieties he soothed, and whose problems he sympathized with? The answer, of course, is that he thought different things about different women, but this answer will be thought by some to be evasive, because Lewis has often been accused of being a misogynist. I think this accusation largely rests on misunderstandings, but there is no question that Lewis shared the attitudes toward women common to men, and especially Christian men, of his time (and, we should add in fairness, of many other times). He believed, for instance, that God had ordained the "headship" of man over woman, especially in marriage: he even explores and defends this teaching at some length in *Mere Christianity*. But the very fact that it is in *Mere Christianity*—the book devoted to a general summary of "the belief that has been common to nearly all Christians at all times"—tells us that he did not think it a very controversial idea. This may tell us something about the limits of his acquaintance and his experience, or it may tell us how little progress feminism had made in England to that date, or perhaps it tells us both things. Nevertheless, Lewis did not believe he was weighing in on an issue of great controversy among Christians when he described the doctrine of male headship.

This also helps to explain a decision that may seem surprising: his entering into the debate about the ordination of women, in a 1948 article with the innocuous title "Notes on the Way" (though his editor, Walter Hooper, later changed the title to the more pointed "Priestesses in the Church?"). He argues that, because a consistent and central image of the Church in the New Testament is the "Bride of Christ," the priest, who "represents the Lord to the Church," must "wear the masculine uniform" in order to act as the Bridegroom. Lewis insists that this is a matter of using the appropriate image to represent a divine mystery; it is not, in his understanding, a commentary on the moral or spiritual excellence of men as opposed to women. Morally and spiritually a woman "may be as 'God-like' as a man; and a given woman much more so than a given man." Rather, there is for Lewis a divinely ordained way of enacting or performing the drama of Redemption, especially in the Eucharistic service, and this performance requires that the priest, impersonating (as it were) the Lord Jesus Christ, be a man.

This book is not the place to evaluate the argument. (I will content myself with noting that the high view of the priestly role that Lewis articulates is *not* shared by most Protestants, including many of his fellow Anglicans; it is curious that he forgets this.) Here I wish simply to ask a question: why does Lewis make this argument *at all?* Why does he set aside his commitment to Christian unity and intervene in this dispute? The answer is quite simple: belief that men alone can be ordained was, when Lewis wrote, one of the beliefs "common to nearly all Christians at all times." Arguments for the ordination of women were then rarely made by people committed to traditional Christian orthodoxy; that is why he brings into the argument the different question of whether it is appropriate to speak of God as "Father, Son, and Holy Spirit." He assumes that people who want women to be ordained will also have serious reservations about all sorts of other beliefs that have historically constituted orthodoxy and that if we follow their recommendations we will find that we have "embarked on a different religion" than Christianity. What has emerged since Lewis's death is a large body of orthodox Christians, many of whom revere C. S. Lewis and wish to promote traditional Christianity as vigorously as he did, who see no difficulty with the ordination of women. If

Lewis were writing today, he would surely leave that subject alone, but in his time it had a different resonance, a different set of contexts.

Matters like this can be clarified, but beyond them, Lewis's attitude toward women becomes difficult to understand, much less to explain. The evidence points in several different directions. It was adult *male* laughter that he loved, and he rarely sought the company of women. For many years he invited groups of undergraduates to his rooms to drink beer and sing bawdy songs, and it was understood not only that no women would be invited to such sessions but also that there would be no other kinds of gatherings at which women *were* welcome. Yet, at a time when many Oxford dons openly resented the increasing presence of women in their lecture halls and among their tutorial pupils, Lewis was unfailingly kind and supportive of his female students. (One of them, Mary Neylan, even asked Lewis to be the godfather of one of her children.) June Flewett also was touched and encouraged by the respect with which Lewis treated her whenever they discussed books and ideas, and she was deeply pleased to learn from Mrs. Moore that he thought her intelligent. Moreover, the tone he uses with female writers such as Dorothy Sayers and female scholars such as Helen Gardner and Joan Bennett is fully as respectful and serious as the tone he uses with their male counterparts, though it is sometimes a bit more courtly.

Nevertheless, he could say some extraordinarily silly things about women. "What makes a pretty girl spread misery wherever she goes by collecting admirers?" he asks in *Mere Christianity*. "Certainly not her sexual instinct; that kind of girl is quite often sexually frigid." Even if such a ludicrous statement were true, how in the world would *he* know? And it is hard not to cringe at the long passage in *The Four Loves* where Lewis describes the unfortunate consequences of bringing an uneducated woman into a social gathering of educated men: "Her presence has thus destroyed the very thing she was brought to share," and this problem is not ameliorated by the fact that such a woman has learned "to drink and smoke and perhaps to tell *risqué* stories." She "has not ... drawn an inch nearer to the men than her grandmother. But her grandmother was far happier and more realistic. She was at home talking real women's talk to other women and perhaps doing so with great charm, sense and even wit." Yes, "even wit"—it is possible that an undereducated woman could be witty. Grating also is the idea of what "real women" think and talk about, a note also struck in *Mere Christianity* when he argues that in every household there must be a "head," an authority who makes the final decisions, and then adds: "There must be something unnatural about the rule of wives over husbands, because the wives themselves are half ashamed of it and despise the husbands whom they rule." The strong implication of the whole passage is either that a woman is unsatisfied unless she is properly ruled, or that a woman who does not want to submit to male headship is *ipso facto* less of a woman, or both.*

And yet, even in such passages Lewis can introduce complexity. When, for instance, he laments the inclusion of uneducated women in the conversations of educated men, he makes it perfectly clear that such a situation is not the result of women's intrinsic deficiencies but rather stems from the fact that society often lacks a "common ground" of education on which men and women can meet. He not only gives the example of an uneducated woman among educated men but also points out that men learned only in making money can, among cultivated women, seem like "barbarians among civilised people." And taking a position that many of his fellow dons and fellow traditional Christians would have strenuously objected to, he affirms the existence of real friendship between men and women: "In a profession (like my

---

* The passages on sexuality in *Mere Christianity* are more badly dated than anything else in that book, though it is likely that they were never very successful. To be sure, Lewis says properly orthodox things about sexuality and strives to correct the common misconception that Christians believe sex to be intrinsically sinful: "Christianity is almost the only one of the great religions which thoroughly approves of the body.... If anyone says that sex, in itself, is bad, Christianity contradicts him at once.... The sins of the flesh are bad, but they are the least bad of all sins." Nevertheless, he gets little credit for this because his writing about sex tends to be rhetorically miscalculated or just strange. The comment about the frigidity of attractive women is one example; another, more notorious, example involves the attraction of striptease acts: "Now suppose you come to a country where you could fill a theatre by simply bringing a covered plate on to the stage and then slowly lifting the cover so as to let every one see, just before the lights went out, that it contained a mutton chop or a bit of bacon, would you not think that in that country something had gone wrong with the appetite for food?" This analogy is so bad it is hard to know where to begin explaining why. For one thing, mutton and bacon are readily available to anyone who wants them and is interested in eating them, whether in public or in private; for another, Christians are not expected to profess fidelity to a particular piece of meat and to forgo eating any others; moreover, I need food simply in order to survive, while my sexual desires are of a different order. I have met several people over the years who remember nothing that Lewis says about sex except this bizarre metaphor and who therefore go about with the conviction that *all* Lewis's ideas about sexuality are perverse or inexplicable.

own) where men and women work side by side, or in the mission field, or among authors and artists, such Friendship is common." (Erotic complications and misunderstandings can arise, of course, but they need not do so. And though Lewis does not say so in this context, he knew perfectly well that the same problems can arise in same-sex relationships.) After reading such thoughts, one may still cringe a bit at the portrait of the smoking, drinking "modern" woman as so much less happy than her grandmother, but one is forced to see that the point Lewis is making is not nearly as offensively sexist as it might appear when taken out of context.

In his fiction and his theological fantasies, the picture is equally complex, though perhaps rather more troubling. One of the most powerfully recurrent themes in Lewis's work is the evil of love gone wrong—love become possessive, voracious, even consuming—and invariably it is a woman who embodies that evil. One sees a relatively lighthearted portrayal of such a perversion of true affection in the portrayal of "Mrs. Fidget" in *The Four Loves,* the woman who "lived for her family":

> She always sat up to "welcome" you if you were out late at night; two or three in the morning, it made no odds; you would always find the frail, pale, weary face awaiting you, like a silent accusation. Which meant of course that you couldn't with any decency go out very often. . . . Mrs. Fidget, as she so often said, would "work her fingers to the bone" for her family. They couldn't stop her. Nor could they—being decent people—quite sit still and watch her do it. They had to help. Indeed they were always having to help. That is, they did things for her to help her to do things for them which they didn't want done.

And on it went, until her death. "The Vicar says Mrs. Fidget is now at rest. Let us hope she is. What's quite certain is that her family are."

A darker side of this compulsion appears in *The Great Divorce* when one of the Ghosts begs that her husband, Robert, be returned to her care (from which he had escaped by dying and going to Heaven); she had worked so hard during their life together to "make something of him":

> Put me in charge of him. He wants firm handling. I know him better than you do. . . . Give him back to me. Why should he

have everything his own way? It's not good for him. It isn't right, it's not fair. I want Robert. What right have you to keep him from me?

Lewis's fullest, deepest, most powerful exposition of this theme is *Till We Have Faces*—indeed, the single purpose of that powerful book is to reveal such passion for what it is. There the misbegotten "love" is revealed to the person consumed by it, and by that revelation she is redeemed and transformed. About this there will be more to say later.

It is impossible not to guess that this particular complex of sin was so fascinating to Lewis because of his long experience with Mrs. Moore, nor to suspect that he knew these tendencies firsthand. It is not likely, however, that he thought men were immune to such temptations: a page or two after describing Mrs. Fidget to us, he introduces Dr. Quartz, a university professor absolutely devoted to his students—until they disagree with him about something. Such "ingratitude" he cannot forgive. This is the domineering spirit of Mrs. Fidget, simply transposed from a domestic setting to an academic one. In the world Lewis knew, women were likely to dominate the domestic realm, men the workplace; each gender suffered the same temptations, practiced the same sins, but in different forms because of the different contexts.

On the one hand, on the other hand—on we go. It is perfectly clear that Lewis thoroughly condescends to Jane Studdock in *That Hideous Strength* almost from the first page: "Jane was not perhaps a very original thinker," we are told, and key to her growth as a person is her willingness to abandon, or at least set aside, her scholarly dreams in order to accept the bearing of children. But of course, Lewis condescends to her husband, Mark, too, as we have already seen. Neither of them has any idea what it means to be truly *married;* both of them must learn, and at the book's end they do begin to learn. But there is no hint that Mark needs to abandon his career as a scholar in order to become the husband, the *person,* he needs to be; certainly that career needs to be transformed, but he need not put it aside altogether. He need not do what Jane is asked to do. The impression many readers have received from this story is that Mark has a good mind that needs to be properly educated, whereas Jane has a sufficiently limited mind that she had better give up hopes of scholarship and focus her attention on having and raising children.

Of course, it is possible that a person like Jane *would* be happier raising children than trying to finish her dissertation on Donne. There are in the world people of whom that could rightly be said. But this judgment would be easier to take if there were elsewhere in Lewis's fiction women of greater stature but within the range of ordinary human experience. (I make that caveat because the great saintly figures known in their contexts just as "the Lady"—the Eve-figure of *Perelandra* and, in *The Great Divorce,* the one who was once Sarah Smith of Golders Green—clearly do not count. They are not part of our fallen human world.) There are no female characters at all in *Out of the Silent Planet,* no ordinary human ones in *Pelelandra.* In *That Hideous Strength* we get only the gentle "Mother Dimble" and the sadistic bull dyke "Fairy" Hardcastle.

It is when we turn to Narnia that the picture grows brighter. For one thing, in those tales there is a strong tendency toward pairing characters, a boy and a girl, of roughly equal narrative interest and with a general moral equality as well: Lucy and Edmund, Polly and Digory, Jill and Eustace, Aravis and Shasta. None of these characters is perfect: all are flawed, but flawed in very familiar ways, and all are capable of virtue when the going gets rough. Probably the boys are a little worse; certainly the two "problem children" of the series are Edmund and Eustace, but they both improve. And when Lewis's narrative calls for us to see the story through one particular character's eyes, that character is as likely to be a girl as a boy. The one major character who seems to have some moral or spiritual insight denied to others is, of course, Lucy: she is the one who finds the Wardrobe; in *Prince Caspian* she is the one granted a unique vision of Aslan; when the various characters enter into the True Narnia near the end of *The Last Battle,* we are told that Lucy fell silent for a while because "she was drinking everything in even more deeply than the others."

Yes, there is the White Witch. But if the perfectly saintly Ladies of *Perelandra* and *The Great Divorce* are not going to count in Lewis's favor as a creator of female characters, why should the single demonic one count against him? Besides, doesn't every fairy tale need a Wicked Witch? Some have discerned that Lewis was making a dig at feminism when he gave Experiment House (the school that Eustace and Jill attend) a headmistress, but it seems clear to me that her problem is that she is a psychobabbling bureaucrat, not that she is a woman. (*That Hideous Strength* is full of such creatures, and they are all men.)

Most troubling to many readers, though, is what the American writer Neil Gaiman has called "the problem of Susan"—an analogy, I guess, to "the problem of pain." The problem is that, as we are told in

The Last Battle, Susan is "no longer a friend of Narnia"—she does not appear with her brothers and sisters when they return to Narnia, that is, the Real Narnia, Narnia remade. According to Jill, "she's interested in nothing nowadays except nylons and lipstick and invitations." For the gifted children's writer and fantasy novelist Philip Pullman, the meaning of this is all too plain: Susan has undergone puberty, and her sexual maturation is "so dreadful and so redolent of sin that [Lewis] had to send her to Hell." But this is nonsense on several counts. First, it is clearly not sexuality that is Susan's problem but rather an excessive regard for social acceptance: she wants to be "grown-up" because she is at an age when being grown-up is the greatest possible good and being childish the worst possible crime. Susan has been distracted from Narnia not by sexual desire but by the desire to be within the Inner Ring. (As Lewis had written years earlier, some young people pursue their first sexual experience less because they want sex itself—that prospect can be as frightening as it is desirable—than because they want the social acceptance that sexual experience can bring.)

More important, Susan cannot have been "sent to Hell" because she has not died—something that Pullman could easily have discovered if he had been concerned with the truth of his accusation against Lewis. In 1957 a boy had written to Lewis with some concern for the fate of Susan, and here is the reply he received: "The books don't tell us what happened to Susan. She is left alive in this world at the end, having turned into a rather silly, conceited young woman. But there is plenty of time for her to mend, and perhaps she will get to Aslan's country in the end—in her own way." But I am sure that this bit of information, however inconvenient it may be to the boldness of Pullman's assertion, would not get Lewis off the hook that Pullman wants to impale him on. For whether Susan makes it in the end to Aslan's country is only a "perhaps": in Lewis's understanding of the cosmos, people do indeed manage to get themselves damned—though he always insists that each of us goes where we choose to go, where we prefer to be. All the Ghosts in *The Great Divorce* can stay in Heaven if they choose; most of them do not so choose, because in their lifetimes they made themselves into the kinds of people who no longer desire what Heaven has to offer. "It is only to the damned that their fate could ever seem less than unendurable," he writes in *The Problem of Pain;* indeed, the "doors of Hell are locked," but they are locked "on the *inside.*" One could, perhaps, convince the critics that Susan had not been condemned for sexual sin, and even that she had not been "sent to Hell" at all, but that would not be likely to alter their essential judgment of Lewis: his greater crime remains, which is that he believes that God gives people the freedom to choose Hell rather than choose to dwell in Heaven. The *exclusivity* (as they might put it) of Lewis's vision is more dreadful than any sexism of which he might be guilty.

I suppose it would be easy enough to say that Lewis can represent women only as virtuous little girls, inaccessible saints, or domestic tyrants. But even if that were true, it would indicate a broader range of female characters than many noted novelists can boast and would drop him right into the same boat as, for example, Charles Dickens. And if every negative female character an author creates is evidence of that author's misogyny, then few writers can escape censure. It is in the end useless to point to fictional characters and declare that they prove something about the character of their creator. In any case, one would not need to read a single word of Lewis's fiction in order to learn that he had very traditional, old-fashioned ideas about gender differences. This is scarcely surprising. Oxford in his time was an overwhelmingly masculine society, still retaining, in its social practices, many of the traditions that had been established when the dons were not allowed to marry and the university was for all practical purposes a monastic institution. He therefore had a very limited female acquaintance; despite the long commitment to Minto, he was in effect a bachelor living among bachelors. (I find myself wondering whether his attitudes would have been any different if his intellectually ambitious and relatively nontraditional mother had lived longer.) What is surprising is the extent to which he strove, in his writing and in his daily life, to compensate for the prejudices that he knew his way of life created in him. His treatment of his female students and colleagues testifies to that effort; so too, I think, in a subtler way, does his writing. We cringe when we see those prejudices emerge, but few of us work as hard as Lewis did to confront our hidden assumptions, bring them to light, and deal strictly with them.

Yet, all that said, one character from Lewis's fiction remains to be considered: Orual, the protagonist of *Till We Have Faces*. I have already noted something of Orual's complexity: she reveals to us the limits of language and argument when we are confronted with the mysteries of divinity, and she embodies the tyrannical, consumptive perversion of love with which Lewis seems to have been deeply concerned. But he also told Katherine Farrer that Orual's story is "the story of every nice, affectionate agnostic whose dearest one suddenly 'gets religion,' or even every luke-warm Christian whose dearest gets a Vocation." That is, in *Till We Have Faces* he returns to, and more deeply explores, the "fiendishness" that conversion can produce in the families of new Christians—the fiendishness that Minto, almost certainly, exhibited when Lewis started inconveniencing the family by getting up on Sunday morning to go to church. If Lewis "is" anyone in this book, it is not Orual, but rather Psyche, whose love for the god of the Grey Mountain enrages Orual, even though, in Psyche's understanding, her love for her new husband will only strengthen and deepen her love for her family. Psyche is in a sense the Church, the Bride of Christ, but also every believer insofar as every believer is a member of the Church. As Lewis wrote in his article on the ordination of women, "We are all, corporately and individually, feminine to Him."

And insofar as Psyche is in the same position that Lewis found himself in when he became a Christian, so Orual is a version of Minto: an old, angry, embittered woman. She is also the most skilled and competent of his adult female characters: a good and wise monarch, much loved by her friends and revered by her people. But bitterness dominates her life—that is, until the very end of the book, and of her life, when she is granted the vision that reveals to her her real complaint, the real source of her bitterness. We have seen Lewis do this before: when, in *The Magician's Nephew*, he gives to Digory's mother the healing he could not give to his own mother, and when he gives to Digory himself (Professor Kirke to be) the revelatory experience that his old tutor, the original Kirk, never received. Now he offers the same gift, retrospectively and fictionally, to Minto: the gift of insight, the gift of getting outside her obsessions and seeing them for what they really are, the gift of forgiveness (granted and received). One feeling he had when Minto was taken to the hospital, he told Arthur, was "fear"—but fear for what? Perhaps fear for his own loss, but certainly fear for the old unbeliever's soul. Surely, as he went daily to her bedside in the nursing home, he must have wanted more than almost anything for his companion of so many years, the love of his youth, to be reconciled to the God whom she despised. It is not likely that he saw any evidence that his prayers on that score were granted; in a sense, through the vision that transforms the last days of Orual's life, he granted them himself.

•　　•　　•

After Minto's death, when nurses were no longer needed, the Kilns became for a time something like the reincarnation of Little Lea, with the role of Albert being played by the gardener and handyman, Fred Paxford. Paxford, an Oxfordshire countryman just Lewis's age, had virtually come with the Kilns: Minto had hired him almost immediately after the house's purchase, and he moved into a little hut on the property, where he lived until Lewis's death. He spent several years clearing and organizing the nine acres of grounds surrounding the Kilns, planting an orchard, and creating a vegetable garden. He also did the grocery shopping for the household, though with a notable, and rather neurotic, degree of frugality: he seems to have been concerned, at least half-seriously, that the world could come to an end with the larder of the Kilns full of sugar and flour. He sang hymns constantly, in a voice loud enough to anger the neighbors, but it was the incessant gloominess of his predictions, especially about the weather, that most caught people's attention and led to his employment as the model for Puddleglum the Marsh-Wiggle in *The Silver Chair*. If Lewis found Paxford amusing and even endearing, Warnie was maddened by him—or rather, by the excessively high value Minto came to place on his opinions, which were many, wide-ranging, and firm. All Minto had to do was to begin a sentence with the words "Paxford says" for Warnie to suffer an immediate spasm of rage. Fortunately, Warnie knew he was wrong to blame Paxford, and after the old lady's death they got along much better.

It would have been possible for the three men, bachelors of late middle age, to continue living in harmony for some time, if also in disorder: the Kilns became so smoky and ashy and filthy in those years that Hugo Dyson started calling it "the Midden." But events at Oxford were loosening Lewis's ties to the university that had long given him an intellectual and vocational home. The dispersal of the Inklings contributed to it, though probably was not decisive. If Thursday evenings had gone quiet, there could still be much bustle and mirth at the pub, and the 1949 letter in which Lewis praised the final version of *The Lord of the Rings,* with its plaintive "I miss you very much," indicates at least a ghost of a hope for the renewal of his relationship with Tolkien. But within the workings of the university itself things were not going so well.

At one point early in their time on the Oxford English faculty, Lewis and Tolkien had had great plans and high hopes for the cause of literature—especially the kind of literature they both loved—at Oxford. In their first years as dons they had thrown their energies into revising the "English syllabus," that is, the whole course of study for what Americans would call English majors. They managed to make philological study, focusing on Old and Middle English, central to the curriculum, and they had ended the syllabus quite abruptly at 1832 (the date of the great Reform Bill, which had, among other things, reconstructed Parliamentary representation and which is usually seen as the beginning of the Victorian age, though Victoria would not come to the throne for another five years). Emboldened by this achievement, Lewis decided in 1938 to promote his friend Adam Fox—the Dean of Divinity at Magdalen and the author of some poems—in an election for Oxford's Professor of Poetry. Enlisting the aid of the other Inklings, Lewis managed a powerful campaign for Fox, counting on the support of voters other than Oxford dons: the Professor of Poetry is elected by all holders of the MA degree from Oxford, a group that then included many clergymen, who were attracted by the support of a rising young spokesman for the Christian faith. Fox won, though with very little support from the Oxford faculty, and in some ways this was a Pyrrhic victory for Lewis. A. N. Wilson explains:

> The election did much to harm Lewis's reputation in Oxford. The dons felt that he could not be trusted: that he was populist, bullying, showy, and hostile to them. By his campaign for Fox, Lewis probably destroyed his own chances of promotion in the University, even though he was very obviously the most distinguished member of the English faculty.

And of course, his very public championing of the Christian faith added to his poor reputation: even some Christians within the Oxford community thought that Lewis's evangelistic zeal, however appropriate it might have been for Billy Sunday (or, later, Billy Graham), was rather embarrassing in a member of the faculty. It began to be said regularly that Lewis was wasting his time on cheap popular sermonizing and science fiction, time that would have been better spent on scholarship. (As Tolkien told Walter Hooper after Lewis's death, Oxford dons allow their peers to write two kinds of books: scholarly ones and detective stories, the latter "because all dons at some time get the flu, and they have to have something to read in bed.")

But some of this resentment, it must also be said, was a function of what the kindly disposed would call the strength of Lewis's personality and what others would call his tendency to bully people. He was always a forceful speaker and an enthusiastic debater, as we have seen, and whether he always meant well or not, he was not always *thought* to mean well. One of the semi-regular Inklings, Peter Bayley, said, "I always remained a little frightened of him, and so did Hugo Dyson"— and if this could happen to Lewis's friends, one can imagine how his enemies felt. Humphrey Havard—like Dyson a true intimate, not just an acquaintance like Bayley—loved Lewis deeply, but admitted, "He could be intolerant, he could be abusive, and he made enemies." If there is one word that comes up most often in the comments of people who knew Jack Lewis well, it is that he was "kind," but his kindness was not invariable, and when he employed his great verbal dexterity and his booming voice in order to refute some perceived error, the recipient of the tongue-lashing was not likely to forget or forgive.

To Lewis's friends, even those who recognized his faults, the key fact about his career was this: that if one ignored all the dialectical overaggressiveness, all the sermonizing, all the fiction, and all the theological fantasies, what remained (by the late 1940s) was a body of scholarly work that no one on Oxford's English faculty could rival. *The Allegory of Love*, as we have seen, had a powerful effect throughout medieval studies; *A Preface to "Paradise Lost"* was read and deeply considered by all Miltonists; his essays about Shakespeare and Spenser had generated great discussion among specialists in those fields; and then, to top it all, the OHEL volume was soon to be released. But many dons were not inclined to ignore all those other traits and activities, and despite Lewis's great scholarly achievements, he could not get himself elected to a chair—that is, a professorial position that would relieve him of tutorial duties. Tolkien had been a professor since 1932 and in 1945 had moved to the prestigious Merton Chair of English Language. When its twin, the Merton Chair of English Literature, came open in 1947, Lewis was overlooked. When the Professor of Poetry elections came around again in 1951, Hugo Dyson tried to do for Lewis what Lewis had done for Fox, mounting a vigorous campaign, but Lewis lost, fairly narrowly, to Cecil Day-Lewis. His friends did not think he was particularly upset by this, but Lewis now had every reason to think that he would have to spend the rest of his career as a tutor, when far less accomplished men throughout the University had long since settled into the easier duties of professorship. (Frustration over the loss of the Merton Chair may even have

contributed to his exhaustion and near-despair at the end of the forties.) To add to his professional miseries, the English faculty were busy
tearing down the great edifice of the English syllabus that he and
Tolkien had built a quarter-century earlier. For many men it all would
have been humiliating; whether Lewis felt it that way or not, it was
perfectly clear to him and all his friends that his university placed very
little value on his work.

It is not surprising, then, that Lewis was moved when he learned, in
May 1954, that the electors for a newly created chair at Cambridge
University in medieval and Renaissance literature had chosen him as
its first occupant. Moved, yes, but he turned them down, even though
it would have meant release from tutorial duties and a raise in salary
from £600 a year to nearly £2,000. He thought he was too old for the
job; he had recommended that someone else apply for the position and
now felt it wrong to make himself a candidate; and above all, he was
concerned about abandoning Warnie and Paxford. When pressed to
reconsider, he admitted to the chair of the committee that had elected
him, Sir Henry Willinck, that his primary concern was for Warnie:
"My brother, in your ear, is not always in perfect psychological
health"—which, of course, meant that his alcoholism had grown
worse. At this point Sir Henry relented.

But someone else did not: Tolkien. For a brief moment, all that had
clouded their relationship was swept away. Tolkien talked to Lewis at
length about the chair, pointing out that he could continue to live at
the Kilns during vacations, and perhaps even on weekends if he was
willing to take the train back and forth between the two university
towns. He enlisted the aid of other friends and corresponded with the
electors of the chair, encouraging them not to give up. "Besides being
the precise man for the job, Lewis would probably be happy there,
and actually be reinvigorated by a change of air," he wrote to Sir
Henry. "Oxford has not, I think, treated him well, and though he is incapable of 'dudgeon,' or of showing resentment, he has been a little
dispirited." (The tribute to Lewis's character is noteworthy.) Tolkien
also lobbied other members of the committee. One gets the sense that
he was in a sense attempting to repay Lewis for the years of unrelenting encouragement that had enabled him to finish *The Lord of the
Rings*—which was just at this time being published, to unexpectedly
positive reviews (overall) and unexpectedly good sales. Eventually he
got Lewis to write to Sir Henry to say that he was ready to reconsider,
provided that one of the Cambridge colleges—the chair was not at-

tached to any particular college—could provide him rooms in which he could stay in term-time.

This was an awkward letter for Sir Henry to receive, because, taking Lewis's refusal seriously, the committee had already voted to offer the job to another candidate: Lewis's younger colleague Helen Gardner. They were friends, of a sort, but they had been on opposing sides in the matter of revising the English syllabus; moreover, Gardner's Christianity, while very real, was less traditional than Lewis's. Worse yet, she had made her name by writing a book about, and in praise of, T. S. Eliot. But when Gardner, a gracious woman as well as a gifted scholar, heard through the grapevine that Lewis might well accept the chair after all, she turned it down. It would have been a great coup for her, but as she later put it, "It was obvious that this ought to be Lewis's chair." And indeed so it became. Sir Henry Willinck, in addition to being the Vice-Chancellor of the University and the head of the committee that elected Lewis, was also the Master of Magdalene College—with the same pronunciation as Oxford's Magdalen despite that ultimate "e"—and in that capacity offered Lewis rooms. As Lewis put it to Sister Penelope, he was delighted to remain "under the same patroness" despite his academic relocation.

Once his acceptance had been announced, authorities at Oxford began to question their treatment of Lewis and scrambled to put together a chair for him, but he refused to consider it (and refused again when he was asked to apply for the Merton Professorship the next time it came open). As he told Nevill Coghill, "I have exchanged the *im*penitent for the *penitent* Magdalen."

Now that all these events of the early 1950s have been sketched out, it is time to turn to the most important event of that period, and indeed the only really well-known part of C. S. Lewis's life: his meeting and marrying Joy Davidman Gresham. Thanks largely to the film *Shadowlands* (with Anthony Hopkins as Lewis and Debra Winger as Joy) and the BBC television drama that preceded it (with Joss Ackland and Claire Bloom), the story is familiar—or at least a neatly trimmed and highly dramatized version of it is. The actual story is not understood at all, nor, I believe, can it be; too much about it is unclear. Perhaps Joy understood the situation; perhaps even Warnie, to some extent, did; but Lewis certainly did not, and even in retrospect he failed, I think, to comprehend what had happened to his life, except in the most general outlines.

As long as Mrs. Moore lived Lewis did not feel himself free to marry or even to engage in a serious relationship.* But after her death he could think freely, and indeed did. In fact, he even had a person in mind, a poet and painter named Ruth Pitter with whom he had been corresponding since 1946, when she had written him to thank him for his books. He already knew and admired her poetry and frequently sought her advice about and commentary on his own poems. His respect for her mind was great, and his letters to her are almost uniquely affectionate. When, in 1953, his friend George Sayer drove Lewis to visit her at her home in Buckinghamshire, he was surprised to discover that Lewis "seemed to be on intimate terms with her." They had a teasing sort of banter: "each suggested amusing and improbable books for the other to write," Sayer noted. Pitter herself recorded one conversation, which took place during a luncheon at her house with Lewis, Warnie, and the sometime Inkling Lord David Cecil and his wife, Rachel. She even gave her account a title: "Ruth Pitter Defeats C. S. Lewis in Argument." Here is the relevant portion, concerning the first of the Narnia tales:

RP: The Witch makes it always winter and never summer?
CS: (in his fine reverberating voice) She does.
RP: Does she allow any foreign trade?
CS: She does not.
RP: Am I allowed to postulate a *deus ex machina,* perhaps on the
        line of Santa Claus with the tea-tray? (This is where CS lost
        the contest. If he had allowed the deus-ex-m., for which
        Santa gives good precedent, he would have saved himself.)
CS: You are not.
RP: Then how could the Beavers have put on the splendid lunch?
CS: They caught the fish through holes in the ice.
RP: Quite so, but the dripping to fry them? The potatoes—a
        plant that perishes at a touch of the frost—the oranges and

---

* At least, this is what Warnie and his biographers have consistently said. But one curious and suggestive comment has been made, in a brief recollection of Lewis, by Roger Lancelyn Green: he mentions a "young lady (the daughter of the head of an Oxford college) who seems to have represented his only thought of marriage in his twenties or thirties." And that is all he said. Whether Lewis ever seriously considered marriage, or even embarked on a courtship, and what that could have meant for his commitment to Minto, we will surely never know.

sugar and suet and flour for the lovely surprise Marmalade
Roll—the malt and hops for Mr. Beaver's beer—the milk for
the children?

CS: (with great presence of mind) I must refer you to a further
study of the text.

Warnie: Nonsense, Jack; you're stumped and you know it.

Perhaps it is not surprising, then, that (as Sayer tells it) "after one visit
in 1955, he remarked that, if he were not a confirmed bachelor, Ruth
Pitter would be the woman he would like to marry." But he did not
pursue her, and Ruth Pitter, being a mannerly and decorous woman,
did nothing to pursue Lewis.

In January 1950—when the subject most on his mind was the onset
of old age—Lewis had received his first letter from a Mrs. Gresham of
New York. Of course, receiving letters from American women was a
daily occurrence for Lewis, as we have seen, but this letter was a little
different. For one thing, it was funny and well written—as might be
expected from a woman who had been a reasonably successful writer
(of fiction, poetry, nonfiction, even film screenplays) for quite some
time. For another, it asked for neither help nor counsel: it was merely
an expression of Mrs. Gresham's gratitude for the role that Lewis's
books had played in her recent conversion to Christianity and—what
was probably more welcome—an attempt to argue with one or two
points. He replied; she wrote again; soon enough, as Warnie noted,
they had become "pen-friends."

Her story was a fascinating one, almost utterly different from
Lewis's, and yet, like his, a characteristic twentieth-century life—except for the conversion-to-Christianity part. Helen Joy Davidman was
born in New York City in 1915; her parents were Jews, but while her
mother was occasionally observant, her father was an atheist. The
Great Depression hit when she was fourteen years old and in the midst
of intellectual self-discovery: "In 1929 I believed in nothing but American prosperity," she later wrote; "in 1930 I believed in nothing." As a
student at Hunter College and then Columbia, she became absorbed
in the political tensions that dominated New York cultural life in those
years. It was a world in which supporters of Trotsky were thought to
occupy the far right of the political spectrum and in which friendships
were permanently destroyed by disagreements over the Moscow
show trials. Like many young artists and intellectuals, Joy Davidman
found the Party's lure irresistible, and she became a staff writer for

their magazine, *New Masses*. Her first book was a collection of largely political poems called *Letters to a Comrade,* and one may get some sense of how talented she was by noting that the book won the prestigious Yale Younger Poets Prize in 1938. After a very brief stint as a screenwriter in Hollywood, she came back to New York and, in 1940, published a novel called *Anya.*

Soon thereafter she met a fellow writer, and fellow Party member, named Bill Gresham, and they were married in 1942. Gresham had been a troubled man: married once before, then separated from his wife, he had gone to Spain (like many young intellectuals of the day) to fight in the Spanish Civil War. Eventually he had a breakdown that led to a suicide attempt, but he felt that a course of psychoanalysis and participation in the Party had stabilized him. And when he and Joy had had two children—David in 1944 and Douglas in 1945—and both had embarked on successful writing careers, it might have seemed that they were on their way to an ideal life. But Bill remained unstable: he had affairs with other women, and he veered close to another breakdown. Joy was crushed both by his infidelity and by his often cruel treatment of her and the children, and in the midst of that devastation this lifelong atheist—she had proclaimed herself an unbeliever at age eight, after having read H. G. Wells's thousand-page *Outline of History*—received a fleeting but unforgettable visitation: "A Person [was] with me in the room, directly present to my consciousness—a Person so real that all my previous life was by comparison mere shadow play. And I myself was more alive than I had ever been; it was like waking up from sleep." This "perception of God lasted perhaps half a minute," but it was enough to set her on a journey to discover who this God was and what It wanted from her.

The journey led to, among other things, the writings of C. S. Lewis, and Bill, to whom she had been reconciled during the search, found— or seemed to find—faith along with her. Joy and her sons were all baptized in 1948. But Bill was fundamentally unstable and soon began to spiral out of control again: he began to dabble in various odd religious traditions, including the Scientology movement founded by the science-fiction writer L. Ron Hubbard. Eventually, as Joy was corresponding more and more regularly with C. S. Lewis, he fell in love with Joy's cousin Renée Pierce—herself married with children—and declared that it would be best for Joy to grant him a divorce, for Renée to divorce her husband, for Renée to marry him, and for Joy to marry "some really swell guy." Which is pretty much how it worked out.

It is all too easy to look back into the past of a given situation from a secure knowledge of what would eventually transpire and declare that the acute observer could have seen it all coming. ("Backshadowing," the critic Gary Saul Morson calls this tendency.) But it is hard not to discern infatuation in Joy's tone as she writes in 1950 to Chad Walsh, whose book on Lewis—one of the first—had been helpful to her. What she refers to here is Lewis's reply to her first letter:

> Just got a letter from Lewis in the mail. I think I told you I'd raised an argument or two on some points? Lord, he knocked my props out from under me unerringly; one shot to a pigeon. I haven't a scrap of my case left. And, what's more, I've seldom enjoyed anything more. Being disposed of so neatly by a master of debate—all fair and square—it seems to be one of the great pleasures of life, though I'd never have suspected it in my arrogant youth.

When she finally managed to get to England, in September 1952—a trip she made for the quite explicit purpose of escaping her husband's influence and replacing it with that of "one of the clearest thinkers of our time"—she, along with a friend, had lunch with Lewis at the Eastgate Hotel and then, at his invitation, at Magdalen. Reading George Sayer's account of the first meeting—he had come to substitute for an indisposed Warnie, a second masculine presence being necessary to balance the two women—one fairly blushes at how outrageously Joy flattered her host: "Small farm life was the only good life, she said. Lewis spoke up then, saying that, on his father's side, he came from farming stock. 'I felt that,' she said. 'Where else could you get the vitality?'" For a man in late middle age—a man moreover increasingly prone to melancholy over the onset of physical and intellectual decline—to be complimented by a woman seventeen years his junior on his "vitality," well, that must have been nice.

But if indeed Joy already had, as the Victorian novelists used to say, "designs" on Lewis, he was quite innocent of them. In his youth his father had feared that Mrs. Moore would somehow take advantage of him because he was "an impetuous, kind hearted creature who could be cajoled by any woman who has been through the mill." Apparently little had changed. Lewis was *so* innocent that, when in February 1954 he invited Ruth Pitter to lunch at the Eastgate, he impetuously and kindheartedly—but without mentioning it to Ruth—asked Joy along too.

•   •   •

Lewis could ask Joy to that lunch because by then she and her sons
were living in England. Her 1952 visit had extended into 1953, and
Lewis had invited her to spend Christmas at the Kilns. He had come to
feel sufficiently close to her that he gave her, as a Christmas present, a
copy of George MacDonald's *Diary of an Old Soul* that had been
signed by MacDonald himself. She stayed at the Kilns for two weeks,
and it was while she was there that she received the letter from her
husband counseling her to marry "some really swell guy." Lewis felt
that she should divorce him immediately; Joy resisted. But her son
Douglas later came to feel that his mother not only accepted her husband's desertion but actually welcomed it, and in a sense had encouraged it: it gave her a means of escape "from a marriage that was fast
disintegrating."

Warnie—and to a great extent this was true of all Lewis's friends—
found Joy strangely fascinating. He had never met a woman like her:
she seemed to him like every Englishman's caricature of a brash, loud
New Yorker. She drank with the boys and laughed with the boys, even
coming to the pub with them; they never would have tolerated such
behavior from an Englishwoman. When she was given her first tour of
Magdalen, George Sayer says, "her enthusiasm, interest, and many
impudent questions made us roar with laughter." (He then adds, mod-
estly, "I suppose the quantity of good wine that we had drunk contributed to our hilarity.") To Warnie she was "quite extraordinarily
uninhibited," and he cites as evidence the first time he met her, also at
a Magdalen lunch: "She turned to me in the presence of three or four
men, and asked in the most natural tone in the world, 'Is there anywhere in this monastic establishment where a lady can relieve herself?'"

What we have seen of Warnie reveals his irascibility more than anything else, but that tendency was greatly exacerbated by his difficult
relationship with Mrs. Moore, and in any case Warnie released far
more hostility to his diary than he ever would have allowed to have
public expression. (He had, after all, become long since the English
gentleman his father had wanted him to be.) One of the later Inklings,
John Wain, wrote that Warnie was the most courteous man he had
ever met, "not with mere politeness, but with a genial, self-forgetful
considerateness that was as instinctive to him as breathing." But between his public courtesy and private wrath, Warnie was a careful and
intelligent observer of his brother's life and friends and was prone nei-

ther to over-sunny optimism nor to cranky critique. Some years after meeting Joy, and reflecting on her lack of inhibition, he wrote, "I was some little time in making up my mind about her." But when he did make up his mind, he came to respect, love, and deeply admire Joy, and this is especially commendable on Warnie's part because Joy's arrival in the Lewises' life would bring a thorough disruption of the peaceful bachelors' household that, after all those miserable years with Mrs. Moore, Warnie had so recently and blissfully achieved. Nevertheless, his approval of Joy did not blind him to her purposes: he understood from early on that Joy was straightforwardly pursuing Lewis.

Ruth Pitter understood this too and, as might be expected, resented it deeply. Interviewed in her old age, she declared of Joy, "She was bad. I think she was a predatory person." It is interesting that even though Warnie recognized that, in an old phrase, Joy had her cap set for Jack, he never resented this or cast any disapproving light on her. Perhaps that is because he saw how happy Jack was when Joy was around.

In November 1953 Joy brought her sons to England. She found a flat in Belsize Park, near Hampstead—that famously artsy community north of central London—and found a preparatory school in Surrey for the boys, who thus began their education as Englishmen. She declared that she loved England and saw no reason why she should ever return to the States. (A few months later her divorce from Bill Gresham would become final.) After bringing the boys to the Kilns for a few days in December—their energy, to which Lewis was unaccustomed, overwhelmed him—she retired discreetly to Hampstead. For the next year or so they saw each other irregularly: in October 1954 Lewis came to London to participate, along with Dorothy Sayers, in a debate about the influence (good or ill) of Christian intellectuals; on that occasion he met Joy's parents, who were visiting their daughter in her new home. A month later Lewis gave his inaugural lecture at Cambridge; Joy made sure to be there. Visiting the Kilns in March 1955, she found that Lewis was struggling to come up with an idea for a new book, and over a couple of whiskies they "kicked a few ideas around till one came to life"—that one being, ultimately, *Till We Have Faces*. As Lewis worked on the book, Joy wrote in a letter to her ex-husband, "He says he finds my advice indispensable." In August she moved to Lewis's section of Oxford, Headington, within walking distance of the Kilns. According to Walter Hooper, Lewis almost immediately began to visit her every day.

• • •

One of the early sources of tension in Lewis's relationship with Tolkien had been a passage in one of his broadcast talks in which he recommended a clear distinction between Christian and civil marriage. His reasoning had been that the State has its ideas of what marriage is, while the Church has its (very different) ideas of what marriage is, and the two should be kept clearly distinct. Tolkien found this idea "abominable" and "ridiculous" and said so in a long letter, a draft of which was found inside his copy of the original brief 1943 volume called *Christian Behaviour*. It is not clear whether he ever sent the letter, but there is reason to believe that he made his feelings clearly known to Lewis. In any event, neither of them ever imagined at the time the controversy arose that the question could have personal implications for either of them. But it did.

Soon after Joy's move to Headington, she discovered that she would not be allowed to remain in England and would soon be deported to the United States. She and Lewis discussed it and came up with a plan: if all appeals were to be exhausted, he would marry Joy—in a civil ceremony only—so that she could remain in England and her sons could be given the status of British subjects. Lewis told several close friends what he was doing and why: as he put the matter to Roger Lancelyn Green, he did not consider that, in the Christian sense that mattered most to him, he would be "married" at all. It was "a pure matter of friendship and expediency . . . simply a legal form." (But he did not tell Tolkien: it was all too obvious what Tolkien would say. In fact, Tolkien knew nothing at all of Lewis's relationship with Joy, and in the end this would be the final blow to their friendship.) The "legal form" was signed on April 23, 1956. It was a Monday, and on Mondays in term-time Lewis took the train to Cambridge. By that evening he was in his rooms in Magdalene, and the next day he resumed his lectures.

In early November 1956, Warnie turned once more to his diary, where he could say all the things that his peculiar relationship with his younger brother would never allow him to say openly:

J assured me that Joy would continue to occupy her own house as "Mrs. Gresham," and that the marriage was a pure formality designed to give Joy the right to go on living in England: and I saw the uselessness of disabusing him. Joy, whose intentions were obvious from the outset, soon began to press for her rights, pointing out with perfect truth that her reputation was suffering from J's being in her house every day, often stopping until eleven at night.

"I saw the uselessness of disabusing him." It was obvious to Warnie that Lewis was in love with Joy, just as it was obvious to him that Joy was drawing Lewis closer and closer to a "real" marriage. It was equally obvious to Joy's younger son Douglas. (What David thought no one knows—he kept to himself then and still does so today.) But Warnie knew from long experience—he would never forget the resoluteness with which Lewis shut down any attempt to initiate a discussion about Mrs. Moore—that there was nothing he could do or say. Events would have to find their own course, and if Warnie was troubled by them, he could but turn to the diary or the bottle for consolation. He had no other options. Lewis denied that at this point he had any erotic or romantic feelings for Joy, and Green and Hooper, dutiful biographers that they are, take his word for it. This seems crazy to me. A man does not visit a woman every single day he is in the same town with her, staying with her until bedtime, unless he is in love with her, and a woman does not tolerate such a constant presence unless she is in love with him. Moreover, Joy had come to England with almost no money, and almost from the start Lewis had been paying (even before he acquired his Cambridge professor's salary) not only her rent but the costs of her sons' education. Not to put too fine a point on it, but the Christian leader a London newspaper once dubbed "ascetic Mr. Lewis" had become an American divorcée's sugar daddy. It is really astonishing, in a comical sort of way, that at the very time Lewis was spending every free hour at Joy's house he was telling George Sayer that if he were not a "confirmed bachelor" he would marry Ruth Pitter. (Did he have on some level the feeling that Ruth Pitter—lacking an ex-husband and children and sharing with him age, country, and class—would be a more appropriate match than the rather extravagant Mrs. Gresham?) In any case, for whatever reasons, Lewis was in denial, but Warnie was not, nor was Doug Gresham, and there is no reason for Lewis's biographers to be less acute than his brother and his stepson.

So, as Warnie put it, by mid-October "all the arrangements had been made for the installation of [Joy and her] family at the Kilns." It is not clear how Lewis planned to explain *this* to his friends—at the very least he must have been steeling himself for a barrage of "surprised by Joy" jokes. But such problems were soon eclipsed by a far greater one.

On October 18, after the plans for her "installation" in the Kilns had been settled, Joy was in her Headington house when the phone rang. As she got up to answer it, she tripped over the cord and fell, and when she hit the ground she felt her left femur snap. In agony, she reached for the receiver: it was Katherine Farrer, who called an ambulance. (Farrer had been seized with a sudden and inexplicable impulse to call Joy.) The femur, Joy learned the next day, had broken so easily because the bone had been eaten away by cancer; the doctors also found tumors in her left breast, in her right leg, and in her right shoulder. She had been feeling pain in her back and leg for some time but did not think it especially serious. She was only forty-two years old.

Green and Hooper insist that "there was still no Eros or romantic love on Lewis's part," but because he felt "a great pity for Joy," and because "it seemed certain that Joy was dying, he wanted to take her to the Kilns where she could die as his wife." They go on to say: "He felt this would be wrong without a Christian marriage." But if that is true, then why was Lewis planning to move Joy and her boys into the Kilns *before* the discovery of her cancer—a sequence of events to which, again, both Warnie and Douglas Gresham testify? Had he, then, already been planning to marry her in a Christian ceremony? (According to Douglas, he even told the two boys that one of the reasons he accepted the Cambridge position was that he was thinking of marrying their mother and wanted to be able to support the whole family comfortably. He could not have been contemplating the civil marriage in this way, because he insisted always that that was something that he simply had to do as a matter of plain Christian charity to allow Joy to stay in the country.) After all, it would make no sense to say that such a ceremony was unnecessary *before* her illness came to light but suddenly became necessary when she was dying.

One wonders if there is not an implicit commentary on this situation in *The Four Loves*, which he wrote after all these events had unfolded. Writing about Eros, he discusses—and dissents from—the idea that real Eros, romantic love, develops out of a preexisting sexual attraction:

> I doubt if this is at all common. Very often what comes first is simply a delighted pre-occupation with the Beloved—a general, unspecified pre-occupation with her in her totality. A man in this state really hasn't leisure to think of sex. He is too busy thinking of a person. The fact that she is a woman is far less important than the fact that she is herself. He is full of desire, but the desire

may not be sexually toned. If you asked him what he wanted, the true reply would often be, "To go on thinking of her." He is love's contemplative. And when at a later stage the explicitly sexual element awakes, he will not feel . . . that this had all along been the root of the whole matter.

Like the comment he makes in *Mere Christianity* about those pretty girls who are "quite often sexually frigid," this passage makes a generalization for which there is no apparent warrant. Certainly my own experience of falling in love was not so divorced from sexual desire, nor would I have even comprehended the idea of separating my beloved's identity "as a woman" from her identity "as herself." Moreover, I have reason to think that many other men are, in this regard, more like me than like Lewis: the experience of a fifty-five-year-old man in rather poor health is not likely to be the norm among all men who fall passionately in love with a woman. And in this passage Lewis surely must be describing his own experience. He can have no grounds for knowing whether it is "common" or not; he is simply disguising as a general observation the course his own Eros took. (What else *could* such a statement mean? Do we really imagine that he went around and asked men about the stages in which they experienced romantic love and the point at which sexuality emerged as a meaningful factor?) If we read the passage in the light I have suggested, then it looks like an explanation for his own earlier denial that he was in love with Joy. Not feeling, at first and indeed for a while, a strong sexual response to her, he believed that what he did feel was not Eros but rather a form of Friendship. It was only retrospectively that he could see the Eros that had been there all along.

But before he could even have time for such reflection, much had to be done. Though Joy had several operations to remove her cancers, the extent and invasiveness of them gave her little hope for survival. Whatever Lewis's feelings for her at the time, and however well or badly he understood them, he knew that he wished to be joined to her in Christian marriage as soon as possible, and she more than anything wished the same. As Warnie would later write, he found "heartrending . . . Joy's eagerness for the pitiable consolation of dying under the same roof as J: though to feel pity for any one so magnificently brave as Joy is almost an insult."

But an enormous obstacle loomed in their path: the Church of England did not allow remarriage after divorce. Lewis understood this policy well enough that he did not even ask Austin Farrer—who, along with his wife, Katherine, was close both to Lewis and to Joy—to marry them; instead, he went to Harry Carpenter, the Bishop of Oxford, to seek an exception to the rule. Lewis argued that since Bill Gresham had been married once before, and his first wife was still alive, then his marriage to Joy—by the very standards of the Church of England—could not have been valid. Unfortunately, as Bishop Carpenter pointed out, it was also the policy of the Church to recognize every legal marriage as valid, even marriages conducted under different rules than the Church's own. Though Lewis refused to admit the rightness of the reasoning—he insisted in a letter to Dorothy Sayers that Joy's previous marriage had been no marriage at all—the bishop was technically correct.

At this refusal Lewis had become desperate and no longer willing to be the dutiful son of the Church that he had been since his conversion. He turned to a young friend, a priest named Peter Bide, and asked if *he* would marry them. According to canon law, Bide simply could not do this: he was not even a priest in the diocese of Oxford, and the bishop had already said that such a marriage was not legitimate. Lewis knew this: Bide could have followed church order only by marrying the two poor lovers within his own diocese and with the permission of his own bishop. But Bide, it seems, did not consider canon law final in its authority. Instead, he asked himself what Jesus would do, and believing on reflection that the answer was obvious, on the twenty-first of March 1957 he married Lewis and Joy in her hospital room. Warnie and one of the nurses served as witnesses; the five of them shared Holy Communion. And then Bide did something else: he placed his hands on Joy and prayed that she be healed.

Lewis never told Tolkien of his marriage. "I learned of it long after the event," Tolkien would later tell his son Michael; probably Humphrey Havard had filled him in, as he had informed Tolkien (vaguely and discreetly) a year or two earlier that Lewis had some sort of liaison with an American woman. But to his other friends Lewis was forthright. Three months after the wedding Lewis wrote to Dorothy Sayers and acknowledged that, though in a previous letter he had been quite insistent that he had no romantic feelings for Joy, "my feelings have changed." And the deadliness of her disease had much to do with it. "They say a rival often turns a friend into a lover. Thanatos [Death], certainly (they say) approaching but at an uncertain speed, is a most efficient rival for this purpose. We soon learn to love what we know we must lose. I hope you give us your blessing: I know you'll give us your prayers."

Not long after the wedding Lewis had lunch with Nevill Coghill, whom he had known since his undergraduate days but who was not one of his closest friends. Nevertheless, he opened up to Coghill to an unusual degree, and for an instant (thanks to Coghill's report) we get a glimpse—I believe the only glimpse we have—of how far short from the ideal had been his relationship with Minto, even in the early days. As he and Coghill stood together and watched Joy across the college quadrangle, Lewis said quietly, "I never expected to have, in my sixties, the happiness that passed me by in my twenties."

TWELVE

"Joy is the serious business of heaven"

On July 14, 1960, two guests visited Lewis at the Kilns: the composer Donald Swann and the librettist David Marsh. They had come to have breakfast and discuss with Lewis their bold plan—originally conceived by Swann—to make *Perelandra* into an opera. It was a brilliant idea: the stylized but highly dramatic plot of the novel, with its long rhetorical set pieces and unrealistic setting, probably belongs more to the world of opera than to any other artistic form. After breakfast they walked in the garden, discussing the possibilities and the obstacles to the realization of their plan. Then Lewis paused and said, "I hope you will excuse me. I must go now because my wife died last night."

Cambridge had been very good to Lewis, indeed far better than Oxford had ever been. Even apart from the release from tutorial drudgery, he found the town and his college more appealing and more comfortable than he had expected. Cambridge was then significantly smaller than Oxford (even today it *feels* much smaller, though the cities are now of similar size), and Magdalene much cozier and less populous than Magdalen. Plus, most of his colleagues welcomed him warmly—*they* knew that it was a coup to get him, even if the Oxonians did not—and for a number of them his Christianity was to be celebrated rather than lamented. He told Warnie that the majority of his colleagues and students were Christians, or at least that is what Warnie thought he said; it was not true, though the exaggeration is pardonable. The renewal Lewis had experienced when Joy came into his life seems to have spread to his social life more generally: he welcomed new friends into his life with gusto and at the beginning and end of each term brought Joy to Cambridge to celebrate with his new community.

His inaugural lecture, which he gave on his fifty-sixth birthday, November 29, 1954, filled the hall assigned for it to overflowing: Joy (who came to see the show, of course) later wrote that "there were so many capped and gowned dons in the front rows that they looked like a rookery." And what they heard was something remarkable. Lewis devoted some time to a repetition of an argument that he had made many times before: that the conventional separation of the "dark," "ignorant," "superstitious" Middle Ages from the "bright" and "humanistic" Renaissance is simply and utterly a fiction. In repeating this case, he was, in a sense, defending the very idea of a chair in medieval *and* Renaissance literature, but the fact of the chair's existence did not in itself refute the historical error. (When Lewis began making that argument, by the way, almost no one agreed with him; his reading of medieval history would only later come to receive widespread support among historians of culture.) For Lewis there is indeed a great divide that separates one great, long period of European history ("Old Western Culture") from our own world—but that divide was located in a much more recent period than the sixteenth century. In fact, though he was bold to say that most of the members of his audience were simply not members of that ancient civilization, he added that "the vast change which separates you from Old Western [Culture] has been gradual and is not even now complete. Wide as the chasm is, those who are native to different sides of it can still meet; are meeting in this room." And because the cliffs on either side of the chasm can be squeezed into a single room, there is a curious and, for most people, unexpected reason why Cambridge did well to choose C. S. Lewis as the first inhabitant of that Chair in Medieval and Renaissance Literature. The conclusion to his talk is worth quoting at length:

> I myself belong far more to that Old Western order than to yours. I am going to claim that this, which in one way is a disqualification for my task, is yet in another a qualification. The disqualification is obvious. You don't want to be lectured on Neanderthal Man by a Neanderthaler, still less on dinosaurs by a dinosaur. And yet, is that the whole story? If a live dinosaur dragged its slow length into the laboratory, would we not all look back as we fled? What a chance to know at last how it

really moved and looked and smelled and what noises it made! And if the Neanderthaler could talk, then, though his lecturing technique might leave much to be desired, should we not almost certainly learn from him some things about him which the best modern anthropologist could never have told us? He would tell us without knowing he was telling. One thing I know: I would give a great deal to hear any ancient Athenian, even a stupid one, talking about Greek tragedy. He would know in his bones so much that we seek in vain. At any moment some chance phrase might, unknown to him, show us where modern scholarship had been on the wrong track for years. Ladies and gentlemen, I stand before you somewhat as that Athenian might stand. I read as a native texts that you must read as foreigners.... It is my settled conviction that in order to read Old Western literature aright you must suspend most of the responses and unlearn most of the habits you have acquired in reading modern literature. And because this is the judgement of a native, I claim that, even if the defence of my conviction is weak, the fact of my conviction is a historical datum to which you should give full weight. That way, where I fail as a critic, I may yet be useful as a specimen. I would even dare to go further. Speaking not only for myself but for all other Old Western men whom you may meet, I would say, use your specimens while you can. There are not going to be many more dinosaurs.

I noted many pages back that Lewis had begun his career as a scholar by defending the value of "old books," by insisting that they have much to teach us if we can but learn to hear what they say. Here he remains attached to those books, and to the Old Western Culture they represent, but he seems less inclined to defend that culture than merely to embody it. It is the academic version of "Preach the Gospel always, using words when necessary." He will not defend Old Western Culture so much as simply *be* a rare specimen of Old Western Man. And he invites the members of the university to come and peer at the oddity.

With that, he began his brief Cambridge career. He resumed in Magdalene the routine that he had practiced for decades at Magdalen: a walk around the college garden before Morning Prayer or Communion at the chapel, then breakfast, then answering his mail—more of it than ever, and much of that concerning Narnia. He offered the "Prolegomena" lectures that had long been his Oxford stock-in-trade and began to assemble them into book form. He lectured on the odd topic of "Some Difficult Words," and these talks too became a book, the curious but endlessly fascinating *Studies in Words*. (Incidentally, he showed his loyalty to his new university by having these published by Cambridge University Press—all his previous academic books had been on Oxford's list.) His lectures on some Latin writers were attended by some dons, including a young classics scholar named Nan Dunbar, and this led to a comical and semiflirtatious exchange of letters. (Dunbar had thought Lewis wrong in denying that the poet Statius had a strict code of sexual morals; Lewis insisted that Statius was deficient in this regard. When, after exchanging many letters, they finally met at a party, Lewis said, "Ah! Miss Dunbar! I am glad to find you exist—I'd thought that perhaps you were only the personification of my conscience.") Lewis still had one polemical blast left in him, as we shall see, but in general he enjoyed Cambridge. It had but two shortcomings: first, Warnie was not there to help him with his letters; second, he did not have enough time with Joy. And he suspected that time with Joy was limited. This cast a constant pall over his life in that "other" university city. One of his colleagues there, Richard Ladborough, later wrote, "When he learned that his wife was suffering from her deadly illness, he did not mention it at first. I heard of it myself in a rather untypical way. He was looking unusually strained one evening after dinner, and I ventured to ask him if he were tired. He replied very suddenly: 'I am in great mental agony. Please pray for us' and then was silent."

Peter Bide had laid hands on Joy and prayed for her healing because, some years earlier, he had discovered that when he did this people often were indeed healed: he possessed, it appears, what the Church calls the gift of healing. In January 1959 an essay by Lewis appeared in the *Atlantic Monthly;* it was called "The Efficacy of Prayer," and one of its early paragraphs goes like this:

> I have stood by the bedside of a woman whose thigh-bone was eaten through with cancer and who had thriving colonies of disease in many other bones as well. It took three people to move her in bed. The doctors predicted a few months of life, the nurses (who often know better), a few weeks. A good man laid his hands on her and prayed. A year later the patient was walking

(uphill, too, through rough woodland) and the man who took the last x-rays was saying, "These bones are solid as rock. It's miraculous."

(Let us pause for a moment to reflect on an America in which an article on the efficacy of prayer could be published in the *Atlantic*.) It *was* miraculous. But it did not last. From her marriage to the end of her life, three years and four months later, Joy would go through a series of extraordinary crests and troughs, and Lewis would go through them with her. The essay on "The Efficacy of Prayer" would be written from a perch on one of the crests, but the fall from that height would be precipitous.

Soon after the wedding Joy was brought home to the Kilns to die. But she did not die. Not only had Peter Bide prayed for her healing, but Lewis too was praying, in a distinctive way. I noted many pages back that I had yet to mention the most important thing Lewis learned from Charles Williams. One of Williams's most passionately held ideas involved what he called "co-inherence": that is, to put it more concisely and directly than Williams was likely to, the ability of Christians, through the unifying power of the Holy Spirit that Christ had sent to his disciples, to dwell fully with each other and in one another's lives. What Williams desired was to explore the most radical implications of Jesus's commands to "bear one another's burdens" and "weep with those who weep, rejoice with those who rejoice." The "way of exchange," he often called it—"dying each other's life, living each other's death"—a kind of *moral* economy in which prayer and love are the currency rather than money. ("Money is *a* medium of exchange," he writes in one of his poems.) Williams believed that if a Christian sees another person suffering, it is that Christian's duty to pray to take on that suffering him- or herself: to become, in an almost literally Christ-like act, the vicarious substitute for one's neighbor. On these grounds Lewis began to pray for Joy's sufferings to be transferred to him.

Soon thereafter, Joy's bones began to heal, and Lewis's began to weaken. He did not get cancer but rather osteoporosis; nevertheless, as the pain in her bones decreased, his increased. To Sister Penelope he wrote about his worst period: "I was losing calcium just about as fast as Joy was gaining it, and a bargain (if it were one) for wh. I'm v. thankful." In the same conversation in which he told Coghill of his unexpected happiness, he explained that he believed that God had allowed him to accept in *his* body *her* pain: the way of exchange. These were for him very strange times. When he still thought that, despite his osteoporosis, Joy was dying, he wrote to Dorothy Sayers—in the same brief but uncharacteristically self-revealing letter that I quoted from at the end of the previous chapter—"Indeed the situation is not easy to describe. My heart is breaking and I was never so happy before; at any rate there is more in life than I knew about." But at this point he still had little hope, though he noticed that she *seemed* much better than the doctors told him she really *was*, despite her bedridden status. By November he could tell Sister Penelope that Joy was walking with a cane; a month later he could tell a godson that she "has made an almost miraculous, certainly an unexpected, recovery." In August 1958 he wrote to a friend to say that "my wife walks up the wooded hill behind our house"; it seems likely that the image of her doing so was what went into the *Atlantic* essay. "All goes amazing well with us."

But he also told Sister Penelope, "*Of course* the sword of Damocles still hangs over us: or, shd I say, *we* are forced to be aware of the sword wh. really overhangs all mortals." Neither Lewis nor Joy believed that they had any guarantees of long life; so they determined to take the best advantage possible of whatever time they had available. In July 1958 they had been able to take a belated honeymoon in Ireland—they took a plane, a brand-new experience for both of them—where Joy was able to meet Arthur and several members of Lewis's family. The next year they repeated the trip and, with Roger Lancelyn Green and his wife, June, planned a vacation in Greece, a remarkable idea for Lewis, who had not left the British Isles since his service in the Army in the Great War and had never shown any inclination to travel. (He and Warnie both feared that the reality of what they had read about would unquestionably be less impressive than their imagination of it.)

Green and Hooper write, with justice, "This brief halcyon period was perhaps the happiest time of Lewis's life." His Cambridge situation, as we have seen, was superb; he still could visit Oxford friends at the Bird and Baby and have them over to the Kilns, which Joy had rescued from its previous masculine squalor; Lewis and Warnie got along extremely well with Joy's younger son Douglas, though the older one, David, was more difficult and less happy to be there. Still, this was nothing compared to dealing with Mrs. Moore and the succession of unbalanced nurses and maids. After some initial tension, Warnie had been convinced that he was still wanted at the Kilns, and the domestic situation there was better than it had ever been. "I decided to give the new regime a try," wrote Warnie in his brief biography of his brother. "All my fears were dispelled. For me, Jack's marriage meant that our home was enriched and enlivened by the presence of a witty, broad-minded, well-read and tolerant Christian, whom I had rarely heard equalled as a conversationalist and whose company was a never-ending source of enjoyment." (In his biography of Lewis, A. N. Wilson takes great pains to point out that many in the Oxford crowd disliked Joy and even found her brashness offensive, but when the highest opinions of a person come from those who have to live with her day in and day out, that is surely a strong testimony to character.)

Above all, Lewis reveled in the experience of Eros. He had written about it with great festivity and celebration—though with great awkwardness as well—at the end of *That Hideous Strength,* and perhaps then he thought he knew something about it. He wrote about it in his scholarship, especially in *The Allegory of Love,* and looking back on that from the perspective of a married man, he admitted that he was "blind enough" to take as a "literary phenomenon" certain experiences that belong truly to Eros itself. But in that brief period of Joy's improved health he learned what he had never known before. "For those few years," he would write after her death, "[Joy] and I feasted on love, every mode of it . . . solemn and merry, romantic and realistic, sometimes as dramatic as a thunderstorm, sometimes as comfortable and unemphatic as putting on your soft slippers. No cranny of heart or body remained unsatisfied."

One product of this time of excitement and bliss was the rather frank chapter on Eros in *The Four Loves.* Though the chapter is not, Lewis insists, about sex, nevertheless sex comes in (as well it might), and when it does he is quite breezily casual in his language about it. He speaks of Winston Smith, in Orwell's *1984,* "towsing the heroine"—an old bawdy word, "towsing" was probably last used by Robert Burns—and lamenting the influence of modern psychology on sexuality, he affirms that "I could believe some young couples now go to it with the complete works of Freud, Kraft-Ebbing, Havelock Ellis and Dr. Stopes spread out on bed-tables all round them." And bluntest of all, he writes of how the sexual act "can invite the man to an extreme, though short-lived, masterfulness, to the dominance of a conqueror or captor, and the woman to a correspondingly extreme abjection and surrender. Hence the roughness, even fierceness, of some erotic play; the 'lover's pinch which hurts and is desired.'" (The quotation is from

Shakespeare's *Antony and Cleopatra*.) And he then, very carefully, goes on to describe the conditions under which such rough "erotic play" can be "harmless and wholesome."

Lewis never imagined that there would be readers of this passage who knew that he had been prone to sadomasochistic tendencies as a young man; I wonder how he might have explained the passage to such readers. In any case he insists strongly that such play must really *be* play, accepted as such on both sides, both fully voluntary and very temporary. Even so, his exposition was far too vivid for the Episcopal Radio-TV Foundation of Atlanta, Georgia, which had commissioned what became *The Four Loves* as a series of talks to be recorded and distributed on American radio. The bishops who constituted the board of directors for the foundation agreed—did they blush as purple as their shirts while listening?—that "the combination of a high intellectual level and startling frankness" in the talks made them unsuitable to a large radio audience; the recordings were, accordingly, redirected to smaller audiences, mainly at universities. The creator of the foundation, a dignified Southern Episcopalian named Catherine Rakestraw— whose name Lewis repeatedly though inadvertently converted to "Cartwheel"—later told him, "Professor Lewis, I'm afraid you brought sex into your talks on Eros."

Mrs. Cartwheel was someone with whom Lewis had much difficulty: when she came to London to record his talks she kept suggesting ways for him to improve his writing style, and at one point, according to Joy, she "made him sit absolutely silent before the microphone for a minute and a half 'so they could feel his living presence.'" Lewis was soon glad to be done with the Episcopal Radio-TV Foundation. In any case, he had more important matters to deal with.

On October 13, 1959, Joy underwent one of the regular medical checkups that all recovering cancer patients are familiar with. Lewis later wrote to Green, "This last check is the only one we approached without dread—her health seemed so complete." But the cancer had returned, in force, metastasized throughout her skeleton. They prayed for healing again, of course, but (or so it seems) without the same zeal and faith they had had earlier: the blow was too crushing. In any event, the immediate question was whether they should go through with the trip to Greece planned for the spring of 1960. In the end they decided that they would try, and though Joy was much weakened and in great pain by the time April came around, they carried through their plan. (But not without a moment of dark comedy, provided by the melancholy Paxford as the taxi arrived to take Lewis and Joy to the airport. He had just heard on the radio that a plane had crashed. Leaning through the taxi window, he raised his already stentorian voice: "Everybody killed—burnt beyond recognition. Did you hear what I said, Mr. Jack? *Burnt beyond recognition.*")

After their return, Lewis described the experience for his friend Chad Walsh:

> It looked very doubtful if Joy and I would be able to do our trip to Greece, but we did. From one point of view it was madness, but neither of us regrets it. She performed prodigies of strength, limping to the top of the Acropolis and up through the Lion gate of Mycenae and all about the medieval city of Rhodes. (Rhodes is simply the Earthly Paradise.) It was as if she were divinely supported. She came back in a *nunc dimittis* frame of mind, having realized, beyond hope, her greatest, lifelong, this-worldly, desire.
>
> There was a heavy price to pay in increased lameness and leg-pains: not that her exertions had or could have any effect on the course of the cancers, but that the muscles etc. had been over-taxed. Since then there has been a recrudescence of the original growth in the right breast which started the whole trouble. It had to be removed last Friday—or, as she characteristically put it, she was "made an Amazon." This operation went through, thank God, with greater ease than we had dared to hope. By the evening of the same day she was free from all severe pain and from nausea, and cheerfully talkative. Yesterday she was able to sit up in a chair for fifteen minutes or so. . . .
>
> I had some ado to prevent Joy (and myself) from relapsing into Paganism in Attica! At Daphne it was hard not to pray to Apollo the Healer. But somehow one didn't feel it wd have been very wrong—wd only have been addressing Christ *sub specie Apollinis.*

It was Simeon, in Luke's Gospel (2:29), who, having seen the Christ child, sang the *Nunc Dimittis:* "Now lettest thou thy servant depart in peace, having seen thy salvation." Neither Lewis nor Joy thought seriously of healing at this point. And it is touching to see that when Lewis forgives himself for his near-prayer to Apollo, he applies to himself and Joy the very generosity he had extended to Laurence Krieg, the American boy who had feared that he loved Aslan more than Jesus: to the boy's mother Lewis had written, "But Laurence can't *really* love Aslan more than Jesus, even if he feels that's what he's doing. For the things he loves Aslan for doing or saying are simply the things Jesus really did and said. So that when Laurence thinks he is loving Aslan, he is really loving Jesus: and perhaps loving Him more than he ever did before."

To judge from Green's account of the experience—he kept a detailed diary—Lewis's letter underplays both the ecstasy and the misery. Joy was in great pain throughout the trip; the only thing that enabled her to keep going was fairly heavy consumption of ouzo and other indigenous beverages, in which the others usually joined her. If this cast an alcoholic haze over their adventures, it also made for some funny moments—for example, the evening in a taverna, the dinner being slow in coming and the band extremely loud, when Joy occupied herself by rolling bread pellets and flicking them at the nearest musicians. But there were times of nearly visionary quality too, moments saturated in meaning: the silence as the two of them sat atop the Acropolis, having passed along the way the Areopagus, where Saint Paul had proclaimed Christianity to the local philosophers and rhetoricians; Lewis's awe upon entering the excavations at Mycenae, the legendary palace of "Agamemnon king of men," so called by Homer, whom Lewis had "worshipped" when reading the *Iliad* and *Odyssey* nearly half a century earlier at Kirk's house in Surrey. For a man who had saturated himself in Greek literature and the Greek New Testament for almost his whole life, every minute must have been extraordinary. (Lewis even tried to read the newspaper, puzzling over the changes from ancient to modern Greek.) I wish he had had the time and energy to write a book about his voyage.

Upon their return Joy had three months of life remaining to her. They were excruciating. In mid-June she and Lewis and Warnie were certain she was dying; she asked that her son Douglas be called to her side (Douglas was at a school in Wales, his older brother, David, at Magdalen College School) and told the doctor that she would not accept another operation. Warnie greeted David when he came home at the end of the school day and gave him the bad news, while Douglas's kind headmaster drove him all the way from Wales. Warnie wrote a valedictory lament in his diary, expecting never to see her again. But she rallied, and two weeks later was back at home. It is not clear that anyone thought this really good news. On July 13 she awoke early,

screaming with pain; an ambulance took her and Lewis to the hospital. When the doctor, a man named Till, told Jack that his wife had
but hours to live, Jack informed her; he later told Warnie that "she
agreed with him that it was the best news they could now get." She
died late that evening.

On the eighteenth she was cremated, according to her request.
Austin Farrer read the great service for the Burial of the Dead from the
Prayer Book.

> Almighty God, with whom do live the spirits of them that depart
> hence in the Lord, and with whom the souls of the faithful, after
> they are delivered from the burden of the flesh, are in joy and fe-
> licity: We give thee hearty thanks, for that it hath pleased thee to
> deliver this our sister out of the miseries of this sinful world; be-
> seeching thee, that it may please thee, of thy gracious goodness,
> shortly to accomplish the number of thine elect, and to hasten
> thy kingdom; that we, with all those that are departed in the true
> faith of thy holy Name, may have our perfect consummation and
> bliss, both in body and soul, in thy eternal and everlasting glory;
> through Jesus Christ our Lord. *Amen.*

For whatever reason, few mourners came; A. N. Wilson says (without citing a source) that Lewis was greatly distressed by this. Joy had
loved a poem of her husband's called "Epitaph," and at her request he
revised it and had it engraved on a plaque, erected in her memory at
the Headington Crematorium:

> Here the whole world (stars, water, air,
> And field, and forest, as they were
> Reflected in a single mind)
> Like cast off clothes was left behind
> In ashes, yet with hope that she,
> Re-born from holy poverty,
> In lenten lands, hereafter may
> Resume them on her Easter Day.

Almost all his life Lewis had been an impassioned opponent of vivisection—indeed, his first recorded opposition to the practice may be
found in a letter he wrote when he was ten. Cruelty to animals (under
the guise of scientific research) is a prominent practice of NICE in

That Hideous Strength, and Lewis must have very much enjoyed writing the scene in which the animals are liberated and encouraged to indulge any amorous inclinations. For him, vivisection is a sign of that instrumentalism, that degeneration into the will to power, that always threatens the practice of science. It is therefore darkly telling that, in the harrowing account he wrote of his own grief in the weeks following Joy's death, he considers at length the possibility that God is not just inscrutable but, worse, the "Cosmic Vivisector"—that God had, for His own purposes, which no doubt He could have explained in the noblest of terms, decided to make an experiment of Joy (and therefore also of Lewis). Even, or especially, the periods of health and energy were part of the cruel experiment. Within Lewis's own moral vocabulary he could scarcely have written anything angrier or more damning. In this account Lewis refers to Joy as "H.," presumably for Helen, her real first name:

> What chokes every prayer and every hope is the memory of all the prayers H. and I offered and all the false hopes we had. Not hopes raised merely by our own wishful thinking, hopes encouraged, even forced upon us, by false diagnoses, by X-ray photographs, by strange remissions, by one temporary recovery that might have ranked as a miracle. Step by step we were "led up the garden path." Time after time, when He seemed most gracious He was really preparing the next torture.

Having made this accusation, Lewis immediately continues: "I wrote that last night. It was a yell rather than a thought." Indeed, for a while he had become Orual. Though he never explicitly makes the connection, one cannot avoid recognizing the likeness. A few pages after letting out that "yell" he writes: "All that stuff about the Cosmic Sadist was not so much the expression of thought as of hatred. I was getting from it the only pleasure a man in anguish could get: the pleasure of hitting back. It was really just Billingsgate—mere abuse; 'telling God what I thought of him.'"

Later on his reflections come even closer to the portrait he painted of Orual: he has repeatedly called for his beloved to "come back," but now, thinking about what an answer to that call would really mean, he has an insight: the cry "is all for my own sake. I never even raised the question whether such a return, if it were possible, would be good for her. . . . Could I have wished her anything worse? Having once got through death, to come back and then, at some later date, have all her dying to do over again?" Reflecting seriously upon his response to his bereavement, he sees what Orual saw in that otherworldly courtroom: how small was his faith and how deficient his love.

He never "lost his faith." Faith, in the sense of a basic belief in God, is actually quite hard to lose when one has been seriously cultivating it for several decades. If anything, he was tempted to believe *more* than what Christians do: to return to the spiritualism with which he had been fascinated as a boy and young man, to believe that through a séance or some other occult means he could establish contact with Joy. ("At any rate I must keep clear of the spiritualists. I promised H. I would.") Though he did, as we have seen, seriously question the character of the God in whom he had to believe, that questioning of God would yield to a deeper self-questioning and a significant growth in self-knowledge.

The last book Lewis completed is called *Letters to Malcolm; Chiefly on Prayer.* Some people love it, but generally it is thought to be one of his less successful books. It is certainly different from his other books on Christianity, and the chief difference is the number of questions it contains: question marks are scattered through the book like confetti. He raises far more puzzles than he can solve—more, one might say, than he is inclined to solve. "Have we any reason to suppose that total self-knowledge, if it were given us, would be for our good?" "As for the last dereliction of all"—the moment when on the Cross Jesus cries out, "My God, my God, why hast thou forsaken me?"—"how can we either understand or endure it? Is it that God Himself cannot be Man unless God seems to vanish at his greatest need? And if so, why?" "I think [mystical experience] shows that there is a way to go, before death, out of what may be called 'this world'—out of the stage set. Out of this; but into what?" Related to this questioning, I think, is his reluctance to be as critical of the radical theologian Alec Vidler as his imaginary friend Malcolm wants him to be; likewise he refused to offer a public critique of the Bishop of Woolwich, John Robinson, whose book *Honest to God* created enormous controversy in the last months of Lewis's life by its insistence on the need to jettison most of traditional Christian theology.

Lewis had not changed his mind in the least about the vacuity of "Christianity-and-water"; indeed, in a brief passage near the end of the *Letters* he renews an old critique of the illiberalism of supposedly "liberal" Christianity. Moreover, he declined to write a review of

Robinson's book because he did not feel that he could do so charitably and because he did not want to give Robinson more publicity than he had already received. So he did not come close to endorsing Vidler or Robinson by any means. But after all he had been through in Joy's illness and death, he better *understood* their discomfort with traditional doctrine. They were trying to get beyond "religion," and in his misery Lewis had come to understand that impulse—even if he thought they were going about it in absolutely the wrong way. "Religion" is either a set of cultural practices or a set of doctrines, and in either case— though for Lewis the doctrines were always absolutely necessary as maps toward one's true destination—they should never be the *goal* of the Christian life. (To make such a mistake would be "as if navigation were substituted for arrival, or battle for victory, or wooing for marriage.") Beyond all religion lies Something, or rather Someone, that religion can never capture, Who is more real than any practices or doctrines. "We may ignore, but we can nowhere evade, the presence of God. The world is crowded with Him. He walks everywhere *incognito*. And the *incognito* is not always hard to penetrate. The real labour is to remember, to attend. In fact, to come awake. Still more, to remain awake." Such attention is difficult; we often fail to achieve it, and when we think we are most awake we are often sound asleep. One wonders how much of Lewis's own writing he believed, there near the end, to have been attentive in this true and full sense. It is perhaps telling that at one point in *Letters to Malcolm* he recalls what happened to Thomas Aquinas, who, after receiving an overwhelming and indeed disabling vision of God, thought back on his life's work of theological reflection and said, "It reminds me of straw."

Even as Joy was dying, Lewis was thinking of writing a book on literary criticism, of all things, and after her death, as he was writing *A Grief Observed,* he worked on it too. He would come to call it *An Experiment in Criticism.* It arose from his reflection on intellectual life at Cambridge and its difference from that of Oxford; in 1956 he had written: "You were never safe from the philosopher at Oxford; here, never from the Critic." At Cambridge the freshman who "means to be anybody" has to learn something about "Literary Criticism (with the largest possible capitals for both words)." This intellectual dominance of a single discipline (only within the humanities—Lewis exaggerates its role in the university as whole) was largely the work of one man, the Critic himself: F. R. Leavis. Leavis, who was Warnie Lewis's age and a veteran of the Great War, had begun his teaching career at almost the same time as Jack. Also like Jack, he was never fully recognized by his own university: he did not even get a permanent full-time faculty position at Cambridge until 1936. But by then, through his books and lectures, he had transformed English studies there. As the critic Terry Eagleton put it, "In the early 1920s it was desperately unclear why English was worth studying at all; by the early 1930s it had become a question of why it was worth wasting your time on anything else."

Lewis had, of course, known of Leavis's work all along, having crossed swords with him briefly in A Preface to "Paradise Lost" and elsewhere. But why would he have seen Leavis as an enemy? Leavis had moved the study of literature to the center of the university curriculum and was a vigorous proponent of the power of literature to change lives and even whole cultures. Shouldn't Lewis have perceived him as an ally? Not at all. For one thing, Leavis was a key figure in a movement whose prime initiator had been the Victorian poet and critic Matthew Arnold: for such thinkers, Christianity had been tried and found wanting, and literature was to replace it as the heart and soul of the formation of English culture. The great literary writers would become our guides, now that Jesus had proved inept to the task. Lewis preferred to take Chesterton's view that Christianity had not been tried and found wanting, but had been "found difficult and left untried." And he strenuously insisted—as early as 1940—that there was and could be *no* connection between being "cultured" and being spiritually mature. Lewis was never interested in literature as a substitute for Christian faith.

Moreover, the literature that Leavis promoted was mainly Victorian and modern—he had been a great champion of Eliot, for instance—and there was little or no room in the Leavisian canon for the books that Lewis loved. But still more to the point, there *was* a "Leavisian canon," what Leavis himself called "the Great Tradition." Much of the energy of Leavis and his colleagues at the journal he founded, *Scrutiny,* was devoted to figuring out who was In and who was Out. In the world of *Scrutiny,* literary history was too much like an Inner Ring to suit Lewis. This was, in his view, a threat to the liberty and pleasure of the reader.

So, even as he grieved deeply the loss of his beloved wife, he engaged in his last great polemic, and it had nothing to do with Christianity. Instead, it was an attack on the "literary Puritans" who wished to transform reading into an exercise in spiritual formation—an exercise guided by these strict Critics who would tell you what to read and why it was good for you. They constituted "the Vigilant school of critics. To them criticism is a form of social and ethical hygiene." Their influence creates "families and circles ... where it requires great independence not to talk about, and therefore occasionally to read, the approved literature, especially the new and astonishing works, and those which have been banned or have become in some other way subjects of controversy." He has in mind here D. H. Lawrence's *Lady Chatterley's Lover,* which had been the subject of an obscenity trial in 1959 and 1960 that, in the words of the BBC, "gripped the nation." Leavis was one of the most vocal supporters of the book and of Lawrence's place in the Great Tradition. The ban on the book having been overturned, it went on sale in Britain in November 1960, just as Lewis was writing *A Grief Observed* and beginning *An Experiment in Criticism.* It was sold out in hours.

The key phrase in the passage I just quoted is "to talk about, and therefore occasionally to read." What the Leavisites create in people is not a desire to read, but a desire to have read, and even more a desire simply to be in the know about what one *should* read. The thousands of people who rushed out to buy *Lady Chatterley's Lover* did not, properly speaking, read the book, even if their eyes rushed across every line of every page. Having described the household obsessed by the desire to be part of this literary Inner Ring, Lewis continues: "Yet, while this goes on downstairs, the only real literary experience in such a family may be occurring in a back bedroom where a small boy is reading *Treasure Island* under the bedclothes by the light of an electric torch."

An Experiment in Criticism is a flawed book in many ways—it is essentially a work of literary theory, and that was not Lewis's strength as a writer or thinker—but I find it absolutely wonderful that this tired, sick man, worn down by suffering and loss and an ever-weakening heart, could be roused to polemical fury in defense of a small boy reading an adventure story in ignorance or defiance of the cultural norms of his household. From his earliest youth Lewis had jealously guarded his freedom as a reader: he had craved every moment he could get alone with some book taken from the vast shelves and stacks of Little Lea, and all his life he had treasured mild illnesses as justifications for irresponsible and purely voluntary reading. It was to defend, and more to celebrate, the Reader that this old warrior put on his armor one last time and set forth to slay the dragon named Critic.

• • •

As 1960 ended and 1961 began, Lewis was extraordinarily busy. For one thing, he was now a single parent and had to figure out how best to care for David and Douglas. This was easier in the case of Doug, whom he loved ("a very bright spot in my life," he told Arthur) and who loved him, but David was more difficult. The few comments David has made over the years about his life with Lewis indicate an extraordinary independence; it does not appear that Lewis made any real impression on him at all, whether for good or for ill. His larger concerns were dealing with what he felt to be the irrational anti-Americanism of his schoolmates—Doug, a year younger, seems to have been more adaptable and more willing to become a young English gentleman—and coming to terms with his Jewish identity. As his mother was Jewish, so, technically, was he, and though he had been raised as a Christian, soon after his mother's death he asked for instruction in Judaism and in the Hebrew language, which Lewis willingly provided. Douglas would, as an adult, become a Christian, but David embraced Judaism. In Douglas's memoir *Lenten Lands*, his brother scarcely appears, which is perhaps one of the reasons *Shadowlands* gives Joy but one son. David remains a mysterious figure in this story.

Soon after Joy's death Bill Gresham came to Oxford to visit, and he and Lewis met several times. The meetings must have been exceptionally awkward, not just for the obvious reasons but also because of something that happened when Joy first became ill. Bill had written then to say that if she became incapable of caring for the boys he wanted custody over them, and Joy had had Lewis write a firm letter telling Bill that they would fight against that with every legal recourse available to them. Lewis then wrote a second letter telling Bill, quite bluntly, how unhappy he had made both his wife and his children. (Doug recalled, he says in *Lenten Lands*, a time when he had a bottle broken on his head by his father. He could not have been more than six at the time.) In the end Bill gave up any claim on his sons, and when he met them after Joy's death they were strangers to one another. He lingered in Oxford for a while, then returned to America. In the summer of 1962 he discovered that he too had cancer, and rather than face what Joy had faced, he took his own life.

Lewis had plenty of help with the boys, sometimes from unexpected sources. Even when Joy was still ill, Maureen Blake—Mrs. Moore's daughter, who still lived not far from Oxford in Malvern—took them for a while, though she found David almost unmanageable, and the Berners-Price family, the proprietors of the hotel in Ramsgate where the resourceful Mrs. Hooker had set herself up as the wife of C. S. Lewis, welcomed the boys to some free holidays. Lewis needed the help because he had many obligations: lectures to give at Cambridge, books to write and prepare for the press, Warnie to manage when he was in his cups, even a role on a Committee to Revise the Psalter— that is, the collection of Psalms in the *Book of Common Prayer*. Lewis had largely taken on this task in order to discourage revisions, since he thought the Miles Coverdale version that had been in use for four hundred years more than adequate. His opinion was shared by another member of the committee, T. S. Eliot, whom Lewis finally got to know. (They had met only once, very briefly, in the forties, though they had corresponded for a while about Charles Williams after their mutual friend's death.) The two men got along very well indeed; bygones could at last be bygones, it seems.

But in the midst of the busyness Lewis was in decline. His heart, which had been a concern to his doctors since his collapse in 1949, was wearing out. In August 1961 he had, to his great joy, a visit from Arthur ("one of the happiest times I've had in many a long day"), but though Arthur enjoyed the visit too, he was disturbed to see how ill Lewis looked. In fact Lewis would soon discover that he had an enlarged prostate, on which the doctors did not operate for fear that his weak heart would not allow him to survive the operation. Instead of returning to Cambridge in the fall, he stayed at the Kilns with Warnie— who had stabilized himself for the time being—and underwent a series of blood transfusions that seemed to help. These were comparatively slight measures, and he knew it, but "meanwhile," he wrote to a former student, "I have no pain and am neither depressed nor bored." And in the Easter term of 1962 he was able to return to Cambridge to lecture, which delighted him, as did his work on the Psalter translation committee. Because of his enlarged prostate and associated kidney troubles, he had to begin wearing a catheter—which more than once (it was a strange makeshift thing) broke open when he was in public, dousing his trousers—but he managed to give a series of lectures on "English Literature 1300–1500" in the autumn. Though he returned to Cambridge after the turn of the new year, he did so only to supervise graduate students; he would never lecture again.

He hoped to travel to Ireland in the summer, and indeed he and Warnie planned a visit to Arthur, with Doug Gresham to accompany them, partly for good company and partly to carry Lewis's bags, which he could no longer do for himself. He was by now as feeble as a man fifteen years older. Warnie went early to Ireland, probably to drink himself into oblivion: he had discovered a group of kindly nuns who ran a kind of convalescent hospital and who could be counted on to keep him alive when he otherwise might have died from any number of things, from a bad fall to simple alcohol poisoning. During the monthlong interlude at the Kilns between his return from Cambridge and the scheduled Irish holiday, Lewis had a visitor: a young American, a teacher of English at the University of Kentucky, who admired his work greatly and wanted to write about it. His name was Walter Hooper. Lewis discouraged Hooper from writing about him—as he discouraged everyone who wanted to write about him—but they had a pleasant chat; Lewis liked Hooper very much.

It soon became clear, however, that he was not up to the Irish vacation—"But oh Arthur, never to see you again!" he wrote, agonizingly—and on July 15 he had a major heart attack, fortunately while undergoing a medical examination. He lapsed into a deep coma and the following afternoon was given the rite of Extreme Unction; he was clearly dying. But an hour after the administration of the rite, he woke up and asked for a cup of tea. ("You can never get a book long enough or a cup of tea big enough to suit me," he once told Hooper.) He thought he had merely nodded off for a few minutes.

He remained in the hospital for two weeks, improving physically but going through periods of dementia. He often, especially at first, failed to recognize friends and family members and on several occasions spoke as though Minto were still living. But in his moments of clearheadedness he assessed his own situation quite shrewdly. He desperately needed help, with his unrelenting burden of letters to respond to, all sorts of publishing business to attend to, his finances in serious disorder, and little likelihood of Warnie's ever again being consistently useful. (The Kilns had also relapsed into squalor—fungus grew on the bathroom walls—but neither of the Lewis brothers seems to have cared about that.) Lewis quickly saw that Hooper would be an excellent secretary and general helper and told George Sayer that he was going to offer Hooper that job. Hooper agreed to do all he could while he remained in England: he was obliged to return to Kentucky to teach that fall, but agreed that in January 1964 he would return to serve as Lewis's secretary.

After Lewis returned to the Kilns—there was still no sign of

Warnie—he resigned his Cambridge chair, knowing that he would never be well enough to return, and as a result he had to vacate his rooms there. One of Hooper's first major tasks was to go to Cambridge (along with Doug) and retrieve all of Lewis's books and papers. This meant bringing an astonishing number of books back to the Kilns, a house already filled with them, and some comedy ensued when Lewis talked Hooper into building a wall of books around the sleeping body of Alec Ross, Lewis's live-in nurse, who had chosen the wrong time and place to take a nap. Obviously his sense of humor had not declined with his physical condition. But he understood the nature of his reprieve. In September he wrote to Sister Penelope (echoing words he had written in *A Grief Observed* about Joy's death and his desire for her to "come back"), "I was unexpectedly revived from a long coma ... but it would have been a luxuriously easy passage and one almost regrets having the door shut in one's face. Ought we to honour Lazarus rather than Stephen as the protomartyr? To be brought back and have all one's dying to do *again* was rather hard."

Lewis closed that letter to Sister Penelope by writing, "It is all rather fun—solemn fun—isn't it?" Likewise, in *Letters to Malcolm* he wrote, "Joy is the serious business of heaven." All his life he had struggled with ceremonial occasions, feeling awkward in the midst of them or embarrassed by them: the old collegiate rite by which he had been received as a fellow of Magdalen, all those decades ago, had been agonizing to him, as he told his father. But he recognized this as a defect in himself and greatly admired those friends of his—Charles Williams was most notable among them—who had the gift of ceremony, for there are times and seasons when ceremony is required of us. As he proclaimed in his most famous sermon, "The Weight of Glory," we should not be "perpetually solemn. We must play. But our merriment must be of that kind (and it is, in fact, the merriest kind) which exists between people who have, from the outset, taken each other seriously— no flippancy, no superiority, no presumption." This requires a certain ceremonious dignity, which we have to learn: it does not come naturally to us, and we must begin by playing at it. Only to Adam and Eve was it natural, and in describing them, in the *Preface to "Paradise Lost,"* Lewis had written, "Their life together is ceremonial—a minuet, where the modern reader looked for a romp. Until they are fallen and robbed of their original majesty, they hardly ever address each other simply by their names, but by stately periphrases; *Fair Consort,*

*My Author and Disposer, Daughter of God and man, accomplisht
Eve, O Sole in whom all my thoughts find repose.*" He learned to love
such ceremony when it was offered to him, even though he was not
good at it: "It delights me that there should be moments in the services
of my own Church when the priest stands and I kneel," he wrote in
"Membership." "As democracy becomes more and more complete the
outer world and opportunities for reverence are successively removed,
the refreshment, the cleansing, and invigorating returns to inequality,
which the Church offers us, become more and more necessary." Thus
it is also that High King Peter and Queen Susan and King Edmund
and Queen Lucy only gradually learn to speak the elevated language
of their rank rather than the vernacular of English schoolchildren. But
that elevated language is appropriate to the roles they have assumed,
the monarchial parts they have been called upon to play.

And so it is with us, precisely because "there are no *ordinary*
people. You have never talked to a mere mortal. Nations, cultures,
arts, civilizations—these are mortal, and their life is to ours as the life
of a gnat. But it is immortals whom we joke with, work with, marry,
snub, and exploit—immortal horrors or everlasting splendours. . . .
Next to the Blessed Sacrament itself, your neighbour is the holiest object presented to your senses." It is the eternal life that Jesus promises,
and for which we were made, that requires us to play the great game
of ceremony, and as he prepared to enter into God's presence Lewis
sought to overcome his awkwardness and learn to participate in the
"solemn fun" of proceeding from one world to the next.

Few Christian writers, and certainly no Christian writers of the
twentieth century, have emphasized immortality more than Lewis did.
Though he is best known for his portraits of Hellishness (in *The
Screwtape Letters*), he professed to have little understanding of Hell:
as he insisted in his first work of apologetics, "We know much more
about heaven than hell, for heaven is the home of humanity and therefore contains all that is implied in a glorified human life: but hell was
not made for men . . . : It is the 'darkness outside.'" Therefore in *The
Great Divorce* we spend little time in the drab city from which the bus
departs and much time learning to see and to love the land of the
Blessed. Likewise, *That Hideous Strength* ends with a visionary fore-
taste of Heavenly splendor. We were made to inherit that splendor,
and while many Christian writers have declined to say so—for fear of
being accused of indifference to this-worldly suffering or of hearing
the "pie-in-the-sky" jeer—Lewis never shied from the proclamation.

"I reckon that the sufferings of the present time are not worthy to be compared with the glory that shall be revealed in us," wrote Saint Paul (Romans 8:18), and by the time Lewis wrote that "Joy is the serious business of Heaven," he knew enough about suffering that his taking hold of that promise commands respect.

"Heaven is the home of humanity": this is the hope and the lesson in which the Narnia books culminate, as the vast and disorderly crew of characters from the previous books rush "further up and further in," discovering what Shakespeare's Hamlet (speaking for all of us on this side of the divide) calls "the undiscovered country." Narnia itself, or what they all had thought was Narnia, pales in comparison: "I have come home at last!" shouts Jewel the Unicorn. "This is my real country! I belong here. This is the land I have been looking for all my life, though I never knew it till now." But the last image we are given of Aslan's country is not that of a landscape at all:

> And for us this is the end of all the stories, and we can most truly say that they all lived happily ever after. But for them it was only the beginning of the real story. All their life in this world and all their adventures in Narnia had only been the cover and the title page: now at last they were beginning Chapter One of the Great Story, which no one on earth has read: which goes on for ever: in which every chapter is better than the one before.

This conclusion is, of course, a learned Christian scholar's homage to Dante, who also ends his vision of Paradise with the image of a great Book, but far more than that, it is the dream come true of a small boy alone in a house full of books in Belfast, who wanted nothing more than to be set free from all drudgery and responsibility and pain and loss so that he could sit in a window overlooking the sea, reading the stories he loved hour after hour by the bright calm light of endless day.

In late September Warnie returned, and the brothers became partners and companions for the last time. "The wheel had come full circle," Warnie wrote in his diary: "once again we were together in the little end room at home, shutting out from our talk the ever-present knowledge that the holidays were ending, that a new term fraught with unknown possibilities awaited us both." Warnie's image reverses that of his brother: for Lewis this world is the term, the "Real" Narnia the everlasting holidays—so Aslan tells the children. Warnie could not quite manage to see it that way: lacking his brother's powerful imagination, he could only continue to long (as he had longed all his life) for a restoring of the bliss he had known when he was ten years old.

Meanwhile, Lewis was readying himself and saying his good-byes. Tolkien (with his son John) came by for a visit; they talked of Malory's *Morte d'Arthur* and of the lives of trees. It was not in the nature of either man to be more intimate, nor would there have been much point. Other friends passed in and out. "I have done all I wanted to and I'm ready to go," Lewis told his brother. Austin Farrer would later say, "He was put almost beside himself by his wife's death; he seemed easy at the approach of his own." There were, of course, books he had hoped to write, and he had for several years considered revising the Narnia books in order to correct their inconsistencies, perhaps among them the problem with the Beavers' dinner on which Ruth Pitter had shone so remorseless a light. But none of that mattered in the final days. Let Warnie tell the story:

> Friday, 22 November 1963, began much as other days: there was breakfast, then letters and the crossword puzzle. After lunch he fell asleep in his chair: I suggested that he would be more comfortable in bed, and he went there. At four I took in his tea and found him drowsy but comfortable. Our few words then were the last: at five-thirty I heard a crash and ran in, to find him lying unconscious at the foot of his bed. He ceased to breathe some three or four minutes later.

Warnie could not make himself go to the funeral five days later; instead, he spent the day in his bed, drinking. His chief contribution to his brother's funeral was to decree that the phrase from Shakespeare that had been on their mother's calendar on the day she died (*Men must endure their going hence*) be inscribed on Jack's tombstone. It was left to eighteen-year-old Doug Gresham—who in three years had lost his mother, his father, and his stepfather—to lead the mourners at the family's parish church, Holy Trinity Headington. All Lewis's close friends were there, but many who would have wanted to attend had not heard of his death because of other news that crowded it out: Lewis died on the same day that President John F. Kennedy was shot to death in Dallas, Texas. The day after the funeral would have been Lewis's sixty-fifth birthday; he had come a year short of matching his father's span.

•   •   •

In July, when Lewis was in the hospital after his heart attack and still passing in and out of delirium, one of his visitors was Maureen Blake, whom he had known since she was a little girl, and with whom he had shared many of the most turbulent and difficult and perhaps even rewarding years of his life. After decades as a music teacher, she had had a recent turn of fortune. Earlier that year a very distant relation of hers with the utterly magnificent name of Sir George Cospatrick Duff-Sutherland-Dunbar, Baron Dunbar of Hempriggs, had died at his estate in Caithness, Scotland. Sir George was unmarried, and the lawyers had some difficulty discovering who was to inherit the estate. Astonishingly, the heir turned out to be Maureen.

When she arrived at the hospital she was told that Lewis had not recognized any of his visitors that day. She entered quietly, clasped his hand, and said, "Jack, it's Maureen." "No," he replied—unsurprisingly, given his condition. But he added, "It's Lady Dunbar of Hempriggs." Maureen was stunned: "Oh Jack, how could you remember that?" "On the contrary," he murmured. "How could *I* forget a fairy-tale?"

The Future of Narnia

The only surviving letter from Jack Lewis to Joy Davidman, written in September 1953, chiefly concerns what was then a new science-fiction novel by Arthur C. Clarke, *Childhood's End*. Lewis had recently read and loved it, and at some length he details its virtues and compares them to the vices of much modern writing. Then, at the end, contemplating the vast edifice of modernism as constructed by the Eliots and Joyces, the Pounds and Woolfs, he adds, "Twenty years ago I felt no doubt that I should live to see it all break up and great literature return; but here I am, losing teeth and hair, and still no break in the clouds." On a similar topic, but in a more hopeful mood, he had written a year earlier to Katherine Farrer about Tolkien's *The Fellowship of the Ring*, which had just been published: "Wouldn't it be wonderful if it really succeeded (in selling, I mean)! It would inaugurate a new age. Dare we hope?"

In a sense, the Narnia books and *The Lord of the Rings*—in their different ways, and for their different audiences—*did* inaugurate a new age. Not that the edifice of modernism has been toppled like Minas Morgul: the Eliots and Joyces, the Pounds and Woolfs still dominate at least the academic arena (as, in my judgment, which in this respect is quite different than Lewis's, they should). But between them Tolkien and Lewis generated a forceful countertradition, one that finds its strength less in the academy—though American universities feature plenty of courses in Tolkien or Lewis or the Inklings—than among ordinary readers. If the literary pooh-bahs selected by the Modern Library name Joyce's *Ulysses* as the greatest novel of the twentieth century, the "common readers" of England (in a poll commissioned jointly by the BBC and Waterstone's bookshops) counter by

giving *The Lord of the Rings* that title. The influence of the Narnia series is seen more in children's stories: having encouraged a renewal of
fantasies by writers such as Lloyd Alexander, Susan Cooper, and
Madeline L'Engle, that influence has culminated in the spectacular success of J. K. Rowling's Harry Potter books (of which there will be
seven, in part, Rowling has said, in tribute to the seven Narnia stories).

Indeed, this countertradition has become so powerful that many recent writers have seen the need to overthrow it, as though Tolkien and
Lewis were two tyrants ruthlessly suppressing alternative ways of
telling stories. China Miéville, an immensely gifted author of dark and
disturbing fantasies, has written that

> Tolkien is the wen on the arse of fantasy literature. His oeuvre is
> massive and contagious—you can't ignore it, so don't even try.
> The best you can do is consciously try to lance the boil. And
> there's a lot to dislike—his cod-Wagnerian pomposity, his boys-
> own-adventure glorying in war, his small-minded and reac-
> tionary love for hierarchical status-quos, his belief in absolute
> morality that blurs moral and political complexity. Tolkien's
> clichés—elves 'n' dwarfs 'n' magic rings—have spread like
> viruses.

Miéville has since modified some of these statements, but not really re-
tracted them (except to admit than one can have a "wen" only on
one's face, not one's arse). The novelist Philip Hensher shows that
Miéville has a thing or two to learn about invective when he writes,

> Let us drop CS Lewis and his ghastly, priggish, half-witted,
> money-making drivel about Narnia down the nearest deep hole,
> as soon as is conveniently possible. In fact, I'd more or less as-
> sumed that these frightful books had stopped being read years
> ago.... They are revoltingly mean-minded books, written to
> corrupt the minds of the young with allegory, smugly denounc-
> ing anything that differs in the slightest respect from Lewis's
> creed of clean-living, muscular Christianity, pipe-smoking, mis-
> ogyny, racism, and the most vulgar snobbery.
>
> Don't give your children CS Lewis to read; not the Narnia
> books, not the *Screwtape Letters*, not that appalling Is God an
> Astronaut? science fiction. It looks like rich fantasy, but it is the

product of a mean, narrow little mind, burrowing into their ideas and pooh-poohing them. Give them anything else—*Last Exit to Brooklyn,* a bottle of vodka, a phial of prussic acid, even Winnie the Pooh—but keep them away from *The Voyage of the Dawn Treader.*

Another English writer, Philip Pullman, tried (without success, I think) to match Hensher's delightful tirade, summarizing the messages of Narnia: "Death is better than life; boys are better than girls; light-coloured people are better than dark-coloured people; and so on. There is no shortage of such nauseating drivel in Narnia, if you can face it." Even when Lewis is canonized a saint—by what method I am not sure, since Anglicans don't canonize saints—"those of us who detest the supernaturalism, the reactionary sneering, the misogyny, the racism, and the sheer dishonesty of his narrative method will still be arguing against him." But Pullman's real polemic against Narnia, and indeed against Lewis's whole vision of human life and its possibilities, is to be found in his brilliant but disturbing fantasy trilogy, *His Dark Materials,* the third volume of which, *The Amber Spyglass,* is a mirror-image revision of *The Great Divorce.*

Comical though the exaggerated rhetoric is, a serious point underlies it. Though Hensher and Pullman truly do feel that Lewis's writing is racist and sexist, that is not the heart of their complaint. Neither of them has shown a particular concern with racism and sexism in *other* writers of Lewis and Tolkien's generation, though plenty of examples are there to be found; indeed, Hensher even *says* that he is willing to give Tolkien a pass on these matters because his writing is, he says, more skillful than Lewis's. But this is somewhat disingenuous, because it is not Lewis's limitations as a literary craftsman that enrages people such as Hensher and Pullman: it is his insistence that people are immortal. It is Lewis's holding to—and more, emphasizing—the Christian promise of eternal life that makes Hensher accuse him of "doctrinaire bullying" and leads Pullman to accuse him of believing that "death is better than life." There is no use in telling Pullman that what Lewis really believed was that life in Heaven is better than earthly life; it would just make him angrier. Of all the Christian beliefs with which atheists disagree, the only one that seems to generate real and deep rage is the belief in eternal life—the offer of "pie in the sky by and by"—and the corollary belief that the eternal life that some people choose is a miserable one.

But what about the charge that for Lewis and Tolkien alike "light-coloured people are better than dark-coloured people"? The people of Calormen in the Narnia books—like the "Southern" people of Harad in *The Lord of the Rings*—are indeed described as "swarthy" and "dark." On the face of it this seems odd: after all, the chief enemies of England in the lifetimes of Lewis and Tolkien made a cult of their blue-eyed, blond-haired Aryanism. But the imaginations of those two men were shaped before the great wars of the twentieth century: they belonged indeed to an Old Western Culture to which the chief threat, for hundreds of years, had been the Ottoman Empire. The Calormenes and the Haradrim are but slightly disguised versions of the ravaging Turk who filled the nightmares of European children for more than half a millennium—but whose "exotic" culture (manifested in images of elegant carpets, strong sweet coffee, slippers with turned-up toes, and elaborate storytelling traditions) had also been an endless source of fascinated delight. In short, Lewis and Tolkien had a ready-made source of "Oriental" imagery on which to draw to enrich their fictional worlds, and in a time less sensitive to cultural difference than our own, they saw no reason not to draw upon it. Perhaps this should count against them, but it rarely does. I think that is because readers (and in the case of *The Lord of the Rings*, viewers) can tell the difference between, on the one hand, an intentionally hostile depiction of some alien culture and, on the other, the use of cultural difference as a mere plot device.

(It is worth noting that Lewis is more nuanced than Tolkien in these matters. The Haradrim are undifferentiated servants of evil—none of them is an actual *character* in *The Lord of the Rings*—and W. H. Auden, who adored *The Lord of the Rings*, nevertheless thought Tolkien's decision to make the Orcs damned as a species "heretical." In *The Last Battle*, by contrast, we have the virtuous Calormene Emeth, whose devotion to truth—that is what his name, in Hebrew, means—gains him admission to the New Narnia, even though he was a worshiper of Tash. Aslan is too merciful to damn one who has not followed Him only because of the failures of his education.)

Any controversies of this kind are likely to be intensified by the release of the feature film version of *The Lion, the Witch, and the Wardrobe* in December 2005—just as the controversies surrounding Tolkien were given new life by Peter Jackson's films of *The Lord of the Rings*. But Tolkien is perhaps less obviously a target of criticism than Lewis because his Christian beliefs are expressed only indirectly in his published writings; *The Lion, the Witch, and the Wardrobe* is far more obviously and specifically Christian in its structure, though the film's screenwriter, Ann Peacock, prefers to use more general moral language to describe it. Upon her hiring by Walden Media, she said, "*The Lion, the Witch, and the Wardrobe* is one of my five children's favorite books; I am thrilled to be writing the screenplay for the story that encapsulates universal principles all young people need introduction to such as truth, honor, compassion, loyalty and courage." She made no mention of the fact that even these real and great virtues could not have averted the destruction of the Pevensie children and all their friends and the endless reign of the evil White Witch over Narnia—always winter and never Christmas *forever*—had it not been for Aslan's self-sacrifice.

But perhaps this generalizing description of the narrative, this reduction of its distinctive events into an unexceptionable catalog of basic virtues, is not to be worried over: it is but commentary, after all. The story will speak for itself or it will not; Narnia will go on to gain new friends and fans, or it will dwindle into obscurity; Lewis will continue to be upheld as a brilliant and vigorous spokesman for "mere Christianity," or he will become a historical footnote. As George Orwell once wrote, "There is no argument by which one can defend a poem"—and by poem he meant any work of literary art. "It defends itself by surviving, or it is indefensible." The anger of people such as Hensher and Pullman will last only as long as people love Lewis's stories: no one gets angry at forgotten books or their forgotten writers. Who can say what the future of Narnia holds?

One of the most extraordinary figures of the British theater in the last century was Kenneth Tynan, a flamboyant, irrepressibly gifted man who electrified almost everything he touched. He was perhaps *too* gifted: he excelled as a dramatist, a screenwriter, a critic, an essayist, a director, and a theatrical impresario, and he flitted all his life among these varying roles. In 1950, when he was only twenty-three, he wrote a commanding survey of the British theatrical scene, and rather than being scorned as a young pup presuming to lecture his elders, he was immediately named the drama critic of the influential magazine the *Spectator*. In that capacity he did a great deal to encourage and support the Angry Young Men of the stage (especially the brilliant playwright John Osborne, whose *Look Back in Anger* virtually created a new genre of British drama). In the sixties he became the dramaturg, or literary adviser, of the National Theatre, which had been created by Laurence Olivier. Later Tynan would write a series of brilliant profiles of actors and other "show people" for *The New Yorker,* including one on Johnny Carson that many people think is the best profile the magazine ever published.

From adolescence onward, Tynan was both flamboyant and delicate. He was thin and looked consumptive, a result of lung problems that would kill him at age fifty-three; he also had a pronounced stutter. But he dressed with the outrageous style of an Oscar Wilde and as a student at Oxford was one of the great "characters" of his time. Though he married twice and had three children, to whom he was devoted, all his life he was sexually adventurous and promiscuous and pronouncedly sadomasochistic. He was devoted to the pushing of boundaries, from pointedly saying words that were not supposed to be said on BBC television to directing the first all-nude musical, *Oh Calcutta!* (At age sixteen he had announced his plan to write, not a morality play, but an *amorality* play: "The whole point of it, I feel, is that the Devil is horrified by the goodness of God and considers him *immoral.*")

His college at Oxford, to which he came up in 1945, was Magdalen; his tutor was C. S. Lewis. Though it might seem highly unlikely that so plainly traditional a figure as Lewis and so peacockish an undergraduate as Tynan would get along, they did. In his first month at Oxford he would write to a friend, "C. S. Lewis, my tutor, is terribly sound and sunny." And Tynan was quite overwhelmed by Lewis's "Prolegomena" lectures, saying years later that Lewis had taught all of his students that the question was not whether medieval literature was relevant to *them,* but whether they were relevant to *it.*

But the lectures were not Lewis's greatest gift to Tynan. Writing in his diary on the first of October, 1974, Tynan recalled a crucial moment in his life:

> Yesterday a bald, deaf, elderly Canadian came to interview me on C. S. Lewis, about whom he is writing a book. Into his hearing aid I bellowed reminiscences of the great man, whose mind was Johnsonian without the bullying and Chestertonian without the facetiousness. If I were ever to stray into the Christian camp, it would be because of Lewis's arguments as expressed in books like *Miracles.* (He never intruded them into tutorials.) Because I stammered, he kindly undertook to read my weekly essays aloud

for me, and the prospect of hearing my words pronounced in that wonderfully juicy and judicious voice had a permanently disciplining effect on my prose style.

He was a deeply kind and charitable man, too. Once in the summer of 1948 I came to him in despair: Jill Rowe-Dutton had jilted me on the eve of what was to have been our marriage, and I had spent most of the term in and out of bed with bronchial diseases that I was sure would soon culminate in TB. I brought my troubles to Lewis, asking him whether I could postpone my final examinations until Christmas. To this he at once agreed: after which he got on with the Christian business of consolation. [In an interview Tynan added that he had told Lewis that he saw no reason to go on living.] He reminded me how I had once told him about the parachuted landmine which, dropping from a German bomber during an air-raid in 1940, so narrowly missed our house in Birmingham that next morning we recovered some of the parachute silk from our chimney. (The mine destroyed six houses across the road and blew out all our windows.) But for that hair's-breadth—a matter of inches only—I would already (Lewis gently pointed out) have been dead for eight years. Every moment of life since then had been a bonus, a tremendous free gift, a present that only the blackest ingratitude could refuse. As I listened to him, my problems began to dwindle to their proper proportions; I had entered the room suicidal, and I left it exhilarated.

This is why Lewis was so faithful a tutor: though he found much of the work sheer drudgery, he knew the difference that he could make in the lives of his pupils by sheer kindness. It is noteworthy that this interview between tutor and student occurred in one of the darkest times of Lewis's life; it is also noteworthy that Lewis did not proselytize or invoke specifically Christian doctrines, in which he knew Tynan did not believe: he merely consoled his pupil in terms that Tynan understood and accepted.

When Tynan did take his examinations, later that year, he failed to earn the First that he had hoped for and that everyone had expected he would get. Lewis immediately wrote with further encouragement: "Don't let it become a trauma! It signifies comparatively little." And with such encouragement Tynan gathered himself and immediately wrote the book that made him a central figure in the British theater.

Surely that kindness inclined Tynan to take Lewis's writings more seriously—thus his comment on the power of *Miracles* to sway him toward the "Christian camp." But in the last decade of his life he would return again and again to Lewis's writings, and the tone in which he speaks of them suggests not a mind convinced by argument but a spirit deeply attracted by a *vision* of the life that is best for people to live. Just two months after the diary entry I quoted, Tynan mentions Lewis again: "I note with interest that W. H. Auden wrote in his last book [that] 'Kierkegaard, Williams and Lewis guided us back to belief.' (C.S., of course.) Will he finally guide me?" Three years earlier he had picked up *That Hideous Strength* and written, "How thrilling he makes goodness seem—how tangible and radiant!" In 1975 he visited Shakespeare's grave at Stratford-upon-Avon and noticed in the church's small bookstall some Lewis titles, which he bought and began to read. The next day he wrote, "As ever, I respond to his powerful suggestion that feelings of guilt and shame are not conditioned by the world in which we live but are real apprehensions of the standards obtaining in an eternal world." Even when he disagrees with Lewis, or thinks Lewis has not explained adequately certain kinds of suffering (he is reading *The Problem of Pain*), he writes, "C.S.L. works as potently as ever on my imagination."

What matters in all this is that "C.S.L." presents to Tynan an *imaginative* picture of goodness and love to which he is consistently drawn—even when the arguments do not convince him. Nothing else in his life offered him that picture, that vision, and it would have been unsurprising if he had left Lewis behind; yet he could not. The vision remained to beckon him. Tynan clearly felt something that Austin Farrer noted in the homily he gave at Lewis's funeral: "But his real power was not proof; it was depiction. There lived in his writings a Christian universe that could be both thought and felt, in which he was at home and in which he made his reader at home."

But what did it amount to? Did Lewis ever manage to convert Tynan, to make a Christian of him? Probably not—or perhaps it is best to say, possibly not. In 1980 he wrote a note to his wife, Kathleen, in which he claimed as his own prayer a French sentence of which he did not know the origin: *À l'heure de ma mort, soyez le refuge de mon âme étonnée, et recevez-vous dans le sein de Votre miséricorde:* "At the hour of my death, may You be the refuge of my astonished soul, and receive it into Your merciful breast." A few months later he was dead from emphysema. Kathleen did not understand her husband's religious impulses, nor his fascination with Lewis—about whom she knew nothing except that he was the "improbable guru [who] affected and haunted Ken throughout his life"—but she understood that his ashes should not be buried in his hometown of Birmingham (that "cemetery without walls," he called it), nor in Los Angeles, where he had spent his last years, nor in London, where he had had his greatest successes, but rather in Oxford. She hoped that he could be interred somewhere on the grounds of Magdalen, because she knew he had been happiest there, but when that proved to be impossible—in fact illegal—the college authorities suggested an alternative: Holy Cross Church, a short walk from the college grounds. It was more appropriate than they knew, for already buried there were two people who had meant a great deal to Lewis, even as Lewis had meant a great deal to Tynan: Kenneth Grahame (author of *The Wind in the Willows*) and Charles Williams.

The graveyard is not well kept—or it has not been on my visits—and among the dingy memorials and weedy grass Tynan's gravestone is strikingly visible: a little taller than most of the older stones, a sharp-edged granite rectangle with a simple inscription in a clean modern typeface. The memorial seems a bit out of place, as indeed Tynan himself would have seemed among most of the others buried there. Yet in death he is linked with that world, the world of his beloved tutor, who had offered to him a "tangible and radiant" image of goodness that he could manage neither to forget nor wholly to reject.

In September 1980, when Tynan was buried, Magdalen's Dean of Divinity read the service, and several friends of the family spoke or read poems. The last to speak was thirteen-year-old Roxana Tynan, who read three sentences. They were taken from "The Weight of Glory," the great sermon that C. S. Lewis had delivered at the University Church of St. Mary the Virgin in 1941, just months after young Kenneth Tynan had escaped death in the German bombing of Birmingham. Tynan would have discovered the passage decades later, and perhaps it taught him at last what Lewis had learned through struggle and misery—that there lies in our hearts a longing that is also a delight, a longing that nothing in this world can satisfy and a delight that nothing in this world can match. It was, at any rate, in Lewis's words that Tynan found what he wished to be the final commentary on his own life. The thought expressed in those sentences is everywhere woven into the fabric of Lewis's work; it is the whole of what Narnia represents; it is Aslan's final teaching to his followers in *The Last Battle*.

If this thought has a future, then so does Narnia, and so does the body of C. S. Lewis's writing. These are the words that Roxana Tynan read over the grave of her father:

> The books or the music in which we thought the beauty was located will betray us if we trust to them; it was not *in* them, it only came *through* them, and what came through them was longing. These things—the beauty, the memory of our own past—are good images of what we really desire; but if they are mistaken for the thing itself, they turn into dumb idols, breaking the hearts of their worshippers. For they are not the thing itself; they are only the scent of a flower we have not found, the echo of a tune we have not heard, news from a country we have never yet visited.

Notes

In quoting from Lewis's letters, I have retained his sometimes idiosyncratic spelling. In quoting the Bible, I have used the translation (the Authorized Version, known in America as the King James) that Lewis knew and the *Book of Common Prayer* (the version of 1662) that was his daily companion for the second half of his life.

The source for many of Lewis's early letters and other family correspondence is the collection of eleven bound typescript volumes usually called the Lewis Papers, the original of which is kept at the Marion Wade Center of Wheaton College. Warren Lewis gathered, edited, and typed this family-history-through-letters in the early 1930s. When letters or other commentary from the Lewis Papers are available in published sources, I have usually cited those published sources because they are more readily available to readers. But at times it was necessary to quote directly from the Papers themselves.

As I write these words, Walter Hooper has not yet finished the third and final volume of Lewis's *Collected Letters,* so for letters after 1949 I have relied on the earlier, one-volume *Letters of C. S. Lewis* and on a mass of unpublished letters kept in the Wade Center. When those letters have been cited at any length in existing biographies, I have given those published works as my source, but when only the recipient and the date of the letter are identified in these notes, the source is the Wade Center collection.

All titles listed below are by C. S. Lewis unless otherwise noted. When the date of first publication differs from the copyright date, the former is given in brackets.

Abbreviations

AL	*The Allegory of Love* (Oxford: Oxford University Press, 1936)
AM	*The Abolition of Man* [1944] (San Francisco: HarperSanFrancisco, 2001)
AMR	*All My Road Before Me: The Diary of C. S. Lewis 1922–1927*, ed. Walter Hooper (San Diego: Harcourt Brace Jovanovich, 1991)
B&F	*Brothers and Friends: The Diaries of Major Warren Hamilton Lewis,* ed. Marjorie Lamp Mead (San Francisco: HarperSanFrancisco, 1982)
Biography	*C. S. Lewis: A Biography* by Roger Lancelyn Green and Walter Hooper, revised and expanded edition (London: HarperCollins, 2002)
BT	*C. S. Lewis at the Breakfast Table and Other Reminiscences*, ed. James T. Como (New York: Macmillan, 1979)
Companion	*C. S. Lewis: Companion and Guide* by Walter Hooper (San Francisco: HarperSanFrancisco, 1996)
CR	*Christian Reflections*, ed. Walter Hooper (Grand Rapids, MI: Eerdmans, 1967)
DI	*The Discarded Image* (Cambridge: Cambridge University Press, 1964)
EC	*An Experiment in Criticism* [1961] (Cambridge: Cambridge University Press, 1979)
ECW	*Essays Presented to Charles Williams,* ed. C. S. Lewis (Grand Rapids, MI: Eerdmans, 1966)
ELSC	*English Literature in the Sixteenth Century, Excluding Drama* (Oxford: Oxford University Press, 1953)
FL	*The Four Loves* [1960] (London: HarperCollins, 1977)
GITD	*God in the Dock: Essays on Theology and Ethics* (Grand Rapids, MI: Eerdmans, 1970)
GD	*The Great Divorce* [1946] (San Francisco: HarperSanFrancisco, 2001)
GO	*A Grief Observed* [1961] (San Francisco: HarperSanFrancisco, 2001)
HB	*The Horse and His Boy* [1954] (San Francisco: HarperSanFrancisco, 1994)

L1   *The Collected Letters of C. S. Lewis,* vol. 1, *Family Letters 1905–1931,* ed. Walter Hooper (San Francisco: HarperSanFrancisco, 2004)

L2   *The Collected Letters of C. S. Lewis,* vol. 2, *Books, Broadcasts, and the War 1931–1949,* ed. Walter Hooper (San Francisco: HarperSanFrancisco, 2004)

LB   *The Last Battle* [1956] (San Francisco: HarperSanFrancisco, 1994)

Letters   *Letters of C. S. Lewis,* ed. W. H. Lewis and Walter Hooper, revised edition (New York: Harcourt Brace Jovanovich, 1993)

LJRRT   *The Letters of J. R. R. Tolkien,* ed. Humphrey Carpenter, with the assistance of Christopher Tolkien (Boston: Houghton Mifflin, 1981)

LM   *Letters to Malcolm: Chiefly on Prayer* [1964] (New York: Harcourt Brace Jovanovich, 1991)

LOTR   *The Lord of the Rings* [1955] by J. R. R. Tolkien (Boston: Houghton Mifflin, 1993)

LP   Lewis Papers ("Memoirs of the Lewis Family: 1850–1930"), compiled by Major Warren Hamilton Lewis, 11 volumes (unpublished), Marion Wade Center, Wheaton College, Wheaton, IL

LTC   *C. S. Lewis Letters to Children,* ed. Lyle W. Dorsett and Marjorie Lamp Mead (New York: Macmillan, 1985)

LWW   *The Lion, the Witch, and the Wardrobe* [1950] (San Francisco: HarperSanFrancisco, 1994)

M   *Miracles* [1947, 1960] (San Francisco: HarperSanFrancisco, 2001)

MC   *Mere Christianity* [1952] (San Francisco: HarperSanFrancisco, 2001)

Memoir   *Memoir of C. S. Lewis* by W. H. Lewis, in **Letters**

MN   *The Magician's Nephew* [1955] (San Francisco: HarperSanFrancisco, 1994)

NP   *Narrative Poems* (New York: Harcourt Brace Jovanovich, 1968)

OS   *"On Stories" and Other Essays on Literature,* ed. Walter Hooper (New York: Harcourt Brace Jovanovich, 1982)

OTSP   *Out of the Silent Planet* [1938] (New York: Macmillan, 1965)

PC   *Prince Caspian* [1951] (San Francisco: HarperSanFrancisco, 1994)

PER   *Perelandra* [1944] (New York: Macmillan, 1965)

Poems   *Poems* (New York: Harcourt Brace Jovanovich, 1964)

PP   *The Problem of Pain* [1940] (San Francisco: HarperSanFrancisco, 2001)

PR   *The Pilgrim's Regress,* revised edition (London: Geoffrey Bles, 1943)

PPL   *A Preface to "Paradise Lost"* [1942] (Oxford: Oxford University Press, 1979)

RP   *Reflections on the Psalms* (New York: Harcourt Brace Jovanovich, 1958)

SB   *Spirits in Bondage: A Cycle of Lyrics* [1920] (New York: Harcourt Brace Jovanovich, 1984)

SBJ   *Surprised by Joy* (New York: Harcourt Brace Jovanovich, 1955)

SC   *The Silver Chair* [1953] (San Francisco: HarperSanFrancisco, 1994)

SL   *The Screwtape Letters* [1942] (San Francisco: HarperSanFrancisco, 2001)

SW   *Studies in Words* (Cambridge: Cambridge University Press, 1960)

THS   *That Hideous Strength* [1946] (New York: Macmillan, 1965)

TWHF   *Till We Have Faces* (New York: Harcourt Brace Jovanovich, 1956)

VDT	*The Voyage of the "Dawn Treader"* [1952] (San Francisco: HarperSan-Francisco, 1994)
WG	*"The Weight of Glory" and Other Addresses* (San Francisco: HarperSanFrancisco 2001)
Wilson	*C. S. Lewis: A Biography,* by A. N. Wilson (New York: Norton, 1990)
WLN	*"The World's Last Night" and Other Essays* (New York: Harcourt Brace Jovanovich, 1960)

INTRODUCTION

"tied to an invalid": L2:922

"as good as an extra maid": Memoir 37

"My mother is old": L2:766

"horror of nonentity": SBJ 117

"His kindness remains": B&F 225

"Dog's stools": L2:929

"wonderful talk" and "Nevertheless it was": Biography 307

"I have tried": L2:802

"My knowledge": Letters 504

he never read: See C. S. Lewis, "On Three Ways of Writing for Children," in OS 33

He told a friend: L2:881

"She has a secure place": L2:538

"Dull, if you will": PPL 71

"there was so much else!": *Owen Barfield on C. S. Lewis*, ed. G. B. Tennyson (Middletown, CT: Wesleyan University Press, 1989).

"I was a younger son": Biography 169

"ideal happiness": AL 304

"I am a product": SBJ 10

"I entered": SBJ 54

"nonsense, poetry, theology, metaphysics"

"I am not sure that anyone": Owen Barfield, "The Five C. S. Lewises," in *Owen Barfield on C. S. Lewis*, 120–21

"picture of a Faun": C. S. Lewis, "It All Began with a Picture . . . ," in OS 53

"had very little idea how the story would go"

"When I was ten": OS 34

"horns of Elfland": SBJ 5

"a certain psychic": Barfield, "The Five C. S. Lewises," 25

"In fact his whole life": Quoted in L2:882

"habits of the heart": AM

"It is a reasonable hope": PPL v

"Writing 'juveniles'": Letters 506

"The imaginative man": Letters 444

"the interpenetration of worlds": A. N. Wilson, *God's Funeral* (London: Abacus, 2000), 226. *C.S. Lewis: A Biography* (New York: W.W. Norton, 1990).

"I hope no one": LWW 158

CHAPTER 1

""Jacksie": Memoir 22

"I have a prejudice": Companion 4

"Happy" SBJ 3

"I wonder do I love you?": LP II:248

"sentimental, passionate, and rhetorical": SBJ 1

"Woe to the poor jury man": LP II:98

A hundred years earlier: Marc Mulholland, *The Longest War: Northern Ireland's Troubled History* (Oxford: Oxford University Press, 2002), 15; for a full treatment of Lewis's Irish context, see Ronald W. Bresland, *The Backward Glance: C. S. Lewis and Ireland* (Belfast: Institute of Irish Studies, 1999)

"we Strandtown and Belmont": SBJ 160

"ill and crying": SBJ 18

"I was taught": SBJ 7

"My mother's death": SBJ 20

"produce by will"

"My disappointment"

"And so would you": MN 4

"it would need fruit": MN 92

"all the other words": MN 178

"But please, please": MN 154

"would have looked back": MN 191

"All get what they want": 190

Men must endure"

"as good a woman": LP III:25

"They were vegetarians": VDT 3

"With my mother's death": SBJ 21

"reflections there-on": Biography 7

"a Paradise within thee": SBJ 19.

"nerves had never"

"merciless": Wilson 21

"smothering tendency": Memoir 26

"peculiar cruelty of fate

"two frightened urchins": SBJ 19

"of all the schools": Biography 8

raininess of Ireland: Memoir 21

"the delight": EC 14

"At present Boxen": L1:3

"Animal-Land had nothing": SBJ 15

"grown-up conversation": Memoir 27

"but it said": PC 76

"jeweled slippers": LB 32

"Nothing was forbidden": SBJ 10; my description of the books in Little Lea and Lewis's parents' reading comes from pages 4–5

she wrote *about* children: Gore Vidal, "The Writing of E. Nesbit," *New York Review of Books,* December 3, 1964

"what neither": SBJ 5

"O hark, O hear!"

"that long line": J. R. R. Tolkien, "On Fairy-Stories," in ECW 40

"*Supernatural* is a dangerous": Ibid., 39

"The trouble with the real": Ibid., 41

"that perilous country": J. R. R. Tolkien, *Smith of Wooton Major and Farmer Giles of Ham* [1967] (New York: Del Rey, 1988), 24

"You've noticed how": THS 31

"fair and perilous": LOTR 329

CHAPTER 2

"It was 'Co-educational'": SC 1–2

"The term is over": LB 210

"Life at a vile boarding school": SBJ 36

"I was at three schools": LTC 102

"terrible, all-powerful monsters": George Orwell, "Such, Such Were the Joys" [1953], in *A Collection of Essays* (New York: Harcourt Brace Jovanovich, 1981), 1–47, 46, 44

"The 'best'": Wilson 13

"It will be good": LP III:25; Wilson 14

"When really angry": SBJ 28

"Missis Capron": L1:8

"In spight of all": L1:10

"escaped [the] worst brutalities": Memoir 23

"I am very sorry": L1:9

"Intellectually, the time": SBJ 34

"In spite of Capron's policy": LP III:40

"There were real fights": SBJ 50

"I am strongly inclined": LP II:223

"Jacko has his peculiarities": LP III:225

"the population was": SBJ 50

"the experiment": LP III:230

"very like living": SBJ 51

"the inestimable benefit": AL, preface

"a great decline": SBJ 34

"Just then a scout": From "Lay of Horatius"—the once-famous "Horatius at the bridge."

"Alas! What happy days: Biography 16

"Pogo was a wit": SBJ 67

"made sad work"

"lived under the shadow": SBJ 83

"committed the serious": SBJ 90

"The work here": L1:31

"No true defender": SBJ 96

"Worst of all": SBJ 94

"a noisy, cheerful function": Memoir 24

"has made himself unpopular": LP IV:156

"the classical period": SBJ 119

"Not only does this": This and the following quotations from Jack's letters at this time come from L1:50–59, 67

"Romanticism": SBJ

"bitter, truculent, skeptical": SBJ 107

"It was, of course": SBJ 127

"You've always liked": LWW 46

"When at last": LWW 180

"sucking up to Them": SC 5

"Stone had the look": THS 109

"He is not altogether": LP IV:158

"it is too late now": L1:46

"The verse translation": LP IV:173

"I do not like": L1:7

"what really mattered": SBJ 32

"realization": SBJ 61

"My [Christian] faith was": L2:702

"She was . . . floundering": SBJ 59

"started in me": SBJ 60

Annie Besant: Wilson 383–92

"I am very religious": W. B. Yeats, *The Trembling of the Veil* [1922], in *The Autobiography of William Butler Yeats* (Garden City, NY: Anchor, 1958), 77

"what I must call": W. B. Yeats, "Magic" [1909], in *The Yeats Reader* (New York: Scribner, 1997), 351

"From the tyrannous noon": SBJ 60

"The idea that if": SBJ 176

"They taught me longing": SBJ 7

"There is no greed": Novalis, *Henry Von Ofterdingen*, trans. Palmer Hilty [1802] (Long Grove, IL: Waveland Press, 1990), 15

"is that of an unsatisfied desire": SBJ 16–17

"I heard a voice"

"In a sense the central story": SBJ 17

"I am terribly afraid": PR 160

CHAPTER 3

"How can people advocate": L1:49

"My chief dread": L1:54

"Amidst all the banal": SBJ 112

"We [he and Warnie] had heard": SBJ 133; I cite many passages from this chapter, "The Great Knock"

"If I ever take to religion": THS 379

"Therefore, since the world": A. E. Housman, "Terence, this is stupid stuff," from *A Shropshire Lad* [1896], in *Collected Poems* (New York: Holt, Rinehart, and Winston, 1965), 88

"a settled expectation": SBJ 64

"abstruse and depressing": L1:151

"one of the worst acts": SBJ 161

"The two hemispheres": SBJ 170

"fixity of purpose": L1:263–64

"For instance": LWW 47f

"was only a shadow": LB 195

I am trying here to": MC 52

"If I could please": SBJ 141

"You ask me how": L1:145

"The other day": L1:17

"The woods": SBJ 153, 156

"Where is your favourite": L1:60

"I found Arthur": SBJ 130–31

"He was not a clever boy": Companion 666

women he'd like to spank: see especially the letter from early 1917, e.g., L1: 268, 271, 276, 283, etc.

"But oh Arthur": C. S. Lewis, letter to Arthur Greeves, September 11, 1963. *They Stand Together: The Letters of C.S. Lewis to Arthur Greeves (1914–1963)* (New York: Macmillian, 1979), 576

"closely tethered": SBJ 162

"Jack would have liked": Letters 27

"devastatingly cruel": Wilson 31

"more power of confusing": SBJ 120–21

"By the way": L1:150

"Now what is your grievance": L1:128

"He has read more": L1:178

"He is the most brilliant": Biography 28

"As a dialectician": L1:264

"Great Bookham": L1:89

"Why aren't you out": Quoted in Philip Yancey, introduction to *Orthodoxy* by G. K. Chesterton [1909] (New York: Image, 2001), xvii

"I think we may reasonably": L1:131

"at any rate": L1:179

"I did feel": SBJ 158

"Kirk says it will be": L1:275

"the man Yeshua": L1:234

"I have had a great": L1:169

"To speak plainly": *George MacDonald: An Anthology,* ed. C. S. Lewis [1946] (San Francisco: HarperSanFrancisco, 2001), xxxv

"The place has surpassed": L1:262

CHAPTER 4

nearly 15,000 "members": Jan Morris,
The Oxford Book of Oxford (Oxford:
Oxford University Press, 1978), 335

"Junior officers were being": John Barth,
Tolkien and the Great War (London:
HarperCollins, 2003), 138

"by 1918 all but": Preface to LOTR,
2nd ed., xvii

"I have been to see": L1:296

"really belong": L1:297

"Visconte de sade": L1:313

a shilling a lash: L1:319

"with Moore at the digs": L1:334

"HAVE ARRIVED BRISTOL": L1:345

"unskilled butchery": SBJ 158

"DON'T UNDERSTAND": L1:345

"anyone in England": Memoir 29

"It has shaken": Wilson 54

"The chief effect": John Keegan, *The
First World War* (New York: Vintage,
1998), 310

"I am present[ly]": L1:348

"They are very deep": L1:351

"There are cliffs": L1:356

"I was a futile officer": SBJ 196

"would have been a life-long friend":
SBJ 191

"I had had him so often": L1:388

"not much the worse": L1:366

"Murder! Fascists! Lions!": SC 252

"horrible things were": LWW 176

"Peter did not feel": LWW 131

"The Fox lay dead": LB 136

"Tirian knew he could": LB 148

"Three dogs were killed": LB 136

"But for the rest": SBJ 196

"health report": L1:417–18

"No, I haven't joined ": L2:258

"Never a day passes": L1:400

"For these decay": SB 7

"Thus with the year": *Paradise Lost,*
III.40ff

"We for a certainty": Housman, "The
chestnut casts its flambeaux," in
Collected Poems, 107

"The ancient songs": SB 7

"I also glanced": L1:832

"Among people who were": George
Orwell, "Inside the Whale," in *A
Collection of Essays,* 221

"Nothing's wrong, Doug": LL 104
Douglas Gresham, *Lenten Lands*
[1988] (San Francisco:
HarperSanFrancisco 1994), 104

"Is it good to tell": SB 12

"It's truth they tell": SB 14

"And if some tears": SB 19

"Come let us curse": SB 20

"Milton was of the Devil's"

"Pain is my element"

"On a slab": L1:298

"Were you much frightened": Leo Baker,
in BT 6

"Nearly all that I loved": SBJ 170

"One would have thought": Letters 30

"Arthur managed to drift": L1:455; for
Michael White's judgment, see his
C. S. Lewis: A Life (New York: Carrol
& Graf, 2004), 56

"Perhaps you don't believe": L1:353

"However, we may have": L1:355

"all the 'gilded youth'": L1:387

"After keeping my MS.": L1:397

"Indeed my life": L1:414

"It seems wonderful": B&F 4

CHAPTER 5

vivid picture of Oxford: These anecdotes
can be found in Morris, *Oxford Book
of Oxford,* and Humphrey Carpenter,
*The Brideshead Generation: Evelyn
Waugh and His Friends* (Boston:
Houghton Mifflin, 1990)

"We found the University": Robert
Graves, *Good-Bye to All That* [1929]
(Garden City, NY: Doubleday,
1957), 291

"I did not go back": Morris, *Oxford Book of Oxford,* 336

"I remember five of us": L1:416

"A red letter day": L1:423

"I don't know any": L1:428

"Those who cannot conceive": FL 91

"dialectical sharpness": SBJ 192

"I can hardly believe": L1:388

"the thing rather sniffs": L1:433

"One day over the tea cups": BT 4

"He is not so much": SBJ 199

"In vain do I tell": undated letters in the Wade Collection

"some withering discourse": B&F 257

"a strange fellow": Baker, BT 3

"After breakfast I work": L1:425f

"current literary set": L1:450

"it would have put": Wilson 66

Keble built a whole row: Graves, *Good-Bye to All That,* 291

"I confess I do not know": L1:451 (edited version) and LP VI:123 (unedited version)

"And so ends": B&F 236

church every Sunday morning: Wilson 64

"may have started": Biography 46

"In twenty years": Letters 33

"ebullient temperament": BT 4

"spoiling" him: *Owen Barfield on C. S. Lewis,* 125

"I have heard from Jacks": LP V1:129

"It is sometimes difficult": LP V1:145

"He said he had no respect": L1:462

"I have during the past four weeks"

"As regards the other matter": L1:470

"I am sure that the old"

"the family sends": L1:467

"being at home": L1:471

"I am writing": L1:479

"I shall have to spend": L1:509

"I am inclined to rate": Letters 24

"In the last fifteen": B&F 237

Maureen would later recall: Maureen Moore Blake, oral history interview,

Marion Wade Center, Wheaton College

"Lewis valued time": John Lawlor, *C. S. Lewis: Memories and Reflections* (Dallas: Spence, 1998), 7

"go and do Mrs. Moore's jars": *Owen Barfield on C. S. Lewis,* 125

"try and meet this"

Once Victor Gollancz: Morris, *Oxford Book of Oxford,* 347

"After Smugy and Kirk": L1:444

"'Greats,' being more philosophical": L1:438

"I am more worried": L1:507

"are always graceful and polished": Companion 144

"'It wasn't a *subject*": SBJ 225

"You will be interested": L1:509

"Now what, I asked myself": SBJ 204–5

"I have been taken recently": L1:524

"That room and that voice": L1:565

"'I was overawed": Preface to *Dymer,* NP 5

"we listened to Hitler's speech": L2:425

"The last two or three years": L1:565

"an old, dirty, gabbling": SBJ 201–2

"There was not to be": L1:539

"At the same time": L1:539

"Though I sometimes feel": L1:567

"hardly precedented migration": L1:570

"I am very grateful": L1:601

"the better man": L1:600

he had been encouraged: L1:591

"second string to [his] bow": SBJ 212

"I walked home": AMR 293

CHAPTER 6

"My father is dead": L2:161

"The stone seemed softer": AMR 307

"I turned up to the left": AMR 338

"I spent the first": L1:637

"What I 'found'": Preface to *Dymer,* NP 3

"I sat in my own bedroom": AMR 15

"Of Heaven or Hell": William Morris,
opening lines of *The Earthly Paradise*
(1868)

"execrebly bad": L1:432

"At Dymer's birth": NP 8

"And from the distant": NP 91

"We felt ourselves": NP 4

"We, dearest Theobald": Samuel Butler,
The Way of All Flesh [1903] (Harmondsworth: Penguin, 1971), 82–83

"A Fellowship in English": L1:640

"This was enough": L1:643

"I went up to his room": L1:642

"the only one in which": L1: 601

"My dear Papy": L1: 642

"Very pleasant, not a cloud": L1:649

"I don't see the use": Quoted in Richard
Ellmann, *Oscar Wilde* (New York:
Vintage, 1988), 39

"My external surroundings": L1:650

"Indeed in turning": L1:649 (the next
three quotations are all from this
letter to Albert of August 14, 1925)

"hard, cold, thin people": Quoted in
Yancey, introduction to Chesterton,
Orthodoxy. Yancey's piece is a nice
overview of Chesterton's career and
character

"To hear Chesterton's howl": Quoted in
Yancey, introduction to Chesterton,
Orthodoxy

"spectacular tournaments": Michael
Holroyd, *Bernard Shaw*, vol. 2, *1898–
1918: The Pursuit of Power* (New
York: Random House, 1989), 219

"Shaw is like": Quoted in ibid., 219

"a thoroughly bad book": AMR 297
(the other references to GKC are listed
in the book's helpful index)

"a pleasant little play": AMR 36

"I shall repeat": from a March 1908
letter quoted by Dale Alquist on the
American Chesterton Society website:
www.chesterton.org/discover/lectures/
25magic.html

"the actual centre: "A Defence of Penny
Dreadfuls" may be found online at
http://www.dur.ac.uk/martin.ward/gkc/
books/penny-dreadfuls.html

"The 'Iliad' is only great": collected in a
book called *The Defendant*
(www.gutenberg.org/extext/12245)

"All Christianity concentrates":
Chesterton, *Orthodoxy*, 143

"The life of man is a story": G. K.
Chesterton, *The Everlasting Man*
[1925] (Garden City, NY: Image,
1955), 251

"The Absolute Mind": SBJ 209–10

"In a sense there is no God": *The
Portable Bernard Shaw*, ed. Stanley
Weintraub (Harmondsworth: Penguin,
1979), 465

"Like all us Celts": L1:713

"Now that I was reading": SBJ 214

"The man of the nineteenth":
Chesterton, *Orthodoxy*, 132

"Poor, poor old Pdaitabird": L1:805

"Things are no better": L1:809

"one for whom I have": L1:820

"I have never been able": L1:821

"They said he might live": L1:823

"Mixed, perhaps rather callously":
L1:822

"in the Trinity term": SBJ 228

"when the human race": Wilson 3

"How I would have": L1:834

the Absolute as the "maker": L1:853

"has really opened a new": L1:857

"I am still inclined": L1:862

"Things are going very": L1:877

"It's not like a book": L1:859

"I think almost more": L1:832

"To-day I got such a sudden": L1:877

"Some have paid me": From the preface
found in some older editions of SL

"They will not let": LB 169

"a most lovely feeling": VDT 108

"the very first tear": VDT

CHAPTER 7

"He is a good boy": George MacDonald,
The Princess and the Goblin [1872]
(London: Puffin, 1996), 17

"not precisely Christianity": L1:887

"Round about": Poems 118

"At my first coming": SBJ 216

"He is a smooth, pale": AMR 393

"Tolkien . . . came back": L1:838

"Men are . . . creatures": Sigmund Freud,
Civilization and Its Discontents
[1930], trans. James Strachey (New
York: Norton, 1961), 68f

"that the borders": Yeats, "Magic," 351

"all the thrills": MC 27

" 'In our world,' said": VDT 209

"Life is only": Quoted in Companion 58

"You look at trees": J. R. R. Tolkien,
Tree and Leaf [1964] (Boston:
Houghton Mifflin, 1989)

"Distinguo, Tollers, distinguo!":
Humphrey Carpenter, *Tolkien: A
Biography* (Boston: Houghton Mifflin
1977), 146

"Do what they will, then": WG 32

"Blessed are the men": Tolkien, *Tree and
Leaf*

"Early in 1926": SBJ 223f

"What I couldn't understand": L1:976

"It was really a memorable": L1:970

"Now what Dyson and Tolkien":
L1:976f

"as if a giant had": LWW 161

"It isn't Narnia": VDT 247

"ought to know": LWW 181

"I have just passed on": L1:974

"Does this amount to": L1:977

"Friendship with Lewis": Quoted in
Carpenter, *Tolkien*, 148

"has long since announced": L1:866

"a place where we can"

"such stuff as dreams": B&F 58

"I am *still* as disappointed": L1:925

"Anything worth doing": G. K.
Chesterton, *What's Wrong with the
World* [1910]; this out-of-print title
may be found at
http://www.ccel.org/c/chesterton/
wrongworld/wrongworld.txt

"On re-reading this book": PR 5

"an English yachtsman": Chesterton,
Orthodoxy, 2

"and when he was far enough":
Chesterton, *The Everlasting Man*, 11

"has knit our hearts": PR 198

"is a kind of Bunyan": L2:94

makes contemptuous reference: PPL 56;
L2:163

"dynasty of Green, Bradley, and
Bosanquet": PR 5

"keep on trying": PR 153

"bold, original, seminal": Norman F.
Cantor, *Inventing the Middle Ages*
(New York: Perennial, 1993), 217

CHAPTER 8

"The plain fact is": Lawlor, *C. S. Lewis*, 6

"many of his pupils": Quoted in Wilson
130

"southern English": L1:766; L2:607

"a short, thickset man": "Oxford's C. S.
Lewis: His Heresy: Christianity,"
Time, September 8, 1947

"tall, fat, rather bald": LTC 45

"chronological snobbery": SBJ 207

"lopsided ethical developments": PP 49

"God might be content": PP 58

"I have made no serious": DI 216

"We can no longer dismiss": DI 222

"The central position": ELSC 3

"not only erroneous": from the preface
found in some older editions of SL

"Historical Point of View": SL 150

"Bulverism": GITD 273

"doesn't think of doctrines": SL 1–2

"It must be remembered": THS 185

"*Him* a magician?": MN 75

"behavior and conversation": MN 114

"watchin' and listenin's": MN 114

"the longer and the more": MN 137

"Well, at any rate": LB 169

"is that in comparison"

"When the man said": Quoted in AM 2

"May not a man": MC xiii

"When a word ceases": MC xiv

"When a man who": MC xv

"Their scepticism about values": AM 29

"St. Augustine defines virtue": AM 16

"On a fine morning": THS 88

"fourth and supreme Jane": THS 151

"You are to be the Prince": LWW 39

"the elimination of war": THS 258

"curried favor": SC

"that horrid school": LWW 180

"You discover gradually": "The Inner
   Ring," in WG 141–57

"Indeed the safest road": SL 61

"next week it will": WG 154

"an invitation from a duchess": WG 147

"'we few' . . . was": SBJ 174

"an invitation that beckoned": THS 268

"The rebel is already": PPL 125

"Your genuine Inner Ring": WG 156

"Of course they'll play": GD 54

"The new magia": ELSC 13–14

"The serious magical endeavour":
   AM 76

"The question is which"

"What we call": AM 55

"is concerned with Fall": LJRRT 145

"He has a mind": LOTR 462

"the only one that": LOTR 47

"Now that she was left": MN 79

"Nothing I can say": AM 75

"was born in an unhealthy": AM 78

"shows the white feather": AM 27

"Oh, I see": MN 21

"You must learn": MN 68

"The better stuff": MC 49

"the scent of a flower": WG 31

"Never forget that": SL 44

"The man who truly": SL 66

"'Ascetic Mr Lewis'—!!!": LJRRT 68

"There is no good trying": MC 64

"Do not despise": LOTR 365

"my old heart": PC 53

"the point at which": ELSC 3

"Each sphere, or something"" DI 115

If a Lewis scholar: Michael Ward,
   "Planet Narnia," *Times Literary
   Supplement*, April 25, 2003

"tingling with anthropomorphic":
   ELSC 4

"towering," and even "vertiginous": DI
   98–99

CHAPTER 9

"My happiest hours": Biography 169

"C.S.L. had a passion": LJRRT 388

he was gratified especially: LJRRT 122

"No one ever influenced": Letters 481

"I begin to suspect": L2:228

"I think he was a man": Eliot's preface
   to Williams's *All Hallows Eve* [1948]
   (New York: Noonday, 1977), xiii

"For the first time": W. H. Auden,
   Modern Canterbury Pilgrims, ed.
   James Pike (London: Mowbray,
   1956), 41

"one in whom": Preface to ECW, x

"wholly alien": LJRRT 362

"for the first time": ECW viii

"my dearest friend": L2:656

"distressing and in parts": LJRRT 352

"And instead of confessing": LJRRT 127

"the world might have": letter dated
   "Whitsunday 1956" from the Wade
   Center

"*rejected* is perhaps": L2:991

"his innocence and ignorance": Quoted
   in Biography 156

"this real, hard, dirty": L1:95

"In a perfect Friendship": FL 67f

"immeasurably dropping": Preface to
   ECW xiii

"used to say that": Ibid. xii

"Every real friendship is": FL 75

"the Royal Society": FL 64

"Alone among unsympathetic": FL 74

"dreadful man": L2:350

"Friendship (as the ancients saw)":
FL 75
"It was wonderful when": FL 74
"Some who have read": LOTR xvi
"a loathing for him": LJRRT 82
"is not full of": FL 82
"On Thursday we had": L2:288
"We meet . . . theoretically": L2:501
"Perhaps we may now hazard": FL 81
"a common religion": FL 62
"items or particulars": WG 163
"The quaternion of Mole": FL 34
"A trio such as Rat": WG 165
"it was not for societies": WG 172
"a boot crashing down": Orwell,
"England Your England," in *A
Collection of Essays,* 259
"One or the other": P. G. Wodehouse,
The Code of the Woosters [1938]
(New York: Vintage, 1975), 222
"mess about in boats": Kenneth
Grahame, *The Wind in the Willows*
[1908]
"the grandfather, the parents": WG 164
"Now that Charles is dead": FL 58f
"threw him in free": VDT 63
"You'd think me simply": VDT 109
"It would be nice": VDT 112
"I am going to venture": WG 167
"there is no question": WG 174
"In His will is our peace"
"The one principle": *George
MacDonald: An Anthology,* ed. C. S.
Lewis [1946] (San Francisco:
HarperSanFrancisco, 2001), #203
"You will be dead": Ibid., #363
"Nothing that has not died": WG 172
"To enter hell": PP 128
"Eat or be eaten": SL
"Those who are members": WG 167
Richard Baxter: See the brief but sound
summary of Baxter's career in
Christopher Hill, *The Experience of
Defeat: Milton and Some*

Contemporaries (Harmondsworth:
Penguin, 1984), ch. 7
Churches throughout the island: See the
account in John Stevenson, *British
Society 1914–1945* (Harmondsworth:
Pelican, 1984), 356ff.
"The process whereby": ELSC 37
"And is Eustace": VDT 248
"the belief that has": MC viii
"I myself was first": GITD 202
"One of our great allies": SL 5
"I have believed myself": PP xii
"Christianity-and-water": MC 40
"boys' philosophies": MC 40
"next to Christianity": MC 42
"Certainly I have met": MC xii
"the liberal and 'broad-minded'":
GITD 60
"The truth is we": L2:657
"the easy conscience": Reinhold
Niebuhr, *The Nature and Destiny of
Man,* vol. 1 (New York: Scribner,
1942), ch. 4
"depth under depth": L1:862

CHAPTER 10
"Those to whom evil": W. H. Auden,
Selected Poems, 2nd ed. (New York:
Vintage, 1979), 86
"my memories of the last": L2:258
"the iniquity of Hitler's": L2:128
"if I am to understand": LJRRT 37
"If its got to be": L2: 258
"As [Warnie] said": L2:274
"not to hope": SL 22
"I write to ask": L2:469
"The first step is": L2:470
"If you know the address": L2:602
"I'm still wading": L2:509
"As you will have": L2:549
"It is extraordinary how": GITD 61
"Few things in the ordinary": FL 46
"Pray for *Jane*": L2:496
"I'm pretty well": L2:549
"sign themselves 'Jehovah'": L2:504

"a very silly, tiresome": Biography 296
"And if Mr. Lewis": LTC 53
"a tremendous crush": L2:1034
"I have met no one": B&F 181
"a perfectly saintly girl": L2:623
"I went in fear": Quoted in Biography 274
"argument . . . has a life": GITD 128
"One last word": GITD 103
"I have, almost all": SBJ 117
"has greatly increased": L2:656
"I . . . have been v. much": L2:648
"There are no *ordinary* people": WG 4
some very odd ideas: Wilson 189, 201, 202
"merely subjective events": M 28
"with real horror": Biography 290
"his argument for the": George Sayer,
    Jack (Wheaton, IL: Crossway Books,
    1994), 307
"to the foot of the Cross": Wilson 213
"Neither Dr. Havard": Biography 291
"All that had happened": Wilson 214
"Of course, she is far": BT 223
"but it was, by": L2:803
"This book is about": Companion 402
"So my mother and I": [indicated in
    text]
"Modern children are poor creatures":
    L2:277
"Minto reads him the Peter Rabbit":
    L2:171
"For my own 'flu": L2:881
"However, cheer up": L1:187
"I can't write a book": L2:674
"I am going to be": Letters 415
"One cannot be": WG 14
"I say, therefore, that": TWHF 249
"Lightly men talk of": TWHF 294
"Send me away, Minos": TWHF 295
"While I was reading": TWHF 292
"I am not quite sure": OS 37
According to Green and Hooper:
    Biography 112
"its severe restraints on": OS 46
"Everything began with images": OS 46
"It is better not": OS 41

"I was being unmade": TWHF 307
"the association of children": Tolkien,
    "On Fairy-Stories," ECW 58
"theoretically we are all": ELSC 342
"Myth and fairy-story must": LJRRT 144
"The 'doctrines' we get": L1:976
"At first I had": OS 53

CHAPTER 11

"I feel my zeal": L2:905
"No Inklings tonight": B&F 231
"the subject that is": L2:986
"I come of a stock": Quoted in
    Biography 341
"I wish that for your love": *The Latin
    Letters of C. S. Lewis,* trans. Martin
    Moynihan (South Bend, IN: St.
    Augustine's Press, 1998), 89 (the next
    quotation is from this letter as well)
"Joyful news": B&F 232
"I remember coming over": Maureen
    Moore Blake, oral history interview,
    Marion Wade Center, Wheaton
    College
"I hardly know how": Letters 380
"And so ends": B&F 236
"I am (like the pilgrim in Bunyan)":
    Letters 390
"It isn't chiefly *men*": Letters 422
"shock him into an answer": Biography
    377
"I never saw Justice": Companion 57
"represents the Lord to": GITD 239
"embarked on a different": GITD 237
"What makes a pretty girl": MC 123
"Her presence has thus": FL 70
"There must be something": MC 113
"Christianity is almost the only": MC 98
"Now suppose you come": MC 96
"barbarians among civilised": FL 69
"lived for her family": FL 48
"Put me in charge": GD 94f
"Jane was not perhaps": THS 2
"she was drinking everything": LB 161

"the problem of Susan": See Gaiman's story of that title in *Flights: Extreme Visions of Fantasy*, ed. Al Sarrantonio (New York: Roc, 2004), 393–402

"no longer a friend": LB 154

"so dreadful and so": Quoted in Gregg Easterbrook, "In Defense of C. S. Lewis," *Atlantic Monthly* (October 2001)

"The books don't tell us": LTC 67

"It is only to the damned": PP 128

"the story of every nice": Companion 77

"We are all, corporately": GITD 239

"The election did much": Wilson 158

"because all dons at": Biography 340

"I always remained": Quoted in BT 80

"He could be intolerant": Quoted in BT 225

"My brother, in your ear": Quoted in Companion 67

"Besides being the precise": Quoted in Biography 342

"It was obvious that": Quoted in Biography 344

"under the same patroness": Letters 439

"I have exchanged": Biography 345

"young lady": Quoted in BT 212

"seemed to be on": Sayer, *Jack,* 347

"RP: The Witch makes it": Quoted in Companion 721

"pen-friends": B&F 244

"A Person [was] with me": Quoted in *And God Came In* by Lyle W. Dorsett (New York: Macmillan, 1983), 59

"some really swell guy": Quoted in Companion 62

"Backshadowing": Morson, *Narrative and Freedom: The Shadows of Time* (New Haven: Yale University Press, 1994)

"Just got a letter": Quoted in Companion 59

"Small farm life was": Sayer, *Jack,* 353

"an impetuous, kind hearted": L1:451

"from a marriage": LL 45

"her enthusiasm, interest": Sayer, *Jack,* 353

"quite extraordinarily uninhibited": Companion 61

"not with mere politeness": Companion 700

"I was some little": B&F 244

"She was bad": Ruth Pitter, oral history interview, Marion Wade Center, Wheaton College

"kicked a few ideas": Companion 77

"He says he finds"

"abominable" and "ridiculous": LJRRT 62

"a pure matter of": Biography 375

"J assured me that": B&F 245

"all the arrangements": BGF 245

"there was still no": Biography 376

According to Douglas: Douglas Gresham, *Lenten Lands* (San Francisco: HarperSanFrancisco, 1988), 67

"I doubt if this": FL 86f

"quite often sexually frigid": MC 123

"heartrending . . . Joy's eagerness": B&F 246

"I learned of it long": LJRRT 341

" my feelings have changed": Letters 466

"I never expected": Biography 385

CHAPTER 12

"I hope you will excuse": Donald Swann, *Swann's Way: A Life in Song* (London: Thames Publishing, 1991), 205

"there were so many capped": Companion 72

"the vast change which"

"Ah! Miss Dunbar!": Wilson 254

"When he learned that": Quoted in BT 104

"I have stood by the bedside": Reprinted in WLN 3–4

"dying each other's life": Charles Williams, *Taliessin Through Logres and The Region of the Summer Stars*, ed. C. S. Lewis (Grand Rapids, MI: Eerdmans, 1974), 63

"I was losing calcium": Letters 450

"Indeed the situation": Letters 466

"has made an almost": Biography 385

"my wife walks up": Letters 474

"*Of course* the sword": Letters 450

"belated honeymoon"

"This brief halcyon period": Biography 386

"I decided to give": Letters 44

"blind enough": FL 102

" For those few years": GO 7

"towsing the heroine": FL 87

"I could believe some": FL 91

"can invite the man": FL 95

"the combination of a high": Biography 388

"Professor Lewis, I'm afraid": Biography 388

"made him sit absolutely silent": Biography 387

"This last check is": Letters 462

"Everybody killed—burnt": Biography 392

"It looked very doubtful": Letters 468

"But Laurence can't *really*": LTC 52

"she agreed with him": B&F 250

"Here the whole world": It is from this poem that Douglas Gresham took the title of his memoir *Lenten Lands*

"What chokes every prayer": GO 30

"All that stuff about": GO 39f

"is all for my own sake": GO 41

"At any rate I must keep": GO 6

"Have we any reason": LM 32

"As for the last dereliction": LM 41

"I think [mystical experience]": LM 63

he declined to write: C. S. Lewis, letter to Edward Dell, April 22, 1963

"as if navigation were": LM 28

"We may ignore, but": LM 73

"It reminds me of straw": LM 80

"You were never safe": Companion 73

"In the early 1920s": Terry Eagleton, *Literary Theory: An Introduction,* 2nd ed. (Minneapolis: University of Minnesota Press, 1996), 27

"found difficult and left": Chesterton, *What's Wrong with the World*

"the Vigilant school of critics": EC 124

"Yet, while this goes on": EC 8

"a very bright spot": Letters 473

"one of the happiest times": *They Stand Together,* 560

"I have no pain": Companion 111

"O Arthur, never to see": *They Stand Together,* 459

"You can never get a book": Walter Hooper, Preface to OS, ix

"I was unexpectedly revived": Letters 488

"It is all rather fun": Letters 489

"Joy is the serious": LM 93

"perpetually solemn": WG 46

"Their life together is": PPL 119

"It delights me that": WG 171

"there are no *ordinary*": WG 46

"We know much more about": PP 129

"further up and further in": LB 196

"I have come home at last!": LB 196

"And for us this is": LB 210

"The wheel had come": Memoir 45

"I have done all": Memoir 45

"He was put almost": BT 244

"Friday, 22 November 1963": Memoir 45f

"Jack, it's Maureen": Biography 428

AFTERWORD

"Twenty years ago I felt": C. S. Lewis, letter to Joy Gresham, September 22, 1953

"Wouldn't it be wonderful": C. S. Lewis, letter to Katherine Farrer, December 4, 1952

"Tolkien is the wen": China Miéville website, http://www.panmacmillan.com/Features/China/debate.htm

"Let us drop CS Lewis": Philip Hensher, "Don't Let Your Children Go to Narnia," *The Independent* (London), December 4, 1998

"Death is better than": Quoted in "The Dark Side of Narnia," the *Guardian* (London), October 1, 1998

W. H. Auden, who adored: letter to Peter Salus, August 11, 1964, in the Berg Collection of the New York Public Library

"*The Lion, the Witch*": Walden Media press release, July 25, 2002: (www.waldon.com/about/news/waldon–07–25–02.jsp)

"There is no argument": *The Orwell Reader* (New York: Harcourt, 1984), 315

"The whole point of it": *Letters of Kenneth Tynan,* ed. John Lahr (New York: Random House, 1998), 32

"C. S. Lewis, my tutor": Ibid., 50

"Yesterday a bald, deaf": September 27, 1974, entry, *The Diaries of Kenneth Tynan,* ed. John Lahr (New York: Bloomsbury, 2001), 194f.

"Don't let it become": Kathleen Tynan, *Kenneth Tynan: A Life* (New York: Morrow, 1987), 121

"I note with interest": December 6, 1974, entry, *Diaries of Kenneth Tynan,* 208

"How thrilling he makes": April 4, 1971, entry, *Diaries of Kenneth Tynan,* 37

"As ever, I respond": May 3, 1975, entry, *Diaries of Kenneth Tynan,* 243

"C.S.L. works as": *Diaries of Kenneth Tynan,* 244

"But his real power": BT 243

À l'heure de": Kathleen Tynan, *Kenneth Tynan: A Life,* 525

"cemetery without walls": Ibid., 31

"improbable guru": Ibid., 84

"The books or the music": WG 30

Index